TIMBER TRADE PRACTICE

TIMBER TRADE PRACTICE

By

R. F. A. MALLINSON, M.B.E.
Mallinson & Eckersley Ltd., Salford
Lecturer, Manchester College of Commerce

and

ROLAND GRUGEON
Technical Wood Expert, Price & Pierce Ltd.
Lecturer, City of London College

With a Foreword by
T. A. STOREY
President, Timber Trade Federation of the United Kingdom

SECOND EDITION
Revised and Enlarged

LONDON
CLEAVER-HUME PRESS LTD.

CLEAVER-HUME PRESS LTD.
Wright's Lane, Kensington
London, W.8

First published - December 1950
Second Edition - September 1953

PRINTED IN GREAT BRITAIN
in 10 *point and* 8 *point Imprint type*
BY HUGH PATON AND SONS LTD
EDINBURGH

PREFACE TO SECOND EDITION

THE first edition of *Timber Trade Practice* was produced to meet the growing demand for a textbook on the commercial practice of the timber trade. This demand was particularly great amongst students attending classes for the optional trade practice examination that had recently been introduced by the T.D.A.

Since the need was urgent, there being no comprehensive book of reference available for the students, the first edition had to be prepared in haste without waiting for the completion of the revision of the various charters, contract forms, etc., that was then being undertaken by the Timber Trade Federation.

Much more time has been available for the preparation of this second edition and the opportunity has been taken to revise the lay-out of the chapters dealing with shipping, marine insurance and contracts, so these now follow a more logical order. Furthermore, considerably more space has been devoted to a closer study of specific charters, marine insurance clauses and contract forms.

Both the softwood and plywood trades have received varying degrees of freedom to import on private account since the first edition was published. The revised charters and contract forms, together with post-war conditions affecting shipping and the inflation of prices and values have all brought with them new problems to both merchants and importers, and as far as possible these new problems have also been examined in this book. Our aim has been to provide a reference book on these matters for experienced members of the trade as well as a standard textbook of trade practice for the student.

It was hoped to include amongst the contract forms reviewed, a revised Albion c.i.f. form. Unfortunately this has not been possible since, although much work has been done towards agreement with the shippers' organisations, there are still some important matters in dispute which are holding up final agreement on the revised contract form. Consequently reference has had to be made to the 1938 Albion c.i.f. contract, the form still officially recognised between shippers and the T.T.F. If and when a new contract is agreed, a copy should be inserted in the end-band, and its terms studied and compared with the old form and with the Uniform 1951 form reviewed in this book.

Statistics of imports have been used in this book to show the relative importance of the different exporting countries to the timber trade. For this reason, the latest figures quoted are those for 1951, a year in which importers had reasonable freedom to purchase what they required. The statistics of imports in 1952, although available, have not been used since, owing to the number of restrictions and controls on imports during that year, they do not present a truly representative picture of the trade.

Manchester-London
June 1953

R. F. A. MALLINSON
ROLAND GRUGEON

FOREWORD to SECOND EDITION by T. A. STOREY

President of the Timber Trade Federation of the United Kingdom

It has been said that when anything ends, it will be the end of everything. Certainly there is no finality of commercial practice in the timber trade, and one can safely predict that there never will be.

This would have been true even had circumstances during the last few years been normal. As it is, the painful emergence of the timber trade from a mass of wartime controls was bound to cause considerable variation of the conditions under which buying and selling of wood is conducted. It is, therefore, not surprising that the Authors of a book so valuable to the trade as this one, should have considered it necessary to produce a second and revised edition.

If, as I believe, this book remains an essential textbook for the education of the trade, the necessity in the future of keeping abreast of changing circumstances will not diminish, though the impetus behind such changes may well decrease. One thing, it seems to me, is quite certain. The impact of day to day world events on industry in general is likely to be infinitely more decisive in the future than it was before the War; and the margins of opportunity within which traders have freedom to operate are likely to be much more limited.

If the political atmosphere clears, and commercial considerations alone begin to dominate international competition, the modern tendency towards all-out production is likely to be intensified, but the profit margins which will be available to industry will be margins obtained as a result of all-out productive effort, and not achieved on scarcity; consequently these margins are likely to contract.

If this is so, it follows that there will be no room for losses of efficiency which arise from incomplete understanding of the way in which a trade operates, or of the administrative detail which should be at everyone's finger tips, and the necessity for a book such as this will become still more evident. Just as it is becoming increasingly the normal practice to leave nothing to chance on the mechanical side of production, so the same procedure will be applied to administration.

This book brings within the reach of those who are finding and will find their living in the timber trade, a first class opportunity of understanding the structure of the industry and the multifarious trading channels through which goods pass in their journey from producer to consumer. It is more than a discursive adventure into the highways and byways of commercial practice in the Timber Trade ; it is a textbook, and a book of reference.

For these reasons I recommend it to every new entrant to the timber trade ; to those who are at present taking advantage of the educational opportunities provided by the Timber Development Association, and also to those who, though they may be experienced in the industry, can still find a thrill in delving into the intricate detail which makes up its fabric.

FOREWORD to FIRST EDITION by N. A. WRIGHT

Past President of the Timber Trade Federation of the United Kingdom

No material product has been so long and so generally used by mankind as has Timber. It was the first material known to primitive man and for thousands of years has entered into every phase of human activity. It is second only to food in its importance to our national economy and although we have been saved from disaster during two world wars by denuding our own forests we are bound to be more dependent in the future on imports from all parts of the world.

If, therefore, those engaged in this essential and fascinating trade wish to make themselves capable of rendering real service it will be necessary for them to have not only a good knowledge of the varieties of timber that are available in various parts of the world but to learn something about the other trades involved in the import and distribution of the commodity:—shipping, chartering, insurance, inland transport, etc. They will also come to understand the necessity for the present structure of the trade—agents, importers and merchants and why it is unsound for the producer to sell direct to the consumer who is usually unable to purchase the full range of sizes falling from the most economical production of the tree.

There are schemes of apprenticeship in different parts of the country and in addition we have educational classes arranged by the Timber Development Association Ltd. This treatise on the commercial aspects of the Timber Trade has been produced primarily for students attending these classes.

The book gives in clear and concise form a fund of information which is essential to the new recruit to the Timber industry and it provides a reliable textbook for all those engaged in the industry.

The authors of *Timber Trade Practice* have rendered a real service to the Trade in publishing this book and I heartily recommend it to all those, especially the youngsters, who have adopted the Timber Trade as their career.

FOREWORD to FIRST EDITION by J. L. BAYNES

Past President, and Chairman of the
Softwood Decontrol Committee,
Timber Trade Federation

FOR nearly eleven years the Timber Trade has been in bondage, but recently the Plywood and Hardwood Sections of the Trade have had a measure of freedom restored to them, which is already resulting in a healthy stock position.

The Softwood Trade, however, is still controlled almost as strictly as it was in the height of the war, and we cannot see even yet, that the end is in sight.

Importers and merchants have been endeavouring to trade in the straight-jacket of quotas, based, for the most part, on the pre-war trading conducted by their elders, which has resulted in enterprise and initiative being discouraged, and inactivity rewarded without merit. It has also meant that young men, deciding to start in business for themselves have been unable to build up anything that was worth while.

Further, as all supplies have been purchased by the Government, merchants have had no control over the quantity, quality, specification or price of the goods handed to them to sell. A graph on page 36 of this valuable book tells the sorry story of Government buying, and the majority of the Trade are sincerely of the opinion that the present shortage will never be overcome until the buying of softwood is once again handed back to the Trade.

This book will prove invaluable to the thousands of young men who may soon be called upon to accept the responsibilities of buying and importing the Softwood so much needed by the country. Many of them have had no previous experience, and in many cases their elders are not there to help them, but this compilation by two experts will prove a veritable *vade mecum* for them, and an invaluable book of reference for all engaged in the Trade. Nothing like it has ever been attempted before and it will fill a long-felt want.

CONTENTS

MAPS AND DIAGRAMS

Fig. *Page*

CONTRACT FORMS

(in band at end)

ACKNOWLEDGMENTS

It would not have been possible to prepare this book without the generous and whole-hearted co-operation of many people and authorities both inside and outside the trade. To all these people, the authors tender their sincere appreciation for the valuable assistance they have received.

In particular they wish to express their thanks to the following authorities for their permission to reproduce the material mentioned :—

Ernest Benn Ltd. (Extracts from " Shipping Marks on Timber ") ; Chamber of Shipping of the United Kingdom (Extracts and Copies of Nubaltwood and other charters) ; Statistical Office, Customs and Excise (Figures of United Kingdom Timber Imports) ; Institute of London Underwriters (Extracts and Copies of Insurance Clauses) ; Lloyd's Underwriters' Association (Extracts and Copies of Insurance Clauses) ; Timber Development Association Ltd. (Reproductions of Graphs of Imports and Prices) ; Timber Trade Federation of the United Kingdom (Extracts and Copies of T.T.F. Contract Forms) ; Wallboard Importers' Distributors' and Merchants' Association (Extracts and Copies of Britfibre Contract Form).

Their grateful thanks are also due to the following, who supplied much detail, information and statistics in the preparation of the copy :—

T. B. Beaton, Liverpool ; J. Bulkely, Churchill and Sim Ltd., London ; B. E. Drew, Liverpool ; The Finnish Sawmill Owners' Association ; E. E. House, C. V. Haerem & Co., Manchester ; Members of the Staff of Mallinson & Eckersley Ltd., Manchester ; A. P. Mayne and Staff of Price, Forbes & Co., Ltd., London ; Members of the Staff of Price & Pierce Ltd., London ; D. F. Money, Russian Wood Agency, London ; the late D. C. C. Ripper, Evans Bellhouse Ltd., Manchester ; R. B. Stoker, Manchester Liners Ltd., Manchester ; The Swedish Wood Exporters' Association ; F. H. Tweedy, Tweedy & Holt (Transport Economics) Ltd., Manchester ; and F. O. Wilson, Secretary, Manchester Timber Trade Association.

and also to the following who read, criticised and corrected the copy after its preparation :—

W. E. Bruce, M.A. (Cantab.), Secretary British Wood Preserving Association, formerly Chief Education Officer, Timber Development Association Ltd. ; H. J. Bocking, Secretary Timber Trade Federation of the U.K. ; H. A. Cox, M.A., Dip. For., Director British Wood Preserving Association, late Principal Scientific Officer, Forest Products Research Laboratory ; G. V. Donnelly, Wm. Brandt's (Timber) Ltd., London, Deputy Chairman, Timber Development Association Ltd. ; F. L. Forge, Secretary Federated Home Timber Association Ltd. ; the late G. T. Hollis, Hollis Bros. Ltd., Hull ; D. B. Irvin, Irvin & Sellers Ltd., Liverpool, Deputy Chairman, Timber Development Association Ltd. ; B. Alwyn Jay, M.A. (Cantab.), F.L.S., Deputy Director Timber Development Association Ltd. ; L. G. Jennings, F.S.S., Statistician and Information Officer, Timber Development Association Ltd. ; R. H. Lindsey-Renton, G. H. Renton & Co. Ltd., London ; the late S. Lisler, Thos. White & Sons Ltd., Paisley ; and Stanley C. Longhurst, E. Longhurst & Sons Ltd., Epsom, Past President of Federated Home Timber Association Ltd.

SOME REFERENCE BOOKS

H. T. Eyres, *Introducing Wood.* (Pitman, 1950.)

H. E. Desch, *Timber: Structure and Properties.* (Macmillan, 1948.)

W. Bullock, *Timber: From the Forest to its Use in Commerce.* (Pitman, 1945.)

Russell Meigs, *Home Timber Production.* (Crosby Lockwood, 1949.)

A. D. Wood and T. G. Linn, *Plywoods.* (W. & A. K. Johnston, 1950.)

T. J. Stobart, *Timber Trade of the United Kingdom.* (Technical Press, 1927; out of print.)

C. F. Laver, *Principles of Log Measurement.* (Ernest Benn, 1951.)

Shipping Marks on Timber. (Ernest Benn, 1951.)

Wood Trade, C.I.F. Contracts. (Ernest Benn, 1930.)

Arbitration in the Timber Trade. (Ernest Benn, 1929.)

S. E. Thomas, *Commerce, its Theory and Practice.* (Gregg Publishing Co., 1932.)

J. Charlesworth, *Principles of Mercantile Law.* (Stevens & Sons, 1949.)

Chalmers Sale of Goods Act, 1893. (Butterworth, Revised 1945.)

C. E. Odgers, *Introduction to the Law of Contracts.* (Sweet & Maxwell, 1948.)

D. B. Buckley, *Companies Acts.* (Butterworth, 1948.)

W. M. Geldart, *Elements of English Law.* (O.U.P., Home University Library, 1948.)

W. J. Thorne, *Banking.* (O.U.P., Home University Library, 1948.)

D. Richardson, *A Simple Guide to Negotiable Instruments and Bills of Exchange Acts.* (Butterworth, 1948.)

C. D. McMurray and M. M. Cree, *Shipping and Shipbuilding.* (Pitman, 1941; out of print.)

Lord Chorley and O. C. Giles, *Shipping Law.* (Pitman, 1947.)

S. Gibbon, *Paynes Carriage by Sea.* (Butterworth, 1949.)

H. A. Turner, *Principles of Marine Insurance.* (Stone & Cox, 1951.)

F. Templeman and G. T. Greenacre, *Marine Insurance.* (Macdonald & Evans, 1934.)

F. Russell, *Law of Arbitration.* (Stevens & Sons, 1952.)

CHAPTER I

Geographical Background

1. General.

Forests cover more than one-fifth of the earth's land surface, although only a proportion are in positions where it is economical and practical to fell and extract the timber. The trees from which we obtain our timber vary considerably in size and quality depending upon their environment. The many varied conditions of weather, soil, altitude and location each have their effect on the growth of the tree and hence on the quality of the timber it produces.

(*a*) Softwoods (Conifers).

Softwoods are found principally in a broad belt stretching across the North American continent, Scandinavia, Russia and Siberia. The commoner softwoods such as European redwood and whitewood when grown in different parts of Europe produce very different grades of timber.

Generally speaking the farther north a conifer grows the better the timber it will produce, as the rate of growth is slower than in the warmer southern climates. The "annual rings" are narrower and the timber is more even in texture and more valuable. It must however be borne in mind that altitude may compensate for latitude; also that trees growing in the north may develop different defects from those growing in the south, such as the black knots in North Scandinavian whitewood. For instance the Scots pine (*Pinus sylvestris*) whilst it is but one species to the botanist, may produce any one of five or six commercial timbers to the timber merchant. It might be "Archangel redwood," "Leningrad redwood," "Finnish redwood," "Swedish redwood," or "Home Grown Scots pine," each of which will be different in quality and have its own value.

(*b*) Hardwoods.

There are two general categories of hardwoods.

Temperate Hardwoods—from Europe and North America,
Tropical Hardwoods—from Central and South America, Africa, India and S.E. Asia, Australasia.

Hardwoods of the same species also vary greatly according to local conditions of temperature, rainfall, etc., which affect the structure of the wood during growth. It is necessary therefore when studying the Timber Trade to have a broad geographical background of the various producing and exporting countries.

In most cases timber is graded, named and priced according to the port from which it is shipped. Very often the timber is given the name of the port as a pre-fix such as "Archangel" redwood, "Memel" whitewood, "San Domingo" mahogany, etc. When the timber comes from sawmills some distance inland from a port it will usually take the name of the district where it was produced such as "Slavonian" beech, "Appalachian" oak.

Many of the northern ports are completely frozen over during the winter months which restricts the period each year during which timber can be shipped from that port. The date when the port is declared open for shipping is known as "first open water" (abbreviated f.o.w.). This date will vary slightly each year depending upon a mild or a severe winter.

The following maps and tables give the most important exporting countries of softwood, hardwood and plywood, showing the principal districts and ports from which timber is shipped. In order to show the relative importance of each country, the volume of their exports to the U.K. of softwood, hardwood and plywood are given for the years 1938, 1948 and 1951.

2. Russia.

Nearly one-third of the world's forest resources are in the U.S.S.R. In these northern forests are large pine trees of slow growth from which is produced redwood of fine texture and close grain and a large proportion of high quality wood which is especially noticeable in the boards which are cut from the outer part of the log. These high quality boards have in the past been much sought after and have commanded a very high price, but owing to the fact that the general quality requirements for joinery are not so high as they used to be, there is no longer quite the same demand for expensive boards.

The sapwood of the redwood is close-grained and of an attractive creamy colour. This well-grown wood is much less liable to warp and twist than sappy open-grained wood and is therefore specially suitable for joinery purposes. The finest redwood comes from the Kara Sea which, owing to ice hindrances, has a very short shipping season since the loading port Igarka lies far up the Yenisei river. The whitewood shipped from the White Sea ports is also of fine quality, but that shipped from the Leningrad area is more similar to the South Finnish productions. Exports consist of sawn softwood (redwood and whitewood), poles, pitprops, sleepers and plywood with a small proportion of planed softwood.

The variations in the c.i.f. prices of Archangel redwood from 1923 to 1952 are shown in Fig. 2. The prices are based on f.o.w. shipments and estimates have had to be made for 1940-41 when there were no purchases of Russian wood by the U.K. During 1942-51 purchases were on f.o.b. basis to which estimated freight rates have been added to make the graph uniform.

IMPORTS FROM U.S.S.R.

	1938			1948			1951		
	Amount	Av. C.I.F. Value	Percentage of Total Import	Amount	Av. C.I.F. Value	Percentage of Total Import	Amount	Av. C.I.F. Value	Percentage of Total Import
		£ s. d.			£ s. d.			£ s. d.	
Sawn Softwood ...	343,500 stds.	13 12 3	23·2	23,200 stds.	54 0 11	2·8	103,000 stds.	103 16 4	6·5
Planed Softwood	4,665 ,,	—	1·7	—	—	—	—	—	—
Pitprops	94,400 piled fathoms	6 10 11	13·8	9,200 piled fathoms	24 0 8	1·7	48,700 piled fathoms	39 19 10	11·7
Plywood	63,700 cubic metres	8 19 10	20·7	—	—	—	71,500 cubic metres	54 5 9	23·5

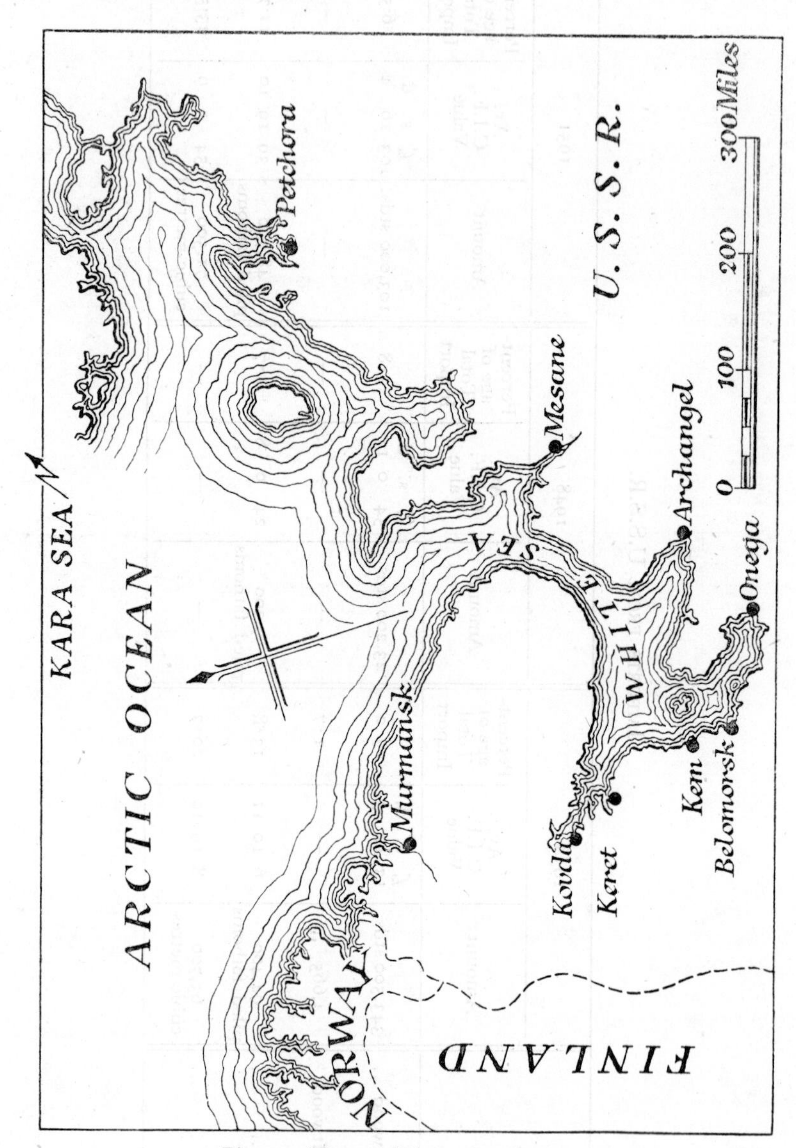

Fig. 1. Map of White Sea Ports.

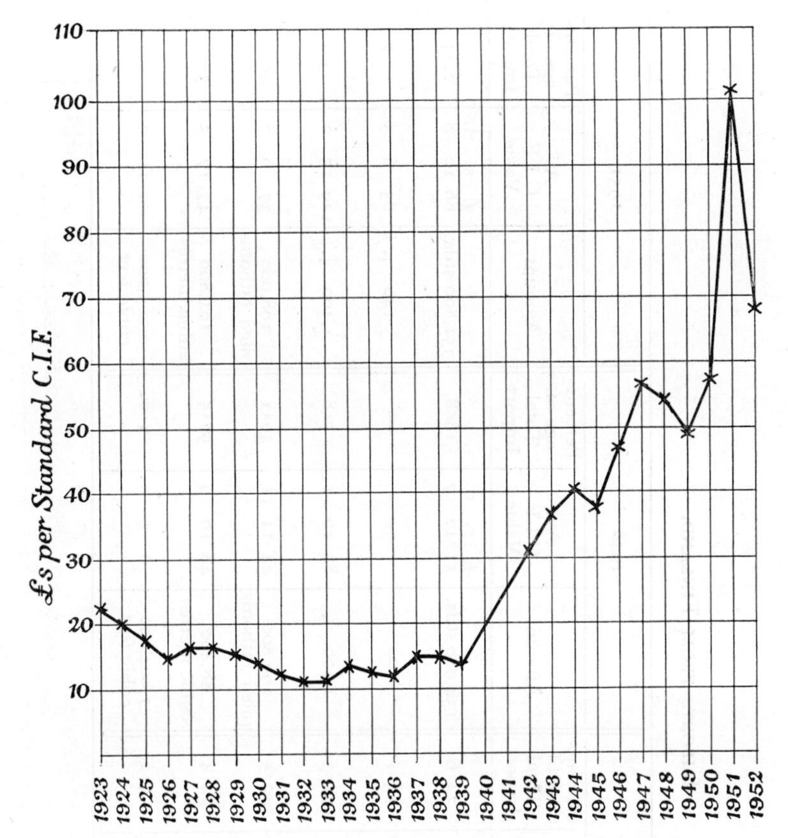

Fig. 2. RUSSIAN SOFTWOOD PRICES, C.I.F. 1923-1952.
Based upon prices for 7″ unsorted Redwood Battens.

3. Finland.

In the years up to 1939 Finland was the largest single exporting country of timber to the U.K. The loss of territory to the U.S.S.R., including some of the finest forest areas, at the end of the Russo-Finnish war in 1940 reduced the forest resources of Finland, but notwithstanding this reduction it remains one of the largest and most important timber exporting countries of the world.

There is a great variety of growth, the product of the northern and eastern parts being close-grained, fine-textured wood, much in demand for joinery. The pine trees producing redwood in the north of Finland are not so large as in Russia, so that the dimensions produced are not so wide, but the narrower boards are usually of very fine quality and the wood of a pleasing reddish colour. The whitewood is also close-grained and fine-textured, but that grown in the north

IMPORTS FROM FINLAND.

	1938			1948			1951		
	Amount	Av. C.I.F. Value	Percentage of Total Import	Amount	Av. C.I.F. Value	Percentage of Total Import	Amount	Av. C.I.F. Value	Percentage of Total Import
		£ s. d.			£ s. d.			£ s. d.	
Sawn Softwood ...	364,300 stds.	12 4 4	24·6	154,900 stds.	51 12 7	18·8	351,800 stds.	86 10 8	22·4
Planed Softwood	39,200 ,,	15 13 8	13·1	—	—	—	140 ,,	85 6 3	·7
Boxboards ...	27,800 ,,	19 14 9	31·3	1,400 ,,	82 16 1	5·8	1,400 ,,	129 15 2	3·6
Pitprops	277,000 piled fathoms	7 12 9	40·5	196,800 piled fathoms	24 11 11	36·1	168,000 piled fathoms	37 6 7	40·2
Plywood	136,500 cubic metres	9 18 1	44·4	88,400 cubic metres	48 16 9	50·5	101,800 cubic metres	47 17 5	33·5
Sawn Hardwood	1,287,000 cubic feet	0 2 2	4·2	1,004,000 cubic feet	0 9 0	5·0	2,265,000 cubic feet	0 11 6	5·9

Fig. 3. Map of Finnish Ports.

(The Finish-Swedish frontier is the river between Haparanda and Tornio.)

usually contains many small black knots. In other parts of Finland the wood is generally more quickly grown and consequently more sappy and open-grained. The so-called "second-grade" stocks consist almost entirely of this sappier wood, whilst the better productions, even from the south of Finland, contain a high percentage of close-grained wood quite suitable for joinery.

Exports are principally sawn and planed softwood (redwood and whitewood), poles, pitprops, boxboards, etc., and plywood, with moderate quantities of hardwood, mainly birch, from the south of Finland.

4. Sweden.

Sweden has always been one of the most important suppliers of timber to the U.K., the redwood shipped from the more northerly ports comparing favourably with redwood from the White Sea. There is considerable diversity of growth and manufacture as the large forest areas of the northern half of Sweden are well cared for and are operated on a large scale with all the latest technical improvements in manufacture, etc. In the southern half of the country, whilst there are some fine forest areas in the interior, there are also coastal areas with a more scattered growth which are converted in small rotary sawmills and are obtainable at a lower price. The best grades of Swedish redwood and whitewood are close-grained, of even texture and easy to work. Swedish redwood has always been a favourite of the joiner, and its pinkish colour is distinctive, something between the darker reddish-brown colour of the North Finland wood and the creamy colour of South Finland wood.

Exports consist mainly of sawn and planed softwood (redwood and whitewood), poles, pitprops, boxboards, etc., and plywood.

Fig. 6 shows the average f.o.b. prices at f.o.w. for Swedish and Finnish timber from 1920 to 1952. These prices show considerable variation.

5. Norway.

Norway has not been an important supplier of timber to the U.K. for many years owing to severe over-exploitation of the forest resources of the country in the nineteenth century. The need for conservation of the Norwegian forests to-day limits very greatly the amount of timber available. The Norwegians make the best of their difficulties by specialising in exports of planed goods and boxboards. They even import timber for the purpose of machining and exporting it. Other exports include telegraph, ladder and scaffold poles.

6. Lower Baltic States.

This includes Poland and the areas that up to 1940 were Estonia, Latvia and Lithuania. The redwood from these areas is generally more open-grained and resinous than from more northerly areas. Although less suitable for joinery, it is often preferred for general constructional purposes as it is cheaper than the higher grades from

IMPORTS FROM SWEDEN.

	1938			1948			1951		
	Amount	Av. C.I.F. Value	Percentage of Total Import	Amount	Av. C.I.F. Value	Percentage of Total Import	Amount	Av. C.I.F. Value	Percentage of Total Import
		£ s. d.			£ s. d.			£ s. d.	
Sawn Softwood ...	218,500 stds.	12 15 1	14·7	174,600 stds.	52 12 11	21·2	322,000 stds.	86 4 10	20·4
Planed Softwood	119,200 ,,	16 13 1	40·1	18,100 ,,	63 15 0	46·1	7,200 ,,	98 4 1	34·7
Boxboards ...	30,800 ,,	22 8 2	34·7	17,400 ,,	76 13 11	71·8	24,600 ,,	126 17 4	66·2
Pitprops	41,000 piled fathoms	6 18 5	6·0	34,300 piled fathoms	23 10 4	6·3	66,900 piled fathoms	35 14 4	16·0
Plywood	6,200 cubic metres	10 2 7	2·0	12,200 cubic metres	47 12 7	7·0	14,400 cubic metres	49 6 5	4·7

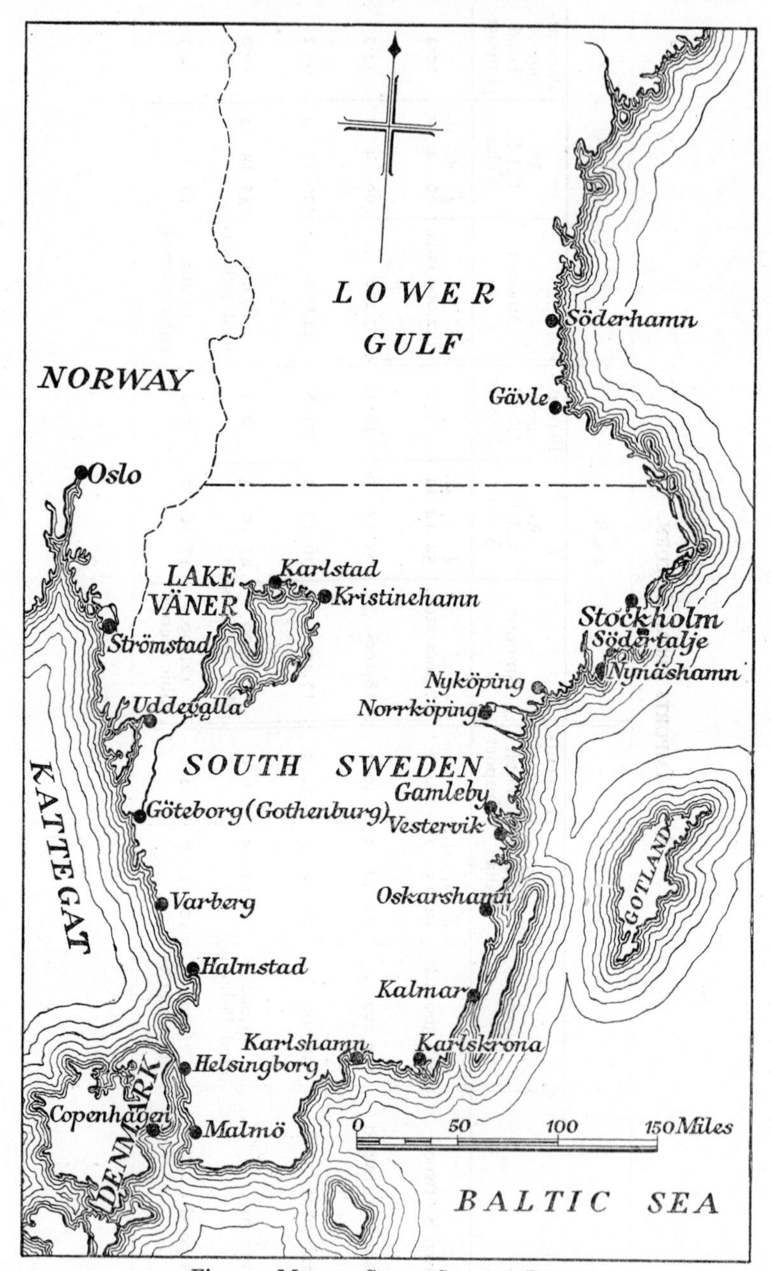

Fig. 4. Map of South Swedish Ports.

Fig. 5. MAP OF SWEDEN—UPPER, MIDDLE AND LOWER GULF PORTS.

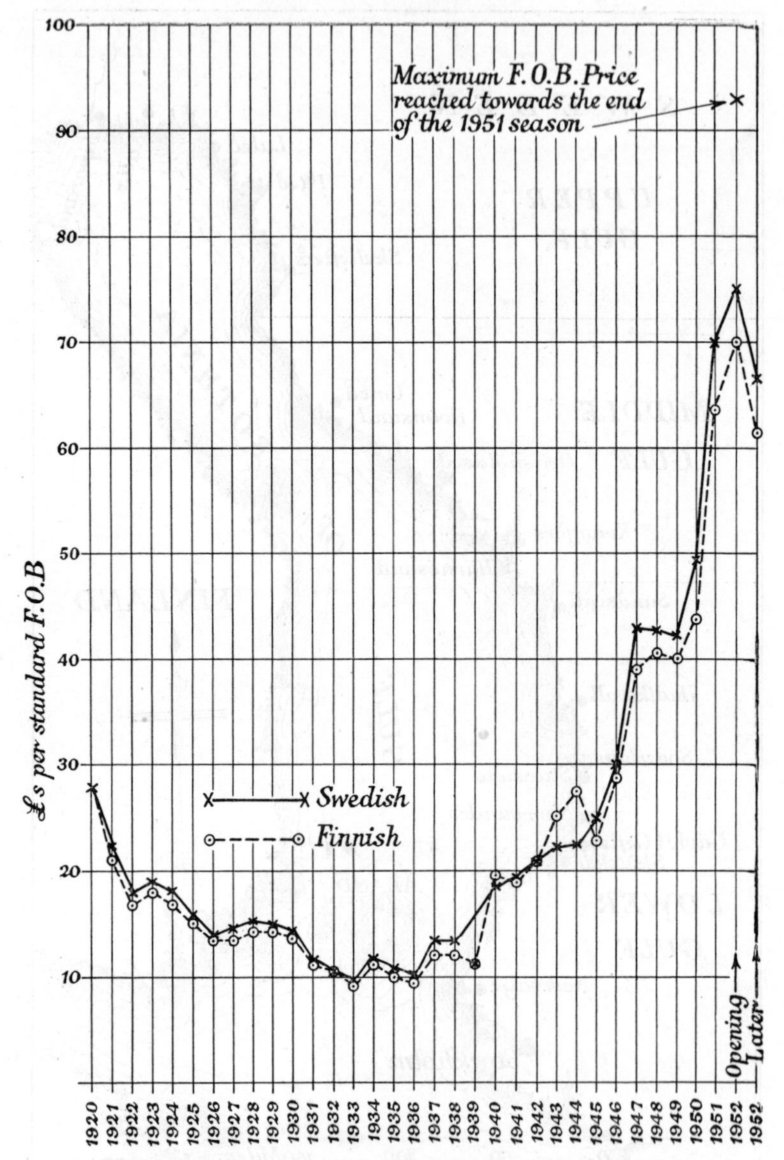

Fig. 6. Finnish and Swedish Opening Prices, F.O.B. 1920-1952.
Based upon prices for 7″ unsorted Redwood Battens.

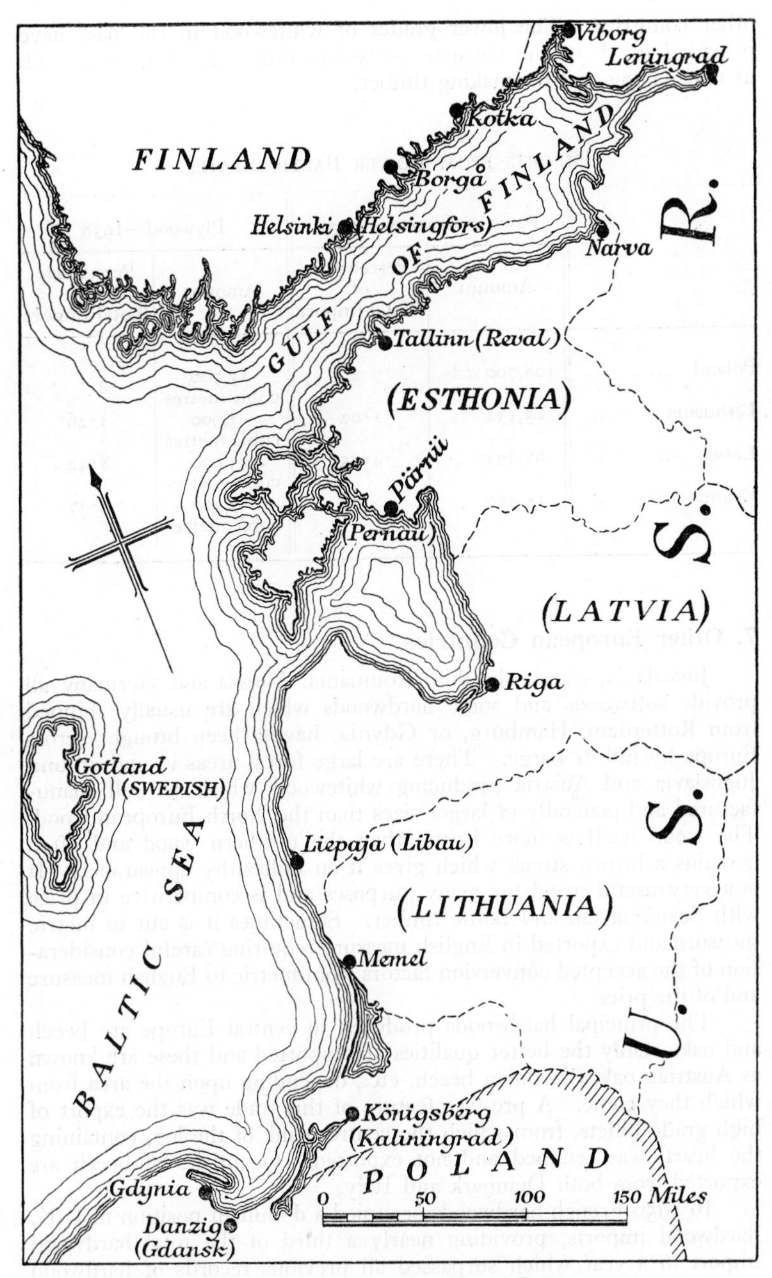

Fig. 7. MAP OF LOWER BALTIC PORTS

other countries. The lower grades of whitewood in the past have provided much of the cheaper carcassing timber for houses as well as casemaking and boxmaking timber.

IMPORTS FROM LOWER BALTIC STATES.

	Sawn Softwoods—1938		Plywood—1938	
	Amount	Percentage of Total Import	Amount	Percentage of Total Import
Poland	108,700 stds.	7·4	15,700 cubic metres	5·1
Lithuania ...	15,132 ,,	1·02	3,900 cubic metres	1·26
Latvia	67,394 ,,	4·55	25,900 cubic metres	8·42
Estonia	14,550 ,,	·98	7,300 cubic metres	2·37

7. Other European Countries.

Jugoslavia, Czechoslovakia, Roumania, Austria and Germany all provide softwoods and some hardwoods which are usually shipped from Rotterdam, Hamburg, or Gdynia, having been brought across Europe by rail or barge. There are large forest areas in and around Jugoslavia and Austria producing whitewood which is well manufactured and generally of larger sizes than the North European wood. The wood itself is more brittle than the northern wood and often contains a brown streak which gives it an unhealthy appearance. It is a very useful wood for many purposes and is competitive in price with Scandinavian and Baltic timber. Sometimes it is cut to metric measure and exported in English measure requiring careful consideration of the accepted conversion factors from metric to English measure and of the price.

The principal hardwoods produced in central Europe are beech and oak. Only the better qualities are exported and these are known as Austrian oak, Slavonian beech, etc., depending upon the area from which they come. A pre-war feature of this trade was the export of high grade billets, from which the centre plank of the log, containing the heart, was retained and not exported. Quantities of beech are exported from both Denmark and Italy.

In 1950 French hardwoods occupied a dominant position in U.K. hardwood imports, providing nearly a third of the total hardwood import in a year which surpassed all previous records of hardwood imports.

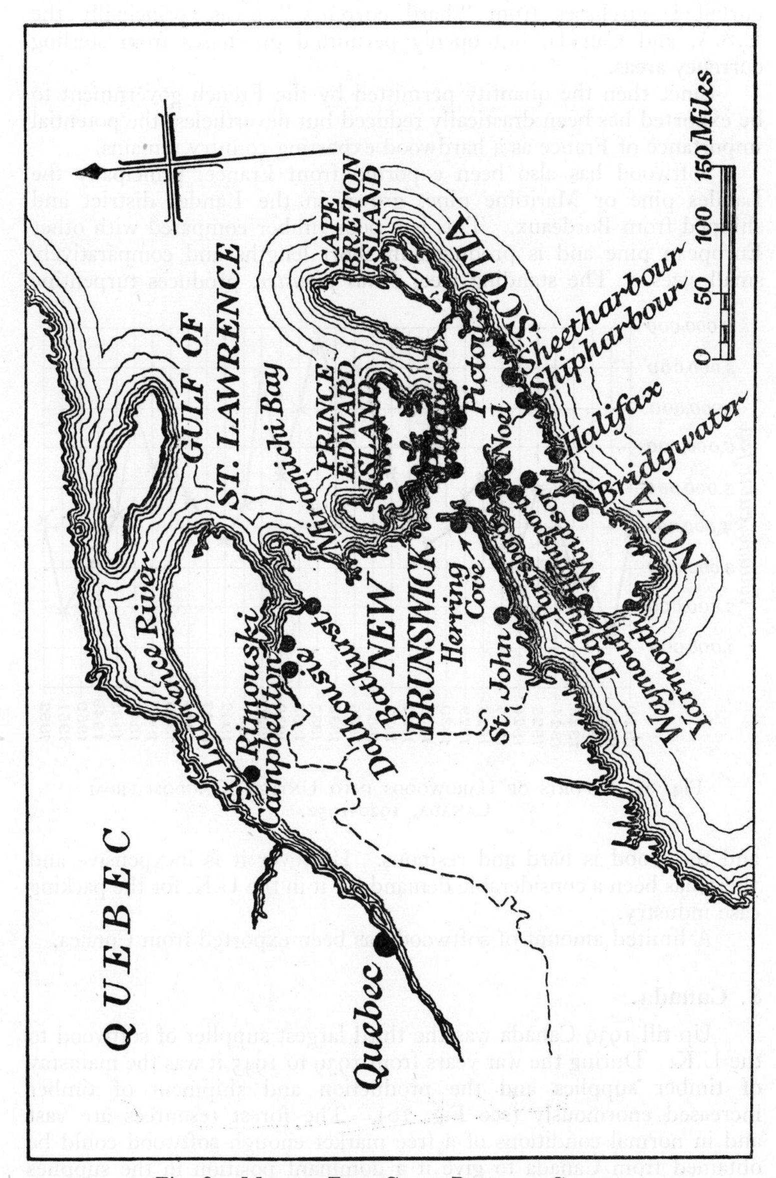

Fig. 8. Map of East Coast Ports of Canada.

Much of this was caused through currency restrictions which curtailed purchases from "hard currency" areas, principally the U.S.A. and Canada, but openly permitted purchases from sterling currency areas.

Since then the quantity permitted by the French government to be exported has been drastically reduced but nevertheless the potential importance of France as a hardwood exporting country remains.

Softwood has also been exported from France, principally the Landes pine or Maritime pine, grown in the Landes district and shipped from Bordeaux. This is a poor timber compared with other European pine and is produced in short lengths and comparatively small sizes. The standing tree, *Pinus pinaster*, produces turpentine

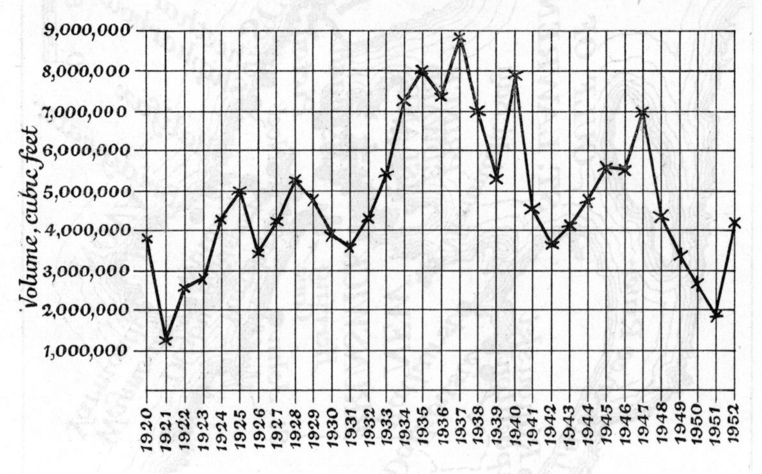

Fig. 9. IMPORTS OF HARDWOODS INTO UNITED KINGDOM FROM CANADA, 1920-1952.

and the wood is hard and resinous. However it is inexpensive and there has been a considerable demand for it in the U.K. for the packing case industry.

A limited amount of softwood has been exported from Corsica.

8. Canada.

Up till 1939 Canada was the third largest supplier of softwood to the U.K. During the war years from 1939 to 1945 it was the mainstay of timber supplies and the production and shipment of timber increased enormously (see Fig. 10). The forest resources are vast and in normal conditions of a free market enough softwood could be obtained from Canada to give it a dominant position in the supplies to this country. Although the freight rates from Canada are obviously very much greater than those from Scandinavia, the lower initial cost of the timber, together with the Imperial Preference of freedom from import duty, means that Canadian timber is competitive in price with the equivalent Scandinavian product.

Timber is exported from both the East and West coasts, the latter coming through the Panama Canal.

EAST COAST.

Spruce is the principal timber exported from the East Coast Maritime Provinces, and shipments vary greatly from one another in value according to the individual shipper, the port of shipment and the method of manufacture. It may be rotary sawn or bandsawn, the

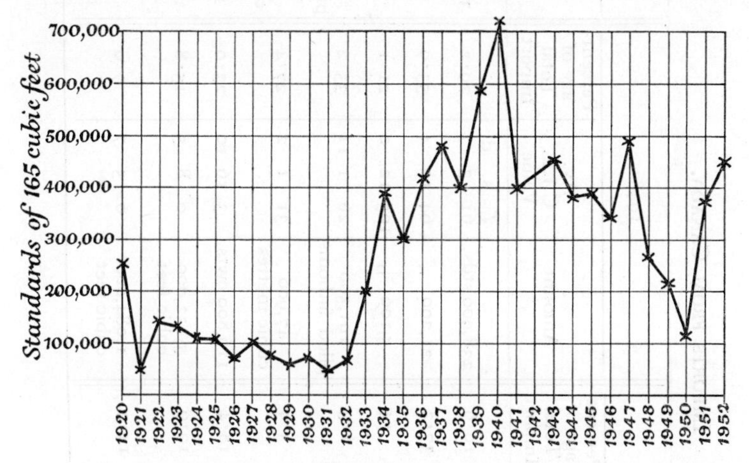

Fig. 10. IMPORTS OF SOFTWOODS INTO UNITED KINGDOM FROM CANADA, 1920-1952.

latter being a superior production as the rotary sawn timber is sometimes very uneven. The best qualities are shipped from Quebec.

White pine (*Pinus strobus*) is the other important softwood, known in this country as Quebec "yellow" pine or Ottawa pine. This even-textured timber is used a great deal by patternmakers. It is expensive, but is easier and more satisfying to work than the highest European grades of redwood.

Birch is the most important Canadian hardwood, and is shipped through Quebec. Other hardwoods that are exported are maple and beech. A certain amount of hardwood plywood is produced and exported from the East Coast.

WEST COAST.

The largest and most important Canadian tree is the Douglas fir, exported from the West Coast through Vancouver and British

IMPORTS FROM CANADA.

	1938			1948			1951		
	Amount	Av. C.I.F. Value	Percentage of Total Import	Amount	Av. C.I.F. Value	Percentage of Total Import	Amount	Av. C.I.F. Value	Percentage of Total Import
		£ s. d.			£ s. d.			£ s. d.	
Sawn Softwood ...	290,100 stds.	13 19 9	19·6	238,900 stds.	61 3 7	29·2	372,200 stds.	93 12 1	23·6
Planed Softwood	110,800 ,,	13 6 5	37·2	21,200 ,,	64 10 4	53·9	7,650 ,,	85 14 8	36·8
Boxboards ...	300 ,,	32 0 7	·4	5,100 ,,	105 12 0	21·1	200 ,,	138 9 4	·5
Pitprops	8,900 piled fathoms	6 16 1	1·3	191,500 piled fathoms	26 1 11	35·2	51,700 piled fathoms	38 14 11	12·4
Plywood	10,600 cubic metres	12 14 2	3·4	47,900 cubic metres	31 1 2	27·4	14,200 cubic metres	59 4 5	4·7
Veneers	45,500 cwts.	0 19 6	18·4	116,800 cwts.	3 16 10	23·0	12,600 cwts.	5 6 7	1·5
Sawn Hardwood	6,108,000 cubic feet	0 2 3	19·9	3,152,000 cubic feet	0 8 5	15·8	1,276,000 cubic feet	0 14 4	3·3
Hewn Hardwood	456,000 cubic feet	0 3 7	14·2	1,084,000 cubic feet	0 5 7	7·0	661,000 cubic feet	0 11 9	2·7

IMPORTS FROM U.S.A.

	1938			1948			1951		
	Amount	Av. C.I.F. Value	Percentage of Total Import	Amount	Av. C.I.F. Value	Percentage of Total Import	Amount	Av. C.I.F. Value	Percentage of Total Import
		£ s. d.			£ s. d.			£ s. d.	
Sawn Softwood ..	34,000 stds.	27 8 7	2·3	66,500 stds.	58 12 10	8·1	122,300 stds.	90 18 8	7·7
Plywood ...	7,900 cubic metres	12 0 0	2·6	8,700 cubic metres	50 19 5	5·0	9,451 cubic metres	54 14 10	3·1
Veneers ...	39,400 cwts.	2 10 7	16·0	76,900 cwts.	5 4 2	15·1	72,900 cwts.	6 1 9	8·6
Sawn Hardwood	9,893,000 cubic feet	0 3 8	32·2	2,989,000 cubic feet	0 12 8	15·0	2,235,000 cubic feet	1 9 8	5·8

Columbia ports. In addition to the normal dimensions of timber the Douglas fir provides the exceptionally large dimensions up to 30 ins. × 30 ins. and of great length, that are required for heavy constructional work and are unobtainable elsewhere.

The West Coast provides two other important structural timbers, Western hemlock and Western red cedar. These two together with Douglas fir are available in " clear " grades, that is to say straight-grained with complete absence of knots. These grades command higher prices than the best European softwoods as they are only available from this area. Other softwoods from the West Coast are Western white pine, a timber very similar to the Quebec " yellow " pine, and the Sitka spruce which is fine textured and long fibred being very strong for its weight. It produces large dimensions of high quality wood and provides the Aero grades required for aircraft construction.

Plywood is now manufactured on a large scale in British Columbia from Douglas fir, and constitutes an important export.

9. U.S.A.

For many years the traditional imports from the U.S.A. have been pitch pine and hardwoods. Economic currency restrictions since 1947 have forced Great Britain to seek new sources for the supply of hardwoods. Notwithstanding this, the hardwood lumber industry of the U.S.A. is one of the most highly productive and efficient timber producing organisations of the world with very high standards of selection, grading and marketing.

There are probably over 30 or 40 species of hardwood being exported from the U.S.A., but by far the most important is oak which is sold as red oak or white oak according to species. Other important hardwoods are ash, gum, walnut, hickory and poplar. The mills producing hardwoods are grouped into two main areas, Northern and Southern. Oak, beech and ash from the Northern area, particularly the Appalachians, being better grown and more valuable than Southern production.

Although practically one third of the sawn hardwood imported in 1938 came from the U.S.A., this proportion is not likely to be attained again. Economic restrictions on imports from hard currency countries will be maintained for several years and alternative sources of hardwoods are being exploited in other countries, most notably in the British Commonwealth (see para. 11—East and West Africa). Furthermore the hardwood industry in the U.S.A. has now long since found internal and external outlets for the production previously exported to the U.K.

10. Central and South America.

The South American continent has very large areas of tropical hardwoods and Brazil has quantities of softwood, mainly Parana pine.

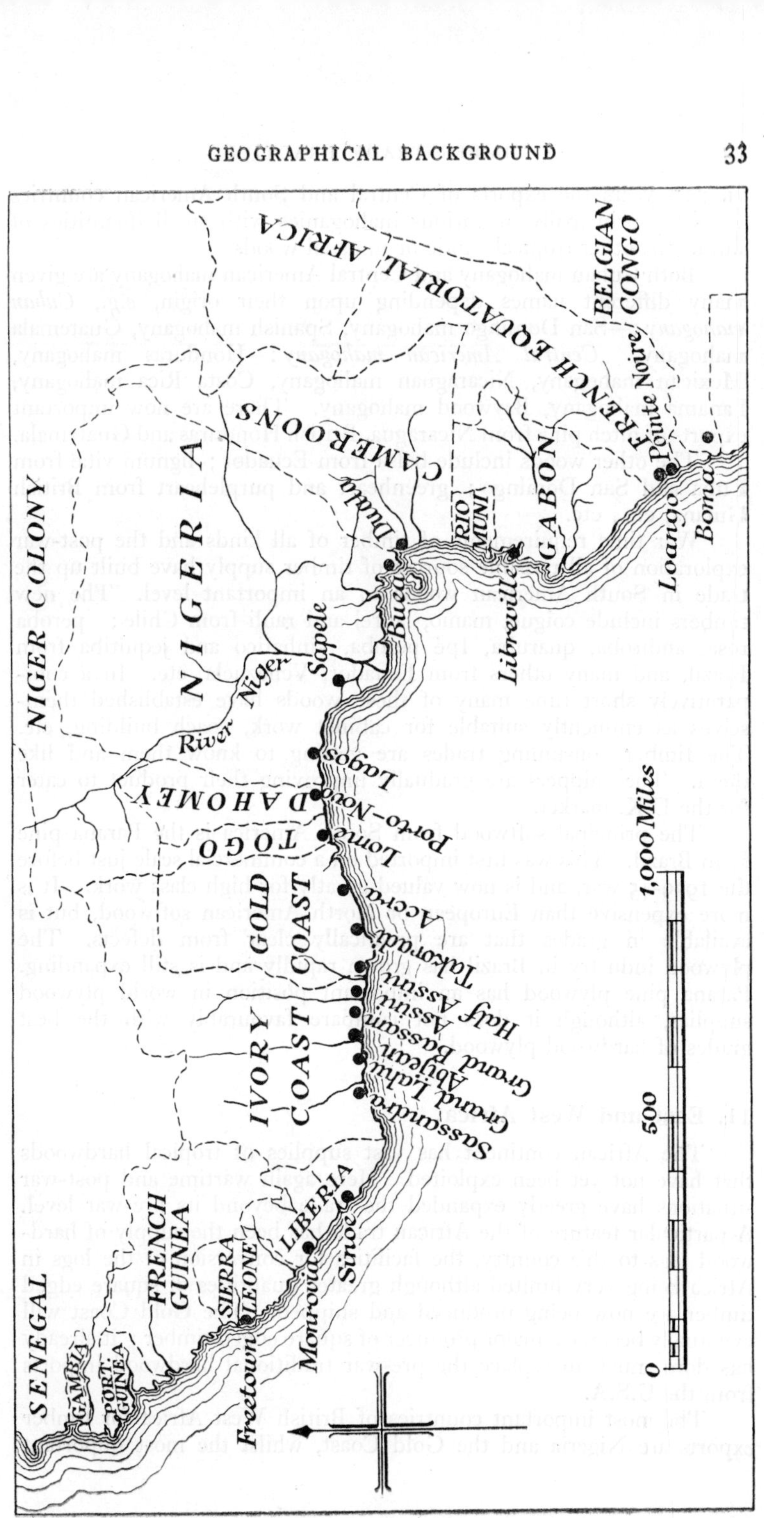

Fig. 11. Map of West African Ports.

In past years the exports of Central and South American countries consisted principally of various mahoganies with small quantities of numerous other tropical exotic or unusual woods.

Both Cuban mahogany and Central American mahogany are given many different names depending upon their origin, *e.g.*, *Cuban mahogany* :—San Domingo mahogany, Spanish mahogany, Guatemala mahogany. *Central American mahogany* :—Honduras mahogany, Mexican mahogany, Nicaraguan mahogany, Costa Rica mahogany, Panama mahogany, Baywood mahogany. There are now important exports of pitch pine from Nicaragua, British Honduras and Guatemala.

The other woods include balsa from Ecuador ; lignum vitæ from Cuba and San Domingo ; greenheart and purpleheart from British Guiana, etc., etc.

War time requirements of timber of all kinds and the post-war exploration of all possible sources of timber supply have built up the trade in South American woods to an important level. The new timbers include coigue, manio, laurel and rauli from Chile ; peroba rosa, andiroba, quaruba, Ipé peroba, vinhatico and jequitiba from Brazil, and many others from Ecuador, Venezuela, etc. In a comparatively short time many of these woods have established themselves as eminently suitable for cabinet work, coach building, etc. The timber consuming trades are getting to know them and like them. The shippers are gradually improving their product to cater for the U.K. market.

The principal softwood from South America is the Parana pine from Brazil. This was first imported on a commercial scale just before the 1939-45 war, and is now valued greatly for high class work. It is more expensive than European or North American softwood, but is available in grades that are practically clear from defects. The plywood industry in Brazil has grown rapidly and is still expanding. Parana pine plywood has an important position in world plywood supplies, although it does not compare favourably with the best grades of hardwood plywood.

11. East and West Africa.

The African continent has vast supplies of tropical hardwoods that have not yet been exploited. Here again wartime and post-war situations have greatly expanded the trade beyond its pre-war level. A particular feature of the African trade has been the supply of hardwood logs to this country, the facilities for conversion of the logs in Africa being very limited although greater quantities of square edged timber are now being produced and shipped. The Gold Coast will eventually become a major producer of square edged timber ; it already has done much to replace the pre-war traditional hardwood imports from the U.S.A.

The most important countries of British West Africa for timber exports are Nigeria and the Gold Coast, whilst the most important

Sawn Softwood Imports to U.K.

	1938			1948			1951		
	Stds.	Av. C.I.F. Value	Percentage	Stds.	Av. C.I.F. Value	Percentage	Stds.	Av. C.I.F. Value	Percentage
		£ s. d.			£ s. d.			£ s. d.	
Finland	364,300	12 4 4	24·6	154,900	51 12 7	18·8	351,800	86 10 8	22·4
U.S.S.R.... ...	343,500	13 12 3	23·2	23,200	54 0 11	2·8	103,000	103 16 4	6·5
Canada	290,100	13 19 9	19·6	238,900	61 3 7	29·2	372,200	93 12 1	23·6
Sweden	218,500	12 15 1	14·7	174,600	52 12 11	21·2	322,000	86 4 10	20·4
Poland	108,700	12 6 4	7·4	31,200	50 18 8	3·8	—	—	—
U.S.A.	34,100	27 8 7	2·37	66,500	58 12 10	8·1	122,300	90 18 8	7·7
Germany ...	400	13 16 6	·03	79,100	46 3 0	9·7	6,600	88 10 8	·4
France	—	—	—	—	—	—	89,600	58 6 8	5·7
Jugoslavia ...	—	—	—	—	—	—	70,400	72 13 2	4·5
Brazil	—	—	—	—	—	—	39,500	90 19 0	2·5
Others	120,800*	12 3 11	8·1	52,200	53 1 1	6·4	99,000	83 4 9	6·3
Total ...	1,480,400		100·0	820,600		100·0	1,576,400		100·0

The average c.i.f. values for imports from U.S.A. in 1938 are high on account of the preponderance of pitch pine in these pre-war imports.

* Softwood imports from other countries in 1938 included the following:—

Estonia ...	14,550 stds.	Norway	3,827 stds.	Roumania ...	4,842 stds.
Latvia ...	67,394 ,,	Czechoslovakia ...	575 ,,	Brazil	1,034 ,,
Lithuania ...	15,132 ,,	Jugoslavia ...	10,612 ,,	Others ...	2,794 ,,

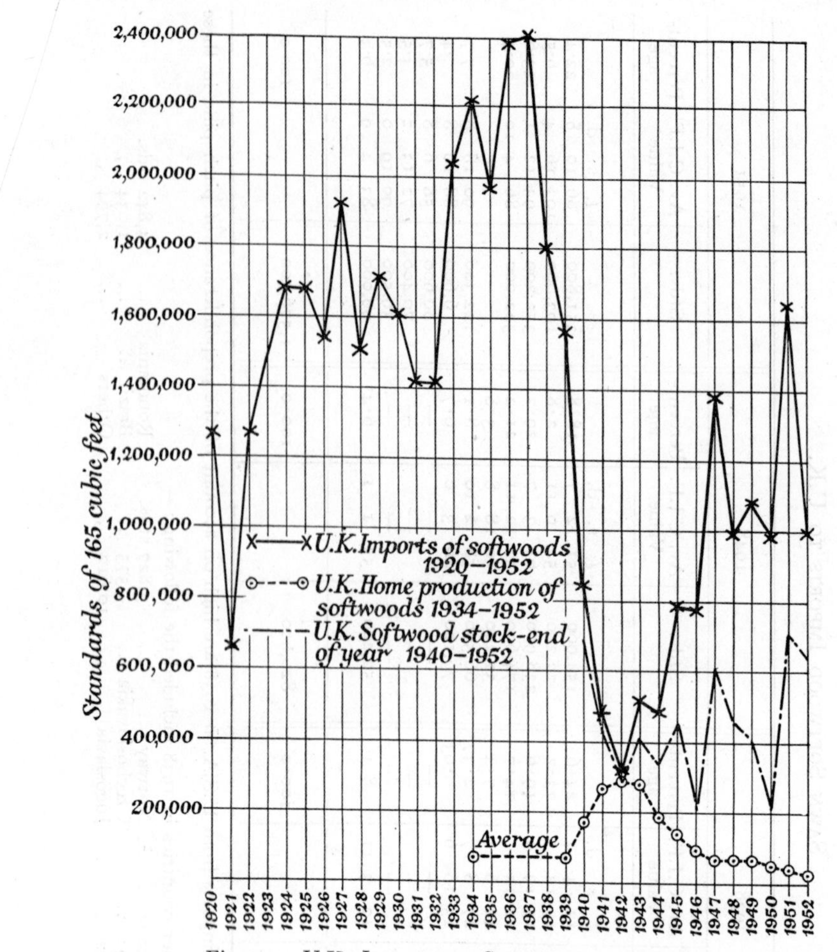

Fig. 12. U.K. IMPORTS OF SOFTWOODS, 1920-1952.

French colonies of West Africa are the Ivory Coast, Gaboon, and French Cameroons. There are many hundreds of species of hardwoods grown in West Africa. The commercial names of these woods are rather confusing particularly since there are sometimes several local names for the same species, and one local name may apply to more than one species of timber.

Place names and port names are also used, particularly with African " mahogany " and African " walnut," *e.g.*, Lagos mahogany, Benin mahogany, Nigerian walnut, Gold Coast walnut. Amongst other timbers regularly shipped from both the Gold Coast and Nigeria must be mentioned Obeche which is now very popular.

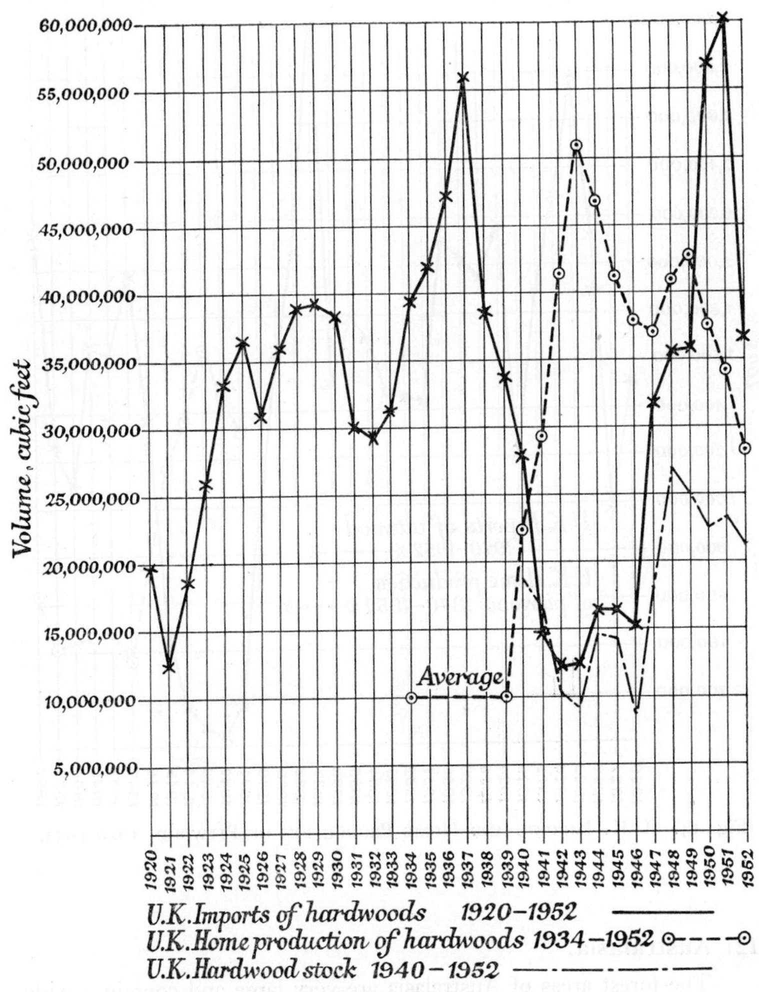

Fig. 13. U.K. IMPORTS OF HARDWOODS, 1920-1952.

British East Africa and Portugese East Africa now export sawn hardwoods and hardwood logs to the U.K. from the port of Mombasa. This trade is only small compared with the older established West African trade.

Valuable softwoods are now coming from Kenya, such as the *Podocarpus* species known as podo.

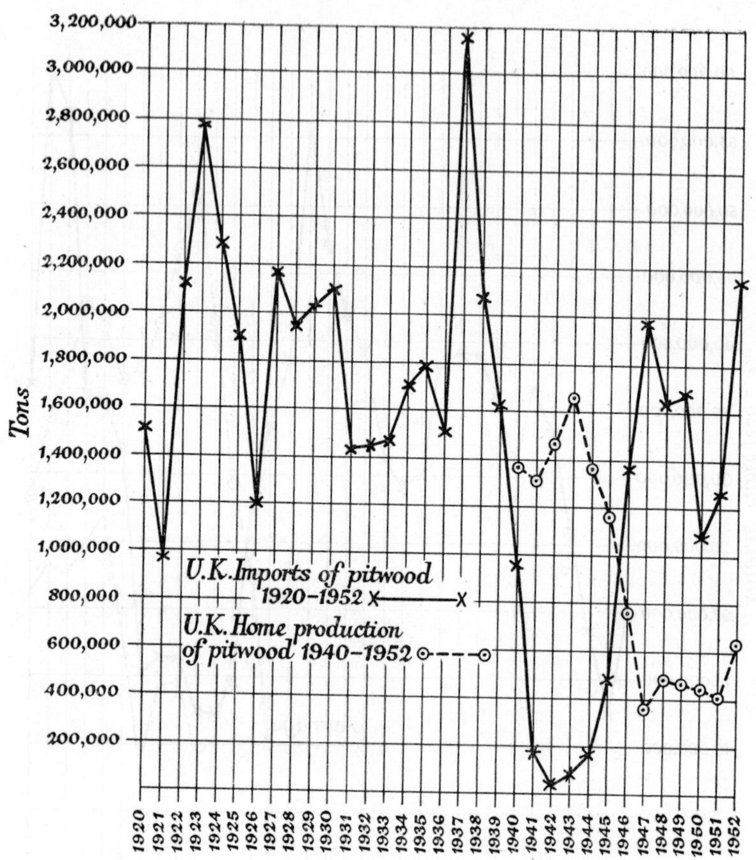

Fig. 14. U.K. Imports and Home Production of Pitwood, 1920-1952.

12. Australasia.

The forest areas of Australasia are very large and contain a wide variety of excellent hardwoods and softwoods, but on account of the distances involved, the freight rates are very high. This limits the timbers that can be imported and used economically to those timbers with special qualities for heavy structural work such as jarrah and karri, or those timbers that are specially decorative such as Queensland "walnut" (*Endiandra palmerstonii*), silky "oak" (*Cardwellia sublimis*), black bean, myrtle, etc. There are certain softwoods, for instance kauri pine and bunya pine, that are exported for high class cabinet work.

13. India, Burma, Siam (Thailand), Malaya.

There are several hundreds of species of tropical hardwoods to be found in the dense forests of S.E. Asia and India. A great range of decorative timbers are exported to the U.K. as well as hardwoods specially suitable for floorings. The most valuable timber economically coming from this area is teak with its unique qualities of durability and resistance to moisture, acid, fire and insects.

Starting in 1949, the export of hardwoods from Malaya to the U.K. expanded greatly. These hardwoods, which often include parcels of mixed species as well as specific timbers such as meranti, melawis, etc., have been well received in the U.K. Much of this is due to the preparation and presentation of the wood. The grading is controlled largely by the Malayan Forestry Commission, with the timber being clearly stencilled with the grade; whilst the sawing, end treatment, etc. is of a high standard.

14. Japan.

There are extensive softwood and hardwood forests in Japan, but only the latter are exported. Japanese oak has long been a favourite timber for the cabinet makers and although considerably more expensive than European oak is easier to work on account of its softer texture.

There is also a large plywood industry in Japan manufacturing oak and lauan plywood, both relatively inexpensive.

15. Statistics of Imports, etc.

The volume of timber imported into the U.K. varies considerably from year to year, as is shown by the tables on pages 40 to 43 and the graphs in Figs. 12, 13, 14 and 17. These graphs also compare the volumes of Home Produced softwood, hardwood, pitwood and plywood, against the volumes of these items imported.

Although 1951 was the first year since the 1939-45 war when sawn softwood imports were comparable in quantity with the pre-war years up to 1938, the year 1952 has revealed a big reduction in spite of an ample supply in the shipping countries. This is accounted for by the severe restrictions on imports imposed in November 1951 by the Government in a drastic attempt to conserve foreign exchange and prevent economic collapse. This reduction therefore has been brought about not by the normal laws of supply and demand, but by the imposition of external controls outside the normal working of the trade.

In consequence, the figures of the 1952 imports give a false impression of the normal importing trade. Since the statistics published in this chapter and in Chapter XVIII are to help the reader to appreciate the relative importance of the various shipping countries, the statistics for 1951 have been selected in preference to 1952.

The result of a severe restriction on imports whilst ample supplies are available for shipment in the principal exporting countries, is

[*continued on page* 44.

Planed Softwood Imports to U.K

	1938			1948			1951		
	Actual Stds.	Av. C.I.F. Value	Percent-age	Actual Stds.	Av. C.I.F. Value	Percent-age	Actual Stds.	Av. C.I.F. Value	Percent-age
		£ s. d.			£ s. d.			£ s. d.	
Canada	110,800	13 6 5	37·2	21,200	64 10 4	53·9	7,650	85 14 8	36·8
Finland	39,200	15 13 8	13·1	—	—	—	140	85 6 3	·7
Sweden	119,200	16 13 1	40·1	18,100	63 15 0	46·1	7,200	98 4 1	34·7
Norway	10,500	16 18 11	3·5	—	—	—	5,800	100 3 11	27·8
Others	18,200*	18 1 6	6·1	—	—	—	—	—	—
Total ...	297,900		100·0	39,300		100·0	20,790		100·0

Canadian planed softwoods contain a high proportion of sizes planed all round to finish ¼ in. scant. Scandinavian planed softwoods are principally floorings, matchings, shelvings, etc.

* Planed softwood imports from other countries in 1938 included the following :—

U.S.S.R.	4,665 stds.	Germany	75 stds.
Latvia	1,988 ,,	Czechoslovakia ...	657 ,,
Poland	8,232 ,,	U.S.A.	1,751 ,,

Boxboard Imports to U.K.

	1938			1948			1951		
	Stds.	Av. C.I.F. Value	Percentage	Stds.	Av. C.I.F. Value	Percentage	Stds.	Av. C.I.F. Value	Percentage
		£ s. d.			£ s. d.			£ s. d.	
Canada	300	32 0 7	·4	5,100	105 12 0	21·1	200	138 9 4	·5
Finland	27,800	19 14 9	31·3	1,400	82 16 1	5·8	1,400	129 15 2	3·6
Sweden	30,800	22 8 2	34·7	17,400	76 13 11	71·8	24,600	126 17 4	66·2
Others	29,800	18 15 5	33·6	300	80 7 3	1·3	11,100	97 6 5	29·7
Total ...	88,700		100·0	24,200		100·0	37,300		100·0

Pitprop Imports to U.K.

	1938			1948			1951		
	Piled Fathoms	Av. C.I.F. Value	Percentage	Piled Fathoms	Av. C.I.F. Value	Percentage	Piled Fathoms	Av. C.I.F. Value	Percentage
		£ s. d.			£ s. d.			£ s. d.	
Canada	8,900	6 16 1	1·3	191,500	26 1 11	35·2	} 51,700	38 14 11	12·4
Newfoundland ...	31,800	6 4 4	4·7	13,300	24 1 11	2·4	}		
U.S.S.R.... ...	94,400	6 10 11	13·8	9,200	24 0 8	1·7	48,700	39 19 10	11·7
Finland	277,000	7 12 9	40·5	196,800	24 11 11	36·1	168,000	37 6 7	40·2
Sweden	41,000	6 18 5	6·0	34,300	23 10 4	6·3	66,900	35 14 4	16·0
Norway	2,600	7 7 11	·4	5,700	21 15 6	1·0	7,000	30 5 2	1·7
Germany ...	1,000	7 10 5	·1	21,900	21 14 3	4·0	2,300	38 15 9	·6
France	89,600	5 0 9	13·0	42,600	20 6 7	7·8	44,200	24 10 3	10·6
Portugal	—	—	—	—	—	—	28,300	27 18 3	6·8
Others	138,300	6 13 9	20·2	30,000	22 12 4	5·5	—	—	—
Total ...	684,600		100·0	545,300		100·0	417,100		100·0

SAWN HARDWOOD IMPORTS TO U.K.

	1938			1948			1951		
	Cubic Feet	Av. C.I.F. Value	Percentage	Cubic Feet	Av. C.I.F. Value	Percentage	Cubic Feet	Av. C.I.F. Value	Percentage
		£ s. d.			£ s. d.			£ s. d.	
British West Africa ...	343,000	0 4 8	1·1	1,542,000	0 8 7	7·7	5,348,000	0 14 4	13·9
British East Africa ...	—	—	—	—	—	—	1,738,000	0 12 10	4·5
Malaya	—	—	—	—	—	—	2,198,000	0 14 10	5·7
Australia	1,359,000	0 4 11	4·4	607,000	0 10 3	3·0	552,000	0 14 2	1·4
Canada	6,108,000	0 2 3	19·9	3,152,000	0 8 5	15·8	1,276,000	0 14 4	3·3
Other Empire Sources	915,000	0 5 0	3·0	633,000	0 13 7	3·2	1,045,000	0 14 3	2·7
Finland	1,287,000	0 2 2	4·2	1,004,000	0 9 0	5·0	2,265,000	0 11 6	5·9
Germany	32,000	0 2 11	·1	3,157,000	0 10 1	15·8	—	—	—
Jugoslavia	2,751,000	0 3 2	8·9	2,303,000	0 10 8	11·6	4,225,000	0 16 3	11·0
Burma	1,509,000	0 9 2	4·9	1,330,000	1 2 1	6·7	621,000	1 5 8	1·6
U.S.A.	9,893,000	0 3 8	32·2	2,989,000	0 12 8	15·0	2,255,000	1 9 8	5·8
Thailand	—	—	—	—	—	—	1,397,000	1 0 4	3·6
France	—	—	—	—	—	—	8,452,000	0 11 3	22·0
Chile	—	—	—	—	—	—	923,000	0 12 11	2·4
Others	6,550,000	0 3 11	21·3	3,210,000	0 13 2	16·2	6,220,000	0 15 4	16·2
Total	30,747,000		100·0	19,927,000		100·0	38,506,000		100·0
Mahogany	849,000	0 5 10	2·8	318,000	0 13 3	1·6	995,000	0 18 4	2·6
Oak	9,198,000	0 4 0	29·8	4,930,000	0 11 4	24·7	5,992,000	0 17 4	15·6
Teak	1,844,000	0 9 0	6·0	1,018,000	1 8 8	5·1	821,000	2 9 8	2·1
Hickory, etc.	320,000	0 6 6	1·1	331,000	1 1 4	1·7	299,000	1 16 10	·8
Ash ... ... }	18,536,000 (Ash, Beech, Birch, Others)	0 2 11	60·3	587,000	0 14 1	2·9	526,000	0 17 8	1·4
Beech ... ... }				3,247,000	0 10 0	16·3	7,898,000	0 14 3	20·6
Birch ... ... }				3,400,000	0 8 6	17·1	3,522,000	0 11 11	9·1
Others ... ... }				6,096,000	0 10 5	30·6	18,453,000	0 12 9	47·8

Mahogany imports in 1938 were divided as follows :—British Countries : 559,000 cubic feet. U.S.A. : 165,000 cubic feet. Others : 125,000 cubic feet.
Oak imports in 1938 were divided as follows :—U.S.A. : 5,844,000 cubic feet. Poland : 1,638,000 cubic feet. Japan : 954,000 cubic feet. Jugoslavia : 453,000. British Countries : 100,000 cubic feet. Others : 211,000 cubic feet.
The dominant position of American oak in 1938 should be noted in relation to its position in 1948 and 1951.
The large increase in imports from Germany was of a temporary nature only. The increase from British West Africa is much more permanent and reflects the additional capital and facilities put into the area in post-war years.

HEWN HARDWOOD IMPORTS TO U.K.

	1938			1948			1951		
	Cubic Feet	Av. C.I.F. Value	Percentage	Cubic Feet	Av. C.I.F. Value	Percentage	Cubic Feet	Av. C.I.F. Value	Percentage
		£ s. d.			£ s. d.			£ s. d.	
Mahogany ...	785,000	0 3 6	24·4	3,157,000	0 9 1	20·4	3,778,000	0 13 5	15·1
All Other Timbers									
Gold Coast ...	9,000	0 2 11	·3	1,850,000	0 7 11	11·9	2,900,000	0 12 10	11·6
Nigeria	509,000	0 2 8	15·8	2,255,000	0 8 3	14·6	11,890,000	0 11 6	47·4
Canada	456,000	0 3 7	14·2	1,084,000	0 5 7	7·0	661,000	0 11 9	2·7
B. N. Borneo ...	—	—	—	—	—	—	983,000	0 8 0	3·9
Other Empire Sources ...	523,000	0 4 6	16·2	797,000	0 11 4	5·2	1,046,000	0 12 5	4·2
French West and East Africa	—	—	—	—	—	—	2,302,000	0 11 5	9·2
Germany ...	4,000	0 6 5	·1	4,760,000	0 3 10	30·7	1,499,000	0 13 7	5·9
Others	933,000	0 3 0	29·0	1,581,000	0 9 2	10·2			
Total ...	3,219,000		100·0	15,484,000		100·0	25,059,000		100·0

The increase in imports of logs from Germany was temporary, but the increases from Gold Coast and Nigeria and the increases in mahogany log imports are likely to remain.

revealed in the considerable drop in c.i.f. prices for softwood from the middle of 1952.

The average c.i.f. price for all softwood imports, from all countries in 1951, was £87, 4s. 4d. per standard, but in the first four months of 1952 the average c.i.f. price had risen to £96, 1s. 4d.

The break in these prices occurred with contracts placed with leading Finnish shippers at £70 f.o.b. (equivalent to approx. £78-£80 c.i.f.) being followed by Russian prices of £75 per standard c.i.f. These two prices refer of course to " offers " and represent the price for Unsorted redwood battens, 7″ wide (see page 64). The graphs of opening prices in Fig. 2 and Fig. 6 are drawn up on the same basis.

The various tables of imports and average prices per country for imports in a particular year are based upon statistics published by the Customs and Excise statistics office. These figures then, in the case of softwood, refer to the average price over the year for all softwood from that country, redwood and whitewood, Unsorted and other qualities, all widths and thicknesses. This fact must be borne in mind when comparing prices on a " 7″ basis U/S redwood battens " with statistics of past imports.

16. Importing Ports.

To complete the Geographical Background the various ports in the U.K. through which timber is imported must be considered. All the major ports and many minor ports are used for importing timber, but the class of trade varies in each. Liverpool has always been a great hardwood port with its natural trade and shipping routes to America and Africa and in conjunction with Manchester and Preston it has been one of the principal ports for Eastern Canadian spruce.

The major trade through Hull and the East Coast ports has always been from Scandinavia. The freight rates from Scandinavia to Hull are very much cheaper than from Scandinavia to Liverpool or Manchester, since the journey is much shorter. On the other hand the West Coast ports enjoy advantageous freight rates with Canada and the U.S.A.

The dock facilities and trade practice at each port vary quite a lot, but a regular feature of the trade for the East and South Coasts is the arrangement of cargoes for " small ports " to be carried in " small ships."

With different labour rates, dock dues and other charges there are considerable differences between one port and another in the cost of importing timber.

The following table gives the names of the Port Authorities at each major port in the U.K., with a summary of the volume of wood goods imported through that port in 1938 and 1948. The total amount imported through any particular port during one year varies with the total amount imported into the U.K. These figures, however, will suffice to show the relative importance to the timber trade of the U.K. ports and at the same time they are a useful guide as to the class of timber imported through particular ports.

MAJOR IMPORTING PORTS IN THE U.K. FOR WOOD GOODS.

Statistics for 1938 and 1948.

 From information supplied by the Statistical Office, H.M. Customs and Excise, 23-27, Brooke St., E.C.1. Ref.: 5498/49.

PORT AUTHORITIES

for Ports included in the following tables.

LONDON ... ... Port of London Authority.

West Coast.

LIVERPOOL ... Mersey Docks and Harbour Board.
GARSTON .... Docks and Inland Waterways Executive.
MANCHESTER ... Manchester Ship Canal Co.
PRESTON ... Port of Preston Authority.

East Coast.

HULL ... ... Docks and Inland Waterways Executive.
GRIMSBY ... Docks and Inland Waterways Executive.
TYNESIDE ... Tyne Improvement Commission.
WEST HARTLEPOOL Docks and Inland Waterways Executive.
YARMOUTH ... Gt. Yarmouth Port and Harbour Commissioners.
KING'S LYNN ... Docks and Inland Waterways Executive.
BOSTON ... ... Port of Boston Authority.

Bristol Channel.

BRISTOL ... ... Port of Bristol Authority.
CARDIFF ... ... Docks and Inland Waterways Executive.
GLOUCESTER AND SHARPNESS Docks and Inland Waterways Executive, South Western Division.
SWANSEA ... Docks and Inland Waterways Executive.

South Coast.

SOUTHAMPTON .... Docks and Inland Waterways Executive.
PLYMOUTH .... Docks and Inland Waterways Executive and Sutton Harbour Improvement Co.
PORTSMOUTH ... City of Portsmouth.

Scotland.

GLASGOW ... Clyde Navigation Trustees.
LEITH ... ... Leith Harbour and Docks Commissioners.
ABERDEEN ... Aberdeen Harbour Commissioners.
GRANGEMOUTH ... Docks and Inland Waterways Executive.
DUNDEE ... ... Dundee Harbour Trust.

N. Ireland.

BELFAST ... Belfast Harbour Commissioners.

IMPORTS: (A)

PORT	Mahogany Logs (cubic feet)		Other Logs (cubic feet)		Sawn Hardwood, Mahogany (cubic feet)	
	1938	1948	1938	1948	1938	1948
London	566,161	1,609,924	976,138	4,709,517	510,270	180,483
West Coast						
Liverpool	975,095	690,513	717,860	5,470,515	282,220	112,050
Manchester ...	—	—	175,498	141,164	14,016	—
Preston	—	—	11,939	—	—	—
East Coast						
Hull	750	2,072	99,208	434,941	4,247	—
Grimsby	—	—	—	56,926	—	—
Tyneside	236,681	392,700	11,590	23,355	573	—
West Hartlepool	—	—	64,286	—	—	—
Yarmouth	—	—	28,912	132,522	—	—
King's Lynn ...	—	—	5,487	13,885	—	—
Boston	—	—	—	138,386	—	—
Bristol Channel						
Bristol	2,676	220,988	13,557	258,681	9,299	—
Cardiff	—	—	9,712	—	1,054	—
Gloucester ...	—	—	138,945	—	—	—
Swansea	—	—	—	—	—	—
South Coast						
Southampton ...	210	—	14,666	401,754	2,581	—
Plymouth	—	—	23,646	—	—	—
Portsmouth ...	—	—	—	125,638	—	—
Scotland						
Glasgow	3,210	222,830	30,761	206,816	18,998	25,073
Leith	—	—	5,114	25,721	1,177	—
Aberdeen	—	—	1,081	—	—	—
Grangemouth ...	—	—	437	—	—	—
Dundee	—	—	1,895	—	—	10
Northern Ireland						
Belfast	—	—	26,549	3,394	4,870	—
OTHERS		20,339	75,583	181,196	—	44
Yearly Totals ...	1,784,783	3,159,366	2,432,864	12,324,411	849,305	317,660

HARDWOODS

Sawn Hardwood, Oak (*cubic feet*)		Sawn Hardwood, Teak (*cubic feet*)		Sawn Hardwood, Others (*cubic feet*)		Planed Hardwood (*cubic feet*)	
1938	1948	1938	1948	1938	1948	1938	1948
4,738,434	2,092,640	896,343	286,973	9,232,055	5,260,360	1,905,009	52,620
2,190,012	1,674,971	358,413	402,679	3,551,713	4,884,557	679,028	23,128
616,442	106,357	—	—	1,410,557	663,450	306,592	2,569
—	—	—	—	3,377		—	—
403,707	101,141	229,281	23,733	1,316,739	475,260	65,414	3,063
—	51,219	—	—	15,151	297,426	—	—
114,789	29,947	2,745	—	268,203	385,743	26,822	—
—	—	—	—	—	55,518	—	—
—	9,812	—	—	—	3,384	—	—
3,186	—	—	—	—	52,946	—	—
5,124	27,916	—	—	—	—	—	—
475,803	184,529	10,920	2,602	207,935	181,674	158,222	—
147,980	66,387	—	—	118,169	82,739	2,503	—
—	—	—	—	6,204	25,328	—	—
6,645	—	—	—	28,944	4,764	2,227	—
9,909	411,160	1,118	—	101,898	83,287	11,536	—
2,495	—	—	—	3,156	21,543	633	—
—	45,056	—	—	—	598	—	—
361,595	34,963	232,342	293,563	1,244,538	692,998	391,854	45,110
9,094	18,151	26,232	7,475	32,632	153,410	12,562	—
2,078	—	—	—	—	—	1,877	—
15,033	49,768	—	—	873,379	79,575	12,604	—
—	13,601	—	73	4,788	2,668	88,962	—
58,649	928	84,631	—	83,421	172,903	2,804	—
37,256	10,191	2,262	849	352,661	81,630	29,994	7,385
9,198,231	4,928,737	1,844,287	1,017,947	18,855,520	13,661,761	3,698,643	133,875

IMPORTS: (B)

PORT	Sawn Softwood (*standards*)		Planed Softwood (*standards*)		Boxboards, Etc., and Other Sawn Softwood (*standards*)	
	1938	1948	1938	1948	1938	1948
London	445,093	239,416	117,965	14,047	30,466	2,432
West Coast						
Liverpool	161,516	86,844	34,324	3,791	14,152	4,180
Manchester ...	52,550	57,435	18,685	3,610	6,569	1,649
Preston	24,148	6,013	10,521	376	455	151
East Coast						
Hull	174,493	89,609	47,173	4,277	14,882	1,942
Grimsby	49,889	32,497	2,643	1,074	242	92
Tyneside	44,918	22,341	12,251	991	1,052	89
West Hartlepool	30,781	19,548	1,968	876	648	—
Yarmouth	25,195	8,985	637	—	2,047	645
King's Lynn ...	23,410	9,777	736	—	283	—
Boston	26,570	24,384	1,135	150	224	—
Bristol Channel						
Bristol	23,558	21,947	5,994	1,990	2,072	203
Cardiff	49,352	35,311	3,274	2,406	19	1
Gloucester ...	35,234	15,754	529	190	—	—
Swansea	3,251	853	3,041	—	1,813	646
South Coast						
Southampton ...	30,316	13,483	4,542	618	42	—
Plymouth	13,181	14,049	4,168	1,890	604	12
Portsmouth ...	9,238	4,161	2,773	245	—	—
Scotland						
Glasgow	17,032	14,930	4,630	914	3,110	5,666
Leith	20,359	12,957	395	531	2,015	2,749
Aberdeen	10,899	3,157	207	—	240	657
Grangemouth ...	66,958	28,380	1,210	—	1,281	307
Dundee	20,504	5,945	192	119	667	340
Northern Ireland						
Belfast	22,419	14,492	1,888	16	1,235	2,254
OTHERS	99,593	38,364	16,991	1,203	4,516	170
Yearly Totals ...	1,480,457	820,632	297,872	39,314	88,634	24,185

SOFTWOODS, ETC.

Pitprops (*piled cubic fathoms*)		Sleepers (*standards*)		Veneers (*cwts.*)		Plywood (*cubic feet*)	
1938	1948	1938	1948	1938	1948	1938	1948
5,307	19	23,514	16,445	175,152	290,027	7,315,339	3,148,549
41,126	43,380	20,687	6,763	29,656	153,121	1,044,781	643,231
12,883	13,210	373	6,272	11,032	19,115	593,793	310,519
4,363	5,147	34	—	—	—	—	—
90,216	103,095	930	4,943	589	—	946,053	1,129,818
11,754	35,703	9,459	4,017	151	—	—	58,285
97,351	37,822	583	2,542	976	—	104,929	23,914
104,089	118,408	12,561	854	—	—	141	9,094
—	1	660	—	—	—	462	—
—	6,400	—	—	—	—	—	—
—	—	5,088	—	—	—	—	—
12	959	—	2,257	1,702	1,529	133,978	121,226
120,685	63,598	857	3,353	16	452	42,675	45,117
—	—	—	—	—	—	—	—
27,058	9,489	78	—	—	—	15,193	2,000
10	—	7,596	1,830	—	—	8,688	107,334
—	—	605	695	—	—	7,231	63,911
—	—	—	—	—	—	374	—
48	1	—	2,782	26,580	26,974	244,108	15,520
1,378	3,542	—	1,834	83	—	113,460	187,842
6,182	—	1,425	—	—	—	2,802	—
20,859	23,053	9,843	116	15	—	99,904	96,367
—	—	1,581	598	—	—	2,608	—
48	—	1,362	944	—	—	80,059	149,540
141,348	81,549	19,975	1,019	1,031	16,240	105,177	64,011
684,717	545,376	117,211	57,264	246,983	507,458	10,861,755	6,176,278

From these figures it will be seen that the main part of the imports of timber came through the following ports. In each case the percentage of the total U.K. timber import is given.

	Percentage of total U.K. import. 1938.	1948.
HARDWOOD (all classes).		
London	48¾%	40 %
Liverpool	22½%	37¼%
Manchester	6½%	2½%
Glasgow	6 %	4¼%
Hull	5¼%	3 %
SOFTWOOD (all classes).		
London	31¼%	29 %
Liverpool	12 %	10½%
Hull	12 %	10½%
Manchester	4 %	7¼%
Grangemouth	4 %	3 %
Grimsby	3 %	4 %
Tyneside	3 %	2¾%
Cardiff	2¾%	4¼%
West Hartlepool	2¼%	2¼%
Southampton	2 %	1½%
Bristol	1½%	2¾%
Boston	1¾%	2½%
PITPROPS.		
Cardiff	17½%	11½%
West Hartlepool	15 %	21½%
Tyneside	14 %	6¾%
Hull	13 %	19 %
Liverpool	6 %	8 %
Swansea	4 %	1¾%
Grangemouth	3 %	4 %
Grimsby	1¾%	6½%
PLYWOOD.		
London	67¾%	51¼%
Liverpool	9½%	10½%
Hull	8¾%	18½%
Glasgow	2¼%	3 %

CHAPTER II

The Imported Timber Trade

1. Structure of the Trade.

(*a*) General.

The Timber Trade must surely be one of the most intricate of trades, dealing as it does with hundreds of species of timber, each of which can be supplied in three variable dimensions of thickness, width and length. Timber is not a homogeneous product like wood-pulp or steel and it requires an elaborate system of shippers, agents, importers, merchants and brokers to arrange its transport and distribution.

(*b*) The Shipper.

The shipper is the man who ships the timber from the sawmills. He may have forests of his own, or he may purchase his logs from landowners or from State forests, take them to his sawmill and convert them into sawn goods for shipment. In the African hardwood trade he may ship the logs to this country without further conversion. Timber is a product of Nature, not a man-made article of guaranteed size, shape and quality. The economic conversion of logs to sawn goods results in a large number of sizes of deals, battens and boards depending upon the diameter of the tree. Each of the sizes of deals, etc., produced will require grading for quality according to the number of defects in it. As a result of the conversion of trees of one species the shipper may have therefore a mixture of sizes varying from say $\frac{7}{8}$ in. × 3 ins. up to say 4 ins. × 11 ins. in two or three qualities. There are certain sizes which after many years have come to be the choice sizes because of most constant demand. These sizes are the centre-piece of stocknotes covering all the sizes produced and they are used as an attraction to the buyer to take the less popular sizes.

The shipper aims to sell his complete output, not merely the choice sizes that are in greatest demand and therefore appoints agents in the U.K. and perhaps elsewhere, to find buyers for his production.

(*c*) The Agent.

The agent acts for the shipper under the authority of an agency agreement. In the course of his business he is well acquainted with the importers who are his customers, as well as the shipper who is his principal. This creates a two-way confidence between the shipper and the importer which would not otherwise be possible. The shipper knows that the agent will only make contracts with reputable importers of some standing. The importers know that the agent would not accept a contract of agency without having first ensured that the principal was a reliable shipper.

The agent works on a small selling commission and for an additional commission he may become a "del credere" agent, when he will guarantee to the shipper the solvency of the buyer. The agent may be a man working on his own, or may be a large firm of great wealth with a network of overseas connections. The agent may finance the shipper in the winter months, particularly in Scandinavia when the ports are frozen and the shipper has no money coming in from shipments of timber.

The agent may also finance the importer by arranging to grant him credit, usually over a period of four months. This is of particular importance when prices are high, in fact without the credit facilities granted by agents many importers in times of high prices would find themselves unable to finance their purchases.

The term "agent" is used here, as in the timber trade generally, to describe the selling agent in the U.K. for a foreign shipper. There are also agents in foreign countries, particularly Finland, who act as selling agents for the smaller sawmills. For the purpose of considering the structure of the trade these may be considered as shippers.

(*d*) The Importer.

The importer buys from the shipper through the agent. He will usually purchase a general specification covering a number of the sizes and qualities that the shipper is producing. The price will depend not only on current market conditions, but on the proportion of choice sizes and qualities in the specification offered. His contract for timber will be made in the majority of cases without having seen the timber he is buying. He relies therefore upon an accurate description of the timber in his contract (see page 127) and upon confidence in the shipper which he obtains through the agent.

Contracts for timber are normally placed many months ahead, and the importer may buy timber from Scandinavia in January or February for shipment at f.o.w. (first open water) that is to say for shipment as soon as the ice clears from the port to enable shipping to load and leave the port without risk of damage to barges.

(*e*) The Merchant.

The importer sells to the merchant. In practice the importer is often a merchant himself as well. The merchant has a stock yard of his own, or he may use a Public Storage Yard operated by a Port Authority or Docks Executive. He buys in smaller quantities from the importer, who may re-sell one shipment of timber amongst several merchants. From his yard he sells specific sizes and qualities to the consumer. Not all sales are quite as simple as this, for the importer may re-sell his timber to another importer whilst it is on the high seas, or the merchant-importer may sell timber to large consumers direct from the quay, thus avoiding additional labour and storage charges.

(*f*) The Consumer.

The consumer is the joiner, cabinet-maker, case-maker, builder, furniture manufacturer, etc. He does not require a multitude of sizes—he has certain requirements for size and quality and he wants those only.

By purchasing from various merchants he can get just those sizes he wants. The merchant in his turn depends upon a wide clientele of consumers each with varied interests and requirements so that he can sell the whole of his stock.

It will now be seen how essential is this system of shippers, agents, importers, merchants and consumers. If the consumer were to short circuit this system and buy direct from the shipper he would have to take a more general specification of sizes and qualities, including those he did not really want. He would have to establish his own confidence in the shipper, and the shipper's confidence in himself, and after considerable financial outlay would still not have only and all the items he wanted. In the case of a claim for quality or measure he would be dealing with a seller in a foreign country, with no representative readily available to assist in the settlement of disputes amicably and quickly.

There are many consumers who are also importer-merchants, such as large casemakers, manufacturing joiners, etc., but if they are going to purchase timber in bulk as importers, they must be prepared to make the financial outlay necessary as a merchant and to re-sell the stocks they are not consuming themselves. In cases of this nature the importer-merchant and the consumer activities of a business can be considered quite apart from each other, and in most firms are clearly separated in different departments.

(*g*) The Broker.

The broker is often an agent as well, but this is not invariable. For a small commission he finds buyers for stocks belonging to an importer or merchant which they have difficulty in selling. In the same manner he will find sellers of special sizes or stocks that a merchant or importer requires and cannot easily find himself. Both these functions are carried out without any great financial outlay, and are made possible by the broker's day to day connections with the principal importers and merchants.

Some brokers sell both hardwood and softwood by auction publicly. This has always been a great feature of the mahogany trade, where logs are rarely sold by description but are usually landed and sold by auction enabling the buyer-importer-merchant to inspect the logs before bidding or purchase.

(*h*) Consignments.

Although not exactly a proper part of the structure of the trade, the question of " consignments " may best be dealt with here.

The normal structure of the trade outlined above applies to the great majority of the transactions that are made. There are some cases, however, when shippers find their goods difficult to sell, possibly owing to some market having failed them and perhaps have their yards overstocked or want to clear sizes for which there is little or no demand, where the shipper ships the goods without having an order for them. These are then said to be shipped " on consignment " and the agents and brokers have to do their best to sell them whilst they are still on passage, find storage accommodation for them if unsold and possibly auction them on arrival.

Opinions with regard to consignments differ greatly. It is easy to understand that an importer who has made large purchases ahead from a shipper on f.o.b. or c.i.f. terms may be put in an uncomfortable position if that shipper unloads his unsold goods on the market in competition with his importer customer: at auction, sales are not even confined to the circle of recognised importers.

On the whole the trade takes the view that consignments are undesirable since they disturb the legitimate efforts of the importer to estimate the market, both as to what it requires and what it can afford to pay. The importer takes risks in purchasing supplies to meet these anticipated requirements and his fear of consignments can sometimes hinder the regular course of trade.

The arrival of consignments has often caused a break in the market which was detrimental to the trade as a whole without any corresponding advantages.

2. Grading and Shippers' Marks.

(*a*) Shipping Marks.

All imported timber and plywood is graded for quality. The grading rules for softwood, hardwood and plywood differ greatly from country to country with the exception that all grading is based primarily on the number of defects present. The higher grades of sawn goods that are practically free from wane, knots, shakes, heart-centre, etc., command higher prices.

The grading of timber is of great importance to the trade and is the basis of all sales. With the exception of the consumer buying timber from the merchant, all purchasers of timber will buy it on description only without an opportunity to inspect the timber beforehand.

After it has been graded for quality it is usual for the timber or plywood to be marked or branded with the *Shipper's Mark*. For sawn softwoods and hardwoods this is usually done on the end of the deal, board or plank by different colours of paint and a stencil or by a hammer mark.

Name of Shipper	Description	Average Annual Production in Standards	Qualities I	II	III	IV	V	Unsorted Non-Classés
Åslands Träföradlings Aktiebolag, Kyrkdal Ship at Nylands Kaj, Hernösand District	Frame-sawn	...	...	..	..	...	N ★ N VI N — N	N ♔ N
Backa-Hosjö Aktiebolag, Sparreholm Ship at Norrkoping and Gothenburg	Sawn	5,000	HB ♔ S	HB + S	HB╳S	HB▼S	HB ★ S	HB — S
	Planed	2,000						
	Boxboards	2,000	..	...	...	..	...	HB — S
Backa Såg & Tegelverks Aktiebolag, Korsnäs Ship also at Gefle	Sawn	2,000	B ♔ Ks	B + Ks	B╳Ks	B ▽ Ks	B — Ks	B.Ks
	Planed	1,000	...	..	..	...	..	BACKA ✱
Bagge (Olof) & Co., Trävaruaktiebolaget Ship at Norrkoping	Sawn and planed	4,000	O ♔ B	O ✱ B	O + B	O — B	O B	O x B
Baltic (Trävaruaktiebolaget), Stockholm	Sawn	..	...	...	..	...	T — B	T ♔ B
Bark & Warburgs Aktiebolag Ship at Gothenburg	Sawn	1,500	BW ♔ AB	BWAB	BWA	BW	BWB	BWFA
	Planed	1,500	BWAB	BWA	BW	BB	..	BWFA
	Joinery	...	Trade Mark B ♔♔♔ W					
	Boxboards	1,500	Trade Mark B ♔♔♔ W					

Fig. 15. Reproduction from "Shipping Marks on Timber"

Plywood shippers' marks are stamped on to one face, or may be in the form of a small gummed label.

Shippers' marks are in the nature of trade marks and each shipper will have a selection of marks covering the qualities of timber or plywood he produces. Each mark will consist of a series of letters, figures or other symbols such as crowns, stars, crosses, etc.

A directory of "*Shipping Marks on Timber*" including hardwood, softwood, joinery and plywood exported from all producing countries in the world is published by Benn Brothers Ltd., Bouverie House, London, E.C.4.

With their permission part of a page from this is published on page 55. With this book a timber merchant can identify any stock that he inspects. The marks are quoted in contracts, sale notes, invoices and specifications and become part of a description of the timber.

The discriminating buyer of timber soon learns that certain marks of timber represent a higher quality than others. These marks enjoy the prestige accorded to a trade mark for any goods that have been established on quality.

(*b*) GRADING—NORTH EUROPEAN COUNTRIES.

Softwood from Russia, Finland, Sweden, Poland and the Baltic States is graded as follows :—

I—First.	IV—Fourth.
II—Second.	V—Fifth.
III—Third.	VI—Sixth, UTSKOTT or WRACK.

The small percentage of higher grades that is now obtained has resulted in the disappearance of 1st, 2nd and 3rd qualities in the ordinary course of trade, except in certain Russian White Sea goods.

Scandinavian timber of 1st, 2nd, 3rd and 4th grade is mixed together into one grade known as Unsorted (abbreviated U/S), but Russian Unsorted grade includes only I, II and III qualities, the Russian IV grade being similar to the V grade of high class Finnish stocks.

The commercial grades of North European wood, in order of quality, are as follows :—

Russia.	*Finland.*	*Sweden.*	
I	—	—	For very high class work only, where cost of timber is of little importance.
II	—	—	
III	—	—	
U/S = III and better.	U/S = IV and better.	U/S = IV and better.	The normal grade for joinery and high class work.
IV	V	V	For carcassing timber, constructional work, floorings, etc.

Russia.	*Finland.*	*Sweden.*	
—	VI	VI	Low grade rough carcassing timber, box and packing case timber: for underground or temporary work or for re-conversion.

Polish timber follows the Swedish and Finnish grading (U/S = IV and better) and Baltic States timber follows the Russian grading (U/S = III and better).

The rules for grading timber are not hard and fast and are not consistent between countries, ports or shippers. They are considered in greater detail in Chapter XV.

It is here that the knowledge of the geographical background of the trade becomes essential, as this greatly affects the quality and description of the goods. The experienced buyer appreciates fully the differences between timbers of the same grade such as "U/S Archangel redwood," "U/S Swedish redwood" and "U/S Finnish redwood." As a general rule one particular grade of softwood will vary from port to port as follows, with the best quality goods at the top of the list.

(1) Kara Sea.
(2) White Sea.
(3) Sweden :—Gefle and Northwards.
(4) Finland :—North and East.
(5) Leningrad.
(6) Finland :—South.
(7) Sweden :—South of Gefle.
(8) Baltic States and Poland.

Usually it is found that Swedish grades are slightly superior to the equivalent Finnish grade, *e.g.*, V Swedish redwood will often be superior to V Finnish redwood from the same latitude, as, although the grading for defects will be the same, the texture of the wood will generally be closer and finer. Generally speaking more wane is permitted in Swedish goods than in Finnish of the same grade.

Torrack is the product of trees which have died standing—it is sold sawfalling, usually at about the same price as Sixths.

This list can only be an approximate guide and it must not be assumed from it that Polish timber for instance is of particularly poor quality, as this is not the case, Polish whitewood in particular being excellent material.

Planed goods show variations in grading amongst the different shippers. In Finland some planed goods follow the sawn goods grading—into U/S and V, whereas others are graded into U/S (consisting of I, II, and III grades) and Inferiors. The latter grading range is also used in Norway.

(*c*) Grading—Canada—West Coast.

Canadian grading rules for timber are much more complicated than their European counterparts and are set out in both Export and Domestic Rules, the latter being very detailed.

The most recent classification, published 1951 by the Pacific Lumber Inspection Bureau is the " Export R List," which supersedes the " Export N List " and W.C.L.A. Lists, and re-groups the principal West Coast timbers, Douglas fir, western hemlock, Sitka spruce and western red cedar mainly into six groups :—

No. 2 Clear and Better (B and Better or Prime)
No. 3 Clear (C clear)
Selected Merchantable
Nos. 1 and 2 Merchantable and
No. 3 Common.

A true comparison with equivalent European grades cannot be made since the dimensions produced in Canada are so much larger. Also the Canadian grading rules are to be applied with reference to the suitability for the use or uses for which the grade was developed.

One important difference between Scandinavian and West Coast Canadian grading rules is that the Scandinavian goods are sawn with sufficient overmeasure to hold up the nominal thickness after normal seasoning, whilst the Canadian goods are sawn to the nominal thickness and permit not only specified variations in sawing, but also natural shrinkage within specified limits.

The comparative values of the different grades, when landed in this country are approximately as follows—

No. 2 Clear and Better	=Russian I and II.
No. 3 Clear	=Best Swedish.
Selected Merchantable	=Good Scandinavian U/S.
No. 1 Merchantable	=South Swedish.
No. 2 Merchantable	=Scandinavian Fifths.
No. 3 Common	=Scandinavian Sixths.

Shippers' quality marks for Canadian timber are not so universal as in the north European countries. In the majority of cases the Shipper's mark identifies the name of the shipper only, without any indication of the quality of the timber. In the future there may be an extension of shippers' marks on Canadian timber with a better identification of grades.

West Coast timber is also graded into special sizes and qualities for particular work such as :—Aircraft Construction (Sitka spruce) ; Ceiling ; Decking ; Door Stock ; Flooring ; Masts and Spars ; Mining ; Scaffolding and Stagings ; Siding ; Sleepers and Crossings, Waggon Sheetings and Bottoms ; etc.

At one time West Coast timbers, particularly Douglas fir, were very irregularly sawn and it became the custom for small sizes to be put through a thicknessing machine to finish $\frac{1}{4}$ in. scant, as the only way to ensure even dimensions. Whilst in recent years the cutting of this timber has improved very greatly, these scant dimensions are still exported. A scant dimension has of course a reasonable reduction in price from the equivalent grade of the full dimension.

(*d*) Grading—Canada—East Coast.

East Canadian spruce follows more closely the North European pattern, since the qualities into which the timber is graded are similar but shipments vary more greatly between individual shippers and ports. There is a considerable difference between the bandsawn production, which represents the highest quality, and the rotary sawn which is at times very uneven. The best spruce comes from Quebec and is shipped from ports on the St. Lawrence. This is usually bandsawn and sorted into six qualities of which I to IV comprise Unsorted, with V (and occasionally VI) shipped separately.

Shipments from New Brunswick ports, principally Miramichi, Campbellton and St. John may be either bandsawn or rotary sawn, the latter being less regular in thickness and width but more over than under measure. These are graded I to III as Unsorted, the IV grade being very similar to Quebec Vs.

Shipments from Nova Scotia are similar to those from New Brunswick, but the average quality is somewhat inferior and the goods mainly rotary cut. The average length is also somewhat shorter.

This is a very broad outline, and to get a truer picture it must be added that some New Brunswick productions are regarded as equal in value to Quebec, and some Nova Scotia productions as equal to New Brunswick and so on. In each case the bandsawn production being more valuable than rotary sawn production.

Wood graded by the Maritime Lumber Bureau is marked on the end with a crown and a star for III and better, and two diamonds for IV.

Quebec " yellow " pine (*Pinus strobus*) is graded into I, II, III, U/S (being I, II and III) and IVs. This is a specialist's timber and commands very high prices.

(*e*) Grading—U.S.A. Softwoods.

Pacific Coast softwoods of U.S.A. follow the same grades as the West Coast of Canada timbers, in fact a common Pacific Lumber Inspection Bureau is maintained by the two countries covering all productions in British Columbia (Canada), Washington (U.S.A.) and Oregon (U.S.A.).

Softwoods shipped from the Gulf Coast of U.S.A. have very different standards and terms for grading.

Pitch pine is graded into :—

Crown or Extra Prime,	Merchantable,
Genoa Prime (Rio),	Square Edge,

with certain dimension grades for heavy structural work.

(*f*) Grading—Brazilian Softwoods.

The grading of Parana Pine in Brazil differs from both the Canadian and North European systems. New rules were published

21st December 1951 detailing defects permitted in the four qualities, broadly speaking as follows :—

FIRSTS may contain slight defects, including some wane on one edge only and small knots on one side only.

SECONDS may contain rather more defects including some wane on both edges, knots on both sides and a few wormholes.

THIRDS may contain still greater defects including some sap-rot on one side.

FOURTHS are the former " Refugo " or " Inferiors."

PRIME QUALITY is a combined grade of 80% I and 20% II and may be guaranteed free from wormholes.

(*g*) GRADING—HARDWOODS.

In the U.S.A. there is one set of grading rules, issued by the National Hardwood Lumber Association, that covers all American hardwoods.

The standard grades are :—

Firsts,	No. 2 Common,
Seconds,	Sound Wormy.
Selects,	No. 3A Common.
No. 1 Common,	No. 3B Common.

Firsts and Seconds are usually combined as one grade, abbreviated F.A.S. Selects and No. 1 Common may be combined as one grade, and No. 3A and No. 3B Common may be combined as one grade called No. 3 Common.

Canadian hardwoods follow the American grading.

The grading of African and European hardwoods is much simpler, and has not been formed into a set of hard and fast rules. The normal export grades of square edged hardwoods being :—

Prime, Selects,

whilst hardwood logs are generally graded into I, II and III quality.

There is no set definition of the grade " Prime," but in general it is composed of I and II with a preponderance of I.

(*h*) GRADING—PLYWOOD.

Plywood grading is based upon the method of manufacture and the number of defects on each face of the sheet. The usual symbols adopted are :—

AA ; A ; B ; BB ; C ; and WG, the last indicating merely well-glued.

Intermediate grades are indicated by combinations of these symbols such as B/BB in which one side of the sheet is graded B, the reverse side graded BB.

The grading of plywood varies from shipper to shipper, but no geographical rule can be applied for quality as in the case of softwoods.

Finnish plywood is rarely graded higher than B, although in quality it equals the A production of other countries.

In addition to the above, plywood from Japan and European countries other than Scandinavia, is sometimes graded into Prime, First and Second grades.

In Canada, Douglas fir plywood of resin-bonded hot-plate production, has its own distinctive grades :—

G 2 S = Good two sides. Solid 2 S = Solid two sides.
G 1 S = Good one side. Solid 1 S = Solid one side.

3. Methods of Importing Timber.

(*a*) GENERAL.

In importing timber the buyer may purchase it at any one of several stages of its journey from the mill where it was produced to the port where it enters the U.K.

The earlier the stage of the journey, the cheaper the timber will be but the greater are the risks undertaken. The method adopted largely depends upon the buyer's experience and judgment.

(*b*) F.A.S. (FREE ALONGSIDE).

The buyer may contract to purchase timber f.a.s. The shipper will deliver the timber alongside the vessel. The buyer is responsible for chartering the ship to load and carry the goods delivered alongside, and for arranging the insurance of the goods on passage.

(*c*) F.O.B. (FREE ON BOARD).

The term f.o.b. indicates that the seller has to put the goods contracted for, free of cost to the buyer, on board the vessel the buyer charters to receive and carry them.

The term f.o.b. here differs considerably from its use in exporting goods from the U.K. In exporting say textiles, f.o.b., the seller or shipper is responsible for the dock labour charges putting the goods "on board." In the timber shipping ports of the world, there are rarely the same craneage and dock facilities that are found in the big ports of the world, and generally the goods have to be loaded from a lighter using the ship's tackle.

It is convenient to use the term f.o.b. in the trade particularly since f.a.s. is a term regularly used in the grading of hardwoods in a different sense altogether, namely a combined grade of Firsts and Seconds.

In an f.a.s. or f.o.b. contract the buyer is taking the risk of the freight market. His contract may be made in February for shipment in June, and he must anticipate the freight market and decide when and at what rate to charter. In times when freight is difficult to charter the buyer is incurring further risks, since if he cannot find a ship to lift his timber he still has his contract obligations to discharge and may have to pay for the timber whilst it is still lying in the shipper's yard.

Note that the T.T.F. " Uniform " contract, generally referred to as an f.o.b. contract, is in fact partly f.a.s. in as much as the seller only has to put the goods free of cost alongside the vessel which the buyer has to provide to load the goods. This is set out in more detail in Chapter VII.

(*d*) C.I.F. (Cost, Insurance, Freight).

The contract price here will include the first cost of the timber (the f.a.s. or f.o.b. price), the insurance covering the passage from the shipper's yard or warehouse to the destination in the U.K. and the freight for that passage.

Generally the c.i.f. price will be a little higher than the f.o.b. price plus insurance and existing freight, as under a c.i.f. contract the shipper undertakes the business of chartering and either charters immediately or takes the risk of what rate he must pay. If the buyer is making a c.i.f. contract in January for goods that are to be shipped in June the shipper, if he does not charter immediately, will now have to bear (within certain limits) the increase of freight that may occur in the intervening period. It is only natural that in these circumstances the shipper will cover himself for any possible rise in freight at the time of shipment.

The c.i.f. contract is completed, not by the delivery of the timber, but by the delivery of certain essential documents that represent the timber. These documents (see pages 119, 151) are in effect a set of title deeds to the timber and possession of them is equivalent to ownership of the timber. If the ship and cargo are lost on voyage the buyer is adequately protected by the insurance policy that has been taken out as a necessary part of the contract.

A c.i.f. contract may be made on a " freight basis," in which a basic rate of freight is stated in the contract upon which the c.i.f. price has been calculated. Any increase or decrease in the freight rate at the time of shipment is passed on to the buyer who thereby is put in much the same position as if he had purchased f.o.b. There are advantages however in this, since the responsibility for chartering freight space still rests with the seller and if it is impossible to charter freight the buyer incurs no liability.

(*e*) C. & F. (Cost and Freight).

This is a variation of the c.i.f. contract, in which the contract price includes cost and freight only, the buyer arranging insurance.

(*f*) C.I.F. Re-sale.

Since the timber on passage in a c.i.f. contract is represented by negotiable documents, it can be bought and sold merely by transferring the documents.

An importer may buy timber c.i.f. from another importer, who in his turn will have bought it f.a.s., f.o.b. or c.i.f. from the shipper.

In this case he may be making a contract to buy the timber whilst it is still on passage, that is to say only a week or so before it arrives in the U.K.

The risk here is much smaller and not so much judgment is required, since he is not having to work so far ahead. On the other hand the timber will be more expensive since he will be paying a little extra in the way of profit to the other importer who made the original contract with the shipper.

These remarks only cover the purchase and sale of timber up to the U.K. port.

Methods of purchase and sale of timber after it has arrived in the U.K. are dealt with in Chapter XIII.

4. Supply and Demand.

(*a*) The Supply.

In countries with a large forest area, such as Finland which is taken here as an example, the export of wood and wood products is one of the main sources of national income. For instance from 1947 to 1951, taken together, the export of wood, woodgoods and woodpulp amounted to almost 70 per cent. of the total export. It is therefore of national importance that the forests should be conserved so as to supply as high a yield of suitable logs as possible and that the logs should be used to the best advantage. It is of course the aim of all sections of the trade to do their part profitably.

The natural supply of logs on a "sustained yield" basis can be calculated fairly closely, but the effective supply is a different matter as it depends on demand. For instance the forests are variously owned by the State, or communities, companies, or private persons and when demand is strong and prices comparatively high, all these owners are anxious to sell and the effective supply is stimulated, but when demand weakens and prices fall, the forest owners, if they are not particularly in need of money, prefer to leave their logs standing in the forest where they increase in volume whilst awaiting an improvement in market value. The matter is, however, not so simple as this in practice, as shippers who are sawmillers and have to purchase logs, must often do so a year or two before the sawn product comes on the market, since felling, floating, ponding, sawing and seasoning may occupy many months, during which market prices may rise or fall very considerably.

(*b*) The Demand.

Assuming that the shipper has bought his logs, he then has to decide how to convert them and in this he will be guided by his estimate of which markets are likely to show the strongest demand and his experience of the particular sizes which those markets normally require. For instance the U.K. usually wants a preponderance of batten sizes, whilst the Continent requires a good proprtion of narrow boards, and so on. But all the time he is limited by what his logs can produce economically. He knows that technically logs of a certain diameter give the best yield when cut to certain sizes and if he is to depart from that he must get a better price to compensate for the waste in conversion. For this reason, if for no other, it is advantageous for shippers to make sales of sawngoods in the Autumn as soon as they know what the bulk of their log-supply consists of and they can cut during the winter as nearly as possible to buyers' requirements. This is not to say that the sawmills do not operate all the year round, but the new season's logs are usually available for cutting during the winter following that in which they are felled. In estimating market requirements the shipper will consult his agents in various countries as to any changes which may have taken place in their particular market; for instance in the U.K. market there has sometimes been less demand for 2½ ins.×7 ins. and more for 2 ins.×7 ins. and at one time it was expected that 1½ ins.×4 ins. would displace 2 ins.×4 ins. as a favourite dimension, and so on.

(*c*) The Stocknote.

Having collected all the information available, the shipper converts his logs on paper to sawngoods and issues his stocknotes showing what he will have available for shipment, properly seasoned, at various shipping dates in the following year. The agent then enters upon his main task of selling by ascertaining what the importers are open to purchase and the price they are willing to pay. In passing it may be mentioned that the agent does a good deal towards stabilising the market for the benefit of all concerned by declining to submit to shippers any offer which he considers unreasonable.

(*d*) The Negotiation.

There are three main factors in any negotiation—specification, price and date of shipment, in that order of importance. Unless the importer wants what the shipper can supply no business can result, but the price may vary according to whether the specification is a difficult one or not. The date of shipment may not always be so very important. As a matter of convenience negotiations are usually based on the f.o.b. price for 7 ins. Unsorted battens, it being understood that anything wider than 7 ins. will cost more and narrower something less. These variations from the basis price are usually fairly stable over a period of time and there is general agreement as to extras for wider widths and for boards and reductions for narrower widths and for Fifth quality. Of late years there has been a tendency for wide widths and especially wide boards to cost comparatively more than formerly and the under 7 ins. to be hardly anything less. This is probably to be accounted for by the average log dimension having diminished in the course of years, old forests of large trees being replaced by younger growth. The extras for board sizes do not apply to Fifths, in which quality all thicknesses are charged alike and the price only varies with the width and even then not so much as in Unsorted.

(*e*) The Importer's Offer.

Having obtained an offer from an importer of a reasonable price for a reasonable specification, the agent airmails, telegraphs or telephones it to the shipper for his consideration. If he accepts it the business is closed and contracts are exchanged, but if he demands a change in the specification or an increase in the price the matter is still in the negotiation stage and the importer is no longer bound by his offer: he may either accept shippers' counter-offer, or renew his offer, or improve or withdraw it. It is always understood that there are no special conditions attaching to an offer unless they are mentioned when the offer is made: the current Albion or Uniform Contract conditions will be assumed to apply, including the description of the goods as " Sellers' usual," whilst in such specialities as slating battens, where lengths are shipped " as falling," one importer may want as many ends as possible to get the advantage of the reduced price and another may want as few as possible because his particular customer has less use for them, in which case shippers would probably make no difficulty about agreeing to a minimum percentage of ends in one case and a maximum percentage in the other.

(*f*) The Transmission of the Offer.

Whilst it is the shipper who decides what he will sell and at what price, the agent's task as negotiator is not always an easy one, especially if, on a falling market, he is instructed by his shipper to " try to get an advance in price of so-and-so, but do not risk losing the business " which is easy enough to put into two five-letter codewords with the aid of the Zebra Code, but is not so easy for the agent to comply with. Coding has generally been supposed to show a great saving in cost, but it is extremely doubtful whether in coming to this conclusion sufficient allowance has been made for the time and labour spent in coding, which is a job requiring considerable experience and extreme accuracy, and the delay involved in decoding. It has been said that nothing annoys a shipper's sales manager more than getting a telegram in code, often at night, which he has to get his codebook to interpret, when a few words in plain English would have told him directly all he needed to know. To balance this argument it may be said that nothing annoys an agent more than to receive from his shipper in reply to an offer a laconic " decline," or codewords to that effect. The agent wants to know WHY and so does the importer. Is it specification, price or date of shipment that is unacceptable ? No agent can serve his principals efficiently unless he has their support and a bare refusal of an offer, without an explanation, stifles the chance of the negotiation leading to business which an explanation might well bring about. There is nothing against codes, which are extremely useful in their place, but to code a message which would cost hardly any more if sent in plain language is one of the worst sorts of false economy, whilst if the matter is a straight-forward one for quick decision, a telephone call will often prove best and cheapest in the end.

(*g*) THE DATE OF SHIPMENT.

The date of shipment is that on which the shipper undertakes to have goods of the contract description ready for loading, properly seasoned, and in an f.o.b. contract if the goods are not removed within a fixed period, usually two months from that date, they have to be paid for as overlying. It is, however, a mistake to suppose that specific goods are allocated to a particular contract in such a way that if one lifts the goods a month later one may expect them to be one month drier : the shipper is not even obliged to carry the same goods over from one season to the next unless this is specifically agreed. The term f.o.w. is seldom used nowadays in contracts as the shipping date, since it is much more satisfactory to have an actual calendar date. Some ports which used to be closed for weeks or months on end during the winter are now kept open by ice-breakers all the year round.

In a c.i.f. contract, such as the Albion, the date of shipment will be based upon the same considerations, but if the goods are not shipped within six weeks of the stipulated time—the buyers have the option of cancelling the contract as far as it concerns those goods.

In the Albion contract there is an obligation on the shippers as sellers to secure freight space " in due time " in order to effect shipment by the date named in the contract. The shipper must take account of this obligation in arriving at the c.i.f. price at which he is prepared to sell the goods, since his obligation is to ship the goods irrespective of the rate of freight he has to pay (with the exception of increases in freight rate due to war, etc.).

(*h*) HARDWOOD NEGOTIATION.

Whilst much of the above is also true of the shipment of hardwoods, this is generally much more an all-the-year-round business. Furthermore the grading, range of lengths, etc., is more closely defined in the respective grading rules and there is less room for negotiation as to specification.

Although the specification is important, and greater widths and lengths will always command the better price, the fact that hardwood is rarely used in the dimension in which it is imported, as is softwood, but is usually sawn down to smaller sections and sizes, emphasises this difference in specification between hardwood and softwood. On page 247, the grading rules of hardwood, based upon this same consideration, are compared with the softwood grading rules.

The specification of imported squares and other hardwood " dimension stock " is a rather different matter, being a specialised business of its own.

On the other hand the date of shipment assumes a greater importance. Practically all hardwood sales are on a c.i.f. basis, with the goods being carried by liners (see page 88) on regular services. Apart from those countries and out of the way places that are badly served with liner services, the shippers can be fairly certain of securing freight space easily and so are in a position to match the dates of shipment on their stocknotes (which are issued the whole year round) with their production.

CHAPTER III

Shipping

1. Elementary Definitions.

The imported trade is bound up closely with shipping and marine insurance which must be fully understood if pitfalls are to be avoided. The following simplified definitions will help to explain the clauses and conditions appearing in shipping and marine insurance documents.

(*a*) TYPES OF VESSEL.

(i) *Liners* are vessels that sail on scheduled journeys between specific ports.

(ii) *Cargo vessels*—more commonly called " tramps " or " freighters " —are in the nature of " free lance " carriers. They will load and carry almost any cargo between any ports in the world suitable to their capacity and type.

(*b*) TONNAGE.

This word occurs in many documents and can have any one of the following meanings :—

(i) *Gross Register Tonnage* (G.R.T.).—The total internal capacity of the ship based upon the calculation—100 cubic feet of capacity = 1 ton.

(ii) *Net Register Tonnage* (N.R.T.).—The tonnage available for cargo or passengers. This represents the earning power of the ship, and is a measure of capacity calculated as 100 cubic feet of capacity = 1 ton. It is the basis on which port and canal dues are paid.

(iii) *Dead Weight Tonnage* (D.W.).—The tonnage available for cargo, passengers and fuel. This is the actual carrying power of the ship.

(iv) *Displacement Tonnage.*—The weight of the vessel including the weight of crew and supplies but *not* including weight of cargo, fuel or passengers. Given in tons of 2,240 lb., and is actually the weight of the volume of water displaced by the ship. Used for warships but not for freighters.

General cargo (other than normal timber cargo) is carried on a tonnage basis, either actual weight or based on the measurement, 40 cubic feet per ton, whichever is the greater.

(*c*) CLASSIFICATION.

For marine insurance purposes, all the more important vessels in the world are classified as to their condition and seaworthiness. The most important classification is that carried out by Lloyd's Register of Shipping. This register covers most vessels in the world, and is the basis for practically all British Marine Insurance policies. Lloyd's Register of Shipping was an offshoot many years ago of Lloyd's Underwriters, and started from the same beginnings. The highest classification that is granted by Lloyd's Register is ✠ 100 A1.

The ✠ signifies that the hull was built under Lloyd's supervision; the 100 reveals that the ship has a steel hull; the A shows that the state of the hull and the 1 the state of the rigging (a relic from the days of sailing ships) are first-class. A1 has thus become an everyday expression for anything first-class. Vessels on Lloyd's Register undergo inspection at frequent intervals, and the older the vessel the more rigorous the inspection.

The insurance of the hull of the ship depends upon the classification; the higher the classification, the lower the insurance premiums. The importer who buys timber f.o.b. and arranges his own insurance (for goods) is affected by the classification in this way. Supposing a very cheap freight rate is offered by a foreign shipowner, and the importer takes this up without checking on the classification of the ship. He may find that if the vessel is not classified at Lloyd's the insurance companies would not be willing to insure the goods in transit.

In addition to the classification, the vessel will be registered at a "port of register" the official document being the "Certificate of Registry."

The "Plimsoll Line" is the white line within a circle painted on the side of the hull to show the safe loading level. The level is fixed by Board of Trade inspectors and varies slightly for different oceans, waters and seasons. It is required by the Merchant Shipping Act. If a vessel is overloaded beyond the "Plimsoll Line," and founders during the voyage, any claim made on the insurance policy covering the goods may be disallowed, unless provision is made to cover this risk which is effected by clause 6 of the T.T.F. clauses regarding seaworthiness, etc.

The phrase ". . . loaded down to her marks" is the common way of expressing that a vessel has been loaded to full capacity down to the level of the "Plimsoll Line" applicable to the voyage and time of year.

(*d*) Ship's Papers.

Each ship carries the following documents relating to the vessel, the crew, the cargo and the voyage:—(i) The agreements with the crew and a description of the voyage for which they are engaged; (ii) Board of Trade Certificate of Registry; (iii) The last Board of Trade survey report (concerning hull, engines, etc.); (iv) Certificates of competency of the master and officers; (v) Pilotage certificates; (vi) Certificate of "entry outwards" stamped and issued at port of departure. This is issued by the customs authorities of the port in exchange for a notification of the vessel's departure together with a certificate of the quantity of bunker coal carried ; (vii) Bill of health ; (viii) Bills of lading, manifests, passenger lists, etc., giving full details of cargo or passengers that are being carried ; (ix) Charter-party ; (x) Board of Trade certificate covering the inspection of the ship's gear and tackle. This must be available for inspection if the ship is going to discharge at a port in the U.K. It must be renewed at stated intervals. If it is not available, or is out of date, the stevedores may refuse to unload the ship.

(*e*) SHIP'S LOG.

This is a complete diary of the life of the ship. In it will be found :—(i) List of the crew and report of character ; (ii) Load line and draught of ship ; (iii) Date of arrival and departure for each port with details of freeboard and draft of water on each occasion that the ship goes to sea ; (iv) Speed, course, wind, depth of wells at stated intervals ; (v) Names of lookouts and watches with their reports ; (vi) A full description of the voyage.

The log book may be inspected by a bill of lading holder when the ship reaches port, and the master of the ship must produce it if reasonably required, or provide extracts of entries having a material bearing on a matter in dispute. In inspecting the ship's log particular attention should be paid to any entries concerning rough weather and the effect of weather and storms on the deck cargo. Sometimes part of the deck cargo may have to be thrown overboard if the vessel is in very heavy seas, on other occasions the violent movement of the ship may displace part of the deck cargo. References to " battening down deck cargo " usually indicate disturbance during the voyage.

If part of a parcel or cargo is shipped on deck, and entries in the ship's log state or infer that part of the deck cargo has been lost or disturbed by rough weather, then the importer is forewarned. A shortage in the deck cargo may be expected and the evidence of the ship's log can be used to support the claim for the shortage (see page 201).

(*f*) ARRIVAL PROCEDURE.

On arrival at a port in the U.K. the master submits his papers to the customs and health authorities and obtains from them a " clearance inwards." After this, unloading of the ship may commence. If the ship has encountered really rough weather on its voyage, the master will take the precaution of " entering a protest " which is done before a notary or British Consul. The protest gives a brief account of the voyage and the weather encountered. It relieves the shipowners and the master of responsibility for damage to cargo on deck or under deck due to the weather.

2. The Charter-Party.

The contract by which a ship is chartered to load and carry goods is known as a "charter-party" (abbreviated to C/P or merely "charter") and is usually prepared by the shipbrokers who have arranged it. If timber is to be shipped from one port to another, shipbrokers are approached and given the details of quantities, the voyage, ready date, and so on. Being in close touch with the shipping world the shipbrokers are able to offer various possibilities of freight that are available by different shipowners.

It may take more than one ship to lift the timber, but the shipbrokers can arrange for whatever is required. When the shipbrokers have found suitable freight space at a rate of freight which the charterer is willing to pay and the owners to accept, they draw up the charter-party.

The charter-party is a very ancient document dating back many centuries. The word is derived from "charter" which is a "document bestowing certain rights and privileges" (a historic example is the well-known Magna Carta) and "party" which is derived from the Latin and means "parted" or "divided." It is said that in olden days the charter-party was torn into two parts after being signed, one part being held by the shipowners and the other by the merchants, called the charterers, and that to complete the document both parts had to be brought together. It has also been thought to signify that it is not merely a "bestowal" by one party on another, but a contract in which the "rights and privileges" are "divided" between the parties. Nowadays however the word has become abbreviated to "charter" as in the Nubaltwood charter itself and is so referred to in the contract forms.

There are two principal types of charter-party,

(i) time charters,
(ii) voyage charters.

In a time charter the vessel is chartered for a particular period and during that period is under the direction of the charterer. The shipowners are paid so much per week or per month for the hire of their vessel irrespective of the amount of cargo it is carrying. Time charters are only made by companies with a large amount of goods to be carried by sea. When shipping lines cannot provide shiproom for all the goods they have to carry, they will often charter other vessels on time charter to supplement their own fleet. The Timber Control, importing government purchased timber, regularly used time charters.

In a voyage charter the vessel is chartered for a particular voyage between two particular ports. The rate of freight in a voyage charter may be based in one of two ways :—

(i) A rate of so much per standard or per ton, possibly varying with one rate for deals and battens and another for boards, with other rates for slatings, etc., or a single rate for a declared composition of cargo limiting the proportions of each kind. In the charter is stated clearly the size of the cargo to be carried.

(ii) A lump sum covering the voyage. The estimated carrying capacity of the vessel is declared at the time the freight is negotiated.

Of these two forms of freight, the first one based on a rate per standard is by far the safest for the importer. He is only required to pay freight on the goods that are carried and delivered (presuming no deadfreight arises) and he does know beforehand how much freight per standard he will have to pay. This information may be vital to him if he is selling his goods forward, *i.e.*, before they have been shipped.

The lump sum freight at first sight may appear attractive and cheaper than a fixed rate per standard but there are many pitfalls. All too often it has been found that the vessel was not able to lift the full quantity of goods expected and that the capacity of the vessel for carrying timber has been over-estimated by the shipowners, particularly in the case of vessels not regularly used as timber carriers. This over-estimation is difficult to prove, the shipowners usually claiming that the goods were insufficiently seasoned or were otherwise heavier than calculated. As a result, as soon as the vessel has been loaded so that it is down to its " marks " (*i.e.*, the Plimsoll line), the master stops loading and sails with only a part of the cargo. On arrival at the port of destination the lump sum freight is payable in full, irrespective of the amount of cargo carried. In such a case, what may first have appeared to be a very cheap freight, is seen to have cost much more than freight based upon a rate per standard. If the difference between the amount of goods carried and the estimated capacity of the vessel is very great, the charterer may have a claim against the shipowners for over-estimating the capacity of the vessel, negligence in stowing the cargo, etc., but in any case it is likely to entail some form of legal proceedings, and these should be avoided if possible, particularly when dealing with foreign shipowners.

The charter-party contains the following details :—

(*a*) Names of the contracting parties, *i.e.*, the shipowners and the charterers.

(*b*) Name, flag, class, registered tonnage, capacity and/or D.W. of vessel and position at time of chartering.

(*c*) Expected loading date.

(*d*) Description and size of cargo (see below), giving maximum and minimum limits and margin allowed to the shipowner for loading.

(*e*) Rate of freight and how it is to be paid.

(*f*) Time allowed for loading and discharge and the amount of demurrage chargeable if these periods are exceeded.

(*g*) Name of the loading port and the discharging port.

(*h*) Clauses protecting the shipowner against various events for which he is not responsible. (In Scandinavian charter-parties the ice clause is particularly important in autumn and winter as it gives the shipowner the option to cancel a charter-party if the port is icebound.)

(*j*) The undertaking to *Load*, *Carry* and *Deliver* the goods detailed in the charter-party.

(*k*) The reverse side of the Nubaltwood charter has a specimen of the form of bill of lading to be used with it.

With reference to (*d*) above, it is extremely important that the cargo shall be correctly and fully described, as otherwise serious difficulties may arise. The most common omission (and therefore need for insertion) is " planed boards in bundles " which the master might refuse to load when sent alongside if not included in the description of cargo in the charter-party.

It is also important to ensure that " unseasoned " goods, such as South Swedish baulks, are correctly described in the charter. This has been the cause of some trouble in recent years, particularly in lump sum charters.

" Demurrage " is a sum paid or agreed to be paid to the shipowners as liquidated damages for delay in loading or discharging beyond certain stipulated times. These stipulated times vary in each form of charter, from a " reasonable time " qualified by such phrases as " in accordance with the custom of the port," to " fixed lay-days."

The " custom of the port " is difficult to define exactly but never-the-less is one of those terms that in the past has been well understood by charterers, shippers and shipowners without much difficulty or dispute.

" Fixed lay-days " means a fixed number of days within which the cargo must be loaded and discharged. It is an exact term without any ambiguity but generally it is much more to the advantage and convenience of the shipowners than the charterers. It has only appeared in timber charters in recent years.

In some charters the fixed lay-days are calculated to start from the date when the vessel arrives at the port, as opposed to the date when the vessel arrives at a *berth* in the port. The difference is important in ports subject to congestion and delay, where vessels may be kept several days awaiting a berth. In such a case a period of time, say 24 hours, is permitted after the vessel has reported at the port, after which the shipowners notify the charterers that they regard the vessel as an " arrived ship " irrespective of the fact that there is no berth available.

For example the Nubaltwood charter states in clause 6 that "... time for loading shall commence at 2 p.m. if the Vessel be ready to load (whether in berth or not) etc. . . ."

Demurrage is calculated usually at a certain sum per day. It is payable by the charterer but the importer is usually protected by clauses in his contract with the seller by which the seller agrees to pay any demurrage caused by him at the loading port. An important exception to this is the Nubaltwood charter (and Uniform 1951 contract) since with these documents the charterer is protected by the demurrage equalisation scheme (see page 82).

Where the importer/charterer has resold the bills of lading and the property in those bills of lading has passed to the new buyer, the latter, as the last consignee, is liable for demurrage at the port of discharge and may also be liable for demurrage at the loading port (see page 171).

In some charters provision is made for an incentive to be paid by the shipowners to the shippers for working time saved in loading the vessel at the loading port. This is known as " despatch money " and may be at half the agreed rate for demurrage. It applies to loading only.

If the charterer does not provide sufficient cargo, within the quantities and margins set out in the charter, the shipowners will claim " dead freight." This is damages for the unoccupied cargo space and is payable at the same rate as if that space were loaded. The provision of the cargo is largely out of the control of the importer buying goods on f.o.b. or c.i.f. terms. Protection is given in the Uniform f.o.b. or Albion c.i.f. contract by which the seller agrees to pay any dead freight admitted or proved to have been caused by them at the loading port. (Uniform 1951 clause 14.)

Demurrage and dead freight do not arise in a time charter since the charterers themselves are the only party to suffer loss, the shipowners are not affected being paid in any case for the full period the vessel is under time charter.

The undertaking to load and deliver the cargo, paragraph (*j*) above, refers particularly to charters for carrying timber from Scandinavia and North America.

There are however other charters, such as F.I.O. charters (Free In and Out) in which the shipowners, for the freight named, only carry the goods from port to port, all costs of loading and discharging being paid by the charterers and nothing at all by the shipowners.

An intermediate form of charter is on " free discharge " terms which means that whilst the shipowners pay for the loading and stowing of the cargo, they make no contribution towards the cost of discharge which is borne entirely by the charterers.

In a c.i.f. contract the sellers are the charterers, in an f.o.b. contract the buyers are the charterers.

The charter for shipments from Norway and the Baltic to the U.K. and Eire is known as the Nubaltwood charter, published in 1951 and superseding the Baltwood charter of 1926.

A copy of the Nubaltwood charter is to be found at the end of this book: its terms are, for the most part, self explanatory. There are several innovations in the Nubaltwood charter so the various clauses are summarised hereunder and major differences from the old Baltwood 1926 charter and other similar charters are pointed out.

NUBALTWOOD CHARTER 1951

This charter has been agreed between the Timber Trade Federation and the Chamber of Shipping. It has not yet (January 1953) been agreed by the Swedish Wood Exporters' Association and Finnish Sawmill Owners' Association although they will review it from time to time. The Baltwood 1926 charter was agreed by all parties concerned, viz. T.T.F., Chamber of Shipping and Shippers' Associations.

Preamble.

Names of charterers and shipowners are inserted, with name of vessel and N.R.T. (see page 68). Dimensions and number of workable hatches are stated, rates of loading and discharge are based upon figures of so many standards per workable hatch per day (see clauses 6 and 15).

The capacity of the vessel, including deckload, is stated in standards and the shipowners are given a margin for loading.

The margin is stated to be 7½ per cent. up to 750 standards and 5 per cent. in excess of 750 standards. It is important to check that the maximum quantity that can be called for by the master of the ship is within the margin of maximum quantity that the shipper is obliged to provide under the purchase contract. This must be done of course *before* the charter is signed. Under the Uniform 1951 f.o.b. contract the margin permitted to the buyer for chartering is 10 per cent., with a maximum of 50 standards (see page 129). For a contract of say 400 standards, the maximum that the seller may be called upon to provide is 440 standards. If a charter is completed for the same quantity of 400 standards, the maximum that the shipowners can call forward under the charter is 430 standards (400 plus 7½ per cent.). The charterer is therefore adequately covered under his purchase contract.

If on the other hand the purchase contract quantity is 800 standards, the margin is 50 standards, so the maximum quantity that the seller is obliged to provide is 850 standards. If the charter is made for 800 standards (the quantity which the charterer has most readily in mind), the shipowners may call forward up to 858¾ standards (800 plus 7½ per cent. of 750 and 5 per cent. of 50), this can result in a dead-freight claim of 8¾ standards. The charter should therefore be made for 790 standards to remain within the maximum margin. On the other hand it must be remembered that the minimum margins similarly restrict the charterer, in the above instance if the shipowners take the minimum margin on a charter for 790 standards they may call forward only 731¾ standards whereas the minimum quantity the buyer may take on his contract for 800 standards is 750 standards. There would therefore be 18¼ standards overlying, but this may be combined with either another shipment, or by taking the maximum margin under the purchase contract there is a sufficient quantity to enable a further charter to be made to lift them. This however is a better alternative than a claim for dead freight.

This problem increases with the quantity chartered. The quantity up to which the Nubaltwood charter and Uniform 1951 f.o.b. contract are in agreement is $666\frac{2}{3}$ standards. Below this figure the charter may be made for the contract quantity.

With other contract forms it is similarly important to check the charter quantities and margins with contract quantities and margins, before they are signed.

The date the vessel is expected to be ready to load is also stated. This must not be before the " ready date " named in the preamble of the Uniform contract, which is the date by which the shipper contracts to have the goods ready to load. On the other hand it should be before the "drawing date " named in clause 11 of the Uniform contract unless the buyer is prepared to pay for his goods and leave them in the shipper's yard for a time.

Clause 1.

The name of the loading port is stated followed by a description of the cargo. It is important to name the loading port exactly as in the purchase contract, especially if there are two loading places with goods at one and/or the other.

The phrase a " full and complete cargo " applies where there is only one charterer for the vessel. If there are several charterers, each with only a part cargo, these words are amended to read " a part cargo of ..... standards " or similar applicable phrase and at the same time the word " proportionate " is inserted before the word " deckload " in line 24, unless the cargo is specified as being " all on " or " all under " deck. Any clause in the charter may be amended in this way by mutual agreement.

The words " . . . described in the purchase contract as properly seasoned for shipment to the U.K." are now included, an addition to the previous wording of the Baltwood 1926 charter. Both the Uniform and Albion contracts provide (clause 2 in each) for the goods being " properly seasoned for shipment, etc. . . . ," but if the importer is buying goods that are not so described, for instance " unseasoned goods," it is vitally important to see that the phrase " properly seasoned etc.," is deleted from the charter and the cargo properly described. Failure to do this can only cause disputes and claims for dead freight.

The clause then gives details of the amount of cargo in different thicknesses and sizes, particularly referring to boards under 1″ thick, slatings, scantlings, laths, planed boards, etc., and which of them are bundled, all of which are more difficult to stow than deals and battens. A memo in the margin defines the sizes of battens and slatings.

Further margins, including those for ends, are included and again these are in agreement with similar clauses in the Uniform and Albion contracts.

The rates of freight " per delivered standard " are set out for deals and battens, boards, boards under 1″ thick, scantlings, slatings, etc., or maybe a single rate for the cargo as specified.

If any of the boards are to be bundled it is safer to add here the words " bundled and/or unbundled."

An alternative paragraph is included by which the cargo may be described in more general terms, and the freight paid in one lump sum.

The clause includes the name of the port of destination, followed by the words " . . . or so near thereunto as she may safely get and deliver the cargo always afloat. . . ." The first part of this phrase permits the master of the vessel, under certain circumstances, to land part of his cargo at ports other than the port of destination. For instance vessels bound for Manchester, that are drawing too much water for the Manchester Ship Canal, under this clause are permitted to discharge part of their deck cargo at Ellesmere Port at the entrance to the Manchester Ship Canal.

In some small ports the vessel may have to lie on the mud at low tide. In these circumstances the words " always afloat " are deleted and substituted by " N.A.A." (not always afloat).

If the vessel is to discharge at a particular wharf, such as a wharf that is part of the importer's own premises, this must be clearly stated in the charter.

Clause 2.

Under this clause the master or shipowners are to give the shippers at least seven *working days* notice of the probable date of arrival of the vessel to commence loading. This covers the buyer's obligation in clause 4 of the Uniform contract. The Baltwood 1926 charter referred to *calendar days* notice. A memo to this clause sets out the holidays which are not working days. If Midsummer day falls upon a Tuesday, then the Sunday, Monday and Tuesday would all be non-working days; notice of arrival on the Wednesday, the day following Midsummer day, would have to be given ten days beforehand to ensure seven working days notice.

If the master or shipowners do not give the required notice, the lay-days are extended and shipowners agree to accept responsibility for demurrage on lighters or trucks caused at the loading port by their failure to give this notice. Under the Uniform contract this responsibility rests with buyers who in turn are covered by this clause in the charter.

Clause 3.

The charterers are given the option of cancelling the charter if the vessel is not ready to load within a certain period.

Clause 4.

If all or part of the goods are destroyed by fire, the charterers have the right to cancel the charter.

Clause 5.

Option of the master to carry ballast.

Clause 6.

The loading clause. This provides that the master "on arrival at the loading port, shall give written notice to the shippers of the approximate quantity of cargo required." This is a departure from the Baltwood 1926 charter, to cover the last paragraph of clause 4 of the Uniform contract. So once again if goods are purchased on a Uniform contract it is important that no other charter than the Nubaltwood is used.

It is customary to insert at line 82 after the words "weather working day" the words "and workable hatch." The clause proceeds to state that "the cargo shall be brought alongside the vessel in the customary manner at charterer's risk and expense." Clause 1 of the Uniform contract stipulates that the goods are to be delivered "all free alongside the vessel," and the Timber Trade Federation Insurance clauses protect buyers against risks from the moment the goods leave the shipper's wharf.

The rate of loading is set out for deals and battens, boards, etc., all per "weather working day." This excludes holidays, Saturday afternoons, Sundays and those working days when weather conditions prevent loading all day. If the weather conditions prevent loading for *less* than half the working hours, that is counted as a full working day. If weather conditions prevent loading for *more* than half the working hours, but not for the full day, that is counted half a working day.

These rates are calculated on the basis of the number of workable hatches given in the description of the vessel in the preamble, and a schedule of rates of loading *per day per hatch* agreed between the Chamber of Shipping, the T.T.F. and the Shippers' associations. These schedules of rates are amended from time to time and are published by the Demurrage Association (see page 82).

The last paragraph of this clause provides for disputes at the loading port to be settled before the bills of lading are signed, but failing this, claims (which will generally be for demurrage or dead freight) are to be endorsed on the bills of lading or, if the master is prevented from so doing, notified to charterers by telegram. Against this, however, is the undertaking by shippers in the Uniform contract to pay all *dead freight* admitted or proved to have been caused by them at the loading port and the undertaking by the shipowners in clause 20 of this charter that neither they nor the master will endorse any bill of lading with a *demurrage* claim or clause (see commutation of demurrage, page 82).

Clause 7.

Advance freight. A proportion of the freight, not to exceed one-third of the total freight, is advanced to the master at the loading port to cover incidental expenses. The amount advanced is endorsed on the bills of lading in sterling, and is ultimately deducted from the total freight leaving a " balance of freight " which is paid to the shipowners in proportions set out in clause 21, only when the vessel has reached the port of destination.

In other types of charter the whole of the freight may have to be paid before the vessel leaves the loading port, this is known as " freight prepaid."

Clause 8.

Ice hindrance. The first part gives shipowners the option of cancelling the charter if ice setting in at the end of the year prevents the vessel from loading or continuing to load. The last paragraph covers charterers for clause 6 of the Uniform contract, which limits seller's liability to supply cargo at f.o.w. (first open water) until 48 hours *after* navigation between shipper's wharf or quay and the vessel is unimpeded by ice. There are often circumstances where there is no difficulty or danger for a steamship to load whilst there is considerable risk of danger and damage to barges from heavy floating ice. The additional 48 hours is to cover the fact that the barges may have to come some distance down a river estuary, where the ice breaks up more slowly than in the open harbour or seaway.

Clause 9.

Strike clause. The first part of this clause extends the period of loading or discharging by the period of the strike. The remainder deals with options given to the shipowners to cancel the charter if there is a strike at the loading port either just before, or after arrival of the vessel. It also gives the shipowners the option of sailing with a part cargo if the strike lasts for more than six calendar days and prevents the vessel from loading the complete cargo.

Clause 10.

Bills of lading (see page 85). This clause governs all the terms and conditions of the bills of lading which " . . . shall be prepared in the form endorsed upon this charter. . . ."

Shipowners accept responsibility for the *number of pieces* signed for by the master, but not for any loss or destruction of cargo in lighters alongside the vessel at the loading port. Here again the importer is protected by the T.T.F. insurance clauses.

The shipowners, however, will only admit claims for shortage in pieces on an ex-ship tally at port of destination, provided they receive notice of this within *six days* of the final discharge of the vessel. This is a departure from the Baltwood 1926 charter where no period for notification was given.

In some ports, such as the Port of London, the landing return may not be available for a considerable period. If importers wish to be in a position to claim for a shortage of pieces, *they must arrange to tally against the ship*, otherwise it is difficult, if not impossible, to notify a claim within the six day period.

Clause 11.

Sets of bills of lading. This sets out the number of bills of lading required. It is customary to alter the first sentence of this clause to make it read " The master shall be obliged to sign more than one set of bills of lading, notice of which is hereby given," and to delete the last sentence as copies of loading instructions are usually supplied by shippers to the master on his arrival in port. It stipulates that charterers will send the goods alongside in such a manner as to enable the cargo under each bill of lading to be kept separate. The importer passes this obligation on to the shipper in Uniform clause 13.

In the final sentence the charterers are called upon to send a copy of the " loading instructions to shippers " to the shipowners for information. This sentence is usually deleted as unnecessary since it has been a long established practice for shippers to give the master a copy of the loading orders on arrival of the vessel at the loading port.

Clause 12.

Exceptions. This is a clause protecting the shipowners against a wide range of occurrences over which they have no control. The importer in his turn is protected by his marine insurance policy including the T.T.F. insurance clauses.

Clause 13.

Deviation clause. A further clause protecting the shipowners that has the effect of defining the scope of the voyage in wider terms to avoid possible claims for deviation. The T.T.F. insurance clauses again protect the importer fully.

Clause 14.

War. Provides for cancellation of the charter in case of war, and protection for the shipowners if vessel is deviated by order of the Government.

Clause 15.

Discharging clause. The first part of this clause defines the limit of shipowner's liability at the port of discharge. If the cargo is discharged by hand this limit is the ship's rail. If the cargo is discharged by ship's tackle or shore cranes, the limit of the shipowner's liability is reached when the cargo is within reach of the ship's tackle or shore cranes. If the vessel is required to do any work beyond these limits the consignees (the bills of lading holders), are required to pay for the additional work. The basis for calculating charges for the additional work is described, and in the following clause 16 the actual charges are set out for deals and battens, boards, etc., where the port is amongst those for which the charges have been agreed between the T.T.F. and the Chamber of Shipping.

In the Albion c.i.f. contract, the sellers (the shippers) are the charterers, but in a clause of that contract the buyers (the importers) accept the liability to pay any of these additional charges. Similarly in the T.T.F. c.i.f. re-selling contract clause 2 these charges are passed on to the new buyers, who become the ultimate bills of lading holders and agree to accept the terms and conditions of the charter.

The second part of the Nubaltwood clause 15 gives the rate of discharge for deals and battens, boards, etc., per " weather working day " and is the counterpart of the loading clause (clause 6). The rates of discharge are calculated from the number of workable hatches (stated in the preamble) and the rate per hatch per day agreed between the T.T.F. and the Chamber of Shipping for each port in the U.K. These vary between 15 standards and 40 standards, and are subject to revision from time to time.

Clause 16.

Apportionment clause. The rates of freight quoted in clause 1 are repeated here, together with the additional charges (if any) payable by consignees for work done by shipowners in discharging cargo beyond the limit of their liability. These additional charges are actually an apportionment between the shipowners and the consignees of the total charges incurred, since shipowners in any case will be responsible for some of them.

In the past there were many disputes concerning the liabilities and duties of shipowners or charterers for these charges, but now, for all the ports regularly used, these apportionment charges are agreed between the T.T.F. and the Chamber of Shipping and adjusted from time to time in accordance with the rise and fall in costs. It is usual to insert against the rate of charges " according to Chamber of Shipping Schedule." Where it is agreed that no extra charges are payable by consignees the word " Nil " is entered.

Clause 17.

Responsibility for dock dues in a London dock. In the case of a part-cargo the words " their proportion of " should be inserted before " the dock dues."

Clause 18.

Demurrage Association clause. This is quite a new clause and together with clause 20, the commutation of demurrage clause, is peculiar to the Nubaltwood charter. The shipowners undertake to become members of the United Kingdom Timber Trade Shipowners' Demurrage Association Ltd. (referred to in this chapter as the Demurrage Association). The charterers undertake when signing the charter to notify this association giving details of name of vessel and name of shipowners.

Clause 19.

Demurrage. The amount of demurrage, in sterling, chargeable if the cargo is not loaded or discharged within the rate stipulated in clauses 6 and 15 is entered in this clause. The amount is based on the vessel's carrying capacity, calculated on a formula laid down by the Chamber of Shipping Schedule.

For example, if a vessel of 1000 standards capacity has four workable cargo hatches and is loading at a port where the rate of loading agreed between the Shipowners, T.T.F. and Shippers' Associations (as shown in the Chamber of Shipping Schedule) is 25 standards per hatch per day, the average rate of loading per day is 100 standards for the vessel. This figure would appear in the average rate in clause 6. At this rate the vessel should be loaded in 10 weather working days. If in fact the loading occupied 12 weather working days, the shipowners are then entitled to demurrage for two days at the rate per day set out in this clause. It has been decided by the Committee of Management of the Demurrage Association that a vessel with one large hatch can be counted as a two-hatch vessel, provided two gangs can work it satisfactorily simultaneously.

Clause 20.

Commutation of demurrage. The holders of each bill of lading agree to pay to the Demurrage Association named in clause 18, a fixed amount per standard. For their part, the shipowners waive any rights that they may have to claim demurrage at loading or discharging ports from charterers or bills of lading holders. Any demurrage claims that the shipowners may have, must be proved to the Demurrage Association who then settle these with the shipowners.

The payment of this fixed charge per standard is therefore the equivalent of an insurance for the bill of lading holder giving protection against the liability of meeting demurrage claims which may prove very heavy. Payment of this fixed charge must be made to the shipowners at the same time that the freight is paid, by means of a separate cheque made payable to the Demurrage Association.

The amount of the fixed charge will be determined for each season and will depend on the amount of demurrage claims that have had to be met ; following a period of heavy claims the fixed charge is bound to rise and *vice-versa*.

Clause 21.

Payment of freight. The freight to be paid is the full freight less advance of freight made under clause 7, plus charges payable under clauses 15 and 16. Fifty per cent. of this is paid when the vessel commences to discharge, further proportions when the cargo starts being discharged from the hold, etc., these proportions varying slightly between different ports and methods of discharging. The final 10 per cent. is usually retained until the final outturn is ascertained. If the outturn has not been ascertained within 30 days of the date of final discharge, a further 5 per cent. must be paid. If the outturn has not been ascertained within 60 days, the final 5 per cent. must be paid. If the outturn is ascertained within 6 months of completion of discharge a refund of any over payment may be claimed.

Most other forms of charter, including liner " booking notes " (see page 89) do not permit this retention by the importer of part of the freight, but stipulate that the freight must be paid in full, " ship lost or not lost."

The freighting of timber has its own problems, and claims by importers against shipowners for shortage in delivery of pieces against bills of lading quantities are frequent. The retention of a percentage of the freight by the importer, until the final outturn is ascertained and therefore any shortage known, greatly strengthens the position of the importer in getting his just claims met by the shipowners. This particularly applies to foreign shipowners who, when they have left the U.K. port after discharging their cargo, are outside the jurisdiction of English courts. To sue foreign shipowners successfully requires taking the matter to court in their own country, or waiting until the vessel once more enters a U.K. port when it may be "arrested" by Court order, the writ being nailed to the mast of the vessel.

These proceedings may be expensive for the importer or bill of lading holder, and certainly they will take time. If, however, a part of the freight is retained, the importer may set off part or all of this retention against the shortage or other claim against the shipowners. This forces the latter to take the initiative to prove their case and if necessary sue the importer. This must be done through the Courts in this country, so foreign shipowners would straight away be placing themselves under the jurisdiction of English (or Scottish) Courts, enabling the importer to pursue his claims as if they were against a British company.

Clause 22.

General average. The York-Antwerp rules govern the procedure for adjustment of general average, and permit a statement of it to be drawn up in a foreign port.

The new Jason clause is applicable where average adjustment is computed under American law.

Clause 23.

"Both to blame" collision clause. A further clause to protect shipowners by reason of differences in American Law. Any possible liability falling on bills of lading holders is covered under the marine insurance policy.

Clause 24.

Lien. The master or shipowners have an absolute lien on the cargo for all freight, deadfreight, average and charges payable under clause 15 and demurrage contribution under clause 20. In other charters (and in the Baltwood 1926 charter) the lien is not for demurrage contribution (the fixed charge per standard) but for the demurrage itself.

Under this clause, if the shipowners do not receive payment or settlement of these items, they can hold the cargo, refusing to give delivery until they receive satisfaction. They cannot, however, sell the cargo themselves to settle their own demands; that can only be done by order of a Court.

Under other charters the most common exercise of lien by shipowners is for settlement of claims for demurrage. This may be particularly hard on the owners of the last bills of lading to come out of the vessel. The first bills of lading will have been discharged and may have been moved away from the quay by the time the vessel comes on demurrage. The shipowners may then place a lien on the remaining bills of lading, until such time as the demurrage, which is for the whole vessel, has been paid. In such circumstances it is conceivable for demurrage at the discharging port, for a vessel chartered under fixed lay-days, to be paid entirely by the holders of the last bill of lading in the vessel.

The demurrage contribution scheme, in clauses 18 and 20, protects the bills of lading holders against this very serious liability.

Clause 25.

Telegrams—is self explanatory.

Clause 26.

Brokerage. Sets out the amount of brokerage and to whom payable.

Clause 27.

Agency. Although this clause states that shipowners shall appoint their own brokers or agents at loading or discharging ports, there may be a stipulation in the purchase contract that brokers or agents named by the shippers shall be appointed at the loading port. In such a case it is important to see that the charter is amended to comply with the shippers' stipulation.

Clause 28.

Substitution. The right to substitute a similar vessel, on giving notice to charterers, is a new clause and sometimes considered objectionable and deleted.

Clause 29.

Overtime. Sets out how additional costs of overtime are to be apportioned between charterers and shipowners.

Clause 30.

Arbitration. Where disputes cannot be settled amicably, provision is here made for reference to arbitration (see page 182).

The Nubaltwood 1951 charter which has been described here in detail, as was its predecessor the Baltwood 1926 charter, is normally the most used charter, covering as it does goods shipped from Norway, Sweden and Finland and Russian goods shipped from the Baltic.

Other charters are the Russwood charter, tied to the Russian contracts for shipment from the White Sea, the Baltwood adopted for Leningrad trade, the Benacon charter for shipments from Eastern Canada and the N. C. B. Europe for props from the Baltic and Scandinavia. All these latter charters are being considered by the Documentary Committee of the U.K. Chamber of Shipping with a view to revision. The Contwood charter for Scandinavian trade to the Continent is also under revision. It may be noticed that " despatch money " for working time saved in loading only (see page 74) is payable by shipowners to shippers in the Scanfin charter, but this incentive is absent in the Baltwood and Nubaltwood charters.

3. The Bill of Lading.

The bill of lading, sometimes abbreviated to B/L, is the most important document in the carriage of any goods by sea, and it is essential for importers to understand their rights and their responsibilities in connection with it.

It contains the following clauses and information :—

(*a*) Name of shipping port.
(*b*) Name and address of shipper.
(*c*) Name of vessel and master, and present position of vessel.
(*d*) Date of charter-party.
(*e*) Description of cargo—given as number of pieces, mark and description.
(*f*) Number of pieces of deck cargo.
(*g*) Name of port of destination.
(*h*) Name of consignee " or Assigns."
(*j*) Signature of Master or Agent.
(*k*) Receipt for freight advance—in British sterling.

(*l*) Clauses protecting shipowner—these are usually references to clauses in a particular charter-party which shall " apply to this bill of lading."

(*m*) The clause—QUALITY, CONDITION AND MEASURE UNKNOWN.

(*n*) The reverse side will often contain the specification of the goods covered by the Bill of Lading.

It fulfills three main functions :—

(i) It is a *receipt* by the *master of the ship* for the goods shipped. It must be remembered however that it is a receipt only for the *number of pieces* shipped. The master of the ship or the shipowners are only responsible for the number of pieces signed for and acknowledged as received.

The master signs for the goods *quality*, *condition and measure unknown* but first of all it is stated that the goods were shipped at the named loading port " in good order and condition " and later the master undertakes that the goods shall " be delivered in the like good order and condition." It is sometimes supposed that this undertaking is cancelled by the words at the foot of the bill of lading, namely " quality, condition and measure unknown." But there are in effect two clauses which, whilst they seem contradictory are not so, but are really complementary, the first being a specific undertaking by the master and the latter a general understanding. Taking the latter (*i.e.*, the general) clause first it is clear that the master of the vessel has no interest in " quality " : the freight rate would be the same whatever the quality. The intrinsic " condition " of the goods whether discoloured or otherwise would not concern him either (except in so far as affects clause 1A of the charter (Nubaltwood) as to their being properly seasoned). The " measure " of the goods certainly concerns the master as the size of the cargo and the amount of freight are calculated upon it, but would be very difficult for the master to check, so it is the custom to accept the evidence of the seller's invoice as to measure, and therefore quantity, on the basis that " what is good enough for the buyer to pay on is also good enough for the ship to be paid freight on." " Actual " and " nominal " are of course another matter, as freight is always paid on " actual " measurement. There remains however the master's specific undertaking to deliver the goods in as good order and condition as he received them, as he is primarily responsible for any damage that may occur to the goods during passage, from the time they were shipped to the time they are delivered and this includes the breaking of pieces which is a common occurrence.

(ii) It is *evidence* of the terms of the *freight contract* made between the seller and the shipowner.

Quite obviously it is not the freight contract itself, as this must be drawn up before the goods are shipped, whilst the bill of lading is drawn up only when the goods are actually being shipped. However, if there is no separate charter-party, the bill of lading does give the necessary legal framework for evidence as to the freight contract.

The Bills of Lading Act, 1855, states that any benefits under a freight contract are vested in the endorsee of a bill of lading, just as if the endorsee had made the freight contract himself. This again is an essential factor of the c.i.f. contract, as the buyer when he acquires ownership of the goods on passage must have the full protection of the freight contract as well as the insurance policy taken out by the shipper.

(iii) It is a *document of title* to the *goods*. Without the bill of lading, delivery of the goods at their port of destination cannot be obtained.

This can be explained in greater detail as follows :—

(*a*) In law—rightful possession of the bill of lading is equivalent to ownership of the goods it represents.

(*b*) The title to the goods can be transferred by *ENDORSEMENT* and *DELIVERY of the bill of lading.*

(*c*) To make it a negotiable instrument a bill of lading must by its terms be deliverable to a *named person* or to *a name left blank* followed by " *or to order or assigns.*" It is not usual to put " deliver to bearer."

(*d*) By the Sale of Goods Act (Section 47) the bill of lading must be " lawfully transferred " by a person who has a right to transfer it.

(*e*) The endorsee of a bill of lading acquires no better title to the goods than was possessed by the endorser. If therefore a bill of lading is in the possession of a person who had *no* title to it because the bill of lading had been stolen or lost, any subsequent transfer of the bill of lading confers no title on the innocent buyer. There is a considerable difference here between the bill of lading as a negotiable instrument and say a bill of exchange or a cheque. An uncrossed cheque that has been lost or stolen may be cashed by any person who endorses it correctly, whether in fact he has a right to endorse it so or not, *e.g.*, an uncrossed cheque made out to " J. Smith or Order " if endorsed " J. Smith " by *anybody*, can be cashed.

There is one exception to this, and that is where an innocent buyer has both obtained *possession* of an endorsed bill of lading from a seller who had no title to it, and *given value* for it, in which case he has a legal title to the goods.

The form of bill of lading used with the Nubaltwood charter has been evolved over years of trading and presents few difficulties to the importer. Other forms of bill of lading, that are used for all classes of merchandise, are not so simple.

In some ports a bill of lading may be drawn up before the goods are loaded, whilst they are in transit sheds or wharves. This form of bill of lading confers a good title to the goods, but is not a clear receipt that the goods have been loaded. In certain French ports a similar document known as a *pris en charge*, duly stamped and sworn before a notary or consul, is used. Its chief advantage lies in the fact that it enables the property in the goods to be transferred to the buyers without delay. Where there is a very short sea voyage of no more than two days, the vessel may have arrived at the port of destination before the normal shipping documents and bills of lading have been received by the importer to enable him to obtain possession of the goods.

Practically all shippers and importers however require a bill of lading referring to the actual goods placed on board the vessel. This is known as an " On Board bill of lading " or a " Shipped bill of lading." With the Nubaltwood charter these phrases are not used since the bill of lading is automatically an " On Board bill of lading " by virtue of the clauses embodied in it and the charter, but it is wise to use this phrase when describing the type of bill of lading required for goods being shipped from other parts of the World. In these other forms of bill of lading the words " On Board " are sometimes endorsed on the face of the bill of lading to indicate that the goods described in the bill of lading were in fact all loaded.

A bill of lading drawn up on the prescribed form and signed by the master or agent without any qualifying terms is said to be a " clean bill of lading." If any qualifying terms are added it is said to be a " claused bill of lading." In recent years the growth of claused bills of lading has presented a serious problem to the timber trade. These qualifications limit the shipowners' liabilities. Although these clauses may cover any condition in which the cargo is received by the vessel, the most common qualifying clauses are " . . . pieces said to be . . ." or " . . . shipper's count said to be. . . ." Thus, although the master of the vessel is signing for a certain number of pieces, the shipowners are not accepting responsibility for that number of pieces. The only way to overcome such a clause is to institute some form of tally, to be acknowledged by the shipowners, as the goods are loaded. This is additional expense and not completely satisfactory. The use of these terms and clauses depends largely on the freight market. With present day values of timber, the loss of a number of pieces can amount to a substantial amount of money. At the same time shortage of freight space places shipowners in a strong position from which, to a certain extent, they can dictate terms to their own advantage.

4. Liner Bill of Lading.

Many shipments of softwood, and the majority of shipments of hardwood and plywood, are carried by liners. If goods are carried by a liner on a scheduled journey, no charter-party is necessary since the shipowners themselves have determined the ports and dates of loading and discharge.

When freight space on a liner service is booked for the carriage of timber, this is confirmed by the shipowners on a " booking note " which describes the cargo and voyage, usually without nominating a vessel. All other conditions are said to be " as per bill of lading," or may refer to some other standard form of charter as " all other terms and conditions as per Nubaltwood charter."

The terms of the freight contract and other terms and conditions normally found in the charter-party, are now embodied in the bill of lading. These liner bills of lading therefore contain much more detail and many more clauses and provisions than ordinary freighter bills of lading.

In considering liner bills of lading it must be remembered that there may be as many as 500 on a particular voyage. The relationship between the shipowners and the bill of lading holders is therefore rather different. The bill of lading holder represents merely a very small part of the interest in the cargo being carried, as apart from a major interest or a total interest in the case of a freighter cargo where the bill of lading holder is also the charterer.

The liner bill of lading holder must accept the shipowners' terms and conditions of carriage, he can rarely make his own stipulations about loading and discharging wharves for instance. On the other hand since small parcels only are being carried, and it is presumed that the liners are making regular passages, there are not the same difficulties in arranging marginal quantities for the convenience of chartering.

A liner bill of lading will nearly always stipulate that the full freight must be paid before the shipowners will release the goods. There is no question of a retention by the bill of lading holder of a proportion of the freight to set off claims against the shipowners. Liner bills of lading are frequently claused " freight payable ship lost or not lost " which is self explanatory and necessitates that the charterer shall insure the full amount of freight as well as the f.o.b. value if he wishes to be fully covered against all loss in the event of the vessel being lost at sea.

Particular care must be exercised in arranging freight on liner terms, to make certain that items normally fully covered in traditional timber charters such as the Nubaltwood, are in fact covered in the liner bill of lading or booking note.

For instance, the cargo must be fully and properly described, particularly with reference to ends. A booking note made out for D.B.B. (deals, battens and boards) should have the following words included " (including ends not exceeding 7½ per cent.)." It is not sufficient in this instance to rely on the words " all other conditions as per Nubaltwood charter etc.," since as far as a liner bill of lading is concerned, ends and D.B.B. are different descriptions of cargo.

Similarly it is not sufficient to rely on a reference to the Nubaltwood charter for a reduction in freight for ends. The rate of freight is one of the prime factors of the booking note, and if it is intended that ends are to be carried at reduced freight, as in the Nubaltwood charter, this should be made quite clear by the introduction of the following wording in the freight payable clause:—" but 2 per cent. of the entire parcel (including deck load) shall be regarded as ends and carried at two-thirds freight."

Most liner booking notes and bills of lading are drawn up by the shipowners concerned, who print their own forms with their own terms and conditions.

There is a standard form of liner booking note, known by the code name " Conlinebooking " and a liner bill of lading, known by the code name " Conlinebill," published by the Chamber of Shipping and approved by the Baltic and International Maritime Conference.

The Conlinebooking booking note sets down the following information, and in this respect resembles a charter in the hands of the importer.

(1) Names of Shipowners and bills of lading holders (referred to as " Merchants."
(2) Name of vessel (with rights of substitution).
(3) Name of loading port.
(4) Name of discharging port.
(5) Approximate time of shipment.
(6) Rate of freight — and whether prepayable or payable at destination.
(7) Whether goods to be loaded on deck or under deck.
(8) Name of bill of lading holder's representatives at loading port (will usually be the shippers).

This form of booking note then proceeds to set down extracts of the more important clauses and conditions of the Conlinebill bill of lading, on which the goods will be carried.

The Conlinebill bill of lading follows the normal bill of lading showing a full detail of the goods carried (" weight, measure, marks, numbers, quality, contents and value unknown") with the amount loaded on deck, together with the rate of freight payable, and amount of any freight advance.

The standard clauses printed are as follows:—

Clause 1. Definition of term " Merchant "—which covers the shipper, importer, etc., as holder of the bill of lading.

Clause 2. Paramount clause—standard shipping clause relating to the Hague rules.

Clause 3. Jurisdiction—unless otherwise provided any disputes on the bill of lading to be decided in, and by the law of, the country of the shipowners.

Clause 4. Period of responsibility, this limits shipowners' liability by disclaiming responsibility for loss or damage before loading or after discharge.

Clause 5. Scope of voyage, a deviation clause which in spite of the more restricted nature of the published voyage, permits shipowners to call at other ports or omit calling at some ports.

Clause 6. Substitution, permits shipowners to substitute another vessel and also permits shipowners to tranship, land, store and re-ship goods if necessary.

Clause 7. Lighterage, at loading or discharging ports to be for account of Merchants.

Clause 8. Loading, discharge and delivery.

No set rates of loading or discharging are laid down, but the shippers (referred to as " Merchants ") must be prepared to supply the cargo without any notice as soon as vessel is ready to load. Furthermore they must supply cargo " as fast as the vessel can receive," during overtime periods if necessary.

At the discharging port the importers (again referred to as " Merchants ") must take delivery of the goods " as fast as the vessel can deliver."

The importer must accept his reasonable proportion of unidentified loose cargo (which may possibly be offered in lieu of shortage on under-deck bills of lading).

Any goods not applied for within a reasonable time (usually referred to as " over-landed ") may be re-sold by the shipowners.

Clause 9. States that deck cargo if carried shall be subject to the Hague rules.

Clause 10. If the importer has an option of having a part of the cargo discharged at more than one port of discharge, this option must be declared at least 48 hours before the vessel reaches the first port.

Clause 11. This deals with any charges payable on the goods and other expenses, all payable by the bill of lading holder.

Where the freight is pre-paid, it is deemed to have been earned when the goods are loaded, and is not then returnable.

Clause 12. Refers to shipowners' lien on the goods for any amount due, and permits the sale of the goods without recourse to a Court Order.

Clause 13. Shipowners' disclaimer of responsibility for any loss sustained through delay, unless caused by gross negligence of the shipowners.

Clause 14. General average clause (see page 83).

Clause 15. Both to blame collision clause (see page 84).

Clause 16. *Force Majeure*, War, Strikes, etc. A clause protecting shipowners against liability if the vessel does not sail or is deviated, or if goods are discharged at another port, due to the *force majeure* circumstances set out.

Clause 17. This clause establishes the bill of lading as evidence of a contract between the bill of lading holder and the shipowners. It proceeds to declare that any shipping line, company or agents who execute this bill of lading for the shipowners, shall not be under any liability arising out of the contract if they are not one of the principals of the transaction. This is declaratory of the law, since in such circumstances they are " agents " for one of the principals, and their position is the same in law as the shippers' agent (see page 119).

The printed form then goes on to state that clauses 1-17 will not be altered, but supplementary clauses may be added.

Three optional additional clauses are given, the most important are relating to demurrage.

Additional Clause A—Demurrage. This sets out the rate of demurrage to be paid per ton if the vessel is not loaded or discharged with the dispatch set out in clause 8 (which states that goods must be supplied as fast as the vessel can receive them), any delay in waiting for berth at or off port to count. If the delay is due to causes beyond control of the bill of lading holder, the time of demurrage will be reduced by 24 hours. The demurrage will not exceed the freight on the goods, the amount being a proportionate part of the whole. Demurrage is not payable where the delay has arisen only in connection with goods belonging to other bill of lading holders.

CHAPTER IV

Marine Insurance

1. General.

Marine insurance is a contract of indemnity, whereby one party (the insurer), in consideration of a specified payment (the premium) undertakes to guarantee another party (the assured), against risk of loss through maritime perils. It dates back to the earliest days of trading between countries and the carriage of goods by sea. Since it is a contract of indemnity, the assured can only recover from the insurer the amount of loss actually sustained.

The assured must have an "insurable interest," which may be in

(i) the hull; (ii) the freight; or (iii) the cargo.

Shipowners have an insurable interest in the hull, importers have an insurable interest in prepaid or guaranteed freight and cargo and also an agreed sum for "imaginary profit." The assured must have the insurable interest at the time of the loss.

If the assured has no insurable interest, it becomes a gaming or wagering contract and is void.

In cases where any possible doubt could arise whether the assured has in fact an insurable interest the insurers should be asked to agree the insertion in the policy of the letters P.P.I., meaning "Policy Proof of Interest."

The utmost good faith must be observed in a contract for marine insurance. The assured must disclose all material facts within his knowledge as to the interest insured. If this is not done, the contract is voidable by the insurer; there are two implied warranties, the seaworthiness of the vessel and the legality of the adventure.

Marine insurance is carried on by "underwriters" and "insurance companies." The most famous name in marine insurance throughout the world is Lloyd's of London.

Lloyd's is an exchange of which these private "underwriters" are the members. It started in the seventeenth century in a coffee house kept by a certain Edward Lloyd in Lombard Street where people connected with shipping and insurance met; hence the phrase in a Lloyd's policy ". . . that this Writing or Policy of Assurance shall be of as much Force and Effect as the surest Writing or Policy of Assurance heretofore made in Lombard Street, or in the Royal Exchange, or elsewhere in London."

Insurance brokers act for the merchant, importer or shipper who approach them to arrange the insurance of their goods for a particular voyage. The insurance brokers draw up the contract of insurance (known as the " policy "), and then " place " the insurance with underwriters or companies, from whom they receive their remuneration.

Underwriters at Lloyd's do not usually accept the whole of any risk (though a group or syndicate of underwriters may do so), particularly if the sum is a large one, but accept varying proportions of the risk, writing their names and the proportions they are accepting on an abbreviated memorandum of the risk, known as the " original slip." Further, all large risks are in fact spread by re-insurance, but that is a matter which concerns the insurer and not the assured.

The merchant, importer or other assured person does not deal directly with the underwriters, who deal only through recognised Lloyd's brokers.

Insurance is also arranged by the brokers with the large insurance companies. For small amounts one company will often be prepared to accept the insurance of the whole, on the other hand for large amounts the broker may spread the insurance over several companies.

English underwriters and insurance companies have the highest reputation, and through their vast network of connections do business in all parts of the World. A foreign shipper requiring to insure goods in a c.i.f. sale can easily do so with a British company. If, however, he wishes to insure with a foreign insurance company, most purchase contracts stipulate that the form of insurance policy and the risks covered shall be the same as if the insurance was undertaken by a British company. Furthermore it is usual to stipulate that a foreign insurance company must be approved by the importers, as although the majority of foreign insurance companies are of the highest integrity, there are some in certain countries, whose reputation for insurance is not of the best.

2. The Policy.

The contract of marine insurance made between the insurer and the assured is known as the " policy." By the Marine Insurance Act 1906, the policy must show :—

(i) The names of the assured or some person who effects the insurance on his behalf. It can *not* be issued blank.

(ii) The subject of the insurance, such as timber, prepaid or guaranteed freight or freight advance. Where the freight is to be paid at destination on delivery of the goods, only freight advance is insured and in an Albion c.i.f. contract the buyer is not entitled to an insurance policy covering the balance of freight.

On the other hand, if the freight has been prepaid, or, as in the case of many liner bills of lading, there is a clause in the freight contract stating " freight payable ship lost or not lost," then the full freight must be insured.

(iii) The risks against which the subject is insured.

(iv) A description of the voyage; it is generally sufficient now to state "via other loading and discharging ports," without naming all intermediate stopping places.

(v) The sum or sums insured. This is usually based on the f.o.b. value plus a 10 per cent. imaginary profit, plus prepaid or guaranteed freight or freight advance as the case may be, but a larger imaginary profit can usually be insured if desired.

(vi) The name or names of the insurers.

Policies are of the following kinds:—

(i) *Voyage policies*, where the contract is to insure the goods for a particular voyage from one place to another. Practically all policies used in importing timber are of this nature.

(ii) *Time policies*, where the contract is to insure the goods for a definite period of time (not exceeding one year).

(iii) *Valued policies*, where the policy specifies the agreed value of the subject matter insured.

(iv) *Unvalued policies*, where the value of the subject matter is not specified but is left to be ascertained subsequently, subject to the limit of the sum insured.

(v) *Floating policies*, where the insurance is in general terms, leaving the name of the vessel, details of voyage and goods etc., to be defined by a subsequent declaration. These declarations may be made by indorsement on the policy, or on special declaration forms, and must be made in order of shipments. The policy is issued for a particular amount and is legally binding.

(vi) *Open cover*. This is not a policy, but is an agreement by insurers to issue an appropriate policy within the terms of the open cover when the necessary details have been supplied. It covers every shipment within the limit of the cover and is in force for an agreed period of time, usually a year. The relevant details for each shipment are supplied on a declaration form as for a floating policy. The premium rates are usually specified in the cover, which may also contain a limitation of the amount of goods to be insured in any one vessel.

On receipt of the declaration form, the brokers prepare a stamped policy in the normal way.

Floating policies or open cover are popular with importers and shippers because of their convenience and the safe assurance that any cargo within the voyage limits is held covered. This latter point is important for the importer who has purchased goods on f.o.b. terms and who will frequently have goods on passage before the relevant shipping documents for those goods reach him.

3. The Policy Form.

One of the characteristics of marine insurance is its flexibility. It must cover every class of goods that are carried by sea, the ships that carry these goods and the value of their carriage or freight. It would clearly be impracticable to issue a fresh policy for each and every type of goods and service insured, and so a standard type of policy form is used, and then amended by additional clauses to suit the class of goods insured.

The most important standard type of policy is known as Lloyd's S.G. policy, the S.G. possibly standing for "Ship—Goods," this is set out in the Marine Insurance Act of 1906. It is not obligatory to use this particular policy, there are others, but it is the policy form most used.

This type of policy has been in use for centuries and the wording has changed very little throughout the years. As a result many of the phrases are archaic and some refer to perils and practices that ceased a century and a half ago. They are still retained in the policy for the very good reason that the form having existed in its present state for so long there is no ambiguity in any part of it. Everyone concerned in the policy is fully aware of the meaning of each of the phrases which have been tested and interpreted in the courts during this long period.

If a new, modernised form of policy were prepared there would inevitably be some matters in dispute, and the legal meaning of many of the phrases would again have to be tested and ruled in court.

The policy takes the following form :—

(i) *Name* of assured.
(ii) *Description* of voyage.
(iii) *Name of vessel.* This is not now essential and it is usual to follow the name of the vessel with such wording as "and/or other approved vessel, etc. . . ."
(iv) *Name of master.* This is unnecessary and is very rarely inserted.
(v) *Description of goods* and value insured.
(vi) *Rate* of premium.
(vii) *Signature* of Superintendent (with seal) of Lloyd's Policy Signing Office.
(viii) Endorsement of numbers of underwriting syndicates.

"*Lost or not lost.*" These words make the contract retrospective, in as much as underwriters are liable for loss which may have occurred before the contract was drawn up, provided of course that the assured was unaware of the loss when the contract was drawn up.

"*At and from.*" These words appear before the name of the loading port. In a voyage policy, the attachment of the insurance (that is the commencement) starts from the moment the goods are loaded on to the ocean going vessel. It does not cover the transit by lighter, etc., to the vessel, and this risk has to be covered by the addition of further clauses (see page 101).

The insurance continues during the voyage, but a major deviation or transhipment could nullify the policy, so these eventualities also have to be covered by additional clauses. The insurance ends when the goods have safely reached their destination.

THE PERILS INSURED AGAINST.

"*Of the seas.*" The foundering of the vessel, collisions, stranding, etc. (but not in tidal harbours, etc.).

"*Men of War, Fire, Enemies, Pirates.*" With the exception of fire, these are now treated as war risks. They are excluded from the policy by the addition of a special exclusion clause, the "Free of Capture and Seizure Clause" (see below). These risks are then covered by a separate war risk insurance with a further premium.

Piracy includes passengers in mutiny, and rioters who attack the vessel from the shore.

"*Rovers.*" An anachronism.

"*Thieves.*" This refers to assailing thieves and not petty pilferers. Where goods are covered under a "warehouse to warehouse" clause, as in the T.T.F. Clause 1 (see page 100) it has been held that thieves who enter a place where the goods are stored by forcibly breaking through doors, etc., are within the meaning of the term.

"*Jettisons.*" The throwing overboard of goods for the safety of the vessel, as opposed to washing overboard by the sea.

"*Letters of Mart and Counter Mart.*" An anachronism.

"*Surprisals, Takings at Sea.*" Treated now as war risks.

"*Arrests, Restraints and Detainments of all Kings, Princes and People of what Nation, Condition, or Quality soever.*" This does not include judicial arrests, riots, etc.

"*Barratry of the Master or Mariners.*" Wrongful acts wilfully committed by the master or crew to the prejudice of ship-owners.

"*All Other Perils.*" This is not comprehensive, it means perils of a similar nature to those already specified.

Sue and labour clause. These are costs incurred by the assured in the defence, safeguarding and recovery of the goods, and are recoverable under the policy.

Free of Capture and Seizure clause. This clause, known as the F.C. and S. clause, excludes the war risks which form part of the perils included in the original form of policy. These risks are normally covered separately (see page 106) the wording including the phrase ". . . to cover the perils excluded by the F.C. and S. clause . . ." but further risks are also covered. It also excludes loss or damage by strikes, etc., if the wording is F.C. and S. S.R. and C.C. (strikes riots and civil commotions) are risks also covered separately.

Franchise clause. With the exception of general average (see page 99) or when the vessel is stranded sunk or burnt (see F.P.A. clause, page 103) a franchise is set on claims on certain classes of goods. This is 3 per cent. in the case of ordinary cargo, also the vessel and freight. This means that in a policy for £100 no claim of less than £3 will be recognised. If the franchise is reached the claim is paid in full. This clause will often be overridden by the addition of clauses stating " . . . to pay irrespective of percentage."

The T.T.F. insurance clauses change the franchise to ½ per cent. or £10 whichever is the less (see page 103).

4. Losses Covered by Marine Insurance.

The main losses normally recoverable under a marine insurance policy are as follows :—

(i) *Total Loss.* (*a*) Absolute or Actual ; (*b*) Constructive.
(ii) *Partial Loss or Damage.* Known as " Particular Average."
(iii) *General Average* loss or expenditure.
(iv) *Salvage Loss.*
(v) *Other charges* incurred on the goods such as (*a*) Salvage charges ; (*b*) Particular charges ; (*c*) Sue and Labour charges ; (*d*) Extra charges.

These items are discussed at greater length in the following pages.

(i) (*a*) *Absolute or Actual Total Loss.*

This is self explanatory. In addition to destruction it includes loss where the goods are so damaged as to cease to be a thing of the kind insured, or where the assured is permanently deprived of the goods.

(i) (*b*) *Constructive Total Loss.*

This is loss where the goods are reasonably abandoned on account of actual total loss appearing unavoidable or else where the preservation of the goods from actual total loss appears to be more expensive than the value of the goods.

(ii) *Particular Average.*

This is any partial loss of or damage to the goods themselves caused by a peril insured against, which is not general average (*q.v.*). (The word average here is derived from the Italian " *avarigio* " meaning risk.)

Particular average occurs where there is :—

(*a*) partial loss.
(*b*) damage or deterioration ; or both.
(*c*) partial loss and damage or deterioration of what remains.

Certain types of cargo are much more likely to suffer damage than others, for instance, a deck cargo of timber may easily be damaged by seawater ; underwriters will usually not accept the risk of damage to such cargo, unless there is a major peril to the vessel or goods, such as fire, collision or stranding of the vessel.

The exclusion of these risks is said to make this type of cargo " *Free from particular average* " usually abbreviated F.P.A.

(iii) *General Average.*

In a way this is quite independent of marine insurance; it is an obligation on all parties with an interest in the vessel, freight, or goods, arising out of the freight contract.

General average loss or expenditure is, however, a loss covered by marine insurance. It is a voluntary sacrifice of one interest for the benefit of all interests. It may occur when it is found necessary to jettison part of the deck cargo in order to lighten the vessel in heavy weather, or to get the vessel off a sandbank. Without the sacrifice of this part of the cargo, the vessel would be in danger and the whole cargo might be lost. The value of the goods sacrificed is therefore carried by the vessel and cargo proportionately to the value of each interest, and is divided between all the holders of bills of lading and the shipowners. These are known as " general average contributions " and they are assessed in accordance with the York-Antwerp rules of 1924. Charterers and holders of bills of lading accept responsibility for paying these contributions in the charter and bill of lading. The amount of these contributions is a loss or expense for which each holder of a bill of lading is responsible for his own share, but is covered by his marine insurance policy.

If there has been a general average loss on a vessel, the shipowners may place a lien on the cargo when the vessel reaches port, until such time as the contributions are paid.

Holders of bills of lading may obtain delivery of their goods by signing a *general average bond*, in which they agree to pay any contributions due from them. If the amount is large, the shipowners may insist on a *general average deposit* being paid into a bank in the name of trustees. In either case the insurers should be consulted first and their approval obtained, so that the bill of lading holder is quite clear that he is covered.

The calculation of the general average and the apportioning of it amongst the interests concerned may be very complicated and not be settled for a long time, especially for instance if the vessel goes into a port of refuge. It is dealt with by specialists who are certified *average adjusters.*

(iv) *Salvage Loss.*

Loss where by reason of the perils insured against, the goods are necessarily sold before they reach their destination.

(v) (*a*) *Salvage Charges.*

Incurred to save a vessel in peril.

(v) (*b*) *Particular Charges.*

Expenses incurred by the assured to minimise or prevent loss of a particular interest in the cargo.

(v) (*c*) *Sue and Labour Charges.*

Expenses incurred by the assured in the defence, safeguarding and recovery of the goods.

(v) (*d*) *Extra Charges.*

These are other charges arising out of damage and claims and they include such items as survey fees, auction charges, etc.

5. The Timber Trade Federation Insurance Clauses.

From sections (2) and (3) above it will be seen that the main body of the policy is in rather open terms, covering the goods only from the moment they are placed on board the vessel, and restricted to a clearly defined voyage with little margin for deviation. Furthermore, a study of charter-parties and bills of lading (see Chapter III) reveals many additional risks that are not covered under the standard form of policy. Some of these risks are sufficiently serious to give rise to cancellation of the policy by insurers, such as wrongful acts by the shipowners, unseaworthiness of vessel, etc.

The T.T.F. insurance clauses have been drawn up and agreed between the T.T.F. and the London Institute of Underwriters and Lloyd's Underwriters Association. They are accepted by all reputable insurers and are acknowledged in practically every timber exporting country in the world. When attached to the policy, which has the words " Including Timber Trade Federation Clauses 1952 " endorsed upon it, the policy is deemed to be extended to cover all the additional risks and contingencies detailed in these clauses.

A copy of these clauses is to be found in the band at the back of this book.

Clause 1. *Transit clause.*

This is sometimes known as the " warehouse to warehouse " clause and extends the cover from the shipper's yard, which may be some distance inland, right through to the " final destination."

The cover afforded by this clause is very wide, and it goes far beyond the cover normally given under general cargo insurance clauses —in particular the Institute Cargo clauses.

A marine insurance policy only attaches when the assured has an " insurable interest " in the goods. In the case of an f.o.b. or f.a.s. contract, the property (and hence risk) usually passes to the buyer when the goods are placed on board, and normally this is the point where the assured assumes an insurable interest. However the Uniform f.o.b. contract clearly states that the goods are at the risk of the buyer from the moment they are loaded on to transport, etc., at the shipper's mill or wharf. Since the goods here are at the risk of the buyers, they clearly have an insurable interest in the goods, and this is conceded by Underwriters.

At the same time it must always be remembered that in spite of the wide ambit of cover given by this clause—the assured *must* have an insurable interest in the goods, and the cover will only commence at the point where that insurable interest starts. This is of great importance where goods are purchased on forms of contract other than the Uniform and Albion. Importers are well advised to check with their insurance brokers that they are adequately protected in the pre-loading period of such contracts, if necessary arranging for their policies to be endorsed to cover the period up to loading on board.

The words " in transit " mean not only the period when the goods are moving in an ocean going vessel or lighter, etc., but they cover ordinary transhipment, delays in transit warehouses, etc. The 1938 T.T.F. Insurance clauses included the phrase " . . . Including all risks of transhipment and/or landing whilst on shore, and of re-shipment wherever incurred . . .," but it has been held that these are unnecessary and all are adequately covered by the phrase " . . . whilst in transit. . . ."

The words " final destination " covers the buyer who is resident outside a port and whose goods are to be delivered to his storage yard inland from the port. They also cover the buyer who resells his goods before arrival on delivered terms or c.i.f. terms to a customer who requires the goods delivered to an inland destination.

However it is vitally important that there is no break in the journey—the goods must remain " in transit " for the full journey. If the journey is broken at all, for instance if the goods are sorted at some intermediate warehouse, or if the goods are stored in a warehouse at the port, for the convenience of the assured, the policy lapses where the original journey is broken. The cover to final destination does not include a further sea voyage, such as by coastal shipping. If the goods are transhipped for delivery by coastal vessel, the policy lapses at the point of transhipment.

In a c.i.f. resale, the benefits and cover of the policy pass to the new buyer, provided there has been no break in the journey. In an ex-ship sale the policy lapses after the goods have been discharged from the ship.

A purchaser on ex-ship terms therefore must ensure that his insurance covers him from the moment the goods leave the ship.

If the goods are stored at a place where they are finally landed, they are only covered under the policy for loss or damage by fire for fifteen days, dating from midnight on the day on which the final landing was completed, even though delivery of the goods cannot be obtained. In such cases (which may occur in docks subject to serious congestion), the assured must make certain that the goods are adequately covered by insurance against fire, at the termination of the fifteen day period.

The words " . . . Assured or Receivers . . . " covers the situation where goods are sold on delivered terms, and delivery is taken not by the Assured but by his customer.

Clause 2. Craft, etc., clause.

This is particularly to cover transit by water to the vessel at the loading port, since the standard policy only covers the goods from the moment they are put on board.

Lightermen in London, under the London Lighterage clause, repudiate all liability for loss or damage to goods, in their contract with the importer. If there is loss from a lighter, the insurers on settling the claim with the assured, are entitled to subrogation of the assured's rights (see page 109) of recourse against third parties. If the assured contracts out of these rights (as in the London Lighterage clause) without informing the insurer, that would amount to concealment of a material fact and would enable the insurers to void the policy. This clause protects the assured against that possibility.

Clause 3. *Deviation clause.*

The normal policy permits of only limited deviation from the voyage described, and does not cover transhipment. The charter grants deviation liberties to the shipowners, and in any case this is a matter well outside the control of the assured.

This clause protects the assured against these contingencies. (See Nubaltwood charter clause 13, page 80.)

However this only covers the goods during the period of deviation against the risks covered by the policy. *It does not cover the goods against damage or deterioration caused by the delay itself.* Delay is specifically excluded in Clause 5.

For instance where timber, shipped as seasoned for a normal voyage to the U.K., is delayed due to breakdown of the ship through a peril of the sea, and is found on arrival to have discoloured and sweated badly (even to the extent of becoming rotten) the underwriters are not liable under the policy. Although the delay to the vessel was caused by a peril or risk insured against, the damage to the timber has been caused by the *delay* and so is not covered under the policy.

Clause 4. *Change of voyage clause.*

The " Held covered at premium to be arranged " gives additional safety to the assured but it is essential that if any change of voyage occurs, or error or omission is discovered, the insurers shall be notified immediately.

Clause 5. *Risks covered.*

(*a*) The words " all risks " are usually construed as meaning all marine risks. It is not an unqualified comprehensive cover against all risks whatsoever. The question of " inherent vice " particularly when associated here with the question of " delay " is important as this may affect claims for deterioration of cargo through sweating, etc., during voyage. It is accepted that woodgoods are " properly seasoned " as stated in the contract and charter for a normal voyage to the country of destination. If the goods when discharged are found to be damaged, stained, commenced to rot, etc., the assured has a legitimate claim provided that it has been caused by a risk covered. Such reasons would include amongst others the following :—

insufficient ventilation in the holds; flooding of the holds; contamination with other goods which have sweated, such as hides.

If on the other hand there are no such circumstances as these to support the claim, the insurers may reject it on the ground that the deterioration has been caused through the goods being insufficiently seasoned for the voyage—in other words "inherent vice."

(*b*) This is the "*Deckload F.P.A. clause.*" The deckload is not covered for particular average, such as damage by seawater, but total loss overboard is specifically included, as also the risk of this during loading, transhipment and discharge.

On the other hand the insurers will pay for particular average damage if the vessel or craft *at any time during the voyage* suffers from the following perils, even though the peril itself may not be directly connected with the particular average damage.

If the vessel or craft is :—

(i) *Stranded.* The vessel must have remained stranded for a reasonable time. It does not apply if the vessel merely touches the bar of a harbour when passing over. Neither does it apply in cases where it is the custom for vessels to lie on the mud in tidal harbours.

(ii) *Sunk.*

(iii) *Burnt.* This means a fire affecting the structure of the vessel itself.

(iv) *In Collision.* Contact with another vessel or any other external substance (ice included) other than water.

The insurers will also pay any loss or damage to deck cargo, which may reasonably be attributed to :—

(i) fire.
(ii) explosion.
(iii) collision (see above).
(iv) discharge at a port of distress, also to pay all the costs incurred in landing, warehousing, forwarding, etc.

This clause extends the insurance cover of under-deck cargo to include "cargo stowed in poop, forecastle, deck house, shelter deck, or other enclosed space. . . ." This is important in connection with the Pacific Coast c.i.f. contract form (see page 163).

(*c*) This overrides the general franchise clause. A lower franchise limit of ½ per cent. or £10 is quoted. It is possible, however, that loss from a raft, etc., might not amount to ½ per cent. of the whole cargo so by stating that each raft, etc., is to be a separate insurance, claims are payable when the amount is ½ per cent. of the raft, etc., in question, as opposed to ½ per cent. of the whole cargo.

Clause 6. *Bill of Lading clause.*

This is to cover the assured against the "exceptions" clauses in charter and bill of lading (see Nubaltwood charter clause 12, page 80).

The seaworthiness of the vessel is a warranty implied in every contract of marine insurance; if the vessel is unseaworthy insurers under the policy alone would be entitled to repudiate the policy. Seaworthiness, however, is another matter beyond the control of a shipper or importer and in fact is a matter about which the insurer will probably have more information. Since the insurers now admit seaworthiness of the vessel, if the vessel is later found to be unseaworthy, the assured's position is not prejudiced.

Clause 7. Termination of Adventure clause.

This protects the assured in the event of the voyage being terminated at any port other than that named in the policy, and covers the goods until they are either sold or forwarded to their original destination *provided notice is given to the assurers and additional premium paid if required.*

Clause 8. General Average clause.

This binds underwriters to accept adjustments drawn up under the York-Antwerp rules, with a statement of general average drawn up in a foreign port if necessary.

Clause 9. Bailee clause.

The object of this clause is to prevent the benefit of the insurance policy passing to the carrier of the goods. The assured is then left to recover loss or damage in this case from the carrier, who in turn should be covered by his own insurance.

However, the insurers undertake that the assured shall not be out of pocket in the matter, and they agree to advance the assured the sum he would normally have received from them, this sum being free of interest. In his turn the assured undertakes to bring the necessary proceedings against the carrier to recover the amount of the loss or the damage. This rather complicated process is necessary because the assured is the only party who can take action against the carrier, since obviously the insurers cannot take action directly against the carrier as there is no contract between them.

Clause 10. War and Strike Risk Exclusion.

This excludes the risks that are normally excluded anyway from the standard marine insurance policy by the F.C. and S. clause (see page 97). The exclusion also covers strike risks etc. These war and strike risks then have to be covered separately by the addition of special War and Strike Risk clauses at an additional premium (see page 106).

Clause 11. Both to Blame Collision clause.

Protects the assured in the event of any liability falling on them under the provision of the charter (see Nubaltwood charter clause 23, page 84).

Clause 12. Increased Value clause.

Where the assured places an additional value on the goods due to changed circumstances, say a rise in market value between the date of placing the insurance and the date of arrival, the agreed valuation of the policy is automatically raised to the new figure. This enables the insurers to obtain subrogation rights for the increased value from the assured, after they have settled claims to the assured.

Increased value can also arise where balance of freight, import duty and other charges are payable after arrival at the port of discharge. This is of particular interest when the goods are still at risk for some time until they reach their ultimate destination. If the insured value is based on the f.o.b. value plus 10 per cent. plus freight advance, there may be a substantial under-insurance after the balance of freight and other charges are paid.

However, from the moment these extra charges are payable there is no risk of total loss, so the increased value can usually be covered by a reduced premium of the order of 25 per cent. of the normal cargo rate.

Clause 13.

This clause must be read in conjunction with the notes appended at the end of these clauses, which read as follows :—" It is necessary for the assured to give prompt notice to the assurers when they become aware of any event for which they are ' held covered ' under this insurance at a premium to be arranged and the right to such cover is dependant upon compliance with this obligation."

The prudent importer notifies the insurers of any event or occurrence which might give rise to a claim, not merely those items where he is " held covered " till a new premium is arranged.

These T.T.F. Insurance clauses, published in 1952, superseded the T.T.F. clauses 1938. They have been redrafted to follow much more closely other standard clauses in use by the London Institute of Underwriters, but in particular the " Institute Cargo Clauses (With Average) " and the " Institute Cargo Clauses (Extended Cover)."

They incorporate several new extensions of cover for the importer, over the old 1938 clauses, but there is one important omission. This is the " dead freight clause " which used to read :—" Including liability for dead freight arising from craft loss at loading port or ports."

Loss of goods owing to loss of a craft at loading port is covered under the policy, but if the vessel sailed without a full and complete cargo being supplied, there would be a claim for dead freight. This would not be recoverable from the shipper, who has discharged his obligations by providing the cargo, but it would fall on the bill of lading holder, *i.e.* the assured in the policy.

Insurers will not accept this liability where the balance of freight is not paid until arrival at destination, since no premium is paid on this balance of freight. A claim for dead freight in these circumstances (bearing in mind that the value of the goods lost with the craft is already covered) would mean that the insurers were accepting liability for the full cost of the goods lost plus full freight, whereas premium has only been paid on the value of the goods plus freight advance.

The importer who wishes to cover this exigency must therefore be prepared to include *the full amount of freight* in his insured value and pay accordingly a premium on c.i.f. value instead of f.o.b. value plus freight advance.

T.T.F. ADDITIONAL CLAUSES FOR NON-ENGLISH POLICIES.

Although not properly a part of the T.T.F. Insurance Clauses, it is convenient to mention these additional clauses at this point.

Most T.T.F. c.i.f. contract forms contain printed in the margin "Additional clauses applicable to Policies issued by Non-English underwriters," these clauses usually being printed below the standard T.T.F. Insurance clauses, in fact they are often assumed to be part of them.

Reference is made in the contract to these additional clauses, making it obligatory for sellers, if arranging insurance with foreign insurers, to ensure that the following conditions are complied with :—

(i) Lloyd's standard form of policy with T.T.F. clauses to be used, and to override terms and conditions of foreign policy form which may be inconsistent therewith.

(ii) All questions regarding interpretation of the policy to be settled according to English law, the assurers admitting the jurisdiction of English Courts.

(iii) Names of paying bankers and/or agents who are authorised to act for insurers (accepting claims, service of writ, etc.), to be stated on the policy.

(iv) If the insured amount is stated in both foreign currency and sterling, claims to be adjusted at the rate of exchange indicated by the two amounts. If insured amount is expressed in foreign currency only, settlement shall be based at rate for sight bills in London on date of the policy.

6. War and Strike Risk Clauses.

War and strike risks are excluded from the standard form of policy and the T.T.F. Insurance clauses. They must be covered by separate clauses for which a separate additional premium is charged. Standard sets of clauses, adopted by the London Institute of Underwriters, are used for this purpose.

INSTITUTE WAR CLAUSES.

(Copy available in the band at the back of this book.)

Clause 1.

The first part of this clause covers those risks previously *excluded* by the F.C. and S. clause in the T.T.F. clauses from the standard form of policy (see pages 97 and 104).

This is merely putting back what has previously been taken out and at first sight appears illogical. The reason is clear to understand. War risk premiums vary very greatly, particularly in periods of political tension, whereas normal marine risk premiums remain reasonably steady always. Insurers are unwilling to calculate premiums to cover both marine and war risks together because of this difficulty. Accordingly the war risks stated in the standard policy have been taken out, leaving the marine risks, and are quoted separately.

This clause recognises " piracy " as a war risk.

The second part of this clause goes on to define war risks as follows :—

> " . . . loss or damage to the interest hereby insured caused by :—
> (1) hostilities, warlike operations, civil war, revolution, rebellion, insurrection or civil strife arising therefrom,
> (2) mines, torpedoes, bombs or other engines of war."

Mine risk insurance used to be a separate cover, but is now included here as a war risk.

Clause 2.

This defines the cover against war risks as restricted to those periods when the goods are waterborne, from the time they are in lighters at loading port, aboard the overseas vessel, during transhipment and in lighters at the port of discharge. It does *not* cover against any war risks whilst the goods are on land, except for the possible limited period during transhipment.

If the freight contract is ended at any port other than the destination named in the policy, such a port is deemed to be the final port of discharge.

Clause 3.

Insurers are not liable for delay, inherent vice, etc. (see page 102).

Clause 4.

The standard General Average clause (see T.T.F. clause 8, page 104).

Clause 5.

The effect of the wording " claims . . . payable without reference to average conditions " is to pay claims " irrespective of percentage." That is to say no franchise limit operates.

Clause 6.

This is the same as the T.T.F. clause 4 (see page 102).

INSTITUTE STRIKE CLAUSES (TIMBER TRADE) EXTENDED COVER.

(Copy available in the band at the back of this book.)

Clause 1.

As with the war risk clauses, this has the effect of covering those risks previously excluded by the F.C. and S. clause and the Institute

Strikes, Riots and Civil Commotions Clause (S.R. and C.C. clause) as in the T.T.F. clause 10 (see page 104).

The policy is also extended to cover " theft, pilferage, breakage and damage directly caused by strikes, locked out workmen or persons taking part in labour disturbances or riots or civil commotions."

Clause 2.

This extends the cover from warehouse to warehouse as opposed to the purely waterborne cover of the war clauses. The remainder of the clauses follow the pattern of the war clauses, giving a full cover to the assured for practically any event that may occur outside his control.

The extent of the cover of these clauses is the same as the T.T.F. clauses and goes some way beyond the cover obtained under the normal Institute Strike Clauses (Extended Cover) applying to other goods.

7. Assignment, Stamp Duty, Certificate, Claims, Subrogation.

(i) *Assignment.*

In a c.i.f. contract, the policy of insurance on the goods is taken out by the shipper as one of his responsibilities under the contract. Any benefits from the policy have to be receivable by the importer since he becomes the owner of the goods long before they reach the port of destination (see page 62).

When the importer becomes the owner of the goods, the risks on those goods automatically pass to him although he may not have taken delivery of them (Sale of Goods Act, 1893).

It is essential therefore that he be covered by a policy of insurance, and that there should be no gap in the insurance cover between the risk passing from shipper to importer. This is overcome by a legal assignment to the importer of the policy taken out by the shipper, by which the importer is put in the same position as if he had taken out the insurance policy himself for his own benefit and protection.

The Marine Insurance Act, 1906, gives the conditions governing the assignment of the policy, and these are summarised as follows :—

(*a*) The policy can be assigned or transferred by endorsement and delivery.

(*b*) In order to be valid, the transfer of the policy must be one of the conditions of the sale. (In a c.i.f. contract this is usually covered by the inclusion of words to the effect that " . . . sellers will arrange insurance for the benefit of buyers, etc., etc. . . .")

(*c*) The importer is entitled as a minimum to the benefit of all subsisting policies upon the goods other than profit policies.

(*d*) Assignment of the policy does not extend the scope of the voyage which is still subject to the original limitations.

(*e*) The importer can demand a policy covering solely his own goods.

(*f*) If the assignment or transfer of the policy is *not* made a condition of the sale (para. *b* above), the policy lapses on transfer of the ownership of the goods and cannot afterwards be resuscitated for the benefit of the importer.

(ii) *Stamp Duty.*

An English insurance policy must be stamped before execution. The duties payable vary for the value insured and are fixed by the Finance Act, 1920. An insurance policy made outside the U.K., but enforceable within the U.K., must be stamped within ten days of receipt in this country. *In any case the policy must be stamped before the documents are handed to the buyer (the importer) in a c.i.f. sale.*

(iii) *Certificate of Insurance.*

Where a shipper or his agent has an open cover or a floating policy, it is sometimes the practice to forward to the importer under a c.i.f. contract a "Certificate of Insurance" in lieu of the actual policy.

This "Certificate of Insurance" is issued by the insurers or brokers, certifying that insurance of the goods in question has been carried out. It must include all details normally stated on the policy itself (see page 94) and the description of cargo, value, voyage, etc., are usually identical with the policy. It must also state all the risks covered, which is normally done by stating that the insurance includes the T.T.F. clauses, etc.

Although certificates of insurance are frequently used, their legality as a substitute for a true policy is doubtful unless the contract for the purchase of the goods expressly states that the shipping documents will include ". . . a certificate or policy of insurance. . . ." A certificate should not be accepted for instance in a sale on the Albion c.i.f. contract form, where no specific reference is made.

(iv) *Claims and Subrogation Rights.*

The submission of claims against the insurers is dealt with in greater detail on pages 201 to 206.

Claims for loss require substantiating with documentary evidence of the quantity short delivered; claims for damage or deterioration will be subject to inspection, negotiation and approval of a qualified insurance surveyor or assessor who will survey and inspect the goods on arrival on behalf of the insurers.

When the claim has been admitted and paid, the insurers will then require to be subrogated to all the rights and remedies of the assured in connection with these goods.

These subrogation rights enable the insurers to recover in certain circumstances some of the value they have paid out to the assured. This they do by taking action against other parties concerned, etc., *e.g.*, by recovery from shipowners where the loss is one for which they are responsible.

CHAPTER V

Timber Contracts

1. Basic Legal Aspects of Sale of Goods.

(*a*) GENERAL.

All transactions involving the purchase and sale of timber are governed by the law of the land. Whilst the great majority of these transactions progress without difficulty, there are inevitably times when differences arise between buyers and sellers. These are settled according to the law which provides for the protection of the interests of both buyers and sellers. It is necessary therefore for any party in commerce to have an understanding of the simple elements of the law affecting the transactions they make, in order that they may benefit fully from the particular protection they receive under the law, and at the same time be fully aware of pitfalls and circumstances where they are not protected.

(*b*) THE LAW.

Reference to " the law " of this country is really reference to three sources of law—all of which on occasion are involved.

Statutes are rules and orders published under the authority of parliament, and in general are inflexible, but also are not ambiguous.

Case Law is legal opinion built upon the precedent and findings of judges in legal cases in the past.

Common Law is an unwritten code of law, built up over the centuries by common usage. Both Statutes and Case Law are interpreted according to common law. Common Law is flexible and often ambiguous but ambiguities are decided one way or the other by case law.

The law is administered by the High Court, which has three divisions, the Queen's Bench (which deals with matters concerning contracts, etc.), Chancery (which deals amongst other things with matters concerning partnership, patents, etc.), and Probate, Divorce and Admiralty.

An action in the Queen's Bench division must first be taken to a County Court if the amount involved is under £200.

An appeal against the judgement of the High Court may be made to the Court of Appeal. If this fails the appeal may be made as a final resort to the House of Lords.

Statutes very often delegate to a government department or public authority, the powers to make Orders in Council or other orders, rules, regulations, etc., all having the force of law. These are known as Statutory Instruments, are given an official number and published in leaflet form. Up to 1948 these were known as Statutory Rules and Orders.

These Statutory Instruments have provided the majority of the detailed regulations to which the trade has been subject since 1939 *i.e.*, consumption licensing, acquisition and disposal of timber, prices (when and where controlled), returns to be made, etc.

Contracts are governed by the law of the place where the contract was entered into. A contract for the purchase of timber by an importer in the U.K. is made with a foreign seller (the shipper) through an agent in the U.K. The acceptance of an offer of timber for sale is normally communicated and the contract is made in this country. The agent usually signs the contract on behalf of the seller. In practice two identical copies of the contract are made, the one signed by the agent on behalf of the seller being retained by the buyer, and the one signed by the buyer retained by the agent who forwards a copy of it to the seller.

Therefore a timber contract is normally governed by English law *unless* there are special stipulations or clauses to the contrary.

It must be remembered that if the buyer visits the shipper in his own country, and completes a contract with him there, the contract will be governed by the law of that country, but if, as is usual, any business discussed abroad goes through the agency firm in the U.K. who make out the contract and sign it as seller's agents, then the contract will have been made in the U.K. and is governed by English law.

(*c*) The Sale of Goods Act.

The law relating to the sale of goods in the U.K. is set out in the Sale of Goods Act, 1893, which codified the many aspects of common law that had previously applied.

In all forms of sale of goods, the term " goods " can have several meanings. These meanings must be clearly understood since they influence the type of sale, the time at which payment is made and the point at which the ownership of the goods is transferred from the seller to the buyer.

Future goods are those which at the time the contract is negotiated, have either not been manufactured or acquired by the seller.

Future goods are therefore sold by " description " (see page 127), the description being a vital part of the contract.

The majority of the purchases of imported timber and other wood goods are therefore purchases of future goods, *e.g.* softwood contracts made in November for shipment f.o.w. the following year, where the goods have not been sawn or seasoned—hardwood contracts for logs which may not have been felled at the time the contract was made.

It is usual in a sale of future goods, to permit the seller to have a reasonable " margin " or tolerance in the quantities supplied, owing to the inherent difficulties in producing exact quantities from a natural product (see page 129).

Existing goods are those that are owned by or in the possession of the seller at the time the sale is negotiated. These goods may either be *Ascertained*, when in fact they become specific goods (see below) or *Unascertained*, that is to say goods that cannot be specifically identified.

The majority of sales of timber from merchants' yards are sales of unascertained existing goods, for instance, say the sale of one standard of softwood from a stack of ten standards. The goods are existing, but not ascertained until the one standard has been measured out.

Specific Goods are goods that can be identified at the time of negotiation of the sale. The sale of a specific log or logs that have first been inspected by the prospective buyer, is a sale of specific goods.

In each of the above cases the ownership of the goods is defined as the "property in the goods." To state that the property in the goods passes from one person to another means that the ownership of the goods passes. This is discussed more fully on page 115.

(*d*) The Contract.

In Section 1 of the Sale of Goods Act, a contract of sale is defined as one ". . . whereby the seller transfers, or agrees to transfer, the property in goods to the buyer in return for a money consideration called the price."

It should be noted that it includes not only the actual sale (which takes place only when certain conditions are fulfilled by each party) but the *agreement to sell.* This agreement to sell covers for instance the sale of future goods whereby the seller agrees to transfer the property at some future date, etc.

If the value of a contract for the sale of goods is over £10, neither party can enforce the contract by law unless :—

(i) the buyer has accepted and received part of the goods sold—or
(ii) the buyer has given something in earnest to bind the contract or in part payment—or
(iii) the contract is made in writing.

The last alternative is the method most frequently used.

The form of the written contract does not matter, it can be any letter, memorandum, etc., setting out sufficient evidence of the contract, *i.e.*, names of the parties, the price and any special terms, and signed by the buyer.

In practice, where specific goods are purchased, the contract merely takes the form of an order made out by the buyer, or a sale note made out by the seller or his agent and signed by the buyer. Where future goods are concerned in the timber trade, the possible difficulties that may arise are greater, particularly since the buyers and sellers are in different countries. Consequently the form of contract is much more complicated, and provision is made for all manner of circumstances that may arise, so that the interests of both buyers and sellers are adequately protected. The next few chapters examine in detail the various forms of contract in regular use in the timber trade.

If there is no written contract, and none of the actions set out in (i) or (ii) above are carried out, the contract is not invalidated at all. It simply means that it cannot be enforced by law.

It should be noted that the word "acceptance" as used in (i) above does not merely mean approval of the goods since acceptance can occur when the buyer makes the slightest act of interference with the goods.

The essentials of a contract for the sale of goods are (i) The offer of the goods for sale and the acceptance of the offer by the buyer. (ii) The consideration or price to be paid.

A contract for the sale of goods is exempt from stamp duty (Stamp Act, 1891).

(*e*) THE OFFER AND ACCEPTANCE.

The offer of goods for sale will depend upon the supply and demand of those goods. This matter is discussed in more detail on pages 65 and 66 in so far as the details of the offer are concerned.

The offer may be made either *generally* (as for instance by means of stock-lists circulated to prospective buyers) or to a *definite* person or firm (as in the case of a quotation from one firm to another) or a counter-offer from a prospective buyer to a shipper.

The acceptance must be made by a *specific* person or persons. Thus although the offer of a stock is circulated widely, the necessary circumstances for a contract to be made are not established until a definite person or firm accepts that offer together with all the terms of that offer.

Any conditions may be attached to the offer provided that all these conditions are brought to the notice of the recipient of the offer at the time when the offer is made.

The offer may be revoked at any time before acceptance, unless an option has been granted whereby the offer will remain open for a certain time. The lapse of a specified time (or a reasonable time if none is specified) or the death of the person making the offer, or the person to whom it is made, all have the effect of revoking the offer. If the revocation of an offer is to be effective it must be communicated to the recipient of the offer before he has accepted, otherwise his acceptance of the offer creates a binding contract.

The acceptance must be unconditional. If an offer is not accepted in all its terms, but certain revisions are suggested, this does not constitute acceptance of the original offer, but is a counter-offer. It will be seen from this that the offer is not only made by the prospective seller to the prospective buyer; there are many cases, particularly where there are protracted negotiations between the two parties, where the offer will actually be made by the prospective buyer. The law concerning acceptance is applicable to both parties of course, whether it be the prospective buyer or seller who accepts. In any case as soon as acceptance has been made, a contract exists, and the general terms of the contract, responsibilities of parties, etc., will be the same no matter who made the final acceptance of the offer.

An important point arises over the communication of offer and acceptance by post. In making an offer, or the revocation of an offer, by post, the offer or revocation are only effective when they reach the recipient of the offer. In other words the post must be delivered. If, for instance, the revocation of an offer is lost in the post, or for any other reason is delayed in the post so that it fails to reach the recipient of the offer *before* he accepts it, the revocation is inoperative and the acceptance stands, so the contract is binding.

On the other hand, an acceptance is complete as soon as it is posted. It does not necessarily have to be delivered. Thus, if the letter of acceptance is lost in the post, or the offer is revoked before the letter of acceptance reaches the person making the offer, the acceptance is nevertheless complete and binding provided proof of postage can be produced if necessary.

Since acceptance must be unconditional, any letters written prior to the conclusion of the contract, have no standing once the contract is signed. Letters written after the date on which the contract is signed do have a bearing on it.

From the above it will be seen that it is important for a seller to exercise care in the manner in which his offer is worded. This is particularly so where a stock-list of goods for sale is circulated widely. Some of the goods offered for sale may be sold quickly, and before the stock list can be withdrawn or amended (the equivalent of revocation) an acceptance may be posted. Since this then constitutes a binding contract, the seller must deliver similar goods to those originally offered, or be in breach of contract. To overcome such a possibility it is usual to include the following wording in the offer, " Subject to remaining unsold at the time order is received," or merely the words " Subject unsold." Sometimes the wider phrase " Subject confirmation and unsold " is used. This is then a condition of the offer.

Where goods have not yet been shipped, there is the added danger that if any peril were to befall them, or if shippers or shipowners were to fail in their obligations, the importer-seller might be in a very difficult position with a buyer who had accepted an open offer of goods without any qualifying condition. In these cases the sellers usually include the following wording in the offer as a protection " Subject to shipment and safe arrival."

(*f*) CONSIDERATION.

No contract for the sale of goods can have any legal effect unless it is made for a " consideration."

This consideration is normally the "price" of the goods. It is possible to have a contract where the price is fixed by "valuation," by a third party.

Where no specific price is made, or where a third party fails to make a valuation if called for, the buyer must then pay a "reasonable" price for the goods.

(*g*) The Parties to the Contract.

The two principals to a contract are the buyer and the seller. There are certain legal formalities to be observed in the different forms of company if full protection under the Sale of Goods Act is to be obtained.

(i) The name of a firm must be registered if it is being carried on in any name other than the name of the proprietor or if the name does not disclose the names of all the partners. If this is not done it is impossible to enforce a contract, or maintain an action in a court of law. (Registration of Business Names Act, 1916; Companies Act, 1948.)

(ii) Every company registered after 23rd November 1916 must state the names of directors in business letters and other printed matter. (Companies Act, 1948.)

(iii) Contracts made by a limited company through its directors, managers, etc., are valid and binding even if they are not concluded under seal. (Companies Act, 1948.)

(*a*) Contracts between private persons if required by law in writing and under seal, may be made by a company under its common seal. (Such as a contract for the sale of land, transfer of shares, etc.)

(*b*) Contracts between private persons if required by law in writing signed by the parties, may be made by a company in writing signed by any person acting under its authority, express or implied. (A director or manager may sign a contract for the purchase of goods.)

(*c*) Contracts between private persons by parol only, if valid by law may be made by parol only on behalf of a company by any person acting under its authority, express or implied.

(iv) Although contracts are made through seller's agents, most agents are not parties to the contract. This is discussed in greater detail on page 119.

(*h*) Transfer of Property in Goods.

Since the very essence of a contract for the sale of goods has been defined in the Sale of Goods Act as ". . . the seller transfers or agrees to transfer the property in goods to the buyer . . ." it is very important to see how and where this transfer takes place.

It must first be understood that "property" and "possession" are quite different, and a person may hold the property in goods without having possession of them. This is particularly important where questions of seller's lien arise, and is discussed more fully on page 134.

Unless there is any agreement to the contrary, the goods are at the risk of the seller until property passes to the buyer, after which all risks pass to the buyer. This is an important matter when considering the marine insurance of goods being imported (see page 108).

If there is no specific agreement in the contract as to when or where the property will be transferred, the transfer of property is governed by the following rules. To avoid any ambiguity on this matter, many contracts specify the time or place where the property passes. In the case of the majority of f.o.b. and c.i.f. timber contracts, the property in goods passes to the buyer when the goods have been put on board the vessel.

If there are no stipulations of this nature, the property passes according to the following rules:—

(i) *Specific goods ready for delivery*. Property passes immediately the contract is made, although delivery of the goods and payment may not take place until a later date.

(ii) *Specific goods not yet ready for delivery* (or where the seller is bound to do something to the goods to put them in a deliverable state). Property passes when the seller has put the goods into a deliverable state and has notified the buyer.

(iii) *Specific goods ready for delivery but requiring measuring, weighing, etc.* Property passes when the seller has measured or weighed the goods, etc., and notified the buyer.

(iv) *Goods sold "on Approval," or "Sale or Return."* Property passes to the buyer when he signifies approval, which may be by word or deed. Retention of the goods without giving notice of rejection within a stipulated or reasonable time, may amount to approval.

(v) *Future or Unascertained goods sold by description.* Property passes when goods of the description in the contract, in a deliverable state, are unconditionally appropriated to the contract. The commonest form of appropriation is the handing of these goods to a carrier for transit to the buyer.

As stated above, in an f.o.b. or c.i.f. contract, this point is usually made quite clear by stating in the contract that the property passes when the goods have been put on board. In any case this is the first moment in an f.o.b. or c.i.f. contract when the goods for the buyer can be determined.

It is normally not possible to determine wood goods accurately before they are loaded, owing to the margins for loading granted to the master of the vessel and the possibility of goods being lost in transit to the vessel. For this reason although a contract may be made on f.a.s. terms, property usually does not pass until the goods are placed on board (see page 134).

In the case of an ex-ship contract, property does not pass till the goods leave the ship. Although the goods are appropriated to the contract, being recognised as certain bills of lading, they are not in a "deliverable state" until they leave the ship (see page 173).

In any of the above five cases, if the seller reserves the "right of disposal" until certain conditions are fulfilled, ***property does not pass until those conditions have been fulfilled.*** The principal condition to be fulfilled is that of payment. Some contracts include specific wording to the above effect, but the seller may be deemed to have reserved the right of disposal if shipping documents are transmitted through a bank, to be released in exchange for payment.

(*j*) AMBIGUITIES.

If a contract is broken, and the case has to be taken to arbitration or to court, it must be remembered that the arbitrator or the judge have only the words of the contract, and other correspondence, to guide them. It is necessary to make a careful examination of the terms and conditions of a contract before it is signed to ensure that the meaning of each party is quite clear and that no other interpretation can be put on the words in the contract.

It is a feature of English law that where two parties completely reduce the terms of a bargain to writing, either of them may not afterwards be heard to say that they "intended to agree something different" from the written contract detail, unless the mistake is common to both parties.

It has been stated that "a man is responsible for his ambiguities in his own expressions, and has no right to induce another to contract with him on the supposition that his words mean one thing, while he hopes the court will adopt a construction by which they would mean another thing more to his advantage."

(*k*) CONDITIONS AND WARRANTIES.

The various clauses in a contract may be divided into two legal categories—"Conditions" and "Warranties."

(i) "*Condition.*" This is a major stipulation of the contract, and if it is broken either party may cancel the contract, and sue the other party for damages. For instance if the contract calls for 3 ins. × 7 ins. Swedish redwood and 2 ins. × 7 ins. redwood is shipped, a condition has been broken. The importer may reject the goods, refuse to take delivery and sue the seller for damages. It must be as obvious as that for a successful action for damages to be maintained. If the breach of the contract is not so obvious or clear cut, it is generally only safe to treat it as a breach of warranty.

(ii) " *Warranty*." A warranty is a stipulation collateral to the main purpose of the contract. Breach of a warranty may give rise to a claim for damages but NOT to cancellation of the contract. A breach of condition may be treated as a breach of warranty, *e.g.*, by accepting the 2 ins. × 7 ins. instead of 3 ins. × 7 ins. in the contract and sueing for damages afterwards.

In the " description of goods " in many contracts the words " other terms and conditions as specified on the back " are used. In these cases it would have been better to use the word " clauses " instead of " conditions " since most of them are actually " warranties " in law.

If a warranty is broken and the seller is sued for damages, the claim for damages may be built up in two ways :—

(1) Claim for difference in price or value between the goods delivered and those contracted for.

(2) Claim for true damages—*i.e.*, loss of profit, dislocation of business, etc., resulting from wrong goods being supplied.

The term warranty here used in a contract for the sale of goods has a different meaning when used in a contract of marine insurance. In this latter case a breach of warranty is sufficient to void the contract.

(*l*) CONDITIONS SUBSEQUENT IN THE CONTRACT.

In the normal course of events a contract will be discharged by its correct fulfilment. When this has happened all rights under the contract cease. On the other hand there are many events that may have occurred to bring about circumstances in which the contract cannot be fulfilled. In these circumstances the contract may be rescinded by :—

(*a*) Payment of allowance by which one party may abandon his rights under the contract.

(*b*) Issue of a new contract in place of the old one.

(*c*) Arbitration or action in law if one party fails to fulfil his part of the contract.

(*d*) War or Government restrictions rendering the fulfilment of the contract unlawful or impossible.

(*e*) Provision of clauses within the contract, by which claims are mutually abandoned.

These clauses are said to be " conditions subsequent " and in law the contract is said to be " defeasible by conditions subsequent."

The difference between conditions and warranties has been explained above. Conditions may be divided, in common law, under three headings.

Conditions Precedent. Conditions that shall be carried out if the contract is to be fulfilled, *e.g.*, the goods shall be of the specification " hereinafter specified."

Conditions Concurrent. Conditions that are carried out simultaneously by each party, *e.g.*, " payment on receipt of and in exchange for shipping documents."

Conditions Subsequent. Conditions whereby on the happening of a certain specified event, either or both parties are relieved of their liability to carry out the contract.

These specified events are named in detail. If these clauses are invoked to provide an excuse for not performing the contract, the specified events must either be *actual* or *operative*. Mere fear or expectancy that these events may happen is not sufficient.

(*m*) The Agent.

Contracts that are made " through the agency of " are between the agent's principal (the seller) and the buyer. The agent is not permitted to make any profit other than his agreed commission and must not place himself in a position where his interests and those of his principal will clash. He must not become a principal party in the transaction.

The agent is responsible for ordinary negligence, but he is not personally liable in a contract between a buyer and his principal if he signs the contract as agent for his principal, by whom he has been either generally or specifically authorised. He is also *not* personally liable if he signs for a principal whose name is not disclosed, although in this case the principal cannot sue upon the contract or be sued upon himself.

The agents are not responsible for the carrying out of the contract by the sellers, nor for the payment of claims awarded by arbitration, or even by the court, against the sellers.

2. The Documents of the Contract.

(i) *Contract Form.* All timber contracts are made out on standard forms already printed with standard clauses and stipulations. These clauses are drawn up and agreed between the T.T.F. and the trade associations of the various exporting countries.

To enable these contract forms to be identified easily they are sometimes given code names. The c.i.f. contract form for contracts with Swedish and Finnish shippers is named the Albion form and the Swedish and Finnish f.o.b. contract is named the Uniform.

These are the most comprehensive forms of contract and are intended to cover every conceivable exigency. They protect the buyer and the seller against the majority of the difficulties likely to arise. Therefore in making a contract with a seller in a country for which no special contract form has been evolved, the buyer cannot do better than adopt as many of these clauses (where applicable) as possible—provided the seller will agree to them.

There is nothing to prevent any particular clause being struck out or amended to cover some particular circumstances. Deleted or amended clauses must be examined very carefully to see how they affect either party, remembering that the deletion of a clause may affect other clauses in the contract that are untouched.

Apart from the names of the agent and the parties to the contract the following detail has to be inserted :—

Name of port of shipment (name of ship if known).
Date of loading or shipment.
Name of port of destination.
Specification of goods.
Prices, etc.

The specification covers :—Quantity, Description, Quality, Dimensions, etc., and is the most important section of the contract. This is explained fully on page 127.

Any additional clauses may be inserted to protect the buyer or the seller provided that both agree to the terms.

Two identical copies of the contract are signed, one by the agent on behalf of the seller to be retained by the buyer; the other by the buyer to be retained by the agent who sends a copy to the seller. Although signed at different times the contract is dated when first drawn up by the agent and this is the "date of the contract."

(ii) *Invoice.* At least two copies of the invoice should be supplied as one copy is required for the customs entry papers. The invoice debits the buyer with the cost of the goods, and in an f.o.b. contract debits the buyer with the amount of any freight advance (which must not exceed one third of the total freight) made to the master of the vessel. In a c.i.f. contract credit is given against the invoice price, for the amount of the "balance of freight" (see page 83) that the buyer will have to pay on arrival of the vessel.

(iii) *Specification.* This is a detailed list of the species, quality, size and measurement of the whole shipment. It will show the numbers of pieces of the various lengths of the various sizes that have been shipped. It is extended into total quantity and supports the figures for measurement in the invoice and number of pieces on the bill of lading.

At least two copies of the specification are required—that is one copy for each copy of the invoice. The specification may be on a separate form, on the invoice itself (if the detail is not great) or on the reverse side of the bill of lading.

(iv) *Bill of Lading.* The bill of lading, normally abbreviated to B/L, is the symbol of the goods. Endorsement and delivery of the bill of lading has the effect of symbolic delivery of the goods. It is the main "Title Deed" to the "property" and the person who rightly possesses the bill of lading, duly endorsed to him, owns the goods—which may be timber, grain, cotton—whatever is being shipped.

See page 85 for full details of the bill of lading.

(v) *Insurance Policy.* The insurance policy is taken out by the buyer in an f.o.b. contract, by the seller in a c.i.f. contract. In the latter case it must be stamped and endorsed when it is passed to the buyer to enable him to claim on it when he becomes the owner of the goods, that is to say when he receives the endorsed bill of lading.

(vi) *Draft.* This is a bill of exchange drawn by the seller or his agent on the buyer (see page 122, Bill of Exchange). The amount of the draft is for the balance shown on the invoice.

(vii) *Charter-Party.* The charter-party is the document by which the ship is chartered to load, carry and deliver the timber. It is taken out by the buyer in an f.o.b. contract, the seller in a c.i.f. contract. In the latter case the buyer is generally entitled to have a copy of the charter included in the shipping documents against which he has to pay. See page 154.

(viii) *Certificate of Origin.* If timber is imported from the Empire, a Certificate of Origin is required in order to obtain Imperial Preference when passing the documents through the customs. Timber from the Empire is duty free, timber from other countries is chargeable with import duty. See page 193.

(ix) *Certificate of Quality and Measure.* There are other local documents which concern particular classes of timber, such as :—

Inspector's Certificate of Pacific Lumber Inspection Bureau given for all parcels of Douglas fir imported from Canada and U.S.A. ; *Inspector's Certificate* issued for U.S.A. hardwoods graded under N.H.L.A. rules, or Malayan hardwoods inspected by Malayan Forestry Service ; *Grading Certificate* by Maritime Lumber Bureau for spruce from Eastern Canada sold on M.L.B. grading rules.

3. Payment Terms.

(*a*) General.

In any timber contract on f.o.b. or c.i.f. terms, provided that the shipping documents (seller's invoice, bills of lading and, in addition in a c.i.f. contract, the charter and a policy of insurance) are in order and agree not only with each other but with the terms of the contract—*payment must be made.*

Although the Uniform contract requires that the method of payment shall be decided when the contract is signed, it is customary for the larger agents to waive a decision until the vessel is advised ready to load. If at that time the importer finds he will have sufficient liquid working capital to pay for the goods in cash, he will usually elect to do so. On the other hand he may require credit terms, to enable him to defer payment for a period of time so that at any rate part of the shipment can be turned into money. This period of time can vary from one month to twelve months, but in the timber trade, particularly with Scandinavia, it is usually four months, this being long enough to cover the length of time between receipt of the shipping documents when the importer is due to pay for the goods and the time when he in his turn receives payment from his customers to whom he has sold the goods.

The convenience and advantage of credit terms such as this is something that has to be paid for (which is why the importer will usually elect to pay cash if he is able).

The credit terms may be granted either by the sellers themselves, but more often by their agents. In granting this credit to the importer they charge interest on the amount of the invoice, the interest rate usually being appreciably higher than interest charged by a bank advance or overdraft.

(*b*) Bill of Exchange.

In the timber trade, as in many trades, the importer is dealing with bulk quantities of goods. There will be a considerable time lag between his paying for the goods, and receiving payment from the sale of them to his customers. He is probably granting his own customers thirty days' credit or asking them for payment during the month following delivery. All these factors impose a heavy burden on the financial resources or working capital of the importer.

It is usual for sellers' agents to take the financial risk of collecting payment from the buyer, so the agent pays the seller the amount due on the invoice, less discount and commission, and collects payment from the buyer in accordance with the payment terms of the contract which refers specifically to " authorised agents." For the service of relieving sellers of financial risk, the agent is given a " del credere " commission. In undertaking " del credere," the agent guarantees the solvency of the buyer and in effect guarantees payment for the goods as from the time when the seller parted with them.

The seller or his agent therefore makes out a *draft* on the buyer, which is a written order requiring the buyer to pay at a specified time a sum of money to a person named (which is usually the seller's agent), and attaches it to the documents which he presents against acceptance of the draft, or the cash equivalent.

The sum of money stated in the draft represents the *nett* invoice price of the goods (after any discounts have been deducted) plus interest for this sum over the period in question. The value of the draft therefore is greater than the nett value of an invoice that is settled in cash, by the amount of the interest. It also includes the value of the stamp duty but this is a minor item. In some cases, however, the amount of the interest and stamp duty is left off the value of the draft, and is settled separately for cash.

The buyer accepts the draft by writing across it :—

"Accepted payable at—(name and address of his Bank)" followed by his signature. A draft may also be "accepted payable" at the office of the acceptor. The draft has now become a "bill of exchange," and is governed by the Bills of Exchange Acts of 1882 and 1906. The parties to a bill of exchange are :—(*a*) The drawer—the person who draws up the bill of exchange ; in this case the seller or his agent. (*b*) The drawee—the person on whom the bill of exchange is drawn, *i.e.*, the buyer. He becomes the acceptor when he has accepted it.

No. *13472* Due *22 October 1950*

£ *5347 10 0*

London, *19 June 1950*

Four months after *date* pay to our Order in London *Five thousand three hundred and forty seven pounds ten shillings*
Value received *per S.S. "Landlecrag" at Manchester.*

STAMP 54/-

To *A.B.C. Timber Company Ltd.,*
Morley Road,
Manchester.

For and on behalf of
X.Y.Z. & Co. Ltd.
J. Smith *Director.*
H. Jones *Secretary.*

A BILL OF EXCHANGE with (*on right*) the crossing, written on it vertically upon acceptance.

Accepted 21 June 1950, payable at Castle Bank Ltd., Birchin Lane, London, E.C.
For and on behalf of
A.B.C. Timber Co. Ltd.
R. Robinson, Director.

Fig. 16. SPECIMEN BILL OF EXCHANGE.

(*c*) The payee—the person to whom the proceeds of the bill of exchange are payable. This will usually be the same person as the drawer.

Bills of exchange are more commonly referred to as "bills."

The same bill of exchange is a bill payable (B/P) to the acceptor (the buyer) and a bill receivable (B/R) to the payee.

A cheque is a bill of exchange drawn on a Bank (the drawee) payable on demand.

The bill of exchange is said to " reach maturity " or to " mature " when the due date specified on it arrives. It must be met at maturity or arrangements made for it to be renewed. If a bill of exchange is renewed, a fresh bill of exchange is made out for the amount of the old bill of exchange, the acceptor paying, usually in cash, the interest for the extended period and the amount of the bill stamp.

A bill of exchange is a negotiable instrument unless it is crossed " not negotiable," which is not usually done. It becomes the property of any person who in good faith gives value for it. It may be negotiated by endorsement and delivery (in much the same manner as a bill of lading).

(i) *Special Endorsement.* Here the bill of exchange is made payable to a definite party who must endorse it before it is any use, *e.g.*, " Pay to J. Smith or Order."

(ii) *Blank Endorsement.* The bill of exchange becomes payable to bearer and may be negotiated by delivery only.

(iii) *Restrictive Endorsement.* This prohibits further negotiation of the bill of exchange, *e.g.*, when made out to " J. Smith " only.

The sum of money stated on a bill of exchange is its " face value."

The holder of a bill receivable has three courses open to him :—

(i) To hold the bill receivable until it reaches maturity when he will receive the full face value of the bill. This he will do if he has plenty of funds and does not require money urgently for other purposes. It is a form of investment.

(ii) To " discount " the bill at a Bank or Discount House. To do this he sells the bill of exchange. What he gets for it will depend on the credit standing of the acceptor, if he endorses it " without recourse," or his own credit as well if he gives a clean endorsement which makes him liable to pay at due date if the acceptor does not.

He gets his money back quickly but does not get as much as he would have done if he had kept the bill to maturity.

The Bank or Discount House however have purchased the bill for less than the face value, and will eventually collect the full face value. Alternatively they may sell the bill of exchange before it reaches maturity. The procedure goes on and the bill of exchange, if for a large amount, may pass through many hands before it reaches maturity. In each case a further endorsement is made on the back of the bill of exchange, and if necessary an additional gummed slip of paper, known as an " Alonge " is added at one end to hold further endorsements.

(iii) To negotiate it in payment. If the holder of the bill receivable owes a similar or a larger amount of money, he may endorse the bill receivable over to his creditor as payment or part payment.

The buying and selling of bills forms the basis of the London Money Market, through which many transactions outside this country are put. These foreign transactions are by bills " payable in London " and caused London to earn its title " The Hub of the World."

A foreign bill of exchange, that is to say a bill not both drawn and payable within the British Isles, is usually drawn in two parts, known as First and Second of Exchange, each part containing a reference to the other part. First part states: ". . . this First of Exchange (Second unpaid) . . ." Second part States: ". . . this Second of Exchange (First unpaid) . . ." Both parts constitute one bill of exchange only, and when either part is paid on presentation the other becomes ineffective. Each part is sent separately to ensure that at least one part reaches its destination safely.

(*c*) UNIFORM AND ALBION CONTRACTS.

In the Uniform and Albion contracts payment is made in several parts.

(i) The freight advance which the seller has made to the master at the port of loading must be repaid to his agents by the buyer in cash, against master's receipt on the bill of lading. The buyer then deducts this from the freight that he pays to the shipowners.

(ii) The balance of freight, after deduction of freight advance, is paid to the shipowners in stages in accordance with the Nubaltwood charter clause 2 (see page 77).

(iii) The invoice amount, or balance of invoice amount in the Albion contract, is paid to sellers in accordance with the payment clause on the front of the contract, which reads as follows:—

> " Payment to be made on receipt of and in exchange for shipping documents
> (*a*) by cash less 2 per cent. (sometimes changed to $2\frac{1}{2}$ per cent.) in London within 3 days of presenting documents
> or (*b*) by approved acceptance of seller's or authorised agents' draft payable in London at 4 months from date of bill of lading
> or (*c*) ...... per cent by cash as per (*a*) above and ...... per cent. by acceptance as per (*b*) above.
> Terms of payment to be agreed before the contract is signed and the alternative NOT agreed to be deleted."

From this it will be seen that in these forms of contract the interest for the period of credit is arrived at, not by adding to the invoice value (as described in section (*b*) Bills of Exchange) but by making the invoice amount the value for a four month credit, and giving a 2 per cent. (or $2\frac{1}{2}$ per cent.) discount where the invoice is settled for cash. This may seem a little confusing at first sight, but a little thought will disclose that both methods amount to practically the same in the end.

The reason for the Uniform and Albion contracts using this method is that the use of these bill credit facilities is a common practice in the softwood trade, particularly at the end of the shipping season when financial commitments are heavy, and also there is a considerable business in the purchase and sale of shipping documents.

These can be purchased for cash less the discount, and resold nett on credit terms, the buyer dealing in bulk quantities and working purely on the cash discount.

The shipping documents, when presented for settlement by cash must be paid for " within three days " of receipt. This differs from the previous (1933) contract forms which required payment " in cash less 2½ per cent. at three days' sight," which, with the added three days' grace, gave six days for the cash payment. Sight bills for three days or more, and period bills carry three days grace but bills for payment " on demand " (such as cheques) have no such grace and must be met when presented.

If the Uniform and Albion clauses are now studied once again it will be seen that the two alternatives are as follows :—

(*a*) By cash less 2 per cent. (or 2½ per cent.) within three days of presentation of documents.

(*b*) By " approved " acceptance of sellers' or authorised agents' draft payable in London at four months from the date of the bill of lading.

The word " approved " is a protection for the drawers who are thus relieved of any obligation to grant credit to buyers who are not considered credit-worthy. The refusal of a draft because the acceptance is not approved is, however, a very rare occurrence.

The clause stipulated for payment " in London," but by the custom of the trade if it is more convenient for buyers to accept payable in their home town, say Liverpool or Hull, the drawers would normally make no objection to that.

Supposing the date of the bill of lading is 15th June and the documents are presented four days later. Payment at four months from date of bill of lading (including days of grace) would mean payment of cash in full on the 18th October, whilst payment within three days would be payment at latest on the 22nd June for 2 per cent. discount (or sometimes 2½ per cent.).

This makes the cost of credit for the period between 22nd June and 18th October (*i.e.*, nearly 17 weeks) the equivalent of 2 per cent. (or 2½ per cent.), a rate which is a trifle over 6 per cent. per annum (or 7½ per cent. on 2½ per cent. discount).

It may, however, quite well pay the buyer to borrow money at this rate if it enables him to increase his profits by increasing his turnover, and it may also pay the seller or his agent to lend money at this rate.

The payment clause in the Uniform and Albion contracts stipulates that the option of payment by cash or acceptance (or part by cash and part by acceptance) shall be settled before the contract is signed, the remaining alternative being deleted. This is a departure from the earlier contract forms where the buyer's option to pay by acceptance (subject to being " approved "—see above) could be made at the time of vessel's arrival out to load. There are obvious difficulties for buyers to know what their financial position will be when the goods arrive. They may wish to take the bill option, but when the goods arrive find they are able to pay cash, or on the other hand several cargoes may chance to be arriving at about the same time, so they cannot very well pay cash as they had hoped to do and would prefer credit.

For this reason, as has been already mentioned, agents may agree if desired to do so, to leave the clause open, on the understanding that buyers will declare their option when the vessel arrives out to load, as has been customary for many years past. There is, however, no obligation on sellers or their agents to modify the contract terms of payment in this way.

4. Description.

The description of the goods in a timber contract is a vital point that is often neglected. Only on rare occasions will the buyer have seen the goods before they are despatched. Normally the contract will be for "future" goods that have yet to be manufactured or measured. The buyer must therefore rely on the written description of the goods in the contract to protect himself. He has none of the safeguards enjoyed by the consumer in this country who can go to the merchant's yard and inspect the timber for quality, condition, measurement, etc., before he buys it.

The Sale of Goods Act (1893)—Section 13—states that in the sale of goods by *description* there is an implied condition that the goods shall comply with that description. However the Sale of Goods Act (1893)—Section 14—states that in a contract for the sale of goods there is no *implied warranty* or condition as to their quality or fitness for any particular purpose. If the goods are purchased by description, the only implied condition is that they shall be of *merchantable* quality. Therefore, if the buyer wishes to ensure that the goods he is buying will be up to the standard he expects, he must strengthen the description in the contract or impose additional warranties on the seller. This will largely depend upon the individual circumstances of each contract, but in general it is the responsibility of the buyer to see that he is fully protected.

Albion and Uniform Contracts.

(i) *Preamble.* "The wood goods hereinafter specified."

These words of description are a *condition* of the contract (see page 117, conditions and warranties). A breach of this clause, being a breach of *condition*, permits the buyer to refuse acceptance of goods materially different from those specified and sue the seller for damages. A buyer is under no obligation to accept a shipment of peas against a contract for beans.

(ii) *Preamble.* "To be loaded at ' . . ."

The name of the port from which the goods are to be shipped is a part of the description of the goods. If they are shipped from any other port, the buyers have the right to maintain that these are not the goods they purchased.

(iii) *Preamble.* " Other terms, conditions and warranties as specified on the back."

Several of these clauses on the back of the contract form refer to the description of the goods. Since most of them are only warranties breach of them does not enable the buyer to reject the goods, although of course he may still sue for damages.

(iv) *Clause* 3. " The goods are to be properly seasoned for shipment to ...., and shall be of Sellers' usual bracking, average length and fair specification for such description of goods. The goods to be delivered to the ship in accordance with the custom of the port, the Sellers not being responsible for any deterioration occasioned by circumstances beyond their control after the goods have left Sellers' wharf properly protected. All bundled goods shall be adequately and securely bound."

(*a*) *Degree of Seasoning.* Normally timber is not " fully seasoned " but only " shipping dry," that is sufficiently seasoned for a normal voyage to the specified port of discharge. Commercially " shipping dry " means in condition which will permit of close piling in the vessel's hold during the ordinary period of a voyage from that port to that destination without deterioration. If the normal voyage is two weeks, but through unforseen circumstances the voyage takes six weeks and the timber suffers as a consequence the seller would not be responsible for the deterioration. There is no standard moisture content for shipping timber. This " properly seasoned " requirement applies very strictly to Scandinavian goods, but the bulk of the Pacific Coast Douglas fir, etc., is sold " green " which permits loading straight from the saw.

(*b*) *Bracking, Average Length, Specification.* The terms of bracking, average length and specification may or may not have been founded upon what was offered by the seller prior to the contract.

A definite agreement of an average length of 14/15 ft. becomes a part of the contract. This is not, as sometimes argued, an average of 14½ ft.—if that were so it could and must be stated—but average neither less than 14 ft. nor more than 15 ft. Expressions of opinion by the seller or his agent describing the goods in glowing terms amount to nothing if not stated in the contract.

It is quite usual for battens to be a foot shorter average length than deals, and boards a foot or two shorter average than battens.

Quality terms provide a description of goods that are saleable as such in the normal market, they do not refer to an absolutely perfect grade.

The basis of the quality is contained in the words " Sellers' usual." It becomes therefore a matter of importance for the buyer to be acquainted with the stock he intends to purchase : this leads to mutual continuity of business between certain sellers and their regular buyers.

The words "properly protected" here mean protection against damage or deterioration during transit from wharf to vessel. In practice goods to be loaded on deck (which are in any case to be exposed during the voyage) need not be so covered.

Ends Clause

"2. Sellers undertake to supply sufficient ends 6 to 8 feet, in reasonable contract specification for broken stowage only at 80 per cent. of contract price for sawn goods and at full contract price for planed goods, but not exceeding 7½ per cent. of the cargo, unless otherwise agreed. Such ends to be regarded as included in the contract quantity but to be disregarded in the calculation of average lengths. Sellers to have the right to supply up to the said 7½ per cent. of ends, whether required for broken stowage or not at 80 per cent. of contract price for sawn goods and at full contract price for planed goods, but such limitation of 7½ per cent. not to apply in the case of slatings, boards 4½ inches and under, and VIth quality."

The shipment of ends is essential for the safe and economical stowage of the cargo to the ship's full capacity. Apart from this consideration there is a considerable demand for ends for the case and boxmaking industries on account of the advantage in price: for this reason large quantities of ends (over 2 per cent. of the contract quantity) are frequently shipped at the full rate of freight.

Goods shipped from Russia are usually in lengths of 9 ft. and up, with ends 5–8 ft.

Depending upon the market situation at the time the contract is negotiated, the figure of 80 per cent. may be reduced to two-thirds This latter figure had been in force for many years, but was increased to 80 per cent. in the 1951 Uniform contract, a contract form negotiated in a strong sellers' market.

5. Marginal Quantities.

The normal timber contract does not specify an exact quantity of goods to be shipped, but an approximate quantity.

Special clauses in the contract cover quantity margins on each or every item. These are necessary to help the seller to ship the goods. Remember that the contract is being made often before the goods have been produced and the seller does not know exactly what his production will be.

They are also necessary to enable the seller in a c.i.f. contract or the buyer in an f.o.b. contract to obtain shiproom to carry the goods. Again there must be differences between cargo space available and the quantity of timber to be shipped.

Albion and Uniform Contract.

Preamble. ". . . subject to a variation in sellers' option of 10 per cent. more or less on any or every item, but not exceeding 20 standards on any one item and items of 2 to 10 standards may be varied to the extent of 1 standard, always provided that the total quantity is not varied except under the provisions of clause 5 . . ."

E

This margin is granted to the seller, but it is a margin only on each item, the total quantity may not be altered under this clause. For instance in a contract for 100 standards consisting of 10 items each of 10 standards, the seller may ship items of 9 or 11 standards *but* the total must still add up to 100 standards.

Uniform Contract—Clause 5.

"5. A margin of 10 per cent. more or less, of the total contract quantity but not exceeding 50 standards, is to be allowed to Buyers for convenience of chartering only, but when two or more shipments are made under the same contract such margin shall only apply to the quantity by the last vessel. This margin does not apply to overlying goods unchartered for and to over-wintering goods. Should Buyers under this clause demand an increase of total contract quantity, Sellers to give such increase in contract sizes, though not more than 25 per cent. increase or 5 standards, whichever may be greater, on any item over 10 standards, or 50 per cent. increase on any item of 10 standards or under."

Under this clause the buyer is granted a margin of 10 per cent., but not exceeding 50 standards, for convenience of chartering. It is this clause that varies the total quantity shipped ; note that it applies only to the quantity shipped by the last vessel if the goods are lifted by more than one vessel. It is vitally important to appreciate the working of this clause when chartering, since charters such as the Nubaltwood embody different margins (see page 75). Below a contract quantity of 666⅔ standards the marginal quantities in the Uniform contract and Nubaltwood charter ensure that the buyer-charterer is covered, but over this quantity great care must be exercised as the quantity chartered may *not* be the same as the contract quantity.

Albion Contract—Clause 5.

"5. A margin of 10 per cent., more or less, on the contract quantity, but not exceeding 50 standards, is to be allowed to Sellers for convenience of chartering, but when two or more shipments are made under the same contract such margin shall only apply to the quantity by the last vessel. Should Sellers under this clause give an increase of total contract quantity, such increase is to be in contract sizes and not more than 25 per cent. increase or 5 standards, whichever may be greater on any item over 10 standards, or 50 per cent. increase on any item of 10 standards or under.

This will be seen to be the same as the Uniform clause except that the margin is now granted to the seller who is now the charterer.

Some other contract forms, such as the Pacific Coast c.i.f. form, grant a margin of 10 per cent. to the seller without any maximum, *e.g.*, on a contract for 1000 standards margin is 100 standards more or less whereas in the Uniform it is still limited to 50 standards.

The "Bill of Lading" clauses in the Albion and Uniform contracts contain this provision, ". . . If the master calls for margin, Buyers authorise Sellers to load such margin on separate bills of lading. . . ."

Subject to these clauses the total quantity of timber delivered must agree substantially with the quantity purchased.

UNDER-SHIPMENT.

Preamble. " . . . In the event of under-shipment of any item of the contract or of the total contract quantity, Buyers are to pay for the quantity shipped, but have the right to claim compensation for such under-shipment."

If the total quantity shipped is less than the quantity purchased, the buyer must accept and pay for the goods shipped at the contract price but may claim compensation for the shortage.

OVER-SHIPMENT.

Albion Contract.

Preamble. " . . . In the event of over-shipment of any item of the contract or of the total contract quantity Buyers shall not be entitled to reject the entire shipment but shall have the option to be exercised without delay of taking up the bills of lading and paying for the whole quantity shipped or of taking up the bills of lading and paying only for the contract quantity rejecting the balance. The same conditions shall apply if the excess is not apparent from the bills of lading but is discovered only on arrival of the goods at their ultimate destination. If Buyers elect to take the contract quantity only Sellers shall pay all extra expenses whatsoever incurred by Buyers in consequence of the over-shipment . . . "

So, if the total quantity shipped is more than the quantity purchased, the buyer has two alternative actions :—(i) To accept the whole—in which case he must pay the full contract price; (ii) To accept only the purchased quantity and to reject the remainder.

Where the over-shipment is obvious from the bills of lading, the course for the buyer to adopt, if the over-shipment is not to his advantage, is immediately to notify the sellers' agents that he rejects it. Simultaneously he may offer to take the excess quantity at a reduced price which should advantage the buyer who is in a strong position to obtain such a concession from the seller.

The clauses in the Albion and Uniform contracts that have been quoted above are quite clear but there are *other types of contract* (for instance, the Unicif hardwood contract) in which these items are not covered in the same detail. In these circumstances an under-shipment or over-shipment is covered by the Sale of Goods Act (1893)—Section 30.

(i) Where the seller delivers to the buyer a quantity less than he contracted to sell, the buyer may reject them; but if the buyer accepts the goods so delivered he must pay for them at the contract price.

(Note difference—in Albion and Uniform contract you must accept an under-shipment.)

(ii) Where the seller delivers to the buyer a quantity of goods larger than he contracted to sell, the buyer may accept the goods included in the contract and reject the rest or he may reject the whole.

(Note difference—in Albion and Uniform contract you may not reject the whole of the goods.)

If the buyer accepts the whole of the goods so delivered he must pay for them at the contract rate.

In cases where the buyer is entitled to reject the whole, and elects to do so, he will refuse the documents, but where he is entitled to reject only part he will proceed by way of notification as indicated above.

It should be noted that in the Uniform 1951 contract these *variations* are specifically stated to be applied, in sellers' option, also to overlying goods. This was not mentioned in the Uniform 1933 contract.

The *margin* for convenience of chartering in the 1951 contract remains the same as in the 1933 contract and does not apply to overlying goods unchartered for and to over-wintering goods.

CHAPTER VI

Timber Contracts (*Continued*)

1. Bill of Lading Clauses. (*See also pages* 85 *to* 92.)

The Albion and Uniform contracts contain clauses relating to the manner in which the goods are to be shipped in bills of lading.

Uniform and Albion Contracts—Bills of Lading Clause.

" . . . Buyers undertake that full loading orders . . . shall be in Sellers' hands not less than . . . (7 working days) before the notified due date of vessels' arrival (at loading port).

The goods to be shipped under as many bills of lading as may be required by Buyers, but if the total number issued should exceed five per 100 standards, Buyers shall for any bill of lading in excess pay 4 guineas.

In addition to this Buyers shall pay :—

In the case of items of 10 *standards or more*

(*a*) 20s. per standard or part of a standard, if at their request any such item is split up on different bills of lading in quantities of 2 standards or more but less than 5 standards ;

(*b*) 40s. per standard or part of a standard, if at their request any such item is split up on different bills of lading in quantities of less than 2 standards ;

In the case of items under 10 *standards*

(*c*) As per (*a*) and (*b*) above, if at their request such items are split up on more than 2 bills of lading.

If Master calls for margin, Buyers authorise Sellers to load such margin on separate bills of lading.

The cargo shall be sent alongside in such a manner as to enable Master to keep separate the cargo under each bill of lading. Quantities of 50 standards or less for which a separate bill of lading is required shall be delivered to the vessel at one and the same time so as to enable Master to make one stowage of that bill of lading in the vessel unless part is stowed on deck."

The number of bills of lading required by the buyer will depend to a certain extent on his business. If he does a large trade selling goods " on passage," re-selling them on a c.i.f. basis or selling goods " ex quay " he will be selling complete bills of lading of timber. The method of handling timber at his port may require a special arrangement of bills of lading, particularly if the timber is being taken direct from the ship into a barge or railway waggon. This latter method saves many of the dock labour charges but it can only be worked with complete bills of lading. All these points therefore affect how the buyer wishes the timber to be shipped.

It is the seller's duty to send the bill of lading to the buyer before the vessel reaches port if possible, but this is not a definite commitment on the seller's part and if he fails to do this, the buyer, although he may be seriously inconvenienced, has no redress. The seller will send the bill of lading as quickly as possible in his own interest, so as to collect payment against it.

It should be borne in mind that in spite of the wording of these clauses, the shipper has no control whatever over the actual loading of the goods and their stowage in the vessel. The utmost that the shipper can do is to send the goods alongside the vessel in such a way as to enable the vessel to load the goods in accordance with the charter (Nubaltwood clause 11) and the loading orders. He is in no way responsible to see that the vessel carries out these orders.

2. Seller's Lien and Stopping the Goods.

In timber contracts and many other forms of sale there is a right of the seller to keep possession of the goods sold until payment for them has been made. This is the seller's "lien" on the goods. Although the "property" in the goods (including the risk of any accident) passes to the buyer when they are put on board ship, the seller's lien or right to hold the goods, if he is not paid, remains.

Albion and Uniform Contracts—Passing of Property Clause.

"Property in goods to be deemed for all purposes, except retention of vendor's lien for unpaid purchase price, to have passed to buyers when goods have been put on board."

There are two distinct legal rights in considering these aspects of contracts :—

(i) Right of property or ownership in the goods. As will be seen above, this passes to the buyer on shipment, subjecting him to the risk of any accident that may befall the goods—against which risks he is of course insured.

(ii) Right of possession of the goods. This normally follows the right of property but it can be defeated if the buyer does not carry out his part of the contract by making payment to the seller in exchange for the shipping documents.

The seller's lien can pass through three possible stages :—

(i) A period of absolute control by the seller over the goods. Although the "property" has passed to the buyer on shipment, whilst the seller still holds the bills of lading made out "to order" or in his agent's name, the right of possession still remains in his hands. Simply by endorsing the bills of lading he can transfer the property back to himself.

(ii) The stage when the seller forwards the bills of lading to the buyer subject to the payment of the price of the goods. If the buyer refuses acceptance of the goods, or refuses to pay for them, he has no right to retain the bill of lading representing them. The seller's lien permits the seller to hold the goods pending the issue of a court order enabling them to be re-sold to re-imburse the original seller, who can then recover any loss sustained by action against the original buyer. However, if the buyer does hold an endorsed bill of lading, and by a further endorsement passes it to an innocent person for value (that is for money, services rendered, etc., etc.) under Section 47 of the Sale of Goods Act, the last holder of the bill of lading obtains a good title to the goods which will defeat the seller's lien for unpaid price.

(iii) Possible final stage in which, provided that possession of the goods has not been lost, the seller's lien revives by reason of non-payment by the buyer. The seller has now become an "unpaid seller." (Defined by Sale of Goods Act, Section 38.)

As soon as possession passes to the buyer, the seller's lien lapses, but it can be revived again on the insolvency of the buyer. Provided that the seller still retains possession of the goods, he has the right to stop the goods in transit, if the buyer becomes insolvent and cannot pay. A person is deemed to be insolvent who has ceased to pay his debts in the ordinary course of business, or cannot pay them as they come due, whether he has committed an act of bankruptcy or not. Goods are said to be in transit from the time they are delivered to a carrier, by land or water, for the purpose of transmission to the buyer, until the buyer takes delivery of them from the carrier. Where part delivery of the goods has been made, the remainder of the goods may be stopped in transit. The carrier is bound to act upon the notice to stop the goods sent to him by the seller. There is no special form for this notice.

Again, the only time when the unpaid seller's right to stop the goods in transit can be defeated is when the buyer has obtained possession of the endorsed bill of lading and sold it to another buyer who obtains *possession* of the bill of lading and *pays* for it. If the last buyer pays for the goods but does *not* obtain possession of the endorsed bill of lading his right is subservient to the rights of the original seller.

If the unpaid seller exercises his seller's lien or his right of stoppage, this does not necessarily cancel the contract. Any sale under these rights confers a good title to the goods on the new buyer as against the first buyer. The unpaid seller may re-sell the goods and recover from the original buyer damages for any loss sustained, provided that the original buyer fails to pay the amount due within a reasonable time after having been notified by the unpaid seller that he is going to re-sell the goods.

However, the seller can only resell the goods after obtaining a court order to this effect. In some contract forms, but NOT in the Albion or Uniform contracts, there is a clause inserted as follows :—

"In the event of non-compliance by buyers with any of the terms of this contract, sellers have the liberty of resale of these goods for buyers' account."

The effect of this clause is to override the normal property clause, and permit an unpaid seller to resell the goods *without* having first obtained a court order.

3. Shipment Under Deck.

It is customary for the higher grades of timber to be loaded under deck, whilst the inferior grades make up the deckload. Vessels carrying whole cargoes of timber usually carry about one-third on deck, consequently when goods are sold without any stipulation as to loading on or under deck, it is assumed that one-third may be loaded on deck.

In this connection there is an obligation on the charterer of the vessel to provide sufficient goods for a full and complete cargo, including deckload. There is also an obligation on the buyer to furnish to the seller full loading instructions in advance of arrival of the vessel to load. These loading instructions specify not only how the cargo is to be divided up in bills of lading, but also which goods are to be loaded under deck and which may be loaded on deck.

There is however an over-riding responsibility on the master to care for the safety of the ship and cargo and he may decline to load all the comparatively light-weight goods, such as sawn laths, or slatings in bundles, under deck, and heavy deals on deck, as that might imperil the stability of the vessel.

The deck cargo is always liable to deterioration through damage by water, also by dirt from coal, cinders, oil, etc. As a matter of experience it is not always the top of the deckload which suffers most, although it is exposed directly to the weather. In heavy weather when the deck is awash it may be the bottom of the deckload which suffers most from saturation, so if there are goods which have to be loaded on deck and yet should be protected as much as possible, the buyer should stipulate that they are " well boxed in " by other cargo.

The deterioration of high grade goods is a serious matter that could involve a buyer in considerable financial loss. For the better grades of timber the buyer can protect himself by insisting that adequate clauses are inserted in the contract to ensure that shipment is made under deck.

If it is clearly a *condition* of the contract that certain goods shall be shipped under deck and words are inserted to that effect, and those goods are in fact shipped on deck, the buyer may reject them. More often however it is not regarded as a condition entitling the buyer to rejection, but a warranty entitling him to damage for breach. In the event of rejection, the buyer may still claim due execution of the contract, or damages for breach of contract, or cancellation of the contract, according to the circumstances. In the case of breach of *warranty*, the buyer can claim damages and should therefore make a written protest as soon as he finds that the goods which should have been shipped under deck have in fact been shipped on deck, holding the seller responsible for any loss or damage to the goods.

The contract form is so comprehensive that provision is made for every move the buyer may wish to make for his protection: it is therefore all the more important for the buyer to act always strictly according to the terms of the contract as, in the unlikely event of any serious dispute developing, his position will then be all the stronger for having acted correctly.

In the case of Plywood and Doors these clauses are already inserted.

Withy Plywood C.I.F. Contract.

"... All goods to be stowed under deck."

Door C.I.F. Contract.

Preamble. "... Prices are per door ... (ocean shipment under deck) to ..."

In both these cases, the fact of shipment "on deck" will be seen from the bills of lading. If the goods are not rejected at that time and the shipping documents are accepted and payment made, then these "conditions" become "warranties."

It should be noted that everything (*i.e.*, all the space) not under hatches is deckload. "On deck" includes cattle deck, bridge deck space, poop deck space and deckhouse shipments.

An exception to this is the Pacific Coast c.i.f. contract form which provides that goods stowed in a covered shelter deck shall be considered as shipped under deck. (See Pacific Coast contract, page 163, T.T.F insurance clauses, page 103.)

4. Claims.

In producing bulk quantities of a natural material such as timber it is inevitable that there will be many variations in the quality of the goods. Added to the variations of quality and manufacture are the many circumstances that can affect the condition of the goods before and during their journey to this country. These variations may bring about claims by the buyer on the seller for quality and condition. In all contracts the procedure for dealing with claims is clearly set out.

Albion and Uniform Contracts—Claims Clause.

"No claim for quality and/or condition will be recognised by Sellers upon any goods shipped under this contract, unless reasonable particulars are given to Agents within fourteen days from date of vessel's final discharge.

Reasonable particulars shall mean a statement as to whether the claim is for quality and/or condition together with a statement of the sizes complained of and an estimate of percentages and of the amount claimed. All such statements are without prejudice and conditional on the facilities for inspecting the goods."

This clause has been constructed with very great care so as to give the greatest possible protection to the buyer without unfairness to the seller. When this form was first adopted some importers considered it necessary to protect themselves by giving "formal notice of claim " automatically on receipt of shipping documents, but a close examination of the clause shows that " notice of claim " has no real value unless accompanied by " reasonable particulars." The giving of " formal notice " on imaginary grounds, without having seen the goods, not only gives the buyer no additional protection, but may give the seller the impression that the buyer is anxious to find some cause for complaint and is therefore not the most desirable customer.

It is however important to the buyer that he shall not overstep the limit of fourteen days from ship's final discharge before inspecting the goods and many importers leave a prominent space in their stockbook, following the dates of bills of lading, ship's arrival and final discharge, for the date of inspection of the goods and notification, if necessary, of any complaint or claim within the fourteen day period.

Although this clause appears to be very wide in its range, it is confined to complaints or claims for quality and/or condition leaving disputes as to measure, for instance, unlimited by time.

" No claim for quality shall be recognised on any item or part item shipped which has been broken into, but otherwise Buyers shall be at liberty to deal with any item or part item on which there is no such claim without prejudice to their right to claim on any intact item or part item under the arbitration clause. An item or part item shall be considered to be intact if it can be produced to the Arbitrator(s) and Umpire in its entirety as discharged.

An item shall mean all goods of the same dimension, quality and description. Where an item is split up on different bills of lading the part of the item shipped on each bill of lading is referred to as a part item."

The breaking into a separate item or parcel is referred to as " breaking bulk."

On comparing the word " item " with its use elsewhere in the contract it becomes clear that it applies not only to a single bill of lading, but to each dimension of each quality on each bill of lading, so that if a bill of lading consists of half-a-dozen different sizes or qualities and only one is complained of, the buyer can dispose freely of the other five items without detriment to his claim on the one complained of. And even then, in the case of a claim for condition, he need not produce the whole item, but only the affected portion. Further, there is no obligation on the buyer to keep the goods in any particular place, but merely intact for production in entirety as discharged. The person most affected by this last consideration is the seller's agent who will be asked to inspect the goods wherever they may be, but his co-operation in this matter for the benefit of both parties can normally confidently be relied on.

" . . . On any claim for condition including discoloration Buyers are at liberty to deal with any portion of the goods on which there is no claim, the claim for condition including discoloration being confined to the quantities which Buyers can produce to the Arbitrator(s) and Umpire. . . . All such statements are without prejudice and conditional on the facilities for inspecting the goods."

The condition of the goods refers to their shipped condition. It does not refer to any condition brought about by damage on voyage. This would form a claim against the Insurance Company covering the goods.

The amount claimed being " without prejudice " leaves it open to the arbitrators to award a sum even greater than that claimed by the buyer, though that is a very unlikely event. On the other hand an exaggerated claim would be taken into account by the arbitrators, to the buyer's disadvantage, in allocating the costs of the arbitration, as between buyer and seller.

If the claim is for quality and/or condition and has not been settled amicably within 10 days, under the Arbitration clause either party may at once proceed to arbitration.

5. Rejection.

Rejection of a shipment is limited to those circumstances whereby a " condition " (see page 117) of the contract has been broken. This generally means that the goods supplied are essentially different from the goods described in the contract. The preamble uses the phrase " The wood goods hereinafter specified " (see page 127) and any major departure from this constitutes a breach of " condition."

Rejection must take place immediately the buyer receives the shipping documents. He cannot wait until he has seen the goods on the quay. If the buyer accepts the documents and pays for them any broken condition becomes a broken warranty, leaving the buyer with the option of making a claim against the shipper but not of rejection of the goods.

The circumstances for rejection depend primarily upon the details contained in the shipping documents. The buyer must inspect these carefully before accepting them, but for a " condition " to be broken there must be something blatantly wrong and it should be immediately obvious to the buyer, such as :—

(i) No insurance policy in a c.i.f. contract.
(ii) Wrong specification or dimensions, *e.g.*, $2\frac{1}{2}$ ins. × 7 ins. shipped instead of 3 ins. × 7 ins.
(iii) Goods shipped " on deck " when contract specified " under deck."
(iv) Average length of parcel say 11 ft. in a contract which has specified say " average length not less than 13 ft."

Any broken " condition " such as these should be obvious from the documents, particularly the bill of lading. If the documents appear to be in order but the goods prove not to be those specified in the contract (*e.g.*, a different dimension, or whitewood instead of redwood etc., etc.), the buyer is entitled to *claim* rejection of those goods and could be awarded rejection at arbitration.

If the shipment is being rejected, all documents must be returned to the seller's agent immediately with a full explanation of the reasons for this action.

Any overshipment beyond the quantity specified in the contract, in excess of the margins allowed, may be rejected, even if the overshipment is not apparent from the bills of lading but is only discovered when the goods have been landed (see page 131).

In a contract which does not contain the overshipment or undershipment clause of the Uniform or Albion contracts, the question of overshipment or undershipment is governed by the Sale of Goods Act which permits the buyer to reject the *entire* shipment for any overshipment or undershipment in excess of the margins allowed.

Earlier contract forms stipulated that the buyers should not reject ". . . the goods herein specified . . ." but should pay for them against shipping documents. The words " herein specified " had the appearance at first sight of being a restriction on the buyer's right of rejection. However a buyer merely had to show that the goods were materially different from those " herein specified," so that the clause did not then cover the goods shipped.

This right of rejection, based upon the assertion that the goods being rejected are *not* the same as the goods purchased, is clear cut and easy to define. Unfortunately in the past this led to a number of rejections on purely technical grounds to suit the convenience of the buyer. For instance, scant sawn goods, purchased as $2'' \times 6''$ but on arrival found to measure $1\frac{7}{8}'' \times 5\frac{7}{8}''$, could be rejected as not being the goods " herein specified."

The new Albion and Uniform contracts limit the buyer's right of rejection where dimension and quality are concerned.

Albion and Uniform Contracts—Rejection Clause.

" Buyers' right of rejection shall not be exercised where the claim is limited to questions of dimensions and/or quality unless the shipment or bill of lading as a whole, if the claim is to reject such shipment or bill of lading, or the item or part item, if the claim is to reject such item or part item, is not in respect of such heads of claim a fair delivery under the contract from a commercial standpoint, of which, in the event of dispute, the Arbitrator(s) or Umpire are to be the sole and final judges.

The phrase a " fair delivery from a commercial standpoint " is a wide term, but it must necessarily be so where commercial aspects of a claim are concerned and each case has to be decided on its own merits. It merely prevents outright rejection, acknowledging that at the same time there has probably been a breach of warranty on which the buyer will claim damages or a reduction in price.

A further right of rejection for the buyers is provided by the marine insurance of the goods. If these deteriorate or are damaged during the voyage *as a result of a peril against which they are insured* to such an extent that they are so different from the goods they were insured as to be of no value to the buyer, he may claim rejection from the insurers. If the insurance surveyor admits the claim, the buyer is paid the equivalent of a total loss on the goods, whilst the goods pass to the insurance company who usually dispose of them at auction.

CHAPTER VII

Timber Contracts (*Continued*)

The F.A.S. and F.O.B. Contract—Uniform 1951.

1. General.

Reference will be made throughout this chapter to the Uniform 1951 contract form. This makes provision for every move of buyer and seller and has been developed as a result of generations of trading. There are several other forms of f.a.s. and f.o.b. contract but none is quite so complete as the Uniform. The basic principles disclosed apply of course to any f.a.s. or f.o.b. contract, modified only by any particular clauses in the contract. A buyer purchasing on f.o.b. terms from a source where there is no regular contract form in use, cannot do better than specify that the contract will be on the " Uniform 1951 form," suitably amended to meet the local circumstances.

There is little practical difference between the terms f.a.s. and f.o.b. as applied to the Scandinavian timber trade, although there are important differences in these terms when used in other parts of the World.

The Uniform contract has always been known in this country as an f.o.b. contract, although the sellers are only responsible for placing the goods " free alongside vessel," the normal terms for an f.a.s. contract. However, in Scandinavia there are rarely sufficient port facilities for the cargo to be loaded by shore cranes on to the vessel and in fact the Nubaltwood charter provides for the vessel to load, so the physical placing of the goods " on board " is beyond control of the sellers anyway. The property or ownership passes when the goods have been placed on board and so it is generally conceded that the Uniform is an f.o.b. contract. If it had been possible for the property to pass whilst the goods were in lighters alongside the vessel, it would probably have become a true f.a.s. contract. Such a position for the passing of property, extremely important from considerations of insurance and insurable interest, was impossible, since within the margins for chartering and loading the vessel the master may send back some of the lighters if the goods they contain are not required.

In other ports of the World the difference between f.a.s. and f.o.b. may be much more important, especially where the charter does not provide for the vessel to load the cargo. In such circumstances a buyer on f.a.s. terms would himself have to arrange with stevedores at the loading port for the loading of the goods.

2. Seller's Responsibilities.

The seller's responsibilities in a Uniform f.o.b. contract are :—

(i) To place *goods of the description contained in the contract* " all free alongside the vessel " at the port of shipment.

(ii) To advance freight if required.

(iii) To deliver to the buyer shipping documents consisting of a specification of the goods shipped, an invoice for them at the contract price and the relative bills of lading.

(iv) To pay any dead freight claims or provide indemnity.

3. Buyer's Responsibilities.

(i) To arrange a freight contract in the form of the usual charter-party, for loading the goods that the seller has undertaken to place alongside.

(ii) To notify the sellers as to the manner in which the goods are to be loaded in bills of lading.

(iii) To arrange insurance for the goods in transit and if required by sellers, produce proof that this insurance has been effected.

(iv) To lift the goods before a date named in the contract, failing which there is an obligation to pay for the goods and thereafter pay storage charges.

(v) *To pay* for the goods on receipt of shipping documents.

4. Description and Price.

The goods are to be of the description contained in the contract, and the prices in standards of 165 cubic feet for sawn and planed goods are " all free alongside the vessel."

The full implications of description are discussed on pages 127 to 129.

5. The Freight Contract.

The buyers arrange freight through a shipbroker or shipping agent, who requires full details of the amount and type of goods to be shipped, the names of loading and discharging ports and the dates when shipping space is required. With this information they will offer the buyer various freights to cover the parcel in question. The quantity being shipped is a great factor in the chartering of shipping space. If the shipping agents offer a vessel of rather more carrying capacity than is required for this contract, the buyer may decide to charter the whole vessel, relying on being able to purchase an additional quantity to fill it, otherwise he must realise the possibility of the shipping agent filling the remainder of the cargo space with another buyer's goods.

The buyer must beware of very cheap freight rates, particularly from obscure foreign shipowners. In chartering a ship of this nature the buyer is wise to make certain that insurance cover is accepted before he completes his freight contract. There have been instances where a foreign ship chartered at a very cheap freight rate has been found to be in such a bad condition that no insurance company would cover the goods being carried.

Uniform Contract.

Preamble. " . . . (goods) to be ready for shipment on the . . ."

Overlying Goods Clause. " Should any of the goods not be removed by . . . (hereinafter called the drawing date). . . ."

The date given in the preamble is the " ready date," and the buyer is at liberty to lift the goods on or after that date. The date given in the overlying goods clause is known as the " drawing date " since if the buyer has not lifted the goods by this date, the sellers will forward a draft for payment with an approximate invoice. The drawing date is usually two months after the ready date, so the buyer has a reasonable period in which to arrange his charter.

Uniform Contract—Chartering Clause.

" Shiproom to be provided in due time by Buyers. Buyers undertake that at least 7 working days' notice shall be given to Sellers direct before arrival of any vessel to load, stating vessel's and Charterer's name. Buyers undertake that full loading orders and Charter party shall be in Sellers' hands not later than the above-mentioned number of days before the notified due date of vessel's arrival.

If due care has not been exercised by Master in giving notice of the probable date of vessel's arrival, Buyers are responsible for demurrage on lighters or trucks due to non-arrival of the vessel on the date stated in the said notice.

Buyers are bound to get inserted in the Charter party a clause that Master has to give written notice of the approximate quantity of cargo required."

The buyer's undertaking to give at least seven working day's notice to sellers before arrival of any vessel to load, and buyer's responsibility for demurrage on lighters, etc., due to non-arrival of the vessel, are covered in the Nubaltwood charter, clause 2 (see page 77) in which these responsibilities are undertaken by shipowners. *If any form of freight contract other than the Nubaltwood charter is used, such as a liner bill of lading, it is imperative that the buyer has a clause inserted in the freight contract to the following effect " . . . subject to all other conditions and clauses of the Nubaltwood charter. . . ."*

If this is not done, buyers may be in breach of their purchase contract by not giving adequate notice of vessel's arrival, at the same time having no redress against shipowners whose charter or bill of lading may state no period at all.

The written notice referred to at the end of the clause is also covered in the Nubaltwood charter.

Ice Hindrance Clause.

" Sellers are not liable to supply vessel with cargo if the navigation of lighters between Sellers' wharves and/or quays and vessel is impeded by ice, nor supply cargo earlier than 48 hours after this hindrance having ceased."

This is covered in the Nubaltwood charter clause 8 (*e*) (see page 79). It is in one sense an effective definition of " first open water," but similar ice hindrances can occur towards the closing of navigation.

Freight Advance Clause.

" Any freight advance for vessel's ordinary disbursement only at port of loading, but not exceeding one-third of the total freight, shall be advanced by Sellers if required by Master subject to cost of insurance only. The amount of the advance shall be endorsed upon the bill of lading in British sterling at the closing rate of exchange at the port of shipment on the day the advance is taken, and shall be settled by Buyers in cash in exchange for Master's receipt at the same rate.

This clause is subject to currency regulations in force at the time of shipment."

This covers the buyer's obligations under the Nubaltwood charter clause 7 (see page 79).

Dead Freight Clause.

" Sellers guarantee to pay all dead freight admitted or proved to have been caused at the loading port by their default. If there is any such claim made against Buyers or bill of lading holders, Buyers shall give prompt notice thereof in writing to Sellers or their Agents. Sellers shall, within ten days after receipt of such notice, either pay the claim or give to Buyers an approved guarantee to indemnify them for any amount and costs which may be awarded to the Shipowners in respect of such claim and for interest at five per cent. per annum or bank rate if higher on any deposit in respect of such claim made to release the goods. In case of arbitration or law suit on such claim Buyers to follow the reasonable instructions of Sellers with regard to the defence and Sellers shall supply all necessary evidence and documents in support thereof."

Before the Nubaltwood charter came into force with its Commutation of Demurrage clause, the sellers also guaranteed to pay demurrage claims admitted or proved to have been incurred by them at the loading port.

Here again the buyer must exercise great care if making a freight contract on liner terms or on any charter other than the Nubaltwood. He may find himself with a charter, or liner booking note, with an obligation to pay any demurrage at the loading port and with no counter obligations accepted by sellers.

The safest action for a buyer to take in these circumstances is either (*a*) if possible to get the phrase " . . . subject to all terms and conditions of Nubaltwood charter " incorporated in the charter or booking note, or (*b*) to get the phrase " . . . sellers guarantee to pay all claims for demurrage admitted or proved to have been incurred by them at the loading port" inserted in the Uniform contract with the sellers. Although the shippers' organisations will not agree to become a party to the Commutation of Demurrage scheme formed under the Nubaltwood charter (see page 82) it is possible that in the future they may accept responsibility for demurrage at loading port as they used to do up to 1951.

6. Insurance of the Goods.

The property clause states that the property in the goods (which includes all risks) passes to the buyer when the goods have been put "on board." The insurance of the goods, however, commences from the moment the goods are loaded into lighters, the buyer being covered during the period of pre-loading whilst the goods are between the wharf and the ocean going vessel and even prior to that. (T.T.F. clauses 1 and 2, see page 100.)

Uniform Insurance Clause.

"Marine insurance of cargo and freight advance to be covered by Buyers. Such insurance to attach as and when the goods are loaded into lighters for shipment after receipt of notice from vessel of her expected arrival or, in the case of goods so loaded prior to the receipt of such notice, when such notice is received. The obligation to insure against War risks shall be on Buyers who shall, if required by Sellers or their Agents, deposit with them before the goods are put on board a cover note or policy of insurance effected with Lloyd's or a first class British Company covering the goods against such risks. If these risks are not coverable or for any reason Buyers do not cover against these risks they shall provide before goods are put on board such security for payment as may be required by Sellers or their Agents and, goods lost or not lost, shall pay against presentation of documents the value of the goods shipped at contract prices plus freight advance, if any, payable under the Charter party.

Buyers shall, if requested at any time after their obligation to insure as above have arisen, furnish Sellers' Agents with sufficient proof of such insurance having been effected."

The buyers have the responsibility for arranging insurance to cover both goods *and freight advance* and must be prepared to furnish proof of this insurance if required.

This clause also visualises that war risks may again become vital and possibly uninsurable in which case sellers must have some security for payment.

7. Marginal Quantities.

Uniform Margins Clause.

"A margin of 10 per cent., more or less, of the total contract quantity but not exceeding 50 standards, is to be allowed to Buyers for convenience of chartering only, but when two or more shipments are made under the same contract such margin shall only apply to the quantity by the last vessel. This margin does not apply to overlying goods unchartered for and to over-wintering goods. Should Buyers under this clause demand an increase of total contract quantity, Sellers to give such increase in contract sizes, though not more than 25 per cent. increase or five standards, whichever may be greater, on any item over ten standards, or 50 per cent. increase on any item of ten standards or under."

The margins in the preamble and the contract generally, and the stipulations concerning overshipment and undershipment have already been described in detail on page 129. The margin for chartering this time being given to buyers. These latter margins do not apply to overlying goods unchartered for and to overwintering goods. These goods have normally been paid for by buyers: it would not be practicable for the sellers either to increase or reduce the quantity overlying.

8. Conditions Subsequent.

Uniform Force Majeure Clause.

" In case the manufacture and/or shipment of any of the goods herein specified be delayed or hindered by floods, droughts, ice, damage to mill and/or timber yard or shipping yard, strike, lock-out or any other cause beyond Sellers' control, causes mentioned in Clause 10 excepted, they shall not be responsible for any damages arising therefrom, provided immediate notice by telegram be given to Buyers. In such event only, Sellers have the right during.................. weeks from the ready date of completing the contract. Should Sellers, however, be unable to deliver within such extended time they shall declare their inability to do so and on receipt of Sellers' declaration Buyers shall have the option, to be promptly declared, of cancelling the contract, or postponing the same to such date of delivery as may be mutually agreed upon, but in any event not later than the following f.o.w.

If, however, the manufacture and/or shipment of the goods specified herein be prevented by destruction of mill and/or timber yard or shipping yard, sellers have the option, to be promptly declared by telegram, to cancel the contract without responsibility for any damages arising therefrom."

This clause differentiates between delay or hindrance, and prevention. Circumstances causing the first of these give sellers the option of extending the period of shipment. If the delay or hindrance prevents shipment within the extended time, buyers have the option of cancelling or putting back the goods for later delivery but not later than the following f.o.w. In the case of prevention of manufacture or shipment, sellers have the option to cancel the contract straight away.

Uniform—War, etc. Clause.

" Should prohibition of export or import (other than export or import conditional only upon licence), war or blockade at any time before the drawing date, original or postponed according to Clause 11, prevent Sellers from manufacturing and/or shipping or Buyers from lifting the goods, this contract shall be cancelled for any unpaid goods."

This clause carries equal rights for buyers and sellers. It is important to note that this clause does not affect goods already paid for by buyers and overlying in the seller's yard, in which the property has already passed to buyers.

Uniform—Licences Clause.

" The obligation to make application for and the cost of obtaining any export or import licence and to pay any export or import duty, charges or taxes which may be payable in respect of the export or import of the goods shall be upon Sellers and Buyers respectively.

If either party having made application has failed to obtain the requisite licence by.., he shall have the right to cancel the contract provided prompt notice is given to the other party.

If a party has not notified the other party by the above date that the requisite licence has been granted, the last mentioned party has the right of cancelling the contract subject to prompt notice being given.

If any requisite licence has been refused to a party or if a licence although granted is subsequently cancelled prior to shipment, such party shall forthwith advise the other party by telegram and either party shall have the right of cancelling the contract provided that notice of cancellation is given, in the case of the first mentioned party, in the said telegram and, in the case of the other party, promptly on receipt thereof."

The amplification of a clause covering the granting and cancelling of import and export licences is a new feature of the contract, brought in by the current " licence-ridden " conditions in which all world import and export trades work to-day.

9. Overlying Goods.

The buyer has a clear obligation in an f.o.b. contract to lift the goods within a specified period, described as " in due time." If he does not do so, even if the reason is that he has been unable to charter suitable freight (unless it is due to war, blockade, etc., as detailed in the war clause), the sellers are then entitled to receive payment for the goods, in return for which they will provide if required, at buyers' expense, a bank guarantee (if requested in time) to the effect that if the goods are not ultimately delivered to the buyers, their money will be refunded.

Uniform—Overlying Clause.

" Should any of the goods not be removed by.. ....(hereinafter called " the drawing date ") payment to be made in the manner provided above but against approximate invoice of the said date and, provided not less than 7 days' notice prior to the said date has been given to Sellers or their authorised Agents, Buyers shall be entitled in exchange for such payment to receive a guarantee by approved Bankers of the country of shipment that if the goods or any portion thereof are not delivered free alongside for any other reason than destruction by fire, if applied for before 1st August of the following year, the contract value of any quantity unshipped will be refunded to Buyers. The cost of the said guarantee shall be borne by Buyers up to a maximum of 1 per cent. Fire insurance on any such goods to be covered by Sellers for Buyers' account and at their expense, unless otherwise agreed."

The Bank guarantee sets out particulars of the contract with the quantity and value of goods prepared and ready for shipment, for which buyers are to pay prior to the shipment thereof, on presentation of the documents specified in the contract, including the guarantee.

The usual form of guarantee is as follows:—

"*The Bank guarantee* if the said goods or any part thereof, payment for which has been made to Sellers by Buyers, are not delivered free alongside or free on board the vessel as may be called for by the said contract for any reason other than by fire, flood, earthquake or naval or aerial bombardment upon request being made to the Sellers so to do, *the payment* to the Buyers by the Sellers on demand *of the contract value* free alongside or free on board as the case may be, *of any quantity short delivered.*

This guarantee is to remain in force until..................................with the option of extension within contract terms, subject to the settlement of all claims made hereunder upon or prior to the said date of termination and subject also to due allowance in respect of the shipment of the whole or any part of the said goods subsequent to any notification of claim hereunder."

The guarantee excludes destruction of the goods by fire, but fire insurance on the goods has to be covered by sellers on behalf of buyers. This being done under the seller's own stock fire policy is obviously a better arrangement than the buyers taking out their own fire insurance on the goods. There are possible difficulties in such circumstances in proving the buyer's insurable interest.

"Buyers' liability to pay for the goods under this clause shall, however, be suspended if the failure to remove the goods is due to any of the contingencies covered by Clause 9 and the drawing date shall be postponed for a period equivalent to the duration of the delay, provided that ice hindrance shall not be a cause for suspension of payment unless shipment of the goods has already been delayed by any other contingency specified in Clause 9."

The setting in of ice at the end of the year to prevent buyers from lifting the goods is one of the risks accepted when buying f.o.b. If this does happen, the goods must be paid for and over-wintered.

"If the goods or part thereof are not removed before the drawing date, rent to be paid from the said date at the rate of 5s. per month or part of a month for the first 6 months and thereafter 7s. 6d. per month or part of a month, all per standard.

If, however, a cause beyond Buyers' control other than ice prevents the lifting of the goods at any time after the rent has become payable Buyers shall pay rent at half of the above rate(s) until such cause ceases to operate.

In case goods sold ready for shipment per 15th November or later in the season and chartered for loading within a week after the ready date cannot be shipped on account of ice hindrance the rent clause in the third paragraph not to be in force until following f.o.w."

Sellers' yards are not unlimited in size, so the continued storing of timber that has been sold but not lifted by buyers represents an inconvenience and an expense. The very fact that the sellers permit the buyers to leave their goods there at all, after the due date by which they should have been lifted, represents a concession to buyers. It is not an uncommon occurrence for buyers to leave their goods in the seller's yard for a considerable time. In view of the space taken up the payment of rent is by no means unreasonable. The increase in rent payable if the goods are left after six months after the drawing date is in the form of a penalty against the buyers.

"Unless over-wintered goods are specified in the contract Sellers may, when executing delivery of goods after the drawing date, deliver goods of later production and/or overlying goods ready for shipment at the drawing date (hereinafter referred to as 'overlying goods').

When delivering overlying goods Sellers shall not be responsible for any deterioration of the goods caused by the postponement of delivery unless such deterioration exceeds what would be normal deterioration between the drawing date and the date of delivery of goods protected as customary."

This clause is an important addition to the Uniform contract, appearing in the 1951 edition for the first time. It takes wood goods out of the category to which a legal decision some years ago applied, namely "vintage" goods. Buyers by that decision in an English court being entitled by law to goods of the vintage of the year in which they would normally be produced for the date of readiness named in the contract. This in fact had not been done for many years, as sellers, having arranged to have "sold goods" ready at certain times, delivered more or less in rotation as they became ready for shipment. In doing this they assumed that buyers would be only too pleased to have goods fairly recently seasoned rather than over-wintered goods which would probably be a bit weathered. Some buyers on the other hand wanted their over-wintering goods to have the benefit of the extra seasoning so there was room for dispute.

The increasingly common change from seasoning and storing timber in open yards to kiln drying and storing in covered store-houses or sheds makes it often physically impossible for sellers to store goods that are not fetched "in due time" by buyers. There are difficulties also under Swedish and Finnish law, since the only manner to identify the goods as those belonging only to the buyer in question would be to segregate the goods completely.

There is never any question of the sellers supplying goods that are not properly seasoned since they must still supply goods of the description contained in the contract.

If the buyer particularly wishes to have over-wintered goods, these must be described as such in the contract.

The preamble states that the *variations* permitted to sellers (10 per cent. more or less, etc.) apply also to overlying goods, whilst clause 5 stipulates that the *margin* for convenience of chartering does not apply to overlying goods unchartered for or to over-wintering goods.

10. Payment, Claims etc.

Payment terms have already been discussed on pages 121 to 127, claims on page 137, right of rejection on page 139 and the arbitration procedure is detailed on pages 182 to 190.

CHAPTER VIII

Timber Contracts (*Continued*)

The C.I.F. Contract—Albion

1. General.

The risks undertaken by a buyer in a c.i.f. contract are far less than those undertaken by him when buying on f.o.b. terms. Unless the contract is on a " freight basis " (see page 62) he takes no risk of an increase in freight rates working against him. The obligation to deliver the goods rests with the seller, and if there is any delay or circumstance preventing a vessel from lifting the goods the buyer is given the option of cancelling the contract. The same circumstances in an f.o.b. contract would leave him with his obligation to pay for the goods and leave them over-lying.

For this reason the c.i.f. form of contract is particularly attractive to the smaller importer. It is used of course by even the largest importers, particularly at the end of the shipping season when the buyers do not want any risk of goods over-lying.

Sellers obviously would prefer to sell all their goods on f.o.b. terms, thus being relieved of all the difficulties of chartering. Sales on c.i.f. terms are to some extent an indication of the strength of the buying market, as sellers will generally (in the Scandinavian softwood trade) only quote c.i.f. when they are finding difficulty in selling f.o.b.

The added safety to the buyer in a c.i.f. contract is not obtained for nothing. The sellers must cover themselves adequately for the risks and difficulties of chartering which have now passed to them and rates of freight can fluctuate very widely. The result is that a c.i.f. price will usually be appreciably higher than the equivalent f.o.b. price plus existing insurance and freight costs.

The main difference from the f.o.b. contract lies in this fact that the sellers must arrange freight and insurance, and the benefits from these must be available to the buyers. It means that bills of lading and insurance policies must be such that they can be transferred to buyers to put them in the same position as if they had arranged the freight and insurance themselves as in an f.o.b. contract. It is accomplished by clauses inserted in the contract form to ensure that the sellers take out a proper form of freight contract and insurance policy.

The broad terms of the contract are the same as for an f.o.b. contract, but the shipping documents have a special significance. Although the Albion contract form (and most other c.i.f. contract forms) states specifically that payment must be made against shipping documents, this is really a declaration of the law. In any c.i.f. contract (unless there are special stipulations to the contrary) the buyer must pay on receipt of shipping documents which *must* include *invoice, bill of lading and insurance policy*.

These are the vital documents of a c.i.f. contract, and in fact it is known as "a contract to be performed by the delivery of documents. . . ."

The Albion c.i.f. contract is now discussed in detail. Like the Uniform f.o.b. contract it represents the most complete form of contract used in the timber trade.

These observations refer to the 1938 Albion contract, since this is the form currently in use. After the 1951 Uniform contract had been agreed between the shippers' organisations and the T.T.F., attempts were made to revise the Albion contract on similar lines. Unfortunately these negotiations resulted in a deadlock, and so no revised Albion form is yet available.

When the new Albion form does make an appearance, it will differ superficially in many ways from the 1938 Albion that is now being discussed, but the general sense, and liabilities and responsibilities of buyers and sellers will remain much the same.

Many of the changes will consist of simplification of wording and layout for greater clarity, the general style of the 1951 Uniform being followed.

2. Seller's Responsibilities.

The seller's responsibilities, once the contract has been signed, are as follows :—

(i) To ship at the port of shipment (named in the contract) *goods of the description contained in the contract.*

(ii) To arrange freight to deliver the goods to the destination named in the contract.

(iii) To arrange insurance of the goods during their passage, such insurance to be available for the benefit of the buyer.

(iv) To make out an invoice at the c.i.f. price less the amount of any freight or balance of freight that the buyer will have to pay when the vessel reaches its destination.

(v) To send to the buyer the following documents :—

Bills of lading.
Insurance policy.
Specification.
Invoice and minor documents, to enable the buyer to—

Ascertain that the goods shipped are those contracted for,
Obtain delivery of the goods when they arrive,
Recover the value of goods lost or obtain compensation for damage,
Know how much cost, insurance and freight he must pay.

3. Buyer's Responsibilities.

The buyer's responsibilities are much less in number than in an f.o.b. contract, but they are no less important.

(i) To notify the sellers as to the manner in which the goods are to be loaded in bills of lading.

(ii) *To pay* for the goods on receipt of shipping documents, provided that these are complete, agree with each other and with the terms of the contract.

4. Description and Price.

The goods are to be of the description contained in the contract (see pages 127 to 129).

The prices, per standard of 165 cubic feet ". . . include first cost, freight and insurance. . . ." "The goods are to be shipped at .... to ....always afloat."

5. The Freight Contract in C.I.F. Sale.

In the c.i.f. sale the freight contract is arranged by the seller. The terms of the freight contract are shown in the charter-party in detail and summarised in the bill of lading. The seller is making the freight contract on behalf of the buyer and it must be a reasonable contract to include all the necessary precautions to ensure safe delivery of the goods. If the seller does not do this, and the goods are lost or damaged during transit, the buyer may refuse to accept the fact of delivery to the carrier as delivery to himself. He may also sue the seller for damages resulting from his failure to make a reasonable freight contract.

The Albion contract covers these exigencies by giving very specific instructions concerning the freight contract.

(i) *Preamble.* ". . . shiproom to be secured in due time by the sellers who shall promptly advise buyers."

The words "in due time" refer to the shipping date stated elsewhere in the contract, so that for instance, sellers may not delay shipment beyond the date stipulated, in the hope that they might be able to charter at a lower rate later in the season.

This notification is usually by telegram and it puts the buyer "in the picture." He now knows approximately when to expect his shipment and can make his arrangements accordingly. By keeping in touch with the shipowners' agents in this country he can follow the course of the ship and learn its expected arrival date.

(ii) *Preamble.* ". . . in the event, however, of vessel chartered under this contract not being ready to load within six weeks after stipulated time of shipment, sellers shall notify buyers that the ship named cannot load within that time, and the buyers shall have the right of cancelling the contract to a corresponding extent, subject to giving notice to that effect to sellers to enable them to cancel the charter party within the time stipulated in same, provided that the sellers' notice states the time for cancellation and has been given instantly on receipt of the shipowners' notice under clause 3(*c*) of the 'Baltwood' charter."

The 1938 Albion, as printed, continues to refer to the 1926 Baltwood charter. It is usual to insert an additional clause in the contract providing for the charter to be on the Nubaltwood form, all references to the Baltwood form being taken as references to the Nubaltwood form.

The "corresponding extent" here refers not necessarily to the full quantity of the contract but merely the quantity that should have been shipped by this particular vessel.

This clause is a protection for the buyer. Quite obviously he must have some power to cancel the contract at the end of a determined time as otherwise there might be circumstances in which a seller had been unable or unwilling to secure shiproom for say six or nine months during which time the market value of timber had fallen badly. Without the power to cancel the contract, the buyer would still be obliged to accept the timber say six or nine months later and to bear the loss.

The buyer must notify the seller within a stipulated time that he is cancelling the contract to enable the seller in turn to cancel the charter-party.

(iii) *Clause* 4. " . . . should any vessel chartered under this contract be lost after being named to buyers and previous to loading, sellers have the option of chartering in substitution other tonnage calculated to be available for loading within the stipulated time of shipment or of cancelling the contract to such an extent upon giving prompt notice to buyers, leaving, however, the buyers option to take the goods on corresponding f.o.b. terms . . ."

The f.o.b. terms are stated to be the c.i.f. price less the cost of insurance and freight at the rate at which it had been secured. The terms and conditions would then be those applying to the normal f.o.b. contract—Uniform.

(iv) *Clause* 7. " Freight advance may be made for ship's ordinary disbursements and is not to exceed one-third of the total freight. Any such advance is to be settled by cash in exchange for Captain's receipt upon the bill of lading together with policy of insurance as above. The amount of the advance shall be endorsed upon the bill of lading in British Sterling."

This advance of freight is made by the seller to the master of the ship. The amount advanced, when deducted from the total amount of freight payable, leaves the "balance of freight" which is paid to the shipowner by the buyer when the cargo has arrived safely. The amount of the advance must also be covered by an insurance policy.

(v) *Clause* 10. " Buyers to pay freight as per charter-party or bill of lading which are to be usual Baltwood form . . . The deduction of freight in the invoice shall be the nett rate only and shall not include the charges which are payable under the Baltwood charter-party for delivery beyond the ship's rail or tackle, unless otherwise provided for in the contract . . ."

Here again references to the Baltwood charter are usually taken as references to the Nubaltwood charter, with a suitable covering clause added to the contract.

The buyer must pay the shipowner the freight due as per charter-party or bill of lading before he can obtain delivery of the goods from the ship. The freight contract covers the carriage of the timber to the port in the U.K. It does not cover any labour charges in handling the timber beyond the ship's rail or the ship's tackle. The buyer is responsible for charges for any additional work and clauses 15 and 16 of the Nubaltwood charter-party shows how these charges are made up.

(vi) *Clause* 13. "The sellers guarantee to pay all dead freight and demurrage admitted or proved to have been incurred by them at the loading port."

If such unsettled claims are notified, the buyer is entitled to obtain from the sellers a written indemnity as essential to complete the shipping documents, and to withhold payment until it is provided.

Although the Nubaltwood charter relieves the sellers of responsibility for demurrage at the loading port at the moment, it is possible that sellers' liability for demurrage may still be included in the new Albion contract.

(vii) *Clause* 10. ". . . on receipt of and in exchange for shipping documents including charter-party and policy of insurance . . ."

The Albion contract states that a copy of the charter-party must be included in the documents forwarded to the buyer, but there are other contract forms that do not make this stipulation.

Although possession of the charter-party (or a copy of it) does not affect the ownership of the goods being shipped, it is a document that the buyer should always insist be produced. Without it the buyer cannot know all the loading port conditions. If these conditions are not fulfilled there may be charges to be paid by bills of lading holders. This is quite apart from the sellers' guarantee in clause 13 Albion contract (see (vi) above).

The freight contract must cover the whole of the journey from the loading port to the discharging port. If the actual point of discharge is specified, such as a buyer's own wharf, this must be fulfilled exactly.

The Nubaltwood charter-party uses the phrase "or so near thereunto as she may safely get, and deliver the cargo, always afloat." The Albion contract preamble states "to . . . always afloat."

If the cargo is to be delivered to a particular quay these two phrases must be altered to an exact description of the wharf or quay concerned.

6. The Insurance of the Goods (see Chapter IV).

Albion Insurance Clause.

"Sellers shall insure the cargo at f.o.b. invoice value plus 10 per cent. and freight advance, if any, with a first-class company or underwriters (if foreign to be approved by buyers) as per Lloyd's form of policy, together with Timber Trade Federation Insurance Clauses, losses payable in London and subject to the provisions of 6*a*, War risks as per Institute War Clause in force at the time of attachment of the insurance."

The buyer is not entitled to an insurance policy on the full amount of freight (*i.e.*, including the freight to be paid only on right delivery at destination) but the amount of freight advanced by seller must be covered.

By the warehouse to warehouse clause in the T.T.F. Insurance Clauses (see page 100) the cover extends till the goods reach their "ultimate destination." As this may be some distance inland, it is possible for the goods to be under-insured after arrival by the amount of the balance of destination freight, import duty, and other charges payable at port of destination. This is covered by an "Increased Value" policy which extends the insured amount to cover the additional charges, etc., paid. Since there is little risk of total loss, other than by fire, after the goods arrive at the port, the premium for the increased value policy is much less than the normal cargo insurance policy.

The property in the goods passes only when the goods have been put on board.

"Property in goods to be deemed for all purposes, except retention of vendor's lien for unpaid purchase price, to have passed to buyers when goods have been put on board the vessel."

War Risks Clause (6*a*).

"Any premium for war risk insurance shall be for account of Buyers except that if owing to the Flag and/or ownership and/or condition of the vessel there is at the time of chartering or, if chartered before the date of the contract, at the date of the contract an increase over the general rate for such insurance such increase shall not be chargeable to Buyers. . . ."

During conditions in which a War Insurance premium is likely to be heavy, the buyer will obviously have no objection to paying the heavy premium since his goods in those conditions will usually be much more valuable.

The second part is a protection for buyers, in case the sellers charter a very old vessel, or a vessel belonging to a nation at war.

". . . If Sellers are unable to effect War Risk Insurance on the goods for a premium of 2 per cent. or less they shall give Buyers immediate telegraphic advice and Buyers shall thereupon have the option of endeavouring to effect War Risk Insurance themselves, accepting the increased premium or of calling upon Sellers to ship the goods uninsured. In either event Buyers to give Sellers' Agents prompt notice after receipt of advice of Sellers' inability to insure at the aforesaid rate of the option they intend to exercise.

Should it not be possible to cover such insurance or should insurance whether effected by Sellers or Buyers be cancelled by underwriters, Sellers or Buyers as the case may be shall give prompt telegraphic advice to Buyers or Sellers, and Buyers shall thereupon have the option of cancelling the contract or calling upon Sellers to ship the goods uninsured.

If Buyers call upon Sellers to ship the goods uninsured they shall provide, before the goods are put on board, such security for payment as may be required by Sellers or their Agents and, goods lost or not lost, shall pay against presentation of documents the value of the goods shipped at contract price less unpaid freight."

The security for payment demanded by sellers if the goods are shipped uninsured against War Risks, is only reasonable. War risks can only fail to be covered when shipping in a particular area is in imminent War danger. In such circumstances if the goods reach their destination safely they become greatly enhanced in value, to the benefit of the buyer. The security given to sellers or their agents will usually be in the form of a Bank credit or guarantee.

7. Marginal Quantities.

These have been discussed on pages 129 to 132. The margins for chartering are, of course, here given to the sellers.

8. Conditions Subsequent.

In the Albion c.i.f. contract provision is made for cancellation or postponement for a number of reasons in addition to the normal War and *Force Majeure* clauses.

Preamble (see C.I.F. Freight Contract, page 152).

Buyers are here given the option to cancel the contract to the extent of the goods chartered for in the event of the vessel that has been chartered, not being ready to load within six weeks of the stipulated time of shipment.

Clause 4 (see page 153).

If the vessel chartered under the contract is lost after being named to buyers and previous to loading, the *sellers* have the option of substituting another vessel or cancelling the contract to the extent of the goods chartered for but leaving the buyer with an option to take the goods f.o.b.

Clause (6*a*) *War Insurance* (page 155).

If War Risk Insurance cannot be covered, *buyers* have the option of cancelling the contract or calling for sellers to ship the goods uninsured.

9. Payment, Claims, Etc.

Payment terms have been discussed on pages 121 to 127. The most important difference in a c.i.f. contract is that the *insurance policy* must be included amongst the shipping documents presented for payment, in addition to the normal shipping documents provided in an f.o.b. contract. The Albion contract form however goes further, and specifies that a copy of the charter will be provided, either with the shipping documents, or before the goods are shipped. The importance of a sight of the charter is discussed on page 154.

Claims (page 137), Right of rejection (page 139) and Arbitration (page 182) are unchanged from the equivalent f.o.b. contract.

CHAPTER IX

Timber Contracts (*Continued*)

Other Contract Forms

1. Unicif Hardwood C.I.F. Contract Form.

(*a*) GENERAL.

This is a c.i.f. contract form for purchases from all countries with the exception of the U.S.A. and Canada. It is therefore set out in much wider terms than the more detailed Uniform and Albion contract forms used in the Baltic trade.

The terms and clauses of the contract form have been negotiated and adopted by the Hardwood Importers' Section of the T.T.F. and the Hardwood Agents' and Brokers' Association Ltd. It has not been negotiated directly between the importers and the various shippers' organisations, this being impossible owing to the number of countries involved. Shippers are therefore not bound to adopt this contract form, but normally their agents will agree with their principals that this form should be used, or at any rate that this form should be the basis for the contract, being amended as necessary to suit the circumstances of the transaction.

(*b*) SELLERS' RESPONSIBILITIES.

This being a c.i.f. contract, the sellers' responsibilities are broadly the same as in the Albion contract (see page 151).

(i) To ship goods of the description contained in the contract. The port of shipment need not be named in the contract unless it is a specific condition in the offer and acceptance.

(ii) To arrange freight to carry and deliver the goods to the destination named in the contract (in the case of prompt shipment, this must be done within 45 days of the date of the contract).

(iii) To arrange insurance of the goods during their passage, such insurance to be available for the benefit of buyers.

(iv) To send the buyer the following documents :—

" On board " bills of lading.
Insurance policy or certificate.
Invoice made out for c.i.f. price, } In triplicate.
Specification of goods, } In triplicate.
Certificate of origin where necessary.

(*c*) BUYERS' RESPONSIBILITIES.

To pay for the goods on first presentation of documents.

(*d*) Description and Price.

As usual, the goods must be of the description contained in the contract. There are no clauses governing the grading, quality, measurement, shipping condition or price basis of the goods. All these items must therefore be included in the description and specification entered on the face of the contract. Much will depend, of course, upon the stated grade or quality of the goods offered, but there are no warranties that the goods must be of " seller's usual " grading, or even that they shall be properly seasoned for shipment to the destination named. It is important for the buyer to ensure that he is adequately covered in these items. Unless otherwise agreed, the goods must be shipped under deck.

(*e*) Freight.

In the case of prompt shipment, sellers must arrange freight to lift the goods within 45 days of the date of the contract. This will normally be done on liner services as the quantities carried will generally be smaller in volume than in the case of softwood shipments.

Sellers must give prompt advice of shipments made under the contract. The freight must include *free discharge* at the port of destination. This is important because many types of charter and booking note will be used with this contract, and in some of them the importer/buyer could be faced with heavy discharging costs over and above the c.i.f. cost of the goods.

Sellers must arrange for " On board " bills of lading to be provided (see page 88). There is no doubt that many importers would have liked the wording here to have been " clean on board " to give them the right to reject if the sellers tendered " claused " bills of lading reading " shipper's count said to be," etc. This, however desirable, would be unfair on shippers at the present moment, they being as powerless as the importers to get certain shipowners to issue clean bills of lading. This can only be achieved when conditions favourable to charterers return, with shipowners competing for the freight business available.

The question of part shipments, which occur frequently in the hardwood trade, is important. Under the Sale of Goods Act, unless otherwise agreed, the buyer of goods is neither bound to accept delivery by instalments, nor entitled to demand delivery of an instalment. If it is intended that there should be part shipments, this together with the detail of the part shipments ; amount, grade, size, etc. and date or period of part shipments, should be entered at the foot of the first page of the contract.

(*f*) Insurance.

Insurance is to be covered by sellers for the c.i.f. value plus 10 per cent., and it must be effected with Lloyd's or a first class British company, claims payable in sterling in the United Kingdom. No option is given to sellers for insuring with a foreign company.

War risks over 5s. per cent. are payable by buyers, but no provision is made in the contract for circumstances where it is impossible to arrange War risk coverage at all, *i.e.*, no option is given to buyers to request goods to be shipped uninsured against War risks, in exchange for some security for payment placed with sellers by buyers. An insurance policy *or* certificate may be presented in the shipping documents.

(*g*) MARGINS.

The margins are quite simple. The term " about " being stated to mean " within 10 per cent. in proportion of the specification under and over the quantity specified or 500 cubic feet whichever is the less." The margins are thus on every item of the specification up to a maximum of 500 cubic feet. It is possible therefore to get a specification in which all sizes were correct with the exception of a considerable shortage or overage on one item. This might well amount to *less* than 10 per cent. of the total specification, but well over 10 per cent. of that item of the specification. It would therefore provide the buyer with the right of claim under the contract.

In the case of dimension stock the margin is reduced to 5 per cent. or 250 cubic feet (whichever is the less) and in the case of logs it is 10 per cent. or 20 tons, whichever is the less. If the word " about " is not used, the sellers are obliged to ship the exact contract quantity, no more and no less.

The most important difference from the Uniform and Albion contract forms is that overshipment and undershipment beyond the margin are not provided for. The question of overshipment or undershipment therefore is regulated entirely by the Sale of Goods Act, *permitting the buyer to reject the goods* in the event of overshipment or undershipment beyond the margins permitted. This should be compared with the Uniform and Albion clause which limits the buyer's rights of rejection to the actual amount of overshipment, leaving him the right to claim damages (see page 131).

Thus in this contract where overshipment occurs the buyer may :—

(i) Accept all the goods shipped, and pay the full contract price.
(ii) Accept the contract quantity and reject the amount overshipped.
(iii) Reject the lot.

In the case of undershipment he may :—

(i) Accept the goods shipped and pay the full contract price.
(ii) Reject the lot.

(*h*) PAYMENT.

Payment must be made in cash on first presentation of documents. There is no discount or provision in the contract form for credit terms. The provision of three or four months bills of exchange has to be negotiated separately between the buyer and the agent, and does not form a part of the contract with the seller. Where the goods are sold subject to a measured and graded outturn (as in the case of West African Logs) payment is made against a *pro-forma* invoice subject to adjustment afterwards.

(*j*) Exceptions and Conditions Subsequent.

The exceptions clause is couched in very wide terms, as follows :—

" Sellers . . . shall not be liable for damage for delay in delivery or non-delivery if arising from any cause or causes whatsoever beyond their control." Furthermore although goods for prompt shipment must be shipped within 45 days of the date of the contract, this is subject to freight space being available.

This should be compared with the Uniform and Albion exceptions clause (see page 146) which limits the circumstances relieving sellers of their obligations, to certain detailed events.

In the case of delay beyond the date of shipment stated in the contract, the buyers have a right of cancellation, provided they give prompt notice to the sellers before the goods are loaded.

A special clause deals with the provision of export and import licences, which must be applied for by the sellers and buyers respectively. The contract may be cancelled by either sellers or buyers if requisite licences are not obtained or are subsequently cancelled.

(*k*) Property.

The usual property clause states that property passes to buyers, except for retention of seller's lien for unpaid purchase price, when goods are placed on board. It differs, however, from the Uniform and Albion contracts in that it is qualified by a non-compliance clause. This states that if the buyers do not comply with the terms of the payment clause, the sellers have the right of immediate resale for buyer's account.

Normally, an unpaid seller, when exercising a lien on goods, has no direct power of resale. He may only hold the goods until a court order is issued authorising the goods to be sold. The effect of the non-compliance clause permits the unpaid seller to resell the goods without reference to the court.

(*l*) Claims.

Claims must be made and formulated in writing within 21 days of final discharge of the goods, except in the case of measurement claims where the period is extended to 30 days. The latter period may be extended if there are delays beyond the control of the buyers, provided they give due notice to the sellers of the delay within the 30 day period.

This again is rather more stringent than in the case of the Uniform and Albion contracts, which specify that " reasonable particulars " of a claim shall be made within 14 days, but no limit of time is placed upon the submission of the formulated claim. In fact claims for measurement may be made at any time, even if the warning notice of " reasonable particulars " has not been made (see page 137).

Pending the settlement of a claim, the goods must be retained intact and " bulk shall not be broken." The question of dealing with items on which there is no claim, is not clearly covered. From this it would appear safer to retain the entire parcel intact until the claim is settled, to avoid any misunderstanding or possibility of the claim being upset. If the goods are moved from the area of the port through which they were imported, they cannot be rejected, although they may be the subject of a substantial claim. In any case the basis of the claim would be as if they were still at the port. In other words, the buyer cannot claim from the seller any charges, etc., incurred in moving the goods from the port to the inland yard.

(*m*) ARBITRATION.

The arbitration clause follows the old T.T.F. arbitration clause of the 1933 Uniform and 1938 Albion contracts, with one important exception. In this arbitration clause the buyers must " accept custody of the goods if and as shipped and make due payment but such acceptance and payment shall be without prejudice." This differs from the Uniform and Albion clause which included the phrase " buyers shall not reject the goods herein specified," a phrase which still left the buyers able to refuse payment if the goods delivered were materially different from those specified in the contract. This point is discussed more fully on page 164. In this contract, therefore, the buyer must pay for the goods shipped, although he has the right afterwards to claim complete rejection if the goods are not in accordance with the contract. No difference in procedure for shipped or unshipped goods is contemplated. In the event of either party not appointing an arbitrator within 7 days of request by the agents, the arbitrator shall be appointed by the Chairman or Deputy Chairman of the Hardwood Importers' Section of the T.T.F., or the Hardwood Agents' and Brokers' Association.

The remainder of the clause states that the arbitration shall be in accordance with the Arbitration Act, 1950.

(*n*) LICENCES.

The clause concerning export and import licences is the same as in the Uniform and Albion contracts (see page 147).

2. Pacific Coast C.I.F. Contract Form.

(*a*) GENERAL.

This is a c.i.f. contract form for the shipment of softwoods from the Pacific coast of Canada or the U.S.A. to the U.K.

It has been negotiated and agreed between the Softwood Importers' Section of the T.T.F. and the softwood agents in the T.T.F.

Although not formally ratified by the shippers' associations, its terms have been agreed by them unofficially and it has become the standard contract form used by them in sales to the U.K.

(*b*) SELLER'S RESPONSIBILITIES.

Here again the seller's responsibilities are broadly the same as in the Albion contract.

(i) To ship goods of the description contained in the contract.

(ii) To arrange freight to carry and deliver the goods to the destination named in the contract.

(iii) To arrange insurance of the goods, such insurance to be available for the benefit of the buyer.

(iv) To send the buyer the following documents :—

Bills of lading.
Policy of insurance (not a certificate in this case),
Invoice and specification,
Certificate of inspection for quality, issued by the Pacific Lumber Inspection Bureau,
Certificate of origin (for Canadian goods).

(*c*) BUYER'S RESPONSIBILITIES.

To pay for the goods in exchange for correct shipping documents.

(*d*) DESCRIPTION AND PRICE.

The goods must be " according to the current grading list " of the Pacific Lumber Inspection Bureau. These grading lists or rules are extremely comprehensive and are discussed in greater detail on page 255. Unless otherwise agreed, a certificate from the Pacific Lumber Inspection Bureau must be included amongst the shipping documents presented for payment.

The price basis is set out in a similar manner to the Albion contract.

(*e*) FREIGHT.

The goods are to be shipped " in the usual and customary manner." The sellers advising the buyers of the approximate loading date when they have secured shiproom.

If the vessel is delayed more than four weeks beyond the latest date for loading, the sellers have the option of substituting another vessel for loading within six weeks, or of cancelling the contract. In the latter event the buyers have the option of taking the goods on f.o.b. terms, provided they give notice to the sellers within 14 days of receiving notice of seller's cancellation.

This varies from the Albion contract, where in the case of a chartered vessel not being ready to load within six weeks of the date for shipment, the *buyers* are given the option of cancelling the contract.

It is likely that in the near future this contract form will be amended to follow the Albion.

Sellers may advance freight for " reasonable disbursements," but no limit is set. Payment of freight advance by buyers is by acceptance of a bill at 30 days sight against the master's receipt on the bill of lading.

A special clause provides that goods stowed in a covered shelter deck shall be considered as shipped under deck, even though such space may not be included in the vessel's registered tonnage, provided the insurance policy specifically accepts this as under deck and provided the buyers do not specifically exclude this method of stowage at the time the contract is signed.

The buyer is adequately covered without further action, since the T.T.F. insurance clauses specifically provide for this matter in clause 5 (*b*) with the words " cargo stowed in poop, forecastle, deck house, shelter deck, or other enclosed space, shall be deemed to be cargo under deck " (see page 103).

(*f*) Insurance.

Marine insurance is to be covered for the c.i.f. price plus 10 per cent. on Lloyd's (or equal) policy including T.T.F. clauses. War and strike risks are to be covered by sellers but any premium in excess of that ruling at the date of the contract has to be paid by buyers.

(*g*) Margins.

These follow the Uniform and Albion contract as far as margins on each item are concerned, *i.e.*, generally 10 per cent. but not exceeding 20 standards on any one item. However, there is no stipulation that the *total* contract quantity shall not be altered (as in Uniform) so the effect is that the 10 per cent. margin if applied to every item in the same sense will result in an increase or decrease of total contract quantity by 10 per cent. Undershipment and overshipment are covered in the same way as in the Uniform.

(*h*) Payment.

Freight is deducted from the invoice and paid in accordance with the charter or bill of lading terms (freight advance, if any, having been paid by 30 day sight bill).

The balance of the invoice price is to be paid in cash less 2½ per cent. discount within three days of presentation of documents, or by " approved acceptance " payable in London at 120 days from *sight* of bill of lading. Note the difference here from the Uniform and Albion contract payment terms (see page 125) where the date from which the bill of exchange runs is taken as the date of the bill of lading, not the *date of sight* of the bill of lading. This is an important point for buyers, particularly where a long voyage is concerned, since the bill of lading may not be *sighted* until 10 or 14 days after the bill of lading is *dated.*

(*j*) EXCEPTIONS.

The sellers are relieved of liability for non-shipment or delay in the case of the usual *force majeure* occurrences, and also in circumstances due to " inability of vessel or vessels chartered for goods under this contract to proceed via the Panama Canal. . . ."

The war clause defines this as a " war between any of the Great European powers *or* in which the U.S.A., Canada or Japan are involved." In the case of war, sellers have the option of cancelling the contract, but buyers may take the goods on f.o.b. terms subject to giving notice to sellers within 14 days.

Sellers also have the option of cancelling the contract (leaving buyers with an option to take on f.o.b. terms), if the vessel named to buyers is delayed more than four weeks after latest loading date in contract (see para. (*e*) above).

(*k*) PROPERTY.

There is the usual property clause, property passing to buyers when the goods are put on board.

(*l*) CLAIMS.

This follows in substance the Uniform and Albion clause (see page 137) with minor differences of wording. The " reasonable particulars " of claim must be notified within 21 days of vessel's final discharge.

(*m*) ARBITRATION.

The arbitration clause closely follows the 1933 Uniform and 1938 Albion arbitration clauses. In this contract the words " . . . buyers shall not reject the goods herein specified but shall accept and pay for them in terms of contract against shipping documents . . ." has been retained. (To be more accurate it should be stated that it has not yet been taken out.) This should be compared with the Unicif arbitration clause (see page 161) and the rejection clause in the Uniform and Albion contracts (see page 139). Where goods are shipped that are materially different from those contracted for, the buyer *in this contract* may still reject them, and not make payment, as not being the goods " herein specified."

In the case of either party failing to appoint an arbitrator, or where arbitrators cannot agree on the appointment of an umpire, these appointments are made by the President or Vice-President of the T.T.F.

An addition to the usual form of arbitration clause is the following wording which is self explanatory :—" It is mutually agreed that either party may apply either to the High Court of Justice in England or to the appropriate courts of Scotland or Ireland or Canada or in the case of the United States the District Court in and for the district in which a party carries on business or resides that a Judgement of the Court shall be entered on the Award."

3. Russian Contract Forms (C.I.F.).

(*a*) General.

There are two contract forms, a " White Sea and Kara Sea " form and a " Baltic " form, for purchases from Russia. These have been negotiated between the Timber Trade Federation and V.O. Exportles, Moscow. The shipment of timber from the White Sea and the Kara Sea presents problems additional to those encountered in shipment from the Baltic. The period of open water is much shorter and sea navigation more difficult. In the case of the Kara Sea, an expedition is sent out to exploit the forest area and load the goods produced that season before the ice sets in.

The difficulties encountered in these operations is reflected in the various clauses of these contracts which differ in several places from the Uniform and Albion contracts.

(*b*) Sellers' Responsibilities.

(i) To ship goods of the description contained in the contract.
(ii) To arrange freight to carry and deliver the goods to the destination named in the contract.
(iii) To arrange insurance of the goods, for the benefit of the buyer.
(iv) To forward the usual shipping documents to the buyer.

(*c*) Buyers' Responsibilities.

(i) To forward loading orders and other instructions regarding which bills of lading may be shut out, within specified times.
(ii) To pay for the goods in exchange for correct shipping documents.

(*d*) Description and Price.

The prices are stated to be c.i.f. the port of destination named in the contract (always afloat), free of all discharging expenses to *sellers*. They are for lengths 9 ft. and up with ends 5 ft. to 8 ft. at two-thirds price. (Up to 1939 the lengths of goods under Archangel bracking were 12 ft. and up with ends 5 ft. to 11 ft.) If the quantity of ends shipped exceeds 4 per cent. of the total quantity, the excess amounts are taken at two-thirds f.o.b. price plus full freight.

The goods are to bear shippers' usual marks, and following the usual Albion and Uniform clauses are to be of sellers' usual bracking and properly seasoned for shipment to country of destination.

(*e*) FREIGHT.

Shiproom must be secured in "due time," see page 152, sellers' not being liable for delays caused by circumstances beyond their control.

The name of the loading port is followed by the period during which shipment must be made, a further 21 days being granted if necessary for "suitable tonnage." Date of shipment is defined as the date of the bill of lading (irrespective presumably of date on which goods were loaded or vessel sailed).

The charter is to be on the Russwood form, and all discharging expenses are for account of buyers. Freight advance is limited to one-third as in Albion.

The sellers have the option of chartering a substitute vessel, if original vessel is lost before loading but after being named to buyers, to load within the same period. They have an alternative option of cancelling that part of the contract that was to be lifted by the lost vessel, leaving the buyers with an option to take the goods on f.o.b. terms (frankly a risky and complicated proposition when considering the White Sea).

The loading clauses are more extensive than in the Uniform and Albion contracts. Buyers' full loading orders are to be in agents' hands not later than a date named in the contract (The Albion contract states "10 days before date of shipment"). Where the goods are to be shipped in more than one cargo or parcel, buyers have to furnish agents with written details of quantities and destinations not later than a date named in the contract. This is for the allocation of freight space, and if buyers do not provide the written loading instructions by the dates named, the sellers may ship the goods as convenient to themselves to any of the ports of destination named in the contract—buyers being obliged by the contract to take delivery if so shipped. These are therefore important dates which the buyer will normally be certain to diarise at the time the contract is signed, to ensure that the loading instructions are forwarded within time.

An addition to the standard Albion and Uniform clauses is an obligation on buyers to give sellers' agents notice of which bills of lading of deck load may be shut out if necessary, this notice to cover at least 10 per cent. of the buyers' cargo.

The provisions regarding the number of bills of lading under which buyers may require the goods to be shipped follows closely the Albion and Uniform contracts but with the following differences :—

(*a*) It is subject to the qualification ". . . providing loading orders are reasonable. . . ."

(*b*) Goods from one mill only to be ordered on the same bill of lading.

(*c*) Goods ordered on one bill of lading are to be shipped by one vessel.

In the case of Kara Sea Contract there is a further limitation in that the total number of bills of lading are not to exceed three per 100 standards (as against 5 per 100 standards in the Uniform, Albion and Russian Baltic contracts) before additional charges are made for dividing into smaller quantities. Furthermore, items of under 10 standards must not be subdivided on different bills of lading (in the Uniform, Albion and Russian Baltic contracts items of under 10 standards may be split up on two bills of lading without extra charges).

The dead freight and demurrage clause follows the 1938 Albion clause—sellers agreeing to pay both dead freight and demurrage admitted or proved to have been caused by them at loading port. The Russwood charter has no commutation of demurrage clause as has the Nubaltwood charter.

(*f*) INSURANCE.

Marine Insurance of cargo and freight advance is to be covered by sellers for the f.o.b. value plus 10 per cent., with a first class company. In the case of a foreign company, this must be approved by buyers. (This is a stipulation that was in the 1938 Albion contract.) The policy must include the T.T.F. insurance clauses, and the Institute War risks, and must be in sterling with losses payable in London.

Any premium for War and Strike risk insurance over 5s. per cent. at date of shipment is to be paid by buyers. If War and Strike risk insurance cannot be covered either party may cancel the contract.

Either the original policy *or* a cover note may be submitted with the shipping documents for payment.

(*g*) MARGINS.

Generally the margins are the same as for the Albion contract (see page 129) except that the margin on total quantity is 10 per cent. with no maximum. Where more than one shipment is made under the contract, the margin will only apply to the quantity shipped by the last vessel for each period of shipment. Furthermore, if more than one port of destination is named in the contract, the margin shall only apply to the last shipment to each port for each period of shipment.

Additional to the Albion clauses, are clauses which absolve the seller from liability if there is any variation between the loading capacity stated in the charter, and the actual intake of the vessel *provided* the 10 per cent. contract margin is not exceeded. Furthermore the sellers' options to shut goods out, or load additional goods (provided these are goods suitable for deck load and not high quality goods normally shipped under deck) are clearly stated—again subject to the margin on the contract quantity of 10 per cent. The clauses dealing with margins are set out more fully than in the Albion, principally on account of difficulties in the past, but virtually the effect is the same as the Albion. Some of the phrases on the Russian contracts are no more than a declaration of the law, others repeat and substantiate earlier clauses. Although it makes the contract form much longer, it does remove any possible element of doubt or ambiguity and is therefore useful.

(*h*) Payment.

Payment of freight is to be made in accordance with charter-party or bill of lading (on Russwood form) and the contract includes a schedule of the percentages of freight to be paid at various stages of discharge. This is actually a copy of the same terms in the Nubaltwood charter (see page 83).

The balance of the invoice is to be paid in cash less 2½ per cent. with the option of a four month bill.

(*j*) Exceptions.

Generally these are much the same as in the Albion and Uniform contracts, with the addition of " delay to vessel chartered." However, although the buyer is given the option of taking the goods on f.o.b. terms, there is no mention of any " drawing date of approx. payment " as there is in the Albion. There is no provision made for overlying goods.

Strikes and lockouts are not included in the exceptions as, in the words of one of the members of the Russian Wood Agency in their explanatory notes on this contract form " . . . these events are not envisaged in the U.S.S.R."

In the event of War, etc. or prohibition of export or import, preventing shipment, the contract (or unfulfilled part of it) is cancelled. If War risk insurance cannot be covered, either party may cancel the contract.

If for *any* reason beyond the sellers' control, there is an increase in sea freight of 20 per cent. above the basic rate of freight which is published in their schedule of prices, the sellers have the option of cancelling the contract unless the buyers agree to pay any excess freight above the 20 per cent. increase on the basic rate. The agreement by buyers to pay this increase must be made to the agents *in writing within three days* from receiving notice from sellers.

(*k*) Property.

Property passes when goods are put on board, as in Uniform and Albion contracts.

(*l*) Claims.

This also follows the general framework of the Uniform and Albion claims clauses, with " reasonable particulars " of claim being made to agents within 14 days but there is an important difference. Under the Russian contracts the goods must be produced ready for inspection within 21 days of the date of the vessel's final discharge. If there is a delay due to circumstances beyond the control of the buyer, this period may be extended to the extent of the delay, upon notice being given to sellers' agents. (Note that in the Uniform and Albion contracts no period is stated.)

This clause has caused difficulty in the past, and on occasions the sellers' ideas of what comprised " ready for inspection " have been very difficult to carry out, the sellers repudiating a claim on the grounds that the goods were not properly " ready for inspection."

For the buyers' protection it is certainly best to anticipate these difficulties and whilst scrupulously observing the periods for notification of reasonable particulars, etc., arrange that in presenting the goods for inspection all sizes are piled separately and each bill of lading kept separate. Although this may take much space and effort, it is worthwhile to assist in the satisfactory settlement of a dispute.

After the buyers have given notice to the agents that the goods are ready for inspection, the sellers must take steps within 14 days to arrive at an amicable settlement. If after this period no settlement has been reached, either party may go to arbitration.

(*m*) ARBITRATION.

The arbitration clause in these Russian contracts presents a serious problem. The 1935 Russian contract forms provided for an arbitration clause on the lines of the 1933 Uniform contract, covering all aspects of the contract and with arbitration being held according to English law and the English Arbitration Act.

In the years from 1936 to 1939 however, the Russians were able to impose more advantageous terms and conditions for themselves, on the U.K. importers (very largely through lack of unity amonst the latter). One of these conditions was an amendment to the arbitration clause, providing for arbitration in Moscow by the U.S.S.R. Chamber of Commerce Foreign Trade Arbitration Commission for *any* dispute *except* disputes for quality, condition, measurement or manufacture of goods, or correctness of documents. In other words disputes on " shipped " goods to be settled by the normal English arbitration, disputes on " unshipped goods " to be settled in Moscow.

The current contract form leaves the arbitration clause to be negotiated by each importer separately, since the Timber Trade Federation were unwilling to perpetuate the Moscow arbitration clause officially. An importer conceding the Moscow arbitration clause must obviously take account of the possible additional risks involved when considering all aspects of the transaction.

4. T.T.F. C.I.F. Reselling Contract, 1952.

(*a*) GENERAL.

This is a c.i.f. contract for sales where goods purchased f.o.b. or c.i.f. by an importer are resold to another importer or merchant on c.i.f. terms. It has been adopted by the National Softwood Importers' Section of the T.T.F. and the Merchants' Section of the T.T.F.

The essential feature in a c.i.f. reselling contract form is that the seller's obligations in his own f.o.b. or c.i.f. purchase contract must be covered, and that all exceptions and rights of cancellation granted to the original seller are incorporated in the contract this time for the benefit of the re-seller. The contract form is designed to cover c.i.f. resale of purchases originally made not only on the Uniform and Albion forms, but on any softwood contract, including the European and North American contract forms.

(*b*) SELLER'S RESPONSIBILITIES.

These are the same as a normal c.i.f. contract, that is to say, to supply goods of the description contained in the contract, delivered to the destination named in the contract and fully insured on the basis of Lloyd's or Institute standard form of policy with current T.T.F. clauses.

(*c*) BUYER'S RESPONSIBILITIES.

These again are primarily limited to paying for the goods against presentation of the correct shipping documents.

(*d*) DESCRIPTION AND PRICE.

The description contained in the contract is particularly important, since the quality and specification of the goods shipped will be quite beyond the immediate control of the seller. He must beware of committing himself in his c.i.f. resale contract, to a description which is more exacting than the description contained in his original contract with the shipper. If the goods are not up to standard or specification and he has a claim made against him by the c.i.f. resale buyer, he must be in a position to sustain a claim successfully against the shipper.

The goods are to be of " shipper's usual bracking," the same as the equivalent Uniform and Albion clause.

The prices are c.i.f., and all discharging expenses (if any) or demurrage contributions (under the Nubaltwood charter) are for buyer's account.

The goods are described as " properly seasoned for shipment," so if unseasoned goods are being sold, this provision must be deleted and the goods clearly described as unseasoned on the face of the contract.

(*e*) FREIGHT.

The rate of discharge and other conditions are to be in accordance with charter-party, freight booking note and/or bills of lading under the terms of which the goods are shipped " *which buyers hereby agree to adopt.*" This places a most important obligation on buyers, since under the contract, sellers have no obligation to provide a copy of the charter-party or freight booking note. It means that the buyers must attempt to obtain a copy of the charter-party or freight booking note to make certain whether or not there are any unusual provisions or obligations falling on holders of bills of lading (which the buyers become after accepting and paying for the shipping documents).

If, for instance, goods are freighted under Nubaltwood terms, they must ensure that they make claims for shortages on under deck bills of lading (in pieces) against shipowners *within six days* of final discharge (see page 79). The responsibility for this notification and claim rests entirely on the buyers, as bills of lading holders ; it does not concern the sellers, who by then have parted with the goods.

The right of the vessel to carry part of the goods on deck is clearly stated. This right of course has already been conceded by sellers in the charter.

(*f*) INSURANCE.

Insurance is to include the current T.T.F. clauses, and a policy or certificate of insurance may be included in the shipping documents.

In the case of War risk insurance, a premium is quoted in the contract, any increase or decrease being for buyer's account.

(*g*) MARGINS.

These are wider to permit the possibility of maximum deviation by shippers and/or shipowners in loading. The general margin is 20 per cent. more or less on any and every item. Overshipment and undershipment are covered as in the Uniform and Albion contracts, except that in the event of the buyers taking only the contract quantity in an overshipment, they must give the sellers a delivery order for the balance overshipped, at the earliest point of segregation. This does not necessarily have to be on the quay, if that is not a convenient point of segregation.

(*h*) PAYMENT.

Payment is to be made in exchange for the usual shipping documents (bills of lading, invoice, policy or certificate of insurance).

(*j*) EXCEPTIONS.

These are extensive and in general favour the seller. In the first place, if loading has not commenced within six weeks of the stated loading date, *buyers* have the right of cancellation.

If the vessel fixed for the contract is lost before commencing to load, or if the charter-party is cancelled, or should it be impossible to find suitable or convenient freight, *sellers* have the option of substituting another vessel or cancelling the contract. Incidentally at no place in the contract is the vessel named, nor are the sellers required to notify to buyers the name of the vessel when fixed.

The usual Uniform and Albion exceptions and *force majeure* clauses are included, giving *sellers* the option of cancelling provided they give notice in writing within six weeks of the latest date of shipment named in the contract. In addition there are the following exceptions giving *sellers* the right to cancel ". . . overestimation of capacity of vessel(s), or of shippers not having carried out seller's loading instructions." Lastly, as mentioned in insurance above, *sellers* have the option of cancelling if it is found impossible to arrange war risk insurance.

(*k*) PROPERTY.

There is no specific clause stating where the property passes to the buyer. In such a case this would normally be at the time of shipment, since this is the first moment that the goods are clearly ascertained (this still being a contract for the sale of future goods by description). However, a non-compliance clause gives the sellers the right of resale if the buyers fail to comply with any of the terms of the contract. This refers principally to the payment clause, so it may be taken that the property passes when the bills of lading are transferred.

(*l*) CLAIMS AND REJECTION.

The claims and rejection clauses follow closely the Uniform and Albion clauses except the period for *notification of reasonable particulars is reduced to ten days*. This must be done to ensure that the sellers can in their turn submit reasonable particulars of their claim against the original shippers within the 14 days required by the Uniform and Albion contracts (see page 137).

(*m*) ARBITRATION.

The standard arbitration clause (based on the Uniform 1933 contract) applies, with the addition of the following clause ". . . buyers shall not be entitled to any allowance or claim unless payment has been made in accordance with the contract terms."

5. T.T.F. Ex-Ship Re-Selling Contract.

(*a*) GENERAL.

This is a contract form for sales where goods purchased f.o.b. or c.i.f. by an importer, are resold ex-ship to other importers or merchants. It has been adopted by the National Softwood Importers' Section of the T.T.F. and the Merchants' Section of the T.T.F.

As in the c.i.f. re-selling contract, the seller is covered in this contract for all obligations, risks and rights of cancellation, etc., undertaken and accepted by him in his original purchase contract.

(*b*) SELLER'S RESPONSIBILITIES.

These are different from the responsibilities undertaken by the seller in any form of c.i.f. contract. They are clearly defined in a special clause headed " Ex-Ship definition."

(i) To deliver the goods described in the contract to the buyer from a ship which has arrived at the port of delivery named in the contract, at the ship's rail (if the goods are discharged by hand), or within reach of the ship's tackle or shore crane (if so discharged).

(ii) To pay the sea freight, and any demurrage or dead freight charges so that the shipowner's lien on the goods is released.

(iii) To furnish the buyer with a delivery order or released bill of lading effectual to give delivery of the contract goods to the buyers.

(*c*) BUYER'S RESPONSIBILITIES.

These are as follows :—

(i) To provide craft or lighters for overside delivery, and to pay any landing charges, etc., incurred through absence of craft or lighters.

(ii) To pay any charges incurred by sellers under the Nubaltwood charter clauses 15 and 16 (see page 81) relating to work done by the ship *beyond* the limit of the ship's rail.

(iii) To pay for the goods in the terms set out in the contract.

(*d*) DESCRIPTION AND PRICE.

As in the c.i.f. re-selling contract, the description of the goods will follow closely the description in the original purchase contract.

Here again the goods are to be of " shipper's usual bracking," etc. The prices are ex-ship, so that all charges up to the ship's rail, including freight, demurrage or dead freight claims, demurrage contribution under the Nubaltwood charter, port charges (other than quay charges), and import duty (if any) are payable by sellers. Goods sold ex-ship have in fact been imported, so import duty is paid by sellers. Sometimes such a price basis is termed " ex-ship duty paid."

Where unseasoned goods are being sold, these must be described as such on the face of the contract, and the provision that the goods are " properly seasoned," must be deleted.

(*e*) FREIGHT.

The rate of discharge and other conditions are to be in accordance with the charter-party, freight booking note or bills of lading. There is no obligation on sellers to supply a copy of the charter or booking note. The buyers, therefore, must take it upon themselves to learn the terms of the charter. As in the c.i.f. re-selling contract, where goods have been freighted on Nubaltwood terms, they must make claims for shortages on under deck bills of lading *within six days* of final discharge.

Sellers are given the option of finding a substitute vessel or of cancelling the contract if any vessel or vessels fixed for the contract are lost before commencing to load, or if the charter-party is cancelled or if convenient freight cannot be found.

A clause stipulates that the vessel is to have the privilege of taking part of the cargo on deck, and buyers are obliged to accept *all* or *part* of the contract goods carried on deck. When a sale is negotiated after loading orders have been issued, it is important that the sellers ensure that the terms of the sale as to whether the goods are to be on deck or under deck, are in accordance with the loading orders.

(*f*) INSURANCE.

The insurance of the goods does not concern the buyer, except in relation to War risk insurance. The prices are stated to be based on a declared rate of War risk insurance, any increase or decrease for buyer's account. If it is not possible to cover against war risks, sellers have the option of cancelling the contract.

The marine insurance policy of the goods lapses as the goods leave the ship.

The T.T.F. " warehouse to warehouse " clause which covers the goods during the period of discharge, and during transit to their ultimate destination, is not therefore available for the benefit of the buyers. It is extremely important, therefore, that the ex-ship buyer should obtain full protection against these risks (which go beyond the normal risks of fire against which he ensures his stock) and normally this is done by means of a separate open cover.

(*g*) MARGINS.

These are the same as in the c.i.f. re-selling contract, a general margin of 20 per cent. and the usual provisions for undershipment and overshipment. In the latter case the buyers are to take delivery of the total quantity, but if accepting only the contract quantity they are to give the sellers a delivery order for the balance overshipped, at the earliest point of segregation.

(*h*) PAYMENT.

The payment clause is left blank, the terms to be negotiated at the time of the sale and then entered on the contract.

(*j*) EXCEPTIONS.

These are similar to the c.i.f. re-selling contract exceptions, namely an extension of the Uniform and Albion exceptions and *force majeure* clauses.

(*k*) PROPERTY.

The property in the goods passes on discharge, but is qualified by a non-compliance clause giving sellers the right of resale in the event of the buyers not complying with any of the terms of the contract.

(*l*) Claims and Rejection.

These clauses also follow the claims and rejection clauses of the Uniform and Albion contracts, with the exception that the period for *notification of reasonable particulars is reduced to ten days.*

(*m*) Arbitration.

The contract carries the same arbitration clause as the c.i.f. reselling contract (see page 172).

6. " Britfibre " Fibre Building Board C.I.F. Contract.

(*a*) General.

This c.i.f. contract form for purchases of all classes of fibre building board, has been negotiated between the Wallboard Importers', Distributors' and Merchants' Association of the U.K. on the one hand, and the Scanboard organisation representing manufacturers and shippers of fibre building boards in Norway, Sweden and Finland. Whilst these two organisations represent the interests of the principals concerned, the contract form has also been agreed in consultations with the Fibre Building Board Agents' Association, representing the agents of overseas shippers, and the Insulation, Building and Hardboard Association—representing the original concessionaires for the first boards imported into the U.K. The concessionaire members of I.B.H.A., besides importing board on their own account, make sales on c.i.f. terms to importer members of W.I.D.M.A. Although the Scanboard organisation in fact represents only about 50 per cent. of the European manufacturers and shippers of fibre building board, the agent members of F.B.B.A.A. and concessionaire members of I.B.H.A. themselves are representatives or agents for every board imported into the U.K.—from whatever source. This contract form, therefore, is used for imports from all countries.

(*b*) Sellers' Responsibilities.

(1) To ship goods of the description contained in the contract.
(2) To arrange freight to deliver the goods at the port named in the contract.
(3) To arrange the marine insurance of the goods.
(4) To forward a complete set of shipping documents to the buyer.

(*c*) Buyers' Responsibilities.

To pay, in nett cash, on the presentation of correct shipping documents.

(*d*) Description and Price.

The prices are stated to be c.i.f. the port of destination named in the contract. The goods are to be of " . . . Sellers' usual quality and manufacture for export to the country of destination." Although normally the manufacturers of fibre building boards are very jealous of their reputation for quality, a number of mills do produce second quality and inferior boards for home consumption, in addition to their export quality.

If a second quality board is being purchased, it must be clearly described as such on the face of the contract.

(*e*) SIZES AND SPECIFICATION.

One stage of the manufacture of hardboard involves the pressing of the board in a multi-daylight hot platten press, with a platten size varying from 4′×12′ up to 4′×18′. This size, known as the " full press size " limits the specification of sizes that can be produced by the factory. For a platten of size 4′×18′, for every sheet produced 4′×10′, there will be one 4′×8′. Similarly for every sheet 4′×12′ there will be a sheet 4′×6′. It is the object of the shippers to sell a specification of complementary sizes that will leave no waste, and this requirement is stated in the contract in clause 2. Much depends upon the circumstances surrounding the negotiation of the sale. The supply of any specification—with the complete elimination of unwanted sizes, etc.—can always be negotiated if price adjustments are made. Where such a specification is detailed on the face of the contract it over-rides clause 2.

Many contracts, however, are made to cover a bulk quantity to be shipped in instalments over a period of time—which may be as long as a year. It is in these cases, where no specification is detailed on the face of the contract, that the buyer is obliged to take complementary sizes. The buyer who does not wish to commit himself to taking complementary sizes, should ensure that the actual specification is detailed on the face of the contract, or that clause 2 is over-ridden by wording to the effect that it is understood that sizes need not be complementary sizes.

(*f*) MARKING AND PACKING.

Under clause 4, the goods are to be " properly packed for export to the country of destination . . .," etc. There is no standard code of packing for fibre building board and so a dispute turning on the words " properly packed " can only be decided by close consideration of the individual circumstances of the dispute, the amount of damage sustained, etc. The question of packing is an expensive one for shippers, but an important factor in their marketing policy. A well packed board is a more attractive purchase for an importer than a board of equal quality but which is packed in an inferior manner. Nevertheless, to claim that one manufacturer's board was not " properly packed," because it was not so well or so attractively packed as the board to another manufacturer, would not be possible under this clause. It would be necessary to show that the goods sustained damage through not being properly packed.

The marking of crates and packages is detailed in clause 5.

(*g*) FREIGHT.

Freight is to be arranged by sellers, and this is usually done on liner terms.

The goods must be shipped at the port named in the contract, within the stated period for shipment. This period may be extended by up to six weeks if manufacture or shipment is delayed " by any cause beyond sellers' control . . ." (clause 9).

All goods must be stowed under deck. Shipping documents must include " original on board bills of lading." If shipping documents are not presented before the arrival of the goods, any charges incurred through this delay are payable by sellers.

(*h*) INSURANCE.

Clause 6 sets out the requirements for marine insurance which is to be covered by sellers for the c.i.f. value plus 10 per cent., with a first class company registered in either sellers' or buyers' country.

The choice of insurance company lies with the sellers but from the moment the goods are shipped all questions relating to the insurance of the goods are of more importance to the buyers than the sellers. This particularly applies in the case of the insurance company insuring the goods. A foreign shipper, tempted by a low insurance premium, might insure goods under a c.i.f. contract, with a less reputable company. In the case of loss during the voyage, the importer would be obliged to pay for the goods against shipping documents, relying then on the policy to safeguard himself. In the event of the insurance company not meeting the claim, the importer would be in a very difficult position. Although he would in all probability have a claim against the shipper for not insuring with a first class company—there would obviously be lengthy and expensive legal proceedings before him.

The 1938 Albion c.i.f. contract, and other timber contracts used to specify that the insurance would be by a " first class company (if foreign to be approved by buyers)."

In practice this was a difficult clause to implement, since in general it meant approval (or otherwise) at the time the shipping documents were tendered. By this time the goods were at risk and on the high seas.

The Britfibre contract has resolved this problem in a very clear and straightforward way that does away with any possible ambiguity. The sellers, if they wish to exercise their option to insure with a foreign company, enter the name of the company on the face of the contract. The buyer, therefore, has an opportunity to check with his own insurance broker, on the standing of the foreign company *before* the contract is signed.

This does not mean that all foreign insurance companies are unreliable. This is far from the case since insurance companies in most countries have a high reputation for integrity. In any case all large foreign insurance companies have their connections with English companies, and many foreign marine insurance companies re-insure their risks with Lloyd's or English companies.

In times of high political tension, of course, there may be the additional risk of a foreign company being prevented from settling a claim for loss, through sudden violent *force majeure*. If the buyers know before the goods are shipped that they will be insured in a foreign country that is likely to be involved in war, they have an opportunity to arrange a re-insurance themselves with an English company.

The policy must include the Institute Cargo "All Risks" and "Extended Cover" clauses, which give a very wide cover but the ambit of the cover is not quite so wide as in the T.T.F. clauses—particularly in regard to warehouse to warehouse cover where the final destination is inland from the port.

War and Strike risk insurance is to be covered by sellers, but any premium in excess of 5s. per cent. is borne by buyers. If the sellers cannot effect War risk insurance for 40s. per cent., the buyers may (i) pay the increased premium or (ii) arrange the war risk insurance themselves (when they must submit proof of the insurance to the sellers representatives before shipment) or (iii) instruct the sellers to ship the goods uninsured.

If for any reason the insurance cannot be effected, or is cancelled, the buyers have the option of cancelling the contract or instructing sellers to ship the goods uninsured. In this latter case they are carrying the full risk of loss themselves, so not unnaturally the sellers require some security or guarantee before the goods are shipped that the buyers will pay "goods lost or not lost."

Either the policy itself or a certificate (providing it specifies the risks covered) may be submitted with the shipping documents.

(*j*) MARGINS.

No special margins are stated, and no provision is made for over or under shipment, so the question of quantities shipped is governed by the Sale of Goods Act (see page 131).

When the term "About" is used, the sellers may ship a margin of $2\frac{1}{2}$ per cent. in superficial footage more or less on any or every item of the specification.

Thus if the term "about" is *not* used—the sellers are obliged to ship the exact quantity specified—no more and no less. Overshipment and undershipment permitting, in law, rejection of the total quantity shipped (or any of the other alternatives described on page 131).

Normally the term "about" will be used which permits the margin of 2½ per cent., but if this is on any or every item, so for the *total* quantity to be exceeded by 2½ per cent. it would be necessary for *each* item to be exceeded by 2½ per cent. It would not be possible to have one item increased by 5 per cent., with another correct—so that the total say was still within 2½ per cent.

Nevertheless, beyond the 2½ per cent. the same conditions described above apply to overshipment and undershipment. Fibre building boards, of course, are manufactured goods of a homogeneous nature. The control of quantities and sizes produced is a simple matter compared to the production of a specification of sawn woodgoods from logs, and consequently it is not difficult for shippers to keep within these margins.

(*k*) Payment.

Payment is to be made in nett cash in exchange for shipping documents. If the contract is signed by agents or representatives of sellers (the latter referring particularly to I.B.H.A. concessionaires) payment is to be made to the agent or representative and not direct to the shipper. This is nothing more than a statement of the accepted method of payment where the agent is taking the *del credere* risk (see page 122).

(*l*) Exceptions.

In addition to the exceptions detailed in the insurance clause 6 (reviewed in para. (*h*) above) which permits the buyer to cancel the goods if marine insurance cannot be effected, there are the usual exceptions provided for in clause 9.

This clause is divided into five parts. Part (*a*) relieves the sellers of liability for damages due to prevention or delay of shipment beyond sellers' control provided prompt notice is given to buyers.

Part (*b*) virtually automatically extends the delivery time by six weeks for "any . . . cause beyond sellers' control." It is important for the buyer to realise that the period of shipment is extended by this six week period, since the buyer is bound to accept delivery if made in this extended period—always provided, of course, that the sellers have submitted proof of the reason for the delay.

If the sellers cannot deliver the goods within the additional six weeks, the date of shipment may be extended by mutual arrangement or *either party* may cancel. If the buyers decide to cancel they must do this in accordance with part (*d*).

Part (*c*) provides for automatic cancellation if manufacture or shipment is prevented by war, etc. or prohibition of import or export, etc.

Part (*d*) gives the buyers a right of cancellation if shipment is delayed beyond the stipulated contract date (it does *not* include the extra six weeks) for any reason—other than those beyond the sellers' control. Generally it must be assumed that any delay will normally be claimed by sellers to be caused by circumstances beyond their control.

This clause also sets out the procedure to be adopted by buyers if they elect to cancel—the important point being that the sellers must receive notice of the buyers' cancellation before the goods are despatched from their mill. It is essential, therefore, for the buyers to notify the sellers immediately they elect to cancel.

Part (*e*) concerns large contracts for shipment in instalments over a period of time where the specification and port of destination are left open, to be notified by buyers to sellers before each shipment. If such notifications are not received by sellers by six weeks before the date of shipment, the sellers have the option of cancelling (to that extent) or of shipping a specification pro-rata to the specification remaining to be shipped—to the nearest port to the buyer's domicile.

(*m*) PROPERTY.

Property passes on shipment, but sellers are given the right of re-sale if buyers do not make payment as set out.

(*n*) CLAIMS.

Clause 10 deals with claims for quality, condition or packing where " reasonable particulars " of the claim must be made in writing within 21 days of final delivery of the goods into public dock, warehouse, etc.

Although this clause limits the buyers' right of rejection by stating ". . . buyers shall not reject the goods herein specified . . .," this does not prevent the buyers from rejecting goods which are materially different from those described in the contract.

This clause limits the number of packages that may be opened by buyers to 10 per cent. of the total consignment (or 10 packages whichever is the greater).

In the case of shortages or overages, wrong dimensions or wrong descriptions, clause 8 (*c*) states that " . . . Invoice to be finally adjusted on proved contents of packages. . . ." This is declaratory of the law since a buyer is not obliged to pay for goods he has not received.

(*o*) ARBITRATION.

A comprehensive arbitration clause is included, providing for arbitration for all disputes to be held in the United Kingdom.

The arbitrators and umpire are to be engaged in or conversant with the Fibre Building Board trade. In the case of either party failing to appoint arbitrator or umpire within a set period, this is to be arranged by the President of the London Chamber of Commerce.

A panel of arbitrators is maintained, made up of importers, agents and concessionaires.

(*p*) Territory of Consumption.

This clause states that the goods are sold for *bona fide* consumption in the United Kingdom and that the buyers undertake not to re-export the goods without the consent of the sellers.

At first sight this appears a rather harsh limitation on the buyers' rights after property in the goods has passed. From the sellers' point of view, they were anxious not to disturb selling arrangements for their products in other countries. Quite apart from this, the strict control of international currency exchange and export licences often means that a shipper must undertake to sell his goods only in certain markets, and would render himself liable to penalties if his goods are re-exported to markets otherwise prohibited to him.

On the other hand, circumstances could easily arise whereby a dock strike and consequent diversion of shipping, resulted in a U.K. buyer's goods being unloaded at a foreign port. In such a case, the buyer must obtain the consent of the seller to the sale of the goods at the foreign port, rather than accept the additional charges involved in lifting the goods at a later date to complete their journey to the U.K.

CHAPTER X

Arbitration

1. General.

The Arbitration Clause in a contract is the ultimate safeguard for the buyer that if in his opinion the seller has failed to fulfil the contract in all respects, he can demand arbitration and if it is decided that he has good cause for complaint he will be awarded compensation. This applies not only to goods shipped but also to non-shipment; in fact *any* dispute under the contract, if not settled amicably, has to be dealt with under the arbitration procedure.

It should not be overlooked that arbitration is something which, if invoked, must be paid for, by one side or both, and may possibly be a costly business, whereas "amicable settlement" costs the buyer nothing. In such a trade as timber, complaints and claims are inevitable, yet some of the largest firms in the trade in the United Kingdom do not have one arbitration in years. Shipper's agents ask no fee for putting their experience at the service of the parties to effect "amicable settlement," but are entitled to any expenses incurred. There are however cases where there is so fundamental a difference of honest opinion between buyer and seller that arbitration is the best course to adopt.

It is important to both seller and buyer, under the T.T.F. contracts, in view of the ultimate allocation of costs according to the efforts of either party to reach amicable settlement, that they should promptly make a serious effort to settle the dispute and to commit those efforts to writing as evidence. The custom is for the seller's agent to supply him with detailed particulars of the buyer's complaint and also usually an unbiased inspection report on the goods complained of, to enable the seller to estimate the justice of buyer's complaint and claim.

Whilst a seller's agent is not legally responsible either for the carrying out of the contract or the payment of an arbitration award, his reputation is involved and it is extremely seldom that ultimate failure to pay a properly executed award has been recorded. Arbitrators and umpires are at liberty to award more than the sum claimed or less than the sum offered which may, in the case of a claim judged to be unfounded, be nothing at all.

In the eyes of the law an arbitration is an adjudication and the powers and position of an arbitrator or umpire are very similar to those of a judge, in fact he is sometimes referred to as a lay judge.

Arbitrations are governed by the English Arbitration Act, 1950. Under this Act, an arbitrator or umpire acting under a written submission has the following powers, though he may never need to exercise them;—(i) To administer oaths; (ii) To take the affirmative of the parties or their witnesses; (iii) To summon witnesses by subpœna.

Where the matter in dispute is more a matter of legal decision than of commercial practise, the arbitrators, or umpire, may, either on the instruction of the party appointing them, or of their own volition, submit the matter to the Court for the ruling of a judge. This is called " stating a case " for the Court's decision and the award will eventually be made in accordance with that ruling. It is however extremely seldom that an arbitrator " states a case " except at the request of the party appointing him.

2. The Reference Note.

The Albion, Uniform and other timber trade contracts actually incorporate the Submission Note, so no further document is actually necessary to enable arbitrators to be appointed and for them to go ahead with the arbitration. It is however customary for a " Reference Note " to be agreed upon between the parties, setting out briefly the limitations of the matters in dispute.

The terms of reference for the arbitrators in a particular arbitration set out in writing in a " Reference Note " contain the following information :—(*a*) Names of the parties concerned; (*b*) A description of the matters in dispute. (The Arbitrators have no power to deal with any matters that are *not* in the Reference Note.); (*c*) Names of Arbitrators.

The Reference Note usually takes the following form :—

Arbitration Note.

A DISPUTE HAVING ARISEN between..the Buyer, and..the Seller, with regard to the (quality) (condition) of..pieces..about ....loads (or Standards), shipped per s.s.............................. at..to.., under Bill of Lading dated ....against Contract dated London the.................................. IT IS HEREBY AGREED to leave the matter to the arbitration of Mr.......................... of..acting for the Buyers, and Mr.. of..acting for the Sellers, who are hereby empowered to appoint an Umpire, thoroughly conversant with the class of goods from the port of shipment named; the decision of the Arbitrators, or of their Umpire, to be final and binding on both parties in the terms of the above-named contract.

. . . .

In the event of SOLE ARBITRATION, then :—
IT IS HEREBY AGREED to leave the matter to the Sole Arbitration of Mr............... ....of..whose decision shall be final and binding on both parties in the terms of the above named Contract.

3. The Rules of Arbitration.

(*a*) GENERAL.

Arbitration is governed by the Arbitration Act, 1950. The rules and regulations laid down in this Act are modified by the Arbitration clauses in various T.T.F. contracts.

These Arbitration clauses include the following wording :—

"... The said Arbitration shall be subject to the English Arbitration Act of 1950 or any subsisting statutory modifications thereof or substitution therefor. . . ."

The question of Arbitration in Scotland is discussed in para. 5 (page 190).

Assuming that the goods shipped are *prima facie* those contracted for, the first essential, before a dispute is taken to arbitration for settlement, is that the buyers shall have accepted and paid for the goods.

(*b*) Appointment of Arbitrators.

The appointment of Arbitrators and Umpire are the points usually covered in most detail in the arbitration clauses in timber contracts. The Uniform 1933 and Albion 1938 contracts set out the following procedure :—

Albion 1938.

"... Should any dispute and/or claim arise under this contract which it may be found impossible to settle by amicable arrangement, the same shall at once be referred to the decision of a third party to be mutually agreed upon or in default of agreement to two arbitrators, one arbitrator to be appointed by the sellers and one by the buyers, . . ."

This clause is the one most generally used in timber contracts other than the Uniform 1951. The Uniform 1951 contract however differentiates between "shipped" and "unshipped" goods and sets out a different procedure for the appointment of Arbitrators and Umpire.

Uniform 1951.

"Any dispute and/or claim regarding shipped goods, which it may be found impossible to settle amicably, shall be referred to the decision of one arbitrator to be mutually agreed upon or in default of agreement to two arbitrators, one arbitrator to be appointed by Sellers and one by Buyers. When the claim is for quality and/or condition and has not been settled amicably within 10 days after receipt of claim as stated in the first paragraph of Clause 16 either party may at once proceed to arbitration."

It is understood in law that where two arbitrators are appointed they will each act as advocate in arguing the case and obtaining the best settlement they can for the party appointing them. A sole arbitrator, or an umpire, is, on the other hand absolutely impartial. In the event of the arbitrators being unable to agree and referring the matter to the decision of the umpire, they will each represent to him their view of the case. The umpire may thus find a considerable measure of agreement, which he does not need to review in detail, and merely has to settle the outstanding differences. On the other hand the umpire may decide that he should consider the whole matter from the start as if he had originally been appointed sole arbitrator : those are matters which are left to his discretion.

Uniform 1951 *and Albion* 1938, *etc.*

" . . . In the event of either side failing to appoint their arbitrator within seven days after being requested through the agents under this contract so to do, the arbitrator thus required shall be appointed by the President, or failing him, the Vice-President of the T.T.F. of the U.K. on the application of either party . . ."

The agent will have acted as intermediary between the buyer and the seller in attempting to arrive at amicable settlement.

A panel of names of experienced members of the trade is maintained by the T.T.F., from which arbitrators can be appointed when required, but selection is by no means limited to any list and usually each side selects some person in whom they have confidence to understand their view of the dispute.

Uniform 1951.

" The said arbitrators shall be selected from members of the timber trade or from the arbitrators recognised by the Timber Trade Federation of the United Kingdom or by the Swedish Wood Exporters' Association and the Finnish Sawmill Owners' Association."

Uniform 1951.

". . . Any dispute regarding unshipped goods which cannot be settled amicably shall be referred to two arbitrators, one to be appointed by each party and in accordance with the English Arbitration Act 1950 or any subsisting statutory modification thereof or substitution therefor. Such arbitrators and their umpire (if any) need not be members of the timber trade.

All such arbitrations shall be held in the United Kingdom. . . ."

A dispute concerning unshipped goods will rarely be a matter in which the commercial experience of a timber trade arbitrator will be of much avail. It is much more likely to revolve around fine points of law and evidence from the seller's country to support either the force majeure or war clause. For this reason the arbitration clause in the Uniform contract is worded to permit the arbitrators if necessary being legal arbitrators.

In the case of hardwood and plywood contracts, arbitrators and umpires are appointed by the Chairman or Deputy Chairman of the Hardwood and Plywood Sections, respectively, of the T.T.F.

Albion 1938 *and Uniform* 1951, *etc.*

" In the case of a claim not exceeding £100 or on less than 25 standards the dispute shall, if not amicably settled, be referred to one arbitrator and in default of the parties agreeing on his appointment he shall be appointed by the President or failing him by the Vice-President of the Timber Trade Federation of the United Kingdom."

Whilst for small claims there is only one arbitrator, it is far better if these are settled without taking them to Arbitration. In general it is unwise to take extreme measures for minor differences.

(*c*) APPOINTMENT OF UMPIRE.

If the two arbitrators cannot agree on an award in the case, the final result must be decided by the umpire who is selected as below:—

Albion 1938.

"... and such arbitrators shall, previously to entering upon the arbitration, appoint an umpire, or if within seven days after appointment they fail to agree as to the umpire, then the President, or, failing him, the Vice-President of the T.T.F. of the U.K. on the application of either party or his arbitrator, shall appoint an umpire ..."

Uniform 1951.

"... Should the Arbitrators fail to agree, they shall appoint an Umpire. If they cannot agree as to such appointment the Umpire shall be nominated by lotdrawing for two names selected from a list of 10 persons drawn up by the Swedish Wood Exporters' Association, the Finnish Sawmill Owners' Association and the Timber Trade Federation of the United Kingdom, 5 persons to be designated by the Swedish and Finnish Association together and the other 5 by the Timber Trade Federation. Each of the two Arbitrators shall select one name from the list and the lot to decide which of the two shall act as Umpire. Should that Umpire be prevented from acting, the Arbitrator who selected that Umpire to appoint another Umpire chosen from the above-mentioned list. The list in question may be revised on May 1st every year. ..."

The umpire must be appointed strictly as above. Unless it is specifically set out in the Reference Note the arbitrators may *not* delegate their duties in the selection of the umpire. The arbitrators are under no obligation to obtain the approval of the buyers or sellers to their selection of umpire. Although it is not necessary to have the appointment of the umpire in writing, it should be endorsed upon the Reference Note.

In the case of softwood contract forms other than the Uniform and Albion, and in the case of hardwood and plywood contract forms; the nomination of the umpire if the arbitrators are unable to agree as to his appointment, is made by the President or Vice-President of the T.T.F. or the Chairman or Deputy Chairman of the relevant section of the T.T.F.

(*d*) AWARD BY ARBITRATORS.

By the Arbitration Act, the arbitrators must make an award in writing within three months after commencing the arbitration. Within these three months the arbitrators may enlarge the time for making the award and if the extended time is insufficient they may enlarge it again.

(*e*) RELEGATION TO UMPIRE.

If the arbitrators allow the time for making the award (that is the three months period or the extended period) to expire without having made an award, or if they cannot agree on an award, then the umpire may enter the arbitration in place of the arbitrators.

(*f*) Award by Umpire—Time Limit.

If the case is relegated to an umpire, he must make his award within one month after the original or extended time for the arbitrators to make their award has expired. Within this time he may in writing extend the time for making his award.

(*g*) Evidence, Witnesses, Examination.

Subject to any legal objections, the arbitrators or umpire may subject either of the parties to examination upon oath or affirmation. The parties must produce, if required, all books, letters or documents in their possession.

If any witnesses are called, the arbitrators or umpire may examine them under oath or affirmation.

(*h*) Award.

An award by arbitrators or umpire is final and binding on the parties concerned. The award must be :—(i) In writing (a usual form of award is appended) ; (ii) Within the required or extended time ; (iii) Certain, final and explicit as to how effect is to be given to it ; (iv) Not bad on the face of it (in the same way that a judge's decision must be legally correct) ; (v) To cover the matters submitted for arbitration, no more and no less ; (vi) The only award made ; (vii) Signed by both arbitrators in each other's presence.

A customary form of Arbitration Award :—

AWARD.

A dispute having arisen between..the Sellers and..the Buyers, in regard to the quality (condition) (manufacture) of about......................standards of......................................marked ...., shipped per s.s..........................at.............................., under Bill of Lading dated..against Contract dated ...., and the same having been referred to the undersigned as Arbitrator(s) by Submission dated...

i (we) having carefully surveyed the goods above referred to where stored at ....on...............................and having considered the documents and correspondence relative to this dispute submitted to me(us)

decide and award that the Sellers pay to the Buyers the sum of £...................... in full and final settlement of all claims under this submission.

i (we) also award that the expense of this Arbitration and award shall be paid (as to...........per cent.) by the Sellers(Buyers).

(Signed)

Expenses of this Arbitration.

Fees ....

Expenses ....

Total ....

(Initialled)

(*j*) Costs

The T.T.F. clause leaves the matter of costs entirely in the hands of the arbitrators and umpire.

"... The costs of such arbitration shall be left to the discretion of the arbitrator(s) or umpire. In deciding as to costs, the arbitrator(s) or umpire shall take into consideration the correspondence between the parties relating to the dispute and their respective efforts to arrive at a fair settlement."

4. The Award.

(*a*) Amount of Award and Damages.

When a warranty in a contract has been broken the buyer may claim either or both of the following :—

(i) *A Reduction in Price.* This might even be a claim for the full amount. If the claim is for the quality of the goods, it is based upon the difference in value between the goods delivered, and those contracted for.

(ii) *Damages*—being the estimated loss to the buyer directly and naturally caused in the ordinary course of events by the breach of warranty by the seller.

(*b*) Taking Up the Award.

When the award has been made by the arbitrators or umpire, signed with a statement of the costs and duly stamped, it is put in a sealed envelope and the parties to the arbitration are informed that the award is ready and will be delivered on payment of costs amounting to so much. It is usually the buyer who "takes up" the award by paying the costs and thereafter proceeds to put it into effect. If the arbitration awards a sum about half-way between what the buyer claimed and the seller was willing to pay, the arbitrators may decide that the costs shall be equally divided between them, and it may then seem to the parties that it was a pity they did not come to "amicable agreement" to split the difference and save the costs. Extreme cases are not unknown where, for instance, the buyer has had to pay costs exceeding the amount awarded to him, leaving him finally out-of-pocket, or on the other hand the seller has had to pay all the costs in addition to an award of the full amount claimed.

If the arbitration awards a sum to be paid by the seller to the buyer, the latter sends the award for collection to the seller's agent, who in turn obtains the seller's authority to pay it.

Although there is no obligation on the arbitrators to do so, it is customary, as a matter of courtesy, for the arbitrator to communicate to the party appointing him how the award was arrived at. This will only take place after the award has been "taken up." It will readily be understood that such information, which may be and often is verbal and confidential, may be of considerable service by way of guidance in handling any future similar dispute.

(*c*) Enforcing the Award.

The Arbitration Act, 1950, states in Section 26 :—

"An award on an arbitration agreement may, by leave of the High Court or a judge thereof, be enforced in the same manner as a judgement or order to the same effect."

For the purposes of enforcement, an award has the same status as a judgment and by taking out the appropriate form of writ, the applicant may seize such property as the defaulting party may have within the jurisdiction of the court. This method of enforcement is quite simple, but is limited by the jurisdiction of the court which does not extend to foreign countries.

When one of the parties is in a foreign country outside the jurisdiction of the court, as is the shipper of timber, the enforcement can only be effected by a legal action on the award. This can be a costly and lengthy process and its success depends to a great deal on the law of the foreign country concerned.

The Pacific Coast contract form overcomes this difficulty with the following clause.

" It is mutually agreed that either party may apply either to the High Court of Justice in England or to the appropriate Courts of Scotland or Ireland or Canada, or in the case of the United States, the District Court in and for the district in which a party carries on business or resides that a judgment of the Court shall be entered upon the award. Notice of application shall be served upon the adverse party in the usual manner and thereupon the Court shall have jurisdiction as though the party served had appeared generally in such proceeding."

(*d*) Setting the Award aside.

If either buyer or seller is dissatisfied with the award, he can endeavour to get it set aside by taking it to court, but that is seldom done and it will be found that the courts are extremely reluctant to set aside the award of a duly appointed commercial arbitrator.

The Arbitration Act, 1950, states in Section 23 :—

" (2) where an arbitrator or umpire has misconducted himself, or an arbitration or award has been improperly procured, the High Court may set the award aside."

Misconduct refers to legal as well as personal misconduct. A sole arbitrator or umpire must not do anything which is not in itself fair and impartial. It is deemed misconduct in an arbitration for him to receive relevant information from one party which is not disclosed to the other. If he receives such a communication from one party he should immediately inform the other. In the same manner he should not grant a private interview to one party without the other being represented.

The improper appointment of the umpire by the arbitrators constitutes misconduct, *e.g.*, relegating the selection of the umpire to another person.

Finally there are the more obvious items of misconduct, fraudulent concealment of matters that should be disclosed, wilful deception of arbitrators or umpire, bribery of the arbitrators, etc.

5. Scottish Arbitration.

Whereas the Sale of Goods Act (1893) makes special provision for those parts of the act affected by the law of Scotland, there are other acts which do not do so. Amongst the latter is the English Arbitration Act, 1950, Arbitration in Scotland being governed by Scottish law and the Arbitration (Scotland) Act, 1894.

This Act differs in several respects from the English Arbitration Act, 1950, the most important difference being that an arbitrator under the Arbitration (Scotland) Act, 1894, has no power to assess or award damages *unless it is specifically detailed in the submission note* (which in this case is the arbitration clause in the contract). In other words the arbitrators merely have power to judge the dispute commercially, leaving the successful party to take their award to the courts to get damages assessed and awarded. This is overcome by including the following wording in the arbitration clause.

" In other respects the said arbitration shall be subject to the English Arbitration Act, 1950, or any statutory modification thereof or substitution therefor except in the case of goods sold to Scottish buyers for shipment to a Scottish port when the said arbitration shall be in Scotland subject to the Arbitration (Scotland) Act, 1894, or any statutory modification thereof or substitution therefor and arbitrators shall have power to assess and award damages."

CHAPTER XI

Importing Timber—Customs and Dock Procedure—Claims.

1. Import Duties, Licences and Dock Procedure.

(*a*) Import Duties.

Under the Import Duties Act, 1932, a customs duty, referred to as " the general *ad valorem* duty," equal to 10 per cent. of the value of the goods, is chargeable on all goods imported into the United Kingdom, with certain exceptions. The " Customs and Excise Tariff " (published by H.M.S.O.) gives in detail the following differences from the general *ad valorem* duty :—

Prohibitions and Restrictions (*Part* 2)—this is a list of items of which the import into the U.K. is restricted or prohibited altogether.

Substituted, Reduced or Additional Duties (*Part* 3). The Treasury has power to make Orders imposing a duty by weight, or quantity, etc., either in addition to or in place of the general *ad valorem* duty. Wood goods are covered in Group XI which must be read carefully if any manufactured or partially manufactured goods are being imported.

Group XI.

(1) Articles manufactured wholly or partly of timber	20%.
A long list of exceptions to this duty are quoted in this section referring to such items as boxboards (sawn or planed including t. and g. but excluding dovetailed), sleepers, plywood, veneers, rough turnings, etc. (These are therefore subject to the *ad valorem* duty of 10 per cent.)	
(2) Builders' Woodwork of the following descriptions :—	
(i) Doors of height and width not less than 6 ft. and 2 ft. respectively.	1s. 6d. each or 15%, whichever is the greater.
(ii) Hardwood flooring blocks or strips planed and tongued and grooved, or planed and otherwise manufactured ...	17½%.
(iii) Hardwood parquet flooring in sections composed of blocks or strips glued or otherwise jointed together ...	17½%.
(iv) Other sorts	15%.

Item	Duty
(3) Wood Wool	£1, 5s. per ton.
(4) Wood Flour	15%.
(8) Wood and timber of coniferous species in the round or hewn or square sawn but not further prepared or manufactured (except boxboards). (10) Softwood boxboards, dovetailed, morised or tenoned at the ends, imported in sets ... ... (Duty for softwood boxboards sawn or planed or t. and g. only is 10 per cent. —see paragraph 1.)	$12\frac{1}{2}\%$.
(11) Articles, excluding boxboards, manufactured wholly of softwood, including the following : ... ... (i) Weather boards. (ii) Boards less than 2 ins. in thickness and 4 ins. or more in width, planed, but not further prepared or manufactured than tongued, grooved, beaded, V-jointed, rebated, chamfered, centre beaded, centre V-jointed or round edged; but not including profiled boards with board and profile not in one piece.	$7\frac{1}{2}\%$.

Generally where goods fall within more than one class or description, the import duty is that chargeable at the highest rate of the various applicable classes or descriptions. However, in paragraphs 2, 8, 10 and 11, these goods are not chargeable at any higher rate under any other heading.

These may be summarised as follows :—

Item	Duty
Softwood	8s. per standard.
Hardwood	10%.
Softwood Floorings, etc.	$7\frac{1}{2}\%$.
Hardwood Floorings, etc.	$17\frac{1}{2}\%$.
Sleepers ... ... Plywood ... ... Veneers ... ... Softwoob doxboards sawn or planed or t. and g. only	10%.
Softwood boxboards with ends machined	$12\frac{1}{2}\%$.
Doors	1s. 6d. each or 15%.

The Value of Goods for *ad valorem* duty purposes is set out in Part I, para. 7 of the " Customs & Excise Tariff." It is based upon the price which the goods would fetch on sale in the open market at the time of importation, if the goods were delivered to the buyer at the port or place of importation, the freight, insurance, commission and all other costs, charges, and expenses of the sale and delivery of the goods having been paid by the seller.

In practice, in the import of wood goods, this is taken as the first cost (f.o.b. price), plus insurance, freight and 0·1 per cent. to cover the other expenses. In some ports a fixed amount per ton is added to cover landing charges, instead of 0·1 per cent. The dutiable value is therefore not the c.i.f. value, but a value taken near the " ex-ship " line—this being the first place that the seller can " deliver " the goods to the buyer.

The general introduction to Part 3 states that no *additional* duty over the 10 per cent. *ad valorem* as quoted above, is payable on :—(*a*) Any goods forming part of a ship or vessel at the time of their import to the U.K., or (*b*) Softwood boxboards of varying descriptions.

Exemptions (*Part* 3). The following wood goods are exempt from import duty :—

(i) Goods which are consigned direct to a shipbuilding yard, to be used for the building, repairing and re-fitting of ships in that yard.

(ii) Goods entitled to Imperial Preference. To claim this it is necessary to show to the satisfaction of the Commissioners of Customs and Excise that the goods have been (*a*) Consigned from the British Empire, (*b*) Grown, produced or manufactured in the British Empire.

(iii) Certain goods named in detail in Group VIII of the list of exceptions, including :—(*a*) Persimmon wood, hickory wood and cornelwood in various forms (specially imported for manufacture into machinery and tool components) ; (*b*) Roundwood logs of pine, spruce and aspen not longer than 50 ins.—top diameter not greater than 12 ins. ; (*c*) Wooden pit props ; (*d*) Wooden telegraph poles ; (*e*) Logs of Gaboon " mahogany " (Okoumé).

The Customs and Excise Tariff provides for repayment of Customs duty where goods are found to be not in accordance with the contract of sale under which they were imported, or to have been damaged in transit. The conditions for this repayment are set out in Notice No. 266.

Drawback. Part 7 of the Customs and Excise Tariff gives the details of imported goods that are eligible for a drawback after the import duty has been paid. The conditions are set out in greater detail in Notice No. 217. Drawback of customs duty is permitted where :—(i) Goods are exported by the importer (or person taking delivery direct from the importer) in the same state in which they were imported. They must not have been used and if they are subjected to any process it must not change the form or character of the goods ; (ii) Goods are brought into a shipbuilding yard for use in the building, repairing or re-fitting of ships.

Refund of Duty. If it transpires that duty has been overpaid for any reason, such as shortage of measure, allowances for quality, condition or damage to the goods, a refund of the overpayment of duty may be claimed. Over a period when substantial quantities of timber are involved, the recovery of overpaid duty may be considerable.

IMPORTANT.—The above data is taken from the 1952 " Import List " and " Customs and Excise Tariff " published by H.M.S.O. There are constant changes and amendments being made to these publications and it is essential to make certain that the most recent amendments have been included before reference is made to them. The Customs and Excise Authorities will always give advice and information on these matters.

(*b*) IMPORT LICENCE.

Before any goods may be imported into the U.K. an import licence must be obtained from the Import Licensing Branch, Board of Trade, Romney House, Tufton Street, London, S.W.1. Import licences may be specific, authorising the import of a definite quantity or value of certain specified goods from specified countries within a limited period ; or they may be " open general " licences permitting the general import of a group of materials, such as hardwood, softwood, etc., from a wide list of countries ; such imports being unlimited in quantity or period.

Specific licences must be produced to the Customs Authorities for endorsement on each occasion goods are imported under that licence. It is most important with this type of import licence to ensure that the units of quantity shown on the licence are the same as those entered on the Customs entry form. It is also most important to make certain that where more than one shipment is made, the licence is sufficient to cover the full quantity by the last ship.

(*c*) PROCEDURE FOR PASSING DOCUMENTS THROUGH CUSTOMS.

A general outline only can be given of this procedure, which is amended in detail from time to time and differs slightly in different ports.

(i) *Form* C. 105 is a certificate to be signed by the importer. It must show the name of the *seller* and the name of the *agent*. It must be signed by the importer himself (if an individual), by a director or secretary of a Limited Company, or by an authorised person employed by the Company. In the last case a letter signed by a director or secretary authorising that person to make the Customs entry must be provided.

Para. 1 must be amplified with the following additional declarations where applicable : " and the price shown together with the charges shown below is the ultimate c.i.f. price, *i.e.*, the last c.i.f. price prior to importation." An alternative declaration used for some ports is : " I declare that the above value includes cost, freight, packing, insurance, and all charges and that a separate invoice has not been issued for any other amount."

Form C. 105 must be completed by the importer or his authorised employee and *not* by an agent on his behalf.

(ii) *Form* 107 *Sale* is the entry form for the shipment and is required in quintuplicate. The description of the goods here must agree with invoice, bills of lading and specification. The class and group must be as per current Import and Export list. The quantities stated must be in the same units as those quoted on the import licence.

The dutiable value is calculated as the sum of the following four items :—(*a*) Value of goods (f.o.b.) ; (*b*) Insurance—in sterling ; (*c*) Freight—as per bill of lading ; (*d*) 1/10th of 1 per cent. of the total of (*a*), (*b*) and (*c*) to cover dock dues and labour charges, or a set amount per ton.

If payment to the shipper or his agent is made in cash less 2 or 2½ per cent., the net amount after discount has been deducted is given at (*a*).

Rates of Import Duty are explained on page 191.

The items of the invoice must be classified on the Form 107 Sale exactly as in the categories laid down in the Customs and Excise Tariff. Where a substituted, reduced or additional rate of duty is chargeable the group number of the Customs and Excise Tariff must be quoted. All the items of one invoice must be kept on one entry form. The Form 107 Sale may be made out by the importer or an agent on his behalf provided that a written authority on Form C. & E. 648 is presented to the Customs.

Very great care must be exercised in completing the Form 107 Sale, as any error however small, will result in the entry being returned for correction and this may result in the discharge of the ship being delayed. At the height of a normal importing season the Customs Authorities have a very large number of entries to deal with, and a corrected Form 107 Sale is liable to have to take its place at the bottom of a very large pile.

(iii) *Imperial Preference*. If the goods are imported from the British Empire and are not dutiable, Form C. 105 is not required, and Form 107 Sale is completed as usual but in the columns for the amount of duty the following is endorsed : " Exempt. Canadian (or other Dominion, etc.) Origin. We claim preference." In addition a certificate of origin for the goods is required.

(iv) *Documents for Customs*. If all the necessary shipping documents are available, a " Perfected Entry " may be made. The following documents must be prepared, following closely the instructions printed on the official forms, and presented.

Form C. 105, or

Certificate of Origin (for Imperial Preference).

Original and copy bills of lading—duly endorsed by importer.

Insurance Policy or Certificate.

Original and copy invoice (one is retained by customs).

If the invoice is not the original seller's invoice, it must be certified by the seller's agents. Sometimes goods from certain countries require special consideration and then an extra copy of the invoice may be required. If it is intended to claim return of duty or part duty at a later date, in respect of goods being exported again or for use in a shipyard, an additional copy of the invoice is required in order to have it stamped by the customs for drawback. The invoice must be endorsed: "To be stamped for drawback."

Form 107 *Sale.* Five copies.

Specification—one for each invoice and copy invoice submitted.

Duty Paid Form 312. In duplicate. This is a summary of the amounts of duty payable by the importer.

These documents are presented to the Customs Authorities together with payment for the duty. If all are in order, they are duly passed, stamped and receipted.

(v) *Entry with Incomplete Documents.* If all the shipping documents are not available, a preliminary customs clearance may be obtained by means of a "bill of sight" on Form 21 Sale. As much information as possible must be obtained from the shipowner's office as to the freight and quantity; the approximate value of the goods may be found from the importer's own records and copy of the contract. From this information an amount is paid to the customs "on deposit." When the full sets of documents are available the "Perfected Entry" is put through in the normal way and any payment of duty "on deposit" adjusted as necessary.

(*d*) Dock and Labour Charges, etc.

Before an importer can obtain delivery of his goods from the ship, he must pay certain charges to the Port Authority. These are known as Dock or Town Dues, and cover the administration and maintenance cost of the docks.

If the ship has reached the port through a canal, such as the Manchester Ship Canal, or if the goods are transferred to barges and taken by inland canal to their ultimate destination, there will be Canal Tolls to pay. These tolls cover the cost of administration and maintenance of the locks and canal walls, etc.

After the goods have come out of the ship, if they are left on the quay over a certain period, Quay Rent is payable for the period they remain there.

The rates of Dock Dues or Town Dues, Toll Charges and Quay Rent are all set out in the Schedule of Charges for the port, which may be obtained from the Port Authority.

Labour in a port may be divided into three sections. Stevedores, master porters and forwarding agents.

Stevedores are responsible for handling goods from the hold of the ship, with or without the use of the ship's tackle depending upon port facilities, and delivering the goods to the rail of the ship.

Master Porters or *Cargo Superintendents* are responsible for taking the goods from the stevedores at the ship's rail and delivering them to the quay alongside the receiver's waggons.

Forwarding Agents are responsible for taking the goods from the quay and putting them on the vehicle carrying them away.

In some ports all three classes of labour will be found working independently, each group working for a self-contained firm. More often however a firm will combine two functions, or possibly all three, and are styled, say " John Smith & Co., Master Porters and Forwarding Agents."

Ports that are controlled by a single authority such as the Railway Executive, or Manchester Ship Canal Co., are generally their own stevedores, master porters and forwarding agents, and do all this work. In these cases the schedule of charges for the port sets out the labour charges as well as the dock dues, etc.

It is convenient to consider the labour handling the goods from the ship under the three headings of stevedores, master porters and forwarding agents, as although they may all come under one employer the men themselves are under different Trade Unions and not all of them may handle the goods if deliveries or sales are made " overside."

Stevedores and master porters or cargo superintendents are separated by the imaginary line of the ship's rail. At this point, where the master porter assumes responsibility, a tally is taken of the number of pieces coming out under each bill of lading. This is the master porter's tally or cargo superintendent's tally, and unless the shipowners or sellers agree to a measurement of the goods by an independent third party, the master porter's tally or cargo superintendent's tally is the basis upon which claims for shortage in measure are based.

This imaginary line of the ship's rail provides the definition for a sale of goods " ex ship " (see page 217).

A proportion of the labour charges may be avoided by arranging for the goods to be taken direct from the ship into road vehicle, rail waggon or lighter without touching the quay. This is known as taking delivery " overside " and although dock dues and toll charges, etc., have to be paid, the labour charges consist only of the stevedore's charges and a small proportion of master porterage charges. The amount that can be saved by this method of delivery varies in every port, but is of the order of 75 per cent. to 90 per cent. of the normal labour charges.

Another allowance that is obtainable at some ports is Terminal Rebate. This is an allowance made by the Railway Authorities where the importer provides the labour to load the waggons at the quayside if rail carriage is used. The amount varies from port to port but in general is about 6d. per ton.

It will be seen that the more people who handle the goods out of the ship, the higher is the ultimate cost of the timber to the importer whereas if he short-circuits some of this labour he will save money. There are other advantages, though, to be gained by taking the goods off the ship " the long way," as there are various other services offered by master porters and forwarding agents.

For a very reasonable charge they will *measure* the timber piece by piece and provide a tally which can be checked against the seller's specification. This is an important service that can save the importer much work himself, and provides accurate figures upon which claims for measurement can be based. Not all sellers or shipowners will accept such measurement details, but insist on the master porter's tally only being adopted for measurement claims.

In certain ports, particularly where the master porters are employed by the Port Authority, there are other services available, such as the "laying out" of a parcel of mixed lengths, widths or thicknesses, to select a particular dimension or length. This depends largely on the time of year and conditions on the quay. In busy days with the quays congested with imports, it is sometimes difficult to arrange for timber to be laid out, but in slack times it is a different matter.

If extremely accurate measurements are required, particularly of valuable timbers such as hardwoods or pitch pine baulks, etc., the importer may employ the " Customs Fund " measurers. These are to be found in all major ports, and application for their services is made to the local " Customs Fund " office.

(*e*) Customs and Dock Procedure Summarised.

On notification of the ship's arrival in the port, the importer must take the following action :—

(1) Pay preliminary deposit to Port Authority to cover dock dues, toll charges and labour charges (if labour employed by Port Authority). This must be paid and a receipt obtained before the Form 107 Sale is presented at the Customs, otherwise the entry will not be accepted.

(2) Submit following documents to customs :—(i) Form C. 105 or certificate of origin ; (ii) Original and copies of bills of lading ; (iii) Insurance policy or certificate ; (iv) Original and copy invoice (with second and third copy invoices if necessary) ; (v) Original and copy specifications (if not already on bill of

lading); (vi) Form 107 Sale—five copies; (vii) Duty Paid form—two copies; (viii) Receipt from Port Authority for preliminary deposit for dock dues, etc., together with a cheque for amount of duty to be paid.

(3) Pay the agreed portion of the freight to shipowners, in accordance with charter-party clauses (see page 83). In receipt for payment of freight, the shipowners will give the importer a "delivery order" authorising him to take delivery of the goods from the ship.

(4) The following documents are then presented to the Customs officer at the dock at which the vessel is berthed:—(i) Customs Entry Form 107 Sale with Duty Paid form; (ii) Copy of seller's invoice; (iii) Delivery order from shipowners. These documents will be inspected and the delivery order then endorsed by customs. It is handed to the master porter or cargo superintendent and the goods can then be removed from the quay.

2. Examination of Shipment—Claims, etc.

(*a*) GENERAL.

The importing of timber from overseas is fraught with hazards. Timber is a natural product, and the grading of sawn timber is often a matter of experience and judgment only. There can be wide differences in quality in the products from the same sawmill. On some occasions small errors in the sawmill may result in sawn timber that is under measure or scant—measuring for instance only $2\frac{7}{8}$ ins. $\times 8\frac{7}{8}$ ins. instead of 3 ins. $\times$ 9 ins.

The quality of the logs going into the mill may vary considerably. A poor run of logs may result in an unusually high proportion of low quality sawn timber being produced, or in an abnormally low "average length." On another occasion average quality and lengths may be better than usual.

During a protracted voyage the timber in a confined hold may deteriorate through "sweating." In rough weather timber carried as deck cargo may be washed overboard or jettisoned. In addition there are all the risks and hazards that are applicable to any goods carried by sea. Pilferage on a greater or smaller scale may take place anywhere in the journey from the shipper's yard to the final destination in this country.

The importer of timber would be very optimistic, to say the least, if he were to assume that by repeating a contract with a shipper he would automatically receive exactly the same specification in precisely similar quality and condition as he received on the previous occasion. There are bound to be differences, and the timber importer must appreciate this fact whilst carefully inspecting and checking the goods he receives.

The importer can make claims against the seller, the shipowner or the insurance company. These claims will fall under the following main headings :—

(i) *Against the seller.* Claims for scant measurement (*e.g.* $2\frac{7}{8}$ ins. × $8\frac{7}{8}$ ins. instead of 3 ins. × 9 ins.) quality, condition (when shipped), quantity supplied (as against contract quantity). In addition the importer may claim damages for any breach of contract warranty.

(ii) *Against the Insurance Company.* Claims for loss of and damage to cargo during the voyage (other than damage to deck cargo by sea-water, etc.). Claims for shortage in deck cargo, which may, for instance, have been caused by rough weather.

(iii) *Against the Shipowner.* Claims for shortages—being difference between bill of lading quantity (in pieces) and quantity delivered over ship's rail (in pieces).

(*b*) EXAMINATION OF DOCUMENTS.

The shipping documents should arrive some time before the ship reaches the port of destination. The first stage in the examination of a shipment of timber consists in the close check and examination of the documents. It is first necessary to see that all the documents are in order and agree with each other and the contract conditions (as detailed in chapters V and IX). If the documents are not in order, or are incomplete, they should immediately be returned to the seller's agent. If in order, the following checks should be carried out on the specification of quantities :—

(i) *Arithmetical check* of accuracy.

(ii) *Check quantities against Contract conditions.* In the case of the last, or only shipment against a contract, this will show any undershipment or overshipment. If there is a considerable overshipment above the marginal quantities allowed, the amount overshipped may be rejected (see page 131).

(iii) *Check average length and width* and compare these against contract description. If contract description states a specific average length or width, and specification reveals that the average shipped is less, the goods may be rejected, but short average is usually treated as a breach of warranty only, to be met by a suitable reduction in price.

(iv) *Check Deck Cargo conditions.* The bills of lading will show which items have been shipped on deck and these should again be compared with the contract.

(v) *Comparison of insurance policy or certificate* with invoice and other documents, to ensure that full value of goods shipped has been covered in accordance with contract, *i.e.*, f.o.b. value plus 10 per cent. plus freight advance or c.i.f. value plus 10 per cent.

(vi) *Check invoice prices* (from contract), quantities (from specification), deductions for freight advance (from bills of lading—

where these are endorsed). Note amount of freight deduction which must not exceed one-third total freight.

The only time that the importer can reject goods out of hand is when he receives the documents. If he accepts and pays for the documents he can only recover any loss by claiming against the seller, and if necessary taking the case to arbitration. Payment however does not affect the buyer's right to claim rejection of the whole or part, which could be awarded at arbitration. For this reason the examination of the shipping documents is of very great importance.

(c) Examination of Goods and Ship.

By the time the ship arrives, the shipping documents will have been checked and the goods paid for. The importer will have followed the progress of the ship and should have notice of its arrival from the shipping agents. The examination of the goods is done on the quay and if necessary in the ship, but the earlier the better. This examination is a skilled job that cannot be relegated to the office boy. The first thing to look at is the ship itself—signs of a rough voyage can usually easily be seen. If signs of a rough passage are seen on boarding the ship, or if news reports have told of bad weather, it may become necessary either to inspect the ship's log or obtain extracts from it.

The log will indicate what has happened during the voyage. There may be references, very slight perhaps, to shifting of the deck cargo or " re-battening down deck cargo." These indicate that some of the deck cargo *may* have gone overboard. If really rough weather has been encountered the log may state that part of the deck cargo has been jettisoned, but in circumstances of this nature the master will enter a protest on reaching port (see page 70). The ship's agent will tell the importer if this has been done, but in any case it is always as well to ask.

When the goods come off the ship, if any are in deck cargo bills of lading and there have been entries in the log as above, *shortages* in the deck cargo items may be expected.

The log may tell of flooding of the holds. This would cause damage to timber there, which can be recovered from the insurance company.

The log therefore is a most vital document, extracts from it will provide the evidence for claims for shortages in deck cargo, or possibly damage to cargo in holds.

The examination of the timber itself must include :—

(i) *Dimension.* A check of the various sizes for dimension, *i.e.*, width and thickness. Some sellers have a reputation for " scant " or under measure : others for " full " measure which gains for the latter considerable sales advantage over the former—perhaps in price, but certainly in preference at the same price—as buyers are quick to notice and record these differences between suppliers. Several pieces in any one parcel must be inspected, and the variation must be general, not just isolated pieces, to justify a claim being made.

(ii) *Pieces and Measurement.* The master of the ship signs the bill of lading for number of pieces only and is only responsible for delivering that number of pieces to the importer.

At the port of destination, the goods are checked or "tallied" over the side of the ship by the master porter, or cargo superintendent. His tally gives numbers of pieces only. If his tally shows a less number of pieces than the bill of lading, that represents a shortage for which :—(*a*) The insurance company is responsible if it is deck cargo lost overboard or jettisoned ; (*b*) The shipowner is responsible if it is hold cargo.

The master porter's tally is not really a very reliable check on measure. All too frequently it agrees *exactly* with the bill of lading number of pieces.

A check should be made of broken pieces, bearing in mind that a piece broken in two crosswise during the voyage may count as two pieces on delivery and is not necessarily laid aside as " damaged." Usually only pieces broken in such a way as to lose their original *width* are " returned " as " damaged." It is the custom when piling, to put the undamaged end of a broken piece towards the front of the pile, so, after piling, broken ends can only be seen by looking at the back of the pile.

In the breaking of a piece, some inches of length are lost in the fracture, so it may be taken for granted that every broken piece delivered as a whole piece represents on the average the loss of something more than half its value : if the broken piece is less than 9 feet long it becomes an " end " and loses a part of its value. If an excess number of pieces is delivered equal to the number of broken pieces, it is not usually considered worth while to make a claim, but if there is no such excess a claim should be made for the missing pieces.

In practice it will be found that several ports have their own customary methods of calculating claims for losses through breakage, which must be followed.

In certain ports, the majority of shipowners will accept a measurement check by a third party. This covers *lengths* as well as numbers of pieces and is obviously much more accurate. These third parties are either the port authorities, if they have timber measuring staffs, or the Customs Fund Measurers.

However under the Nubaltwood charter claims for shortage of outturn must be made *within six days* of discharge (see page 79). The importer therefore must obtain at least a copy of the master porter's tally (overside the ship) if not a third party measurement, for his parcel of timber. An accurate measurement piece by piece in his own yard will rarely be accepted by the insurance company, shipowner or seller for a shortage in measurement.

(iii) *Quality*. The quality of a particular parcel can only be assessed by someone with experience. Grading rules may be obtained for the American and Canadian timbers but even these in the hands of an inexperienced man are not much use. All too often it will be found that they are so full of " escape " clauses that almost any defect seems to be permitted, at any rate in the middle grades for softwoods. The hardwood and plywood grading rules are rather more clear, but still cannot replace sheer judgment in assessing the quality of goods on the quay.

Scandinavian softwoods are graded at the producing mills without reference to any written rules and therefore must be judged for quality without any grading rules. The basis of grading is generally stated in the contract as " sellers' usual " which requires special knowledge and experience to judge.

(iv) *Condition*. The condition of timber is quite different from graded quality. A high grade timber can be ruined by being shipped in bad condition, such as an insufficiently seasoned condition. The *quality* of timber is judged by the presence of inherent *defects* such as knots, wane, rate of growth, checks, etc. *Condition* refers to the *state* of the timber, such as freshness, weathering and discoloration. Deterioration of this nature may have been present when the timber was in the shipper's yard, or it may have occurred during shipment.

If the voyage was normal, bad condition of timber may be shown to be due to insufficient seasoning for voyage to port of destination (see page 128). For this the importer must claim against the seller. On the other hand, if through " perils of the sea " the length of the voyage is increased much beyond normal, resulting in " sweating " of the timber in the hold and fungal moulds forming, the claim should be made against the insurance company.

In cases where the goods arrive in bad condition it may be difficult to decide the cause as it may be either insufficient seasoning, for which the seller is liable, or water damage, for which the insurance company is liable. In that case the buyer is justified in notifying both the seller's agents and the insurance company inviting both of them to inspect the goods.

Damage by water may be freshwater (see T.T.F. insurance clause 5*a*) or saltwater. It is easy to ascertain whether the timber has been damaged by saltwater by applying the following chemical test. If silver nitrate is applied in solution to the wet surface of the timber, a white precipitate of silver chloride will be formed if salt water is present. This blackens almost at once as impurities break up the silver chloride into metallic silver. There is no known test to distinguish sap water from rainwater or snow water.

Where a claim is being made for anything except measurement, there are two essentials to be observed :—

(1) *Inspection.* For claim against seller, inspection is by the seller's agents. For claim against insurance company, the inspection is by the insurance company's surveyor. These are experienced men trained in specialised damage surveyance.

This inspection must be done quickly, if possible the same day the importer himself has seen the parcel. Timber that has developed a fungal growth in the hold of the ship, may appear awful when it first comes out of the ship, but given a spell of fine dry weather much of the fungal growth will disappear. In such a case if the inspection was left for two or three days the timber might appear superficially to be in perfect condition and the importer's chance of a successful claim would be small.

(2) *Retention of Bulk.* If the claim is for "quality" the buyer must not "break bulk." By this is meant that the parcel or item complained of (which may be only a single dimension on one bill of lading) must be kept so intact that, in case of arbitration, it can be produced to the arbitrators in its entirety as discharged.

Sellers' agents are sometimes asked to authorise breaking bulk, but they usually have no authority to do so and in any case the clause is so worded that there is no hardship in letting matters follow the prescribed course. Indeed, if the buyer relies on "permission to break bulk" he may find himself in a less favourable position if the matter eventually goes to arbitration.

If the claim is for "condition" the buyer can dispose of any part without detriment to his claim on the rest. In either case there is no obligation to hold the goods at any particular place, nor even all in one place, so long as the whole item in the case of quality, and the quantity complained of in the case of condition, is available for inspection as discharged.

(*d*) Claims.

If it appears that a claim will have to be made on an Albion or Uniform contract, the seller's agent must be given reasonable particulars within 14 days of the discharge of the ship. This notification merely states in general terms whether the claim is for measurement, quality, condition, etc., without any specific details (see page 137). Other forms give slightly different time limits, for instance, 10 days in the c.i.f. re-selling contract and the ex-ship contract.

If, after closer inspection of the goods, it is decided to proceed with the claim it must be detailed and formulated.

(i) *Dimension claims.* These are simply claims for the difference in measure between the goods supplied and the quantity invoiced, and may be for scantness in thickness, width or length of the whole or part of the goods.

If boards invoiced as 1 in. prove to be scant, *i.e.*, do not hold up to 1 in. in thickness, the claim against the seller would probably be to reduce them to $\frac{7}{8}$ in., or in other words a claim for the return of $\frac{1}{8}$th of the invoice value.

It is possible in certain circumstances to claim also that the smaller dimension is in itself not worth so much per standard as the original dimension. In these cases the claim is made up in two parts, firstly the shortage in measurement and secondly the reduction in price per standard.

(ii) *Quantity claims* against the ship or insurance company for shortage of pieces are based upon the difference between the number of pieces as per seller's specification or bill of lading and the number of pieces checked overside on the master porter's or cargo superintendent's tally.

It is important for the importer to obtain the *original* master porter's or cargo superintendent's tally if there is any dispute over a claim made in this manner.

When the number of pieces short has been established and agreed by the other party, the importer's claim may then be compiled taking the *average* cost per piece over the bill of lading in question, *e.g.*,

645 pieces 3 ins. × 9 ins.—10·261 stds. at £55 std.
=£564, 7s. 1d.
Shortage 23 pieces.
Shortage claim = £20, 2s. 6d.

It is assumed in this method of calculation that any shortage is of the same average specification as the whole bill of lading. If the shortage comprises all long lengths, the importer will be out of pocket, if the shortage is all of short lengths the importer will obviously gain.

The only accurate method of establishing a shortage is on *independent measure* but unfortunately it will not be accepted by every shipowner and insurance company. The measurement, piece by piece, is carried out by trained timber men often employed by the port authority. Where especially accurate measurements are required, the importer may employ the services of the Customs Fund Measurers who can be found in all the major ports. A claim submitted in this manner is compiled simply from the difference between sellers' and third party's measurements. A copy of the specification compiled by the third party will have to be produced to support the importer's claim.

However claims against shipowners under the Nubaltwood charter must be made within six days of final discharge. This not only makes it practically impossible to rely on outturn details from a Port Authority, owing to the length of time these take to be prepared but the importer, to be certain of being able to formulate the claim within this very short period, may have to arrange for a special tally to be taken at the ship's rail.

(iii) *Quality and Condition claims.* There is no set form for compiling claims for quality or condition, the claim depends upon the circumstances and detail of each case. In a claim against a seller for quality, it might be argued that a parcel of U/s redwood was of such poor quality as to be saleable only as V redwood and the claim would be made for the difference between the two prices. A claim for condition, such as discoloration, might be based upon the estimated cost per standard or per cubic foot to bring the timber to a saleable condition, *e.g.*, say the estimated cost of brushing off fungi mould and sticking the timber to dry it out, or if the discoloration had penetrated and become deep-seated, the goods might be reduced to a lower grade.

Where only part of the parcel has been damaged or broken by handling or attacked by insects, the claim is generally based upon the difference between the amount invoiced and the amount of good timber that could be cut out of the parcel. If the good timber so obtained is much smaller in dimension, then the claim can also include the difference in price between wide and narrow boards, the latter invariably being cheaper.

CHAPTER XII

Storage, Handling, Transport, Office Routine.

1. Storage.

When timber has passed from the ship it goes into a storage yard to await its re-sale to the ultimate consumer. The class of storage and the handling facilities available will affect the ultimate price of the timber to the consumer.

Storage yards may be grouped into three major classes :—

(*a*) Public Storage Yards.

These are either at the port of arrival or with direct rail or canal connection to the port. Timber is taken overside from the ship on to the quay, or straight into railway waggons or barge and moved into these yards. They represent the cheapest form of bulk storage of timber and are ideal for the merchant or importer with limited yard space who is re-selling his timber without processing it further. For the importer or merchant with a sawmill, etc., the public storage yard is a convenience but only as an overflow from his own yard.

In the ports controlled by the Railway Executive, the storage yards are often also controlled by them and offer exceptionally low storage rates on the condition that the timber is moved in and out of the storage yard by rail. Stock may be moved by motor transport, but a penalty rent is imposed.

Public storage yards work on the usual system of warehousing rates, *i.e.*, a set charge per ton or per standard for receipt, storage and re-delivery to waggon and a rental charge per week.

(*b*) Private Yards—Direct Rail or Water Access.

Merchant's or importer's own yard may have direct connection by rail or water with the port. Here again timber may be taken direct overside into railway waggon or barge and many labour charges saved. This again puts the merchant at an advantage in the ultimate cost of his timber, as it is possible to obtain special low carriage rates from the Railway Executive where goods are being carried to a private siding over a certain tonnage per year. The siding itself will generally be arranged so that timber can be taken direct from the waggon on to the timber stack without further handling. This also applies to the Docks and to the Inland Waterways Executive.

Private sidings however are very expensive to build, and although there is a saving in cost it depends on a large volume of timber being handled in any one year. Yards with canal wharves outside the London area rarely use this facility these days, although in London docks the lightering of timber to private yards is a major custom of the trade.

When lighters, barges or railway waggons are used there arise the question of demurrage which can prove a very expensive item. In the case of barge traffic it can be overcome by the merchant using his own lighters or barges but here again a great volume of timber must be handled owing to the high initial cost of a modern lighter or barge.

(*c*) PRIVATE YARDS—ROAD ACCESS ONLY.

This represents the greatest proportion of storage yards in the country. The merchant has complete control of his own timber, and can handle much smaller quantities economically. Timber from this type of yard carries all the labour charges that accumulate on the timber after it leaves the ship and therefore the cost per standard or cubic foot of timber to the merchant is greater. On the other hand this class of yard is much more flexible for working. Railway lines, when once laid, cannot be taken up and re-laid light-heartedly because the first layout was found unsuitable. The merchant has no waggon or lighter demurrage problem and generally can carry on his business with less capital tied up in expensive equipment.

2. Handling.

There are immense variations in the handling of timber in bulk. For the merchant who has no mill and is merely selling timber in its imported form, the handling services of a public storage yard represent his most satisfactory method of handling timber. He pays a set amount per standard, ton or cubic foot and that is all. He knows exactly how much it has cost him, and that is something that the average merchant owning his own yard and employing men the whole year round, will never know. For the merchant with his own yard and labour force, handling may vary from plain man-handling, to handling by the most scientific equipment produced.

(*a*) MANPOWER.

There has been so much propaganda on mechanical handling to speed production in various industries, that many people overlook exactly how much a really good gang of timber carriers can handle. Manpower is the most flexible system of handling, and can be used with the very minimum of capital expense in the form of equipment, buildings and roadways. Even in a mechanised yard a certain amount of manpower is necessary, therefore before mechanical handling equipment is installed to run economically, the volume of timber handled must be such that the cost and depreciation of the equipment, etc., will show an advantage over the manpower employed.

(*b*) MOBILE CRANE.

Small mobile cranes on road wheels or road vehicle chassis, capable of lifting three tons are flexible and of comparatively low cost, although they must have at least a cinder track to run on, which will increase the cost.

The principal advantage of all cranes is in the speed with which the merchant's own road vehicles can be loaded or unloaded and turned round. This may make the difference of an extra journey or more each day by each vehicle since hand loading and unloading is comparatively slow. The mobile crane is limited in height of lift and cannot be used to stack timber very high.

(*c*) TRUCKS ON ROADS.

Conveyance of timber round a yard, and particularly a yard attached to a sawmill, can be by small bogey trucks either hand drawn or power drawn. Although the trucks themselves are not expensive, the laying down of a concrete roadway and the electric or diesel power units to draw the bogeys may prove expensive. Again within the limits of the roadways, this system of handling is flexible, but works at its best in conjunction with a crane.

(*d*) STACKER AND STRADDLE WAGGON.

The most modern system of mechanical handling is the stacker and straddle waggon. The stacker, or fork lift truck being able to pile timber up to 24 feet high, and the bow-legged straddle waggon carry it for considerable distances, even along normal highways where the local authorities have no objection. Flexibility is maintained but the initial cost of the equipment is high—to which must be added the cost of the roadways. To cover this cost most effectively, this equipment should be working at maximum capacity for the greater part of the year and this again means that a very great volume of timber must be handled before the equipment can show a reasonable saving and begin to earn a profit itself.

(*e*) TRUCKS ON RAILS.

This system is particularly applicable to sawmills, where the rails are run right up to each machine, and either a crane or "transfer truck" runs at right angles to the feeding rails to move timber from one set of rails to another. Flexibility here is limited and it is necessary to maintain a large number of trucks to make the system workable. This in turn means high initial cost. It is not necessary to have power units to move the trucks provided the site is fairly level and as a system it works well in a large sawmill where bulk quantities of timber are being sawn and machined. Some form of crane is still necessary if full benefit is to be obtained in loading and unloading road vehicles.

(*f*) JIB CRANE.

A large jib crane, mounted high on supports, with a 100 feet or more jib, has advantages of certain flexibility since it can cover such a large area. In addition it is possible to stack timber really high (say up to 60 feet) with it, if crane-driver and slingers are fully experienced. This is important, as rents, rates and taxes are only concerned with the ground area of land in the merchant's yard, and the higher he can stack his timber the smaller becomes the amount of these charges per standard or per cubic foot that the timber has to carry.

(*g*) Gantry Crane.

A gantry crane has less flexibility than a jib crane, normally covering a smaller area and not having such a high lift. On the other hand the usual gantry crane has a more powerful and a faster rate of lift than a jib crane. This is important if the crane is up to its maximum capacity of work. The gantry crane is found in most mills dealing with home grown and imported logs. Where it is used in a mill cutting logs it is found essential not merely by virtue of the volume of logs handled but simply because the handling of a very large log is almost impossibly slow by manpower with block and tackle.

(*h*) Conveyor.

Conveyors are not flexible and not much use in a small yard dealing with a very variable trade, and for this reason they are seldom seen in this country. Where there is a large volume of timber being handled in comparatively the same manner the whole time, a conveyor can be an inexpensive time saver. The Scandinavian and North American producing mills use conveyors extensively, but their problems are different.

The yard must be organised around the conveyor which can consist of a main powered belt or chain, with subsidiary gravity feed rollers going off at right angles to various stacks. Alternatively, powered belt conveyors can be used for lifting the timber to stack level.

Conveyors do not cost a great deal of money since the merchant will usually design and build them himself. The capital cost can be considerably less than other mechanised equipment, yet if kept well maintained they can last considerably longer as there are usually fewer vital components to wear out.

The above remarks apply to power driven conveyors, but there is a great application for plain gravity feed roller conveyors in the average timber yard. These can be kept quite mobile and set up for individual jobs. The use of these time savers with ordinary manpower is not yet fully appreciated by the timber trade, in spite of the lessons to be learned during the 1939-45 war in the handling of stores from landing ships, etc., at beachheads.

Summary.

The ultimate cost of the timber from a merchant's yard therefore is affected by the location and class of yard, and by the method of handling timber in the yard. Expensive handling equipment may be necessary on account of the class of trade handled (*e.g.*, logs or heavy baulks), or to make a particular yard or mill workable (*e.g.*, to effect a rapid turn round of transport) or on account of the large volume of timber to be handled. Only if the mechanical equipment can be fully employed handling a large volume of timber during the year, can the cost of handling be so reduced as to enable the merchant to offer at lower prices than his competitors.

3. Rail Transport.

The rates charged for the carriage of timber by merchandise trains are laid down in two books published by the railway authorities: "The General Classification of Merchandise" and "Scales of Standard Charges." All goods are grouped in classes given numbers from 1 to 21. The classification is based largely on the railway authorities' liability for damage to the goods in transit. Goods easily damaged are put in high grades (*e.g.*, cut glass is class 20g), whereas goods of a simple bulk nature are put in low grades (*e.g.*, coal pyrites in class 1).

The classification refers not only to the goods themselves, but to the nature of their packing. Well packed goods come under lower classifications, *e.g.*, motor cycles, in cases or crates, class 18; if not packed or protected, class 19. These classes apply to all stations and routes, and for any one particular journey the carriage rates vary for each classification, the lower classes being cheaper, the higher classes being dearer.

The scales of general charges give the station to station rates throughout the U.K. for each class of goods. All that is necessary to be known is the classification and the two stations between which the goods are to be carried.

In page 383 of the "General Classification of Merchandise" is given a definition of the word "Timber" together with details for ascertaining measurement and weight. Timber, with the exception of logs, is charged at actual machine weight only, unless otherwise provided for.

In the case of logs, or where arrangements are made to carry the timber on a measurement weight basis, this classification sets down an arbitrary list of the number of cubic feet per ton in the case of sawn timber or round logs for each wood. The tonnage for charging is then calculated from the measurement of the timber, converted to tons by these set factors:—

e.g., Fir or pine (excepting pitch pine) over 4 ins. thickness	Sawn timber	= 53 cube ft./ton.
		= 3·12 ton per std.
	Round logs	= 37 cube ft./ton.
Ditto, up to 4 ins. thick	Sawn timber	= 66 cube ft./ton.
		= 2·5 ton per std.
	Round logs	= 37 cube ft./ton.

The normal classifications for timber are:—

Timber, except where otherwise specified, class 8. Deals, battens, boards, planed, tongued or grooved, class 9. Planks, planed, class 9. Scantlings, planed, class 9. Beadings and mouldings (not carved or embossed) as they leave the moulding machine—Common fir or pine, class 10; Other timbers, class 13. Beadings and mouldings, gilt, lacquered, varnished or polished—In cases or protected by boards, class 18; Covered with paper and packed in corrugated cardboard or straw and canvas, except otherwise herein provided, class 20c. Etc., etc.

All timber rates for 4 tons and over are *station* to *station* only and do not include handling or cartage, which if provided are charged extra.

If the weight of traffic to be carried between two specified stations in any one year exceeds 200 tons, an *exceptional rate* may be obtained showing a reduction on the standard rate of anything from 5 per cent. to 60 per cent. The goods do not have to go all at the same time provided that the yearly aggregate is over 200 tons. The most important point to be remembered when making an application for an exceptional rate, is that the application must be in the railway authorities' hands *before* the goods move. After the application has been sent in, the goods may be moved even though an exceptional rate has not yet been confirmed by the railway authority. These exceptional rates take a little time to get through, but are retrospective to the date of application when once they are granted.

Where there is already a large weight of traffic of a particular kind between two stations, an exceptional rate may exist already. If this is the case, then it is not necessary to make a separate application for the exceptional rate, and it is not necessary to consign a minimum of 200 tons per annum between the two stations. When once one trader has been granted an exceptional rate between two particular stations, that rate should be charged automatically for all other similar consignments of goods from other traders between the two stations in question. The great saving in exceptional rates has naturally resulted in a vast number of them being made. In fact the rate books kept by railway clerks in the various goods stations contain many more exceptional rates than they do standard rates, the number of exceptional rates is estimated to be many millions, as over 80 per cent. of all railway traffic is charged this way.

At the end of the " General Classification of Merchandise " are published various lists of goods for which exceptional rates are in existence. The relative lists for the timber trade are :—

List O : Joiners' work. List V : Timber. List W : Timber.

When consigning any goods contained in these lists, application should be made to the *station from which the goods will be sent* to see if an exceptional rate is in existence. Where possible it is advisable to visit the station as the trader consigning goods has a right to inspect the rate book of the station to verify any particular rate. In making applications for Exceptional Rates, etc., reference should be made to S.R. and O. 989 of 1949 " Transport Tribunal Rules, 1949," which deals with the procedure to be adopted with regard to making applications to the Transport Tribunal.

All goods conveyed by rail must be consigned carriage paid. Monthly accounts are rendered by the railway authorities and these should be checked carefully with the " Schedule of Charges," " General Classification " and the grant of any exceptional rates—if necessary by reference to the consigning station as detailed above.

A great deal of time can be saved in checking railway carriage accounts, if the goods are consigned correctly in the first instance. Particular attention should be paid to the wording of the description of the goods on the consignment note to ensure that it is quite clear under which class the goods will be carried.

It is possible to have goods that can be described in slightly different ways, and consigned under different classes. The timber merchant or manufacturer will normally try and consign them under the lowest classification possible, but it must be remembered that if the goods are liable to damage, such as mouldings or manufactured woodwork, the rate of payment of claims for damage will be smaller on the lower classes. Any amount saved by consigning the goods cheaply may be more than lost if they are damaged and only a small amount is recoverable from the railway authorities.

Railway rates all vary with the quantity consigned at any one time. For timber, the minimum quantity for lowest rate (even if an exceptional rate is granted) is 4 tons. Quantities of 2 to 4 tons are charged at a higher rate, quantities of under 2 tons are charged higher still. Obviously then the maximum quantity possible must be consigned at any one time to ensure that they are carried at minimum rates.

When signing for goods delivered by the railway, it is important to remember that to sign as "unexamined" means nothing and is tantamount to a clear signature, unless a claim is notified within a "reasonable" time, *e.g.*, time enough to examine the goods at leisure without keeping the carman waiting.

The safest way to sign a railway delivery note is :—" (Signature). Weight, Quantity and Condition Unknown," but this is in itself not sufficient unless a notification of claim is sent in.

In the case of damage, breakage, seepage or partial loss, this notification must be sent in within six days of signing delivery note.

In the case of non-delivery the notification of claim must be sent in within twenty-eight days of despatch, being date of consignor's invoice.

These are only ***notifications***, the claims themselves must be sent in within ten days in the case of damage, partial loss, etc., or forty-two days in the case of non-delivery.

These are the periods at present in force, but the Minister of Transport has powers to change them at short notice. Reference should be made therefore to the Railway Executive to confirm the current claim periods.

The procedure for handling claims for damage or loss of goods on railway transit is explained in " Special Instruction Leaflet No. 60003 " published by the Railway Clearing House.

4. Road Transport.

Goods carried by British Road Services are subject to the " Conditions of Carriage " published by the Road Haulage Executive and obtainable from 222 Marylebone Road, London, N.W.1, or any B.R.S. office. These should be studied carefully by any trader consigning goods by B.R.S., particularly in respect of the periods for making claims.

Number 4 of these conditions states that " The Executive shall, subject to these conditions, be liable for any loss, misdelivery of or damage to merchandise, occasioned during transit .... unless the Executive shall prove that such loss, misdelivery or damage has arisen from . . ." Here follows a list of the usual *force majeure* conditions, with the addition of " Act or ommission of the Trader, his servant, or Agent. Inherent .... Vice .... of the merchandise." It is essential therefore for the trader to observe these conditions of carriage in every detail, if a successful claim is to be made against the Executive. This clause goes on to state :—

" Provided that :—

(i) Where loss, misdelivery or damage arises and the Executives have failed to prove that they used all reasonable foresight and care in the carriage of the merchandise, the Executive shall *not* be relieved of liability for such loss, misdelivery or damage.

(ii) The Executive shall not incur liability of any kind in respect of merchandise where there has been fraud on the part of the trader."

In condition number 7 the Executives' liability is further limited where the loss or damage has arisen through " insufficient or improper packing " or " consignees not accepting or taking delivery within a reasonable time." Condition number 8 sets out the manner in which the goods are to be consigned, whilst condition number 9 limits the liability of the Executive to £400 per ton of the gross weight, although not limiting their liability below £10 in any one consignment.

Under condition number 10 the Executive accepts liability for loss *proved by the trader* to have been caused by delay, detention or unreasonable deviation in the carriage of the goods—unless the Executive can prove that this has occurred without negligence on the part of the Executive.

The most important condition is number 19, as this sets out the time limits for notifying loss or damage and making claims. Claims in respect of loss of part of an unpacked consignment or claims for damage, deviation, misdelivery, delay or detention must be notified *in writing within three days* and the claim itself formulated *in writing* and presented *within seven days.* In each case the period is calculated from the date of the termination of the transit.

Claims for non-delivery of a whole consignment, or of a package forming part of a consignment (but *not* loss from a package or loss from an unpacked consignment) must be notified to the Executive *in writing within* 14 *days* and the claim itself formulated *in writing* and presented *within* 28 *days.* In these cases the periods are calculated from the date the goods were handed to the Executive.

5. Office Routine.

The importing of timber and its subsequent sale in this country depends upon an efficient office routine. Long experience by buyers in firms of importers, and high pressure salesmanship by the firm's representatives on the road can be set at naught by an inefficient office. The method or system used matters little, it is the results that count. If an office is to be started, or re-organised, the system or routine that is introduced must be such that accurate information, data and records can be easily produced. Therefore before putting the system into effect, it is essential to make certain exactly what information, etc., is required, and then basing the system on these definite requirements.

In the Timber Trade, an office system may be divided into three main headings: Correspondence and Filing, Financial and Book-keeping, Stock Control and Costing.

It is not proposed here to discuss the questions of labour costing.

The first two of these headings apply to any business and there are a great variety of Filing and Book-keeping systems that can be put into operation depending upon the size and resources of the firm. In putting a modern filing system into operation, it is important to remember that the filing system is the servant of the firm's office requirements, not the master of it. All too often an office routine is re-designed around some patent filing system, when really no tangible increase in efficiency can be obtained, and a simpler system would produce the necessary letters, etc., just as quickly.

It is the third heading, Stock Control, which is the real keystone to a timber office. Outside experts in office management and book-keeping methods can help a timber merchant in planning the correspondence and book-keeping side of his office, since many trades are fundamentally the same in this respect, but in planning a stock control system the timber merchant must not rely on any outside help. Only he really knows what he wants from his stock control system, and if he brings in outside advisors he will have to teach them the timber trade before they can advise him.

Stock control of timber is itself centred around the stock book or stock sheets. The ruling and design of the stock book governs the system. This is the information that is wanted from the stock book :—

(*a*) Details of the particular stock, including details of contract, seller, name of ship, etc.

(*b*) Date received into stock, date placed in stick (if hardwoods). Date of final discharge of ship and date claim for condition or measure submitted.

(*c*) Cost—c.i.f. price (or equivalent) together with all other charges such as dock and labour charges, transport or storage charges that have accumulated on that parcel, to give actual *nett cost* at any time, to the firm.

(*d*) Full specification to enable outturn (amount received from ship) to be checked against seller's invoice and specification and claim for shortage (if any) to be made against the ship.

(*e*) Full specification of goods in stock at any one time. As each sale is made, the quantity is marked off the opening stock figure.

It should be possible to check stock physically at any particular time, and for this stock to agree, with very small variations, with the stock book figure.

(*f*) Balance of stock remaining to be sold. This of course is not necessarily the same as (*e*), as some goods may have been sold, but not removed from stock by the purchasers. To avoid over-selling any parcel, it is necessary to know at all times how much remains to be sold although this figure does not have to be exact and is usually only taken to the nearest quarter fraction.

The stock lists or sale lists, showing what the merchant or importer has available for sale, are made up from these figures on the stock book.

The stock book may be a simple ledger ruled up by an office clerk, or it may be an expensive loose leaf ledger with highly complicated specially printed sheets. Whatever form it takes, it fails in its purpose if it does not produce the information set out above *quickly* and *easily*.

CHAPTER XIII

Inland Sales, Charges and Costs

1. Inland Sales.

Timber may be bought and sold in this country at several stages varying from the purchase of it whilst it is still in transit to this country, to the purchase of it delivered to the ultimate user's factory or yard.

The timber is cheaper at the earlier stages, but must be purchased in quantity with possibly the inclusion of less popular sizes or specifications. In the later stages the timber is dearer by virtue of labour, services, etc., performed on the timber, but on the other hand the buyer has the power to select just what is required, inspect the stock beforehand, and purchase only very small quantities.

(*a*) C.I.F. Resale.

An importer buying timber f.o.b. or c.i.f. may resell it on the same terms but it is seldom resold f.o.b., almost always c.i.f. This is achieved by endorsement and transfer of the relevant bills of lading and insurance policies, thus transferring the property in the bills of lading to the new purchaser. The new purchaser is protected in the same manner as the original importer was, all the terms and conditions applying to a c.i.f. contract protecting the original buyer, also protect the buyer in a c.i.f. resale contract.

For all practical purposes the buyer in a c.i.f. resale contract is in the same position as a buyer in an original c.i.f. contract except that the c.i.f. resale price is usually higher since it includes the working profit, etc., of the original importer. A sale on these terms must be in complete bills of lading to enable the transfer of the property in the goods to be carried out.

The T.T.F. c.i.f. re-selling contract form is discussed on page 170.

(*b*) Ex-Ship.

Timber may be sold by the importer at the point where it crosses the ship's rail. In these " ex-ship " sales the importer pays the import duty (if any), dock and town dues, tolls, etc., and a small proportion only of the labour charges. The buyer pays the porterage charges ; also quay rent, etc., if the timber is taken on to the quay. Some days free of rent and watching after discharge from ship is usual : *e.g.*, Liverpool, three days ; Belfast, seven days.

The importer is responsible for all charges to the ship, such as demurrage or dead freight in addition to the normal freight charges, and must provide the ex-ship buyer with a clear delivery order to obtain the goods from the ship.

The T.T.F. Ex-Ship contract form is discussed on page 172.

An ex-ship sale will enable the new buyer to take the timber overside direct into railway waggon or lighter for transport to his own yard, giving him the advantage of a considerable saving in labour charges. Again the sale must be of complete bills of lading as this is the minimum quantity for which separate disposal instructions can be given to the stevedores unloading the ship.

(*c*) Ex Quay (Landed).

When the importer has taken his bills of lading on to the quay, paying the full labour charges, etc., he may sell either complete bills of lading or else parts of bills of lading for delivery to the customer's vehicle at the quay. The sale of a part of a bill of lading from the quay largely depends upon the labour services available. In some cases it is possible to arrange for the master porters to lay the bill of lading out and to deliver specific widths or lengths from a mixed parcel.

The term " landed " is primarily used to distinguish a sale from an " overside " or " ex-ship " sale, but it may be used in reference to goods that have been moved from the quay to a storage ground. There is no hard and fast definition of " landed," and it must be interpreted by its relation to all other factors of the sale that are disclosed.

(*d*) Ex Public Storage Yard.

The major ports in the U.K. usually have either open or covered public storage yards either at the quayside or with direct rail or water connection with the quays. It is possible in some ports for the importer to take his goods " overside " either into railway waggon or lighter, straight into the storage ground. These storage grounds are very useful to the importer, as they provide an overflow for his own yard. The charges made are usually in two parts: (*a*) Receipt, handling and re-delivery to vehicle, (*b*) Rental charge per week, as for most warehousing, and the importer knows exactly what his handling has cost him.

The rates for handling and storing in public storage yards are generally very competitive, and with the saving obtained by taking the goods " overside " it is possible for timber sold ex public storage yard to be cheaper than the same goods sold ex private yard.

(*e*) Ex Private Storage Yard.

The last stage is the sale from a private storage yard. Here the timber will have accumulated all the labour charges from ship to yard and therefore the ultimate cost of the timber is greater, although some saving can be made where the yard has direct rail or water connection with the quay. In addition to labour charges there is also the cost of carriage of the goods from the quay to the yard, and in the case of yards well inland from the port, these carriage charges can amount to quite a lot. The bulk of the timber stocks in the country are carried in private yards, since there are only a limited number of public storage yards anyway and most of these are around the ports.

Sales from a private yard offer the consumer the greatest service he can get. Here he can pick and choose, inspect the timber before he buys it, specify lengths, widths, qualities and buy whatever quantity he wants from a hundredth to a hundred standards. Frequently the yard is part and parcel of a sawmill so that the consumer may purchase his own particular requirements of sawn or machined timber, in fact if he urgently requires one particular size that is not in stock, it can usually be sawn for him from larger dimensions. A comparison can be made here with a sale of timber from a public storage yard, since if the purchaser wishes to have his timber sawn or machined it must be carried from the public storage yard to a sawmill, handled in and out, sawn, machined, etc., and in the end may cost more than the same timber purchased from the private yard attached to the sawmill.

The ex quay, public storage yard and private yard sales have been considered in relation to relative costs delivered on to the transport that will convey the timber to the purchaser's yard or factory. The importer may deliver the timber on his own vehicles from any of the stages shown above, in which case the price is a " delivered " price.

An inland sale is far less liable to difficulties or disputes as to quality or measurement, since when sales are made of " landed " goods from quay or storage yard the buyer can inspect them before placing his order. For these sales nothing more than a written order is required. The onus is entirely upon the buyer ; " *caveat emptor*," which means " let the buyer beware," expresses the legal attitude.

Where a sale is made ex-ship, ex quay or public storage yard it is necessary for the seller to forward a " delivery order " either direct to the master porters or storage yard, or to the buyers who can present it to the master porters or storage yard. A " delivery order " takes no set form, but is merely an authorisation from the seller for the release of the timber being sold to the buyer.

An inland sale is much simpler than a sale between a foreign seller and an importer in this country. In the latter, delivery is effected by transfer of documents, in the former by the transfer of the goods themselves. It is usual to send with the goods a consignment note or delivery note giving details at any rate of the number of pieces sent. This is signed by the buyers as they take delivery, and the signed note returned to the seller. Sometimes a full specification of the goods is sent either with or on the delivery note but usually it is only practicable for the number of pieces received to be signed for, without an actual measurement check of each piece as it is received.

The invoice will certainly be accompanied by a full specification of the goods, if the specification has not already been sent.

It is important to remember that all the correspondence and documents relating to an inland sale are as important as the contract form in a c.i.f. or f.o.b. sale from the legal point of view. In case of dispute all the letters, memoranda, etc., relating to the sale constitute the terms and conditions of the sale. There is no necessity for any document relating to the sale of goods to be stamped, nor for any special set form to be used; many firms use "sale notes" to confirm the terms of a sale but this is not necessary if the terms are already contained in other documents, such as an order from the customer, memoranda offering the goods, etc., etc. Taken together, all these documents give sufficient detail usually to give written form as a legal contract. That is to say, names of parties, description of goods, price and signature of buyer.

Of course, if the details of the contract (if over £10) are not in writing in a transaction which has been negotiated verbally, there is no question of it being an illegal transaction. However, if the contract is not in writing, or certain other conditions have not been complied with, it is not possible for either party to take legal action to enforce the contract.

2. Conversion and Machining Charges and Costs.

Conversion and machining charges show immense variations between individual firms and different parts of the country. Most sawmills have their own local trade association from which a "sawing and planing list" is issued setting out the rates to be charged for various operations. These lists can only be a guide and each firm will have its own scale of charges. The great variations that exist in sawmill charges are brought about principally through lack of adequate information upon which a rational scale of charges could be drawn up. As a result, guesswork and rule of thumb methods coupled with copying or following sawing lists issued in other areas has been the basis for many of the rates used to-day.

If a sawmill is to be operated economically it is essential to have accurate data as to the cost of various operations, quite apart from an overall financial costing of the trading of a sawmill over a given period of time. In a sawmill that is producing the same articles day in and day out, this is comparatively easy. A sawmill or machine shop attached to a joinery factory or furniture factory can be costed fairly easily, the difficulties occur in the all purpose sawmill.

First of all the units on which sawmill charges are based, themselves vary as follows :—

Log sawing —charged per cubic foot or per 100 sq. ft. of sawing.
Deep cutting—Softwoods—per standard.
Hardwoods—per 100 sq. ft. of sawing.
Flat cutting —Softwoods—per standard or per 100 lin. ft.
Hardwoods—per 100 lin. ft.
Cross cutting—Softwoods—per standard or per cut.
Machining —Softwoods—per standard.
Hardwoods—per 100 sq. ft. or per 100 lin. ft.

etc., etc.

This variation greatly complicates any costing system, but much of it is unnecessary. A typical anomaly arising out of the above methods of charging may be seen from the deep cutting charges for softwood. These are either per standard, with varying rates for the "number of deep cuts" in battens or deals of varying thicknesses or else per 100 sq. ft. of sawing. Both really amount to the same. If the charge is for 1 deep cut in a 2 ins. × 9 ins., then 133 lin. ft. will produce 100 sq. ft. of sawing, which can be charged at X shillings. On the other hand the same charge would be made for 100 sq. ft. of sawing if 2 ins. × 6 ins. were sawn 1 deep, but in this case the lineal footage of sawing would be 200 lin. ft.

Now modern sawmilling equipment is designed with a great amount of "power" in hand, much more power is being applied to the modern motorised sawbench than could be applied in the old days of line shafts. As a result, the modern band re-saw will saw 2 ins. × 9 ins. just as fast as it will saw 2 ins. × 6 ins. with no noticeably increased effort (although an ammeter in the motor circuit would reveal that more current was being used). With modern equipment then it would seem more rational in this case to base costs, and hence charges, on a lineal footage basis. This certainly simplifies the costing system. It is not suggested that 2 ins. × 4 ins. and 2 ins. × 12 ins. should be both charged at the same rate per 100 lin. ft., some graduation is necessary and separate rates for—up to 4 ins., 4 ins. to 6 ins., 6 ins. to 9 ins., 10 ins. and up would be required. Note that the first rate, up to 4 ins., would take care of flat cutting rates as well.

If more rational rates for sawing charges are adopted, costing becomes easier. All that is required is the lineal footage, under say four different headings of depth, produced by a particular sawbench per hour, day or week. The first stage in costing has then been reached. This information can be taken out week by week and provides an accurate basis for comparison of the production of the mill.

The next stage is to calculate as accurately as possible the cost of that amount of sawing. Certain items are directly chargeable such as labour (sawyer, etc.), holiday pay and national insurance. In assessing the labour item, it must not be forgotten that a sawyer is paid for 46½ hours (or whatever applies) during the week. Each hour of that time must be taken up on cost sheets. It is not sufficient merely to put down the time the sawyer was actually cutting timber. Setting up, changing saws, breakdowns, etc., all mean time that must be accounted for. In highly organised engineering works this is all listed under "lost time" but in a sawmill it is simplest merely to include it in the time on a particular job.

The remaining items that cannot be easily or quickly calculated are as follows:—factory expenses, indirect labour charges, overhead charges or on-costs. The method of assessment of these depends upon how accurately the costs are required.

Depreciation, running costs, power consumption, insurance, proportion of factory floor area occupied, may all be calculated or compiled resulting in a value per week, month, etc., of a particular machine. This value is in its turn split out into the various costs of work produced by the machine in a given period.

There remains at the end a hard core of " overhead " charges, which may either be added to the cost of the job as a percentage of direct labour, materials, or based upon time, capital value of machine, etc., etc.

The more difficult items of overheads, factory expenses, etc., can only be based on say six months or twelve months trading figures, but when calculated they remain fixed. It is only necessary then on each costing to take up the amount of direct labour, etc.

The control of materials and their place in costing is also extremely important but does not have a direct bearing in this case on the charging rates. If an adequate stock control system is in operation it is often much simpler to confine costing to labour only. There is always the problem of " off-cuts " in material costing. One dimension of timber will go into a mill for sawing and machining to a particular section. During this process an off-cut may be produced which is used to produce say a standard moulding or slating batten, etc.

Sawmill costing can never be easy whilst a sawmill is flexible in the class of work that it handles, since one machine may not do the same job twice, and may have many variations in class of work in one day. If it is felt though that a full job costing system cannot be started (whereby each job is costed separately) it is often possible to cost a mill or part of a mill as a whole, without trying to account for materials in the costing.

In this type of costing the total amount of work performed by the mill in a week is compiled, *i.e.*, total amount of deep-cutting, flat-cutting, machining, etc. This is then extended into a value of " labour services " performed by the mill during the week, or period. All that is now required is the cost of running the mill for a week, *i.e.*, wage bill and an assessment of overhead charges to be carried by the whole mill for one week. This type of costing system gives a week by week control on the running of a mill and at the same time confirms or disproves the sawmill charging rates in force.

Costing, like office systems, should be based upon the information that is required. In installing a costing system, a sawmill owner can obtain much excellent experienced technical advice, but in the end it is only he who can devise the best costing system for his works since only he knows exactly what information he wants from his costings. Notwithstanding this, there is still much to be learned about costing in the Timber Trade, many lessons could be taken from the Engineering Trades which are so far advanced in these matters, and when the trade in general becomes more advanced in their outlook on costing, sawmill charging rates and price lists will become more rational.

CHAPTER XIV

Measurements, Calculations and Units of Sale

1. Wholesale and Bulk Measurements.

The first measurements and units of sale that affect the Timber Trade are those used in importing timber into the U.K. The standard Albion, Uniform and other contract forms set out the various bases of measurement as follows :—

Sawn goods per St. Petersburg standard of 165 cubic feet.

Planed goods per St. Petersburg standard of 165 cubic feet (nominal measure).

Hewn goods per load of 50 cubic feet (customs calliper measure) excepting Upper Gulf Hewn baulks.

Firewood per fathom of 216 cubic feet.

Pitprops are measured either by piled fathom of 216 cubic feet, or by the Gothenburg standard of 180 cubic feet, or by the cord of 128 cubic feet (mainly to Holland and other parts of Europe), or by the cubic metre of 35·3174 cubic feet, all piled measure.

In Scandinavia the measurement of timber begins in the forest, where the foresters survey the forest area (usually stated in hektares measuring 2·47 acres) and note the number, kind, quality and size of the trees. The trees are measured with a calliper to ascertain the diameter at breast height ($4\frac{1}{4}$ feet to $4\frac{1}{2}$ feet above ground level) and the height of the tree is estimated.

Whilst forests consist mostly of sawlogs, they may also contain trees suitable for telegraph poles 16 feet to 85 feet long which must conform to a very strict specification. In addition there are ordinary poles 24 feet to 35 feet long with $2\frac{1}{2}$ inch top diameter ; rickers 16 feet to 23 feet long with 2 inch top diameter ; sleeper logs, formerly 9 feet now usually $8\frac{1}{2}$ feet long ; pitprops of specified lengths ranging from $2\frac{1}{2}$ feet to 10 feet rising by half feet with a specified range of top diameters from $2\frac{1}{2}$ inches to 8 inches rising by half inches—these are called " short props," long props are over 10 feet up to 13 feet long ; pulpwood mostly 6 feet or 2 metres long.

Trees are felled not more than 4 inches above ground level. In marking the felled tree for cross cutting, the measurer takes into account the diameter and quality in deciding whether to make one or more sawlogs and of what length. Lengths are seldom over 23 feet which is the maximum for a standard log when calculating floating charges that will be made when the logs are floated down the rivers to the sawmill. The average length is about 18 feet and an excess of 4 inches is allowed on each log to cover possible damage to the ends of the log during floating.

Felling takes place during the winter and the sawlogs, pitprops and pulpwood are hauled to the river to await floating when the ice melts. Here a measurement is taken by certified measurers and is final as between the forest owner seller and the sawmill buyer and is the quantity to be invoiced at the pre-arranged price.

The sawlogs are measured for *length* and *top diameter*, and their contents calculated as if they were perfect cylinders of those top diameters. For measuring round logs as cylinders the formula is: *Length × area of cross section.* The area of a circle is πr^2—where $\pi = 3{\cdot}1416$ and r = radius. All the measurements must be in the same units (*i.e.*, the length must be in feet and the radius in feet), so if the radius is measured in inches this must, when squared, be divided by 144. The formula then becomes :—

$$\textit{Length}\ (\text{feet}) \times \pi \times \frac{\textit{radius}\ (\text{inches})^2}{144}.$$

However it is simpler to use the diameter of the tree in these calculations, since this is ascertained immediately from the callipers. The diameter is double the radius and its square is four times the square of the radius, so the calculation is now :—

$$\frac{\textit{Length}\ (\text{feet}) \times 3{\cdot}1416\ (\pi) \times \textit{diameter}\ (\text{inches})^2}{144 \times 4}.$$

This may be resolved still further to :—

$$\frac{\textit{Length}\ (\text{feet}) \times \textit{diameter}\ (\text{inches})^2}{183{\cdot}34}.$$

In practice the divisor is generally accepted as 183 only. It is found that about 235 cubic feet of logs are required to produce one standard of 165 cubic feet of sawn goods, this loss of about 30 per cent. going partly in sawdust which may be used for the power house, and partly in slabs, edgings and trimmings which are converted into chips which are used for pulp for paper and wallboards.

(*a*) Customs Calliper Measure.

The formula given above is used also by the Customs Fund Measurers in the U.K. as one method for measuring round timber. They take the diameter at mid-length of log which gives a reasonably true figure of the cubic contents of the log and is known as customs calliper measure.

(*b*) Piled Fathom.

Pitprops and pulpwood are measured by piling them in a frame 6 feet wide and 6 feet high, which contains one piled fathom of 216 cubic feet of 6-foot lengths. Only one length is framed at a time and if, for instance, the lengths are 4 feet, the frame contains two-thirds of a fathom and so on. This is often referred to as "loose" or "piled" measure. The actual solid content of a piled fathom of

216 cubic feet is very nearly 165 cubic feet, *i.e.*, a standard, so as units of measurement the piled fathom and the standard are practically equal. Statistically it is presumed that a piled fathom contains three-quarters of solid wood.

Roundwood can of course be, and sometimes is, measured in bulk pile, by calculating the average height and width of a pile of any length.

It is customary when loading pitprops from the water, where they are measured in frames on pontoons, to allow 5 per cent. of the total measurement to compensate for the piling in the frames being looser when loaded from the water than from the land.

Another recognised method of calculating a fathom of pitprops is by an agreed scale of running or lineal feet of each top diameter, which has been found to give, on the average, a fair result.

Top diameters ...	2½ ins.	3 ins.	4 ins.	4½ ins.	5 ins.	5½ ins.
Running feet ...	3,000	2,160	1,800	1,440	1,200	960
Top diameters ...	6 ins.	6½ ins.	7 ins.	7½ ins.	8 ins.	
Running feet ...	840	600	480	400	360	

The top diameter stated is the " minimum " top diameter and generally no piece may have a top diameter in inches more than it has length in feet.

In practice whilst pitprops are imported in units of fathoms, they are usually distributed to the mines in units of Gothenburg standards (as follows) and they may require a good deal of adjustment to the particular top diameter and length required to suit the special requirements of the mine owing to variations in the seam to be worked, etc.

(*c*) Gothenburg Standard.

Pitprops are also sold by the Gothenburg standard of 180 cubic feet, the quantity being calculated in lineal or running feet of top diameter.

Sets of tables are issued from which these calculations can be made quickly, as follows :—

Top diameters ...	3 ins.	4 ins.	5 ins.	6 ins.	7 ins.	8 ins.
Running feet ...	1,800	1,116	792	540	396	288

The rules for measuring the pitprops state :—(i) The least diameter at top (or smaller) end of prop is measured (pitprops are generally more oval than round in section) ; (ii) Measurements are taken to half inches, and if a fraction are taken to the nearest lower half inch.

(*d*) Firewood Fathom.

In the conversion of logs into sawn goods in the sawmill, falling lengths under 6 feet become firewood and are cut to lengths in multiples of 6 inches down to 1½ feet or 1 foot. These are also sold per *fathom* of 216 cubic feet. Although there may be a great deal of wane, every piece at the worst must be touched by the saw the whole length on both sides and both edges, but if one edge is quite square, the other may be fully waney. Firewood is often piled for seasoning in open stacks with half as much space as wood in the pile, from which the actual content can be calculated.

All these measurements refer to English feet of 12 English inches. There is also a Norwegian, or Norsk inch, which is nearly 3 per cent. longer than the English inch. This is commonly used for sawing measurements to allow for the normal shrinkage from fresh sawn to shipping dry.

(*e*) Petersburg Standard—Sawn Goods.

Sawn goods are measured in Petersburg standards of 165 cubic feet. This again is a " solid " measure. This originates from the import of Russian timber to the U.K. in the form of " deals " $1\frac{1}{2}$ ins. × 11 ins. × 12 ft. The normal unit was a " hundred " deals, but this was the " long hundred " of ten dozen. The St. Petersburg standard hundred, abbreviated P.S.H., was therefore 120 deals amounting to 165 cubic feet. This unit is now practically universally employed for the measure of sawn softwood and is commonly written std.

The calculation of Petersburg standard quantity is purely a question of mathematics. In general the total lineal measurement of the parcel is obtained in feet (by addition of the lengths of the various pieces) which is then multiplied by the width and thickness in inches divided by 144. This gives the total quantity in cubic feet which, when divided by 165, gives the quantity in standards.

There are many short cuts to these calculations and there are also several sets of tables whereby the standard quantity can be ascertained quickly from the total lineal feet of any particular cross-section.

The reason for the contract forms and charter-party setting out in full " St. Petersburg standard of 165 cubic feet " is that there are other " standards " of local significance in other countries, or past times, though not now current in this country, such as :—

Christiania Standard	—$103\frac{1}{8}$ cub. ft.	—120 pieces	$1\frac{1}{4}$ ins. × 9 ins. × 11 ft.
Drammen ,,	—$121\frac{7}{8}$,,	—120 ,,	$1\frac{1}{4}$ ins. × 9 ins. × 13 ft.
Irish (or *London*) ,,	—270 ,,	—120 ,,	3 ins. × 9 ins. × 12 ft.
Quebec ,,	—$229\frac{1}{6}$,,	—100 ,,	$2\frac{1}{2}$ ins. × 11 ins. × 12 ft.
Gothenburg ,,	—180 ,,	—120 ,,	2 ins. × 9 ins. × 12 ft.

There are also the " freight basis " standards of 120 cubic feet for poles and 150 cubic feet for baulks and spars.

(*f*) Petersburg Standard (Nominal Measure)—Planed Goods.

It is understood that in planing North European softwood $\frac{1}{8}$ inch is lost in thickness and $\frac{1}{4}$ inch in width. A board 1 in. × 6 ins. that is planed plain-edged (P.E.) therefore actually measures $\frac{7}{8}$ in. × $5\frac{3}{4}$ ins. If boards are tongued and grooved (T.G.) a further $\frac{1}{4}$ inch is lost on the tongue and the surface measure of the board would be only $5\frac{1}{2}$ inches, which is important when calculating the surface to be covered when laid.

Planed goods are bought and sold on nominal measure, that is to say on a measurement based upon the timber from which they are produced, and P.T.G. boards measuring actually $\frac{7}{8}$ in. thick × $5\frac{1}{2}$ ins. face are charged as 1 in. × 6 ins.

Freight however is charged on actual and not nominal measure, but whether the boards are tongued and grooved or plain-edged the calculated differences between the actual and the nominal sizes are the same, namely $\frac{1}{8}$ inch in thickness and $\frac{1}{4}$ inch in width, since the width of the tongue (which takes up space in the ship) must be paid for. The saving in freight between actual and nominal measure may amount to a considerable sum, for instance on 1 in. × 6 ins. nominal boards it amounts to over 16 per cent.

Sawn softwood is nearly always carried by rail on a " measurement weight " basis. That is to say the carriage rate is per ton, and the measured volume of the goods is converted to tons. In the case of North European softwood it is converted on the basis of one standard to $2\frac{1}{2}$ tons. Planed goods are carried by rail in the U.K. on a " machine weight " basis, that is to say the goods are weighed on a weighbridge.

The differences between nominal and actual measure that are customary in Scandinavia are not necessarily the same elsewhere. Pacific Coast softwoods are subject to the following rules, and the words " surfacing " or " dressing " are used instead of " planing."

Sizes 4 inches and under in thickness, 6 inches and under in width, worked $\frac{1}{4}$ inch less for one or more sides or edges surfaced ; in other words both width and thickness may be $\frac{1}{4}$ inch scant. Widths over 6 inches, each edge will be surfaced $\frac{1}{4}$ inch less.

In practice, however, it has been customary to import all building dimensions up to 3 ins. × 9 ins. " $\frac{1}{4}$ inch scant " and not according to the rule for widths over 6 inches. Further, the wood may be surfaced when freshly sawn, so that after normal shrinkage during seasoning the scantness may amount to $\frac{3}{8}$ inch.

Sizes over 4 inches in thickness and 6 inches and over in width will be worked $\frac{1}{4}$ inch less for each side or edge surfaced.

Consequently 2 ins. × 4 ins. S4S (surfaced four sides)

		finishes	$1\frac{3}{4}$ ins. × $3\frac{3}{4}$ ins.
3 ins. × 7 ins.	,,	,,	$2\frac{3}{4}$ ins. × $6\frac{1}{2}$ ins.
6 ins. × 9 ins.	,,	,,	$5\frac{1}{2}$ ins. × $8\frac{1}{2}$ ins.

It will be found useful in describing any piece of wood to refer to the wider dimension as the " side " and the narrower dimension as the " edge." Of the two sides of a piece, the better or in the case of planed wood the more perfectly finished side, is the " face," the reverse side being the " back."

Although not current in this country, it is as well to know that the Pacific Coast term equivalent to the Scandinavian P.T.G. is D.&M. standing for Dressed and Matched, *i.e.*, surfaced with tongued and grooved edges. Another American equivalent term is S2S&S.M., *i.e.*, surfaced two sides and standard matched, the main difference being a greater loss in the finished as against the nominal sizes in the American than the Scandinavian.

The degree of seasoning affects the difference between nominal and actual measure. The American terms used are KD for Kiln-dried: AD for Air-dried: G for Green (unseasoned). Their standard Planing patterns (or profiles) show :—

1 in. × 3 ins.	Flooring TG Kiln-dried	$2\frac{3}{8}$ ins. face :	Green $2\frac{1}{2}$ ins. face.
1 in. × 4 ins.	" " "	$3\frac{1}{4}$ ins. "	" $3\frac{3}{8}$ ins. "
1 in. × 6 ins.	" " "	$5\frac{3}{16}$ ins. "	" $5\frac{5}{16}$ ins. "

The face measure does not of course include the tongue, but represents the floor area the board will cover when laid. The face measure is used for calculating the amount required to cover a particular floor area (see page 234); it is not used for freight calculations.

(*g*) LOAD.

The load in imported timber is 50 cubic feet for sawngoods and 40 cubic feet for round timber or trees. This unit of measurement was used by the Board of Trade for statistical returns until they found the Petersburg standard more convenient. It is still used to some extent by many of the port authorities in the U.K., including the P.L.A., which also uses the Mille of 1,200 pieces (which is the unit of sale of hardwood staves), the Ton of 2,240 lb., and the unit number of 120 pieces of Poles, etc.

(*h*) OTHER NORTH EUROPEAN MEASUREMENTS.

In addition there are the following selling units :—

Upper Gulf Hewn Baulks—per standard of 150 cubic feet (as apart from loads of 50 cubic feet); *Telegraph Poles*—per piece; *Other Poles*—per foot run; *Rickers*—per piece or per foot run; *Putlogs* (hewn birch 6 ft. × 3 ins. × 3 ins.)—per piece; *Mouldings*—per foot run or 100 feet run; *Plywood*—per square foot or per 100 square feet; *Doors*—per piece; *Sawn Laths*—per bundle or per standard.

Sawn laths are normally $\frac{1}{4}$ in. × 1 in. from Sweden and $\frac{3}{16}$ in. × 1 in. from Finland, measuring $2\frac{1}{2}$ feet or 3 feet to $4\frac{1}{2}$ feet or 5 feet long, rising by half feet.

The proportion of lengths is usually fixed, as certain localities prefer certain lengths in greater proportion. Sawn laths are always bundled in bundles of 500 feet run, whatever the length, and may be sold either per bundle or per standard.

$\frac{1}{4}$ in. × 1 in. laths are 190·08 bundles to the standard, though usually sold per bundle. $\frac{3}{16}$ in. × 1 in. laths are 253·44 bundles to the standard, and usually sold per standard where 1d. per bundle is equivalent approximately to one guinea per standard.

Handsplit Laths, usually $\frac{3}{16}$ in. × 1$\frac{1}{8}$ ins., seldom seen nowadays, are sold per bundle of 360 feet run; *Lathwood*, seldom imported now, per piled fathom of 288 cubic feet; *Russian Piled Fathom*, for pitprops —343 cubic feet (*i.e.*, 7 ft. × 7 ft. × 7 ft.); *Cordwood* consists mainly of branches and tops of hardwood, intended for fuel, cut to lengths of 4 ft. and piled in a frame measuring 4 ft. high and 8 ft. long (or its equivalent) and comprising one cord of 128 cubic feet piled measure. For statistical purposes it is estimated that a cord contains approximately three-fifths, or about 75 cubic feet, of solid wood, or in other words it takes about 1·66 cords to provide 128 cubic feet of solid wood.

(*j*) Hardwoods.

Hardwood units of measurement and sale are much simpler. With the exception of North America, the unit is usually the *cubic foot*, and the calculation of quantity merely a question of mathematics. As mentioned elsewhere, the "Hoppus foot" is the customary unit for the sale of round logs and this equals 1·273 actual cubic feet.

Some expensive or heavy hardwoods such as lignum vitæ, boxwood, ebony, etc., are sold by weight, but they are the principal exceptions.

In North America the unit of measurement of hardwoods is the *board foot*. This is a square foot of timber 1 inch thick (12 ins. × 12 ins. × 1 in.) and therefore equal to one twelfth of a cubic foot. A full definition of the measurement of a board foot is given in the N.H.L.A. (para. 16) grading rules, and is reproduced on page 259. In calculating the board measure of a parcel of timber, all measurements 1 in. and over are converted to square feet 1 inch thick. If the parcel is of 1 inch boards, then the board measure is simply the sum of the surface area in square feet of each piece. A piece 12 ft. × 9 ins. × 1 in. contains 9 board feet, usually written 9 ft. B.M.

When boards are thicker than 1 in., the surface area (in feet) is multiplied by the thickness. Thus a board 12 ft. × 9 ins. × 2 ins. contains 18 ft. B.M.; one 12 ft. × 9 ins. × 3 ins. contains 27 ft. B.M.

For very large transactions, to avoid being too cumbersome, the measurements are taken "per thousand board feet," 37,000 board feet is then written 37 M.ft. B.M., or more often 37 m.b.m.

Boards under 1 *inch in thickness* are sold per square foot surface measure of that particular thickness, so that M.ft. B.M. of $\frac{3}{4}$ inch contains only three-quarters of the quantity of M.ft. B.M. of 1 inch.

In importing hardwood into the U.K., the quantity in the contract is often given in *carloads*. This is a term used regularly in the American hardwood trade, and simply denotes the amount of timber that can be carried in one of the long American railway covered "cars." In the U.K. it would be called a "waggon load" although the quantity would be much smaller and the British waggons are open. The

American Hardwood Lumber contract defines a carload as follows :— " Unless this contract states a specific quantity of either cubic or superficial feet a carload shall be considered to contain the equivalent of about 15,000 superficial feet B.M. of 1 inch."

Unedged boards are usually measured at the middle, or average, width (including half the wane, calculated by taking the mean of the two sides) to the nearest lower half inch and lengths to the nearest lower half foot. But under $1\frac{1}{2}$ inch thick are usually measured inside the wane. For instance $1\frac{1}{4}$ inch and under Finnish Unedged Birch is measured inside the wane on the narrow side.

(*k*) ROUND TIMBER MEASUREMENTS.

(i) *The Customs Fund Calliper Measurement*, based upon $L \times D^2/183$. Where L is length in feet, and D is diameter in inches at mid length of log, has been described in para. (*a*), page 224.

(ii) *Customs Fund String Measure or* 113 *Divisor.*

Another measurement that may be used to calculate the actual contents of a round log is Customs Fund String Measure, sometimes called " string measure " or " $\frac{1}{4}$ girth measure." The circumference of the log is measured in the middle, or at various places in its length—and an average figure for the circumference of the log thereby obtained. From elementary geometry principles, the circumference (C inches) is equal to $2\pi r$ ($\pi = 3{\cdot}1416$, $r =$ radius in inches). The mean cross section area of the log is πr^2 (presuming it to be cylindrical). Since $C = 2\pi r$, $r = C/2\pi$.

The cross section area is therefore

$$\pi \times C/2\pi \times C/2\pi = C^2/4\pi \text{ sq. ins. or } C^2/4\pi \times 144 \text{ sq. ft.}$$

which may be written $(C/4)^2 \times 1/\pi \times 36 = (C/4)^2 \times 1/113$.

The volume of timber in the log is given by the length $\times$ cross section area and is therefore $L \times (C/4)^2 \times 1/113$, where L is the length in feet $C/4$ is the quarter girth in inches—*i.e.*, the circumference divided by 4.

(iii) *Hoppus System*—144 *Divisor.*

Round timber may also be measured by the Hoppus System, also known as " Hoppus quarter-girth," " string 144 divisor," " quarter-girth 144 divisor," etc. This is a simplified system and is based upon assumptions of what can be sawn out of a particular log, rather than on any attempt to calculate the true volume of the log. The circumference of the log is measured in the middle in inches by string or tape and divided by 4 giving the " quarter-girth." The length is taken in feet. The calculation is then based upon $L \times (C/4)^2 \times 1/144$, the result being in " cubic feet Hoppus measure."

This measure may be visualised by theoretically converting the log into a square baulk of which each side is equal to the quarter-girth, the slabs on the four sides being thrown in as it were for good measure. Incidentally, whilst the baulk would give a clear measurement across any one face, of the amount of the quarter-girth, simple geometrical considerations will show that it would have a small amount of wane on each corner.

Measurement by the 144 divisor method gives about 21½ per cent. less than the true contents as given by the 113 divisor. The units of measurement so obtained are sometimes called "Hoppus feet" or simply "cubic feet." The latter is of course not correct as far as actual volume is concerned, although it represents closely the volume of usable timber that can be produced from the log. Wherever used in this connection, the words "cubic feet" should be qualified by "Hoppus measure." Full sets of calculating tables are obtainable based upon the Hoppus system. (The same result in "Hoppus feet" is obtained by taking the diameter instead of the quarter-girth and dividing by 233.)

Francon and Auquart are the metre equivalents of Hoppus.

There are other systems of log measurement in use in America of which complete tables are set out in Brereton's Practical Lumberman. The following measurements in board feet of a 20 foot log of 20 ins. and of 40 ins. dimeter indicate how these differ from Hoppus and from each other :—

		20 ins diameter	*40 ins diameter*
Actual measurement	....	524	2094
Hoppus measurement	....	412	1648
Scribner Log Table	....	350	1505
Spaulding Log Table	....	345	1481
British Columbia Log Table		326	1411

Swedish shippers have sometimes referred to "Ericson's Log Measurement Tables." These are purely mathematical, showing the actual cubic contents of so many feet run of logs (as cylinders) of certain diameters. As a basis of sale one would, of course, want to know whether the diameter was being taken at the top (as customary) or at the middle.

(iv) *Imported Round and Hewn Logs.*

These are measured by the "Liverpool String or Quarter-Girth" measure, based on 144 divisor as detailed above. Length is called down to the nearest quarter foot and quarter-girth called down to the nearest quarter inch. If measurement of the quarter-girth is made over the bark, an allowance is made by deduction off the dimensions before calculating the quantity. For quarter-girth up to 11¾ inches the deduction is ½ inch, 12 inches to 17¾ inches deduction is 1 inch, 18 inches and over deduction is increased by an additional ½ inch for each increase of 6 inches (or part) of quarter-girth.

(v) *Home Grown Round Logs.*

The 144 divisor is used, the length being taken in whole feet only, down to the nearest foot except if the log has been cross cut to a specified length when the length may be taken to a quarter of a foot. The girth is taken at the middle of the length being measured. Where logs are of irregular shape each straight section of the log is measured separately as above.

(vi) *Railway Measure for Round Logs.*

Logs are carried by rail on a "measurement weight" basis, and specific instructions are given in the "General Classification of Merchandise" as to how these measurements are to be computed. The 144 divisor is normally used, lengths are called down to the nearest half foot. Quarter-girth to be measured over bark, and if bark stripped off (for measuring under-bark girth for invoicing, etc.) the girth for railway carriage purposes to be taken on each side of the stripped place and averaged. Tonnage is then calculated on a set schedule of cubic feet per ton for each species of timber.

(vii) *Bark Allowances.*

Where the volume of round logs is being calculated from measurement of the circumference of the log, the presence of the bark can clearly greatly affect the measurements. By far the most satisfactory method is to strip the bark off and then measure the quarter-girth. If measurement is made over bark, usually abbreviated T.O.B. (tape over bark), the allowance may be in the form of the "Liverpool Conventional Allowance" off the dimension of the quarter-girth, or it may be an allowance in the form of a percentage off the total calculated quantity. The percentage allowance varies between England and Scotland and between the various species of trees.

	England and Wales.	*Scotland.*
Conifers	$7\frac{1}{2}\%$	10%
Ash, sycamore, beech, birch	$7\frac{1}{2}\%$	$7\frac{1}{2}\%$
Poplar, elm, alder, lime	15%	15%
Oak, chestnut and others	10%	10%

(*l*) *Metric Measurements.*

Metric measurements are occasionally encountered in the timber trade. European plywood is usually produced in millimetre thicknesses, but sold per square foot or per 100 square feet. There are occasions however when cubic metres may be used as a measurement of plywood. The normal conversion tables are as follows :—

25·4 millimetres = 1 inch.
1 metre = 3·2809 English feet = 39·37 English inches
1 square metre = 10·764 English square feet.
1 cubic metre or stere = 35·3174 English cubic feet.
4·673 cubic metres = 1 standard.
1 cubic metre fathom = 2×2×2 = 8 cubic metres.

Softwood from Central Europe is sometimes shipped in metric measurements but charged in English measurements. Where this occurs the relation between English and metric measure is usually clearly defined in the terms of the sale, since an approximation is used and not the exact conversion factor of 25·4 m/m to the inch.

2. Retail Measurements.

(*a*) GENERAL.

Retail measurements show a much greater variation of units than bulk measurements. The selection of units upon which a sale is to be made is a local arrangement between buyer and seller. It depends upon the quantity being sold and upon the buyer's own particular trade.

Where reasonably large quantities are involved, the wholesale units of measurement may be used.

Any particular parcel of softwood or hardwood may be sold by any one of 3 or 4 different units of measurement, as follows :—

Standard, of 165 cubic feet—for softwoods.

Cubic foot—for hardwoods.

Lineal foot of 1 *in.*×12 *ins. or per square foot* 1 *inch thick*—equivalent to the American "Board Measure" (board foot or ft. B.M.).

These prices are independent of the dimensions of the timber. The square foot of 1 inch unit of sale is very convenient for retail transactions and a basis for calculating other prices per lineal or square foot.

Square foot or Superficial foot—this will vary according to thickness. Sometimes as "per foot super."

Lineal foot—this will vary according to both width and thickness.

Piece—this will vary according to width, thickness and length.

It is useful to remember that 1d. per square foot of 1 inch = 1s. per cubic foot = £8, 5s. per standard. Therefore 8d. per square foot of 1 inch = 8s. per cubic foot = £66 per standard.

In small sales of the order of $\frac{1}{10}$ standard to $\frac{1}{4}$ standard, it is rather cumbersome to convert measurements to standards and then charge per standard. It is simpler and easier for the buyer if the charge is made per lineal foot or per square foot.

Any price in £ per standard can be quickly converted into a price in pence per lineal foot of 1 in.×12 ins. (or square foot of 1 inch thick, or board foot) by dividing by $8\frac{1}{4}$.

A price per square foot of 1 inch can then be converted to a price per square foot in any other thickness merely by multiplication, *e.g.*, 8d. per square foot of 1 inch is equivalent to

8d.×2 = 1s. 4d. per square foot of 2 inches.
8d.×3 = 2s. per square foot of 3 inches.
8d.×$\frac{3}{4}$ = 6d. per square foot of $\frac{3}{4}$ inch.

A price per lineal foot can then easily be obtained by taking the price per square foot—multiplying by width and dividing by 12, *e.g.*, 8d. per square foot of 1 inch is equivalent to

$8 \times 3/12 = 2$d. per lineal foot of 3 ins. $\times$ 1 in.
$8 \times 3/4 \times 3/12 = 1\frac{1}{2}$d. per lineal foot of 3 ins. $\times \frac{3}{4}$ in.

and so on. Where 550 lineal feet of 3 ins. $\times \frac{3}{4}$ in. are to be charged, it is obviously more simple to charge this at $1\frac{1}{2}$d. per lineal foot—rather than to convert it into a standard quantity and multiply by £66 per standard.

The buyer or seller of timber soon becomes accustomed to the relationship between various prices per lineal or square foot and the basis price per square foot of 1 inch.

There is a limit to the use of these small units, since fine price differences in £ per standard cannot very well be converted to a price per lineal or square foot. A difference of $\frac{1}{8}$d. in the square foot, which is about the smallest difference that can be taken in this way, represents £1, 0s. $7\frac{1}{2}$d. per standard.

Mouldings for builders, etc., may be charged per lineal foot or per 100 lineal feet—the latter enabling finer price differences to be obtained when necessary.

Plywood and other sheet materials may be sold per square foot, per 100 square feet or per 1,000 square feet depending upon conditions of price, etc.

The choice of unit depends mainly on the quantity in question: also on the type of buyer and the salesmanship of the seller. The keen buyer, accustomed to the ramifications of the working of the timber trade, will usually buy his timber per standard or per cubic foot. Another buyer, in different circumstances, would be horrified at paying £66 per standard, but will accept $1\frac{1}{2}$d. per lineal foot of 3 ins. $\times \frac{3}{4}$ in. (the same price, in fact) quite happily. Yet another would accept a price of 16s. 8d. per 100 lineal feet more readily than 2d. per lineal foot. To some people, " per 100 lineal feet " sounds as if they are getting more for their money, it is a matter of the seller studying his customer.

(*b*) Flooring Measurements.

Whilst planed boards are imported at a price per standard (nominal measure) and are often resold on the same basis, they are also sold per " square " in some parts of the country. The *square* is a superficial measure of 100 square feet irrespective of thickness and may be applied to rough boards as well as planed. The number of " squares " in a standard depends on the thickness of the boards and, like the standard, it is calculated on nominal measure.

The *square yard* is also superficial and measures 9 square feet which, if applied to rough boards would of course be the same in actual as in nominal measure, but when applied to planed boards is nominal measure unless qualified by the word " laid " when it becomes the actual surface measure covered when the boards have been laid.

In the same way an actual covered surface after laying 100 square feet is a "laid square," and sometimes quotations are made on that basis.

As trade customs vary considerably in different parts of the country in quoting "nominal," "actual," or "laid" measure, it is very important that there should be a clear understanding between seller and buyer as to what exactly is meant. In quoting for instance for a "laid square" the finished width of the "face" of the board must be taken into consideration to allow for the difference between "nominal" and "laid" measure.

Laid measure is also a superficial measure, but so far from being "nominal" means something more than "actual" (which in tongued and grooved boards includes the measurement of the tongue) being based on the "face" measure, quotations being per "laid square" or "laid yard."

In calculating the quantity required to lay a certain area of flooring, it must be remembered that the actual "face" measure of Scandinavian planed plain-edged (P.P.E.) boards is $\frac{1}{4}$ inch less in width than the nominal and that of planed tongued and grooved (P.T.G.) boards is $\frac{1}{2}$ inch less, the $\frac{1}{4}$ inch tongue being concealed in the groove. Consequently in the case of P.E. flooring there must be added to the running feet of nominal measure enough wood to make up an extra $\frac{1}{4}$ inch in width (in the case of 6 inch nominal an addition to the running feet of one twenty-third or 4·35 per cent.) and in the case of P.T.G. an extra $\frac{1}{2}$ inch in width (in the case of 6 inch nominal one-eleventh or a fraction over 9 per cent.).

Of 1 inch thick there are 1,980 square feet in a standard.

Unplaned or nominal } 19·8 squares in a standard.
220 square yards in a standard.

Of 6 inch width there are 200 running feet in a square.

P.P.E. ... ... 208·7 running feet in a laid square.
P.T.G. ... ... 218·2 ,, ,, ,,

From these basic figures other thicknesses and widths can easily be calculated. Putting it another way, to find :—

Square feet in a *standard*, divide 1,980 by thickness in inches.
Squares in a *standard*, divide 19·8 by thickness in inches.
Square yards in a *standard*, divide 220 by thickness in inches.
Running feet in a *standard*, divide 23,760 by cross-section in inches.
Running feet in a *square*, divide 1,200 by nominal width in inches.
Running feet in a *laid square*, divide 1,200 by actual face width in inches.
Running feet in a *square yard*, divide 108 by nominal width in inches.
Running feet in a *laid yard*, divide 108 by actual face width in inches.

The foregoing "laid" units which are customary in softwoods are also generally used for hardwood block and strip flooring but the difference between "nominal" and "face" measure may not be the same.

(*c*) SPECIAL HARDWOOD MEASUREMENTS.

Frequently hardwood logs, either imported or home grown, are cut " through and through " producing boards sawn on two surfaces but with two waney edges. In these cases it is customary to measure the width, in the middle of the length, including half the wane, but in some cases the 1 in. thick and under are measured inside the wane.

If there is variation in the width of the boards from end to end—mean values for width are taken over the whole board, say by measuring at each end and in two other places—adding total width measurements together and dividing by 4. Alternatively each part of the board where width remains more or less constant may be measured separately for length and width.

3. Terms and Definitions.

Imported sawn softwoods have a wide variety of names, depending upon the dimension. These names vary all over the U.K. The British Standards Institution has standardised them in their B.S. 565—1949, summarised hereunder :—

Imported Sawn Softwood.

Term.	*Dimension.*
Plank ...	2 ins. to 4 ins. thick × 11 ins. and wider.
Deal ...	2 ins. to 4 ins. thick × 9 ins. to under 11 ins. wide.
Batten ...	2 ins. to 4 ins. thick × 5 ins. to 8 ins. wide.
Scantling ...	2 ins. to 4 ins. thick × 2 ins. to 4½ ins. wide.
Board ...	Under 2 ins. thick × 4 ins. and wider.
Strip ...	Under 2 ins. thick × under 4 ins. wide.
Slating ...	½ in. to 1 in. thick × 1 in. to 3 ins. wide.
Square ...	1 in. × 1 in. to 6 ins. × 6 ins.
Baulk	4 ins. × 4½ ins. or greater cross-section.
Flitch ...	4 ins. × 12 ins. or greater cross-section.
Shook ...	Set of pieces of sawn and/or machined timber ready for assembly to form a box or crate.

These have not all been universally adopted, a typical difference from this set of definitions is found in the North West, where the regular deal size is 3 ins. × 7 ins., as against 2 ins. and up × 9 ins. and up in the South East.

In sales contracts this difference in terms (with certain exceptions) does not arise as the actual dimension is always specified, although in negotiations leading up to them the terms may be used generally and should therefore be understood. There are however four occasions when the terms used are of importance :—

(i) In the *Albion and Uniform contracts*, clause 2, reference is made to " slatings, boards 4½ inches and under and VI quality " as being excluded from the limit of ends to 7½ per cent.

(ii) The *Nubaltwood charter* contains the following rule :—" *Memo.*— Battens to be considered 2 ins.×4 ins. and up to 3 ins.×7 ins. Slatings to be considered 1 inch and under in thickness and 3 inches and under in width."

(Remember when chartering for planed goods to insert after planed boards and/or floorings " bundled and/or unbundled " to cover this difference which is particularly likely to occur in the " quantity under 1 inch " mentioned in the same line.)

(iii) *Port Dock Dues and Labour Charges.* It will be found that there are often different rates in different ports for handling deals, battens, boards, etc., so the importer or merchant must acquaint himself with the local customs and terms if these are not already laid down in detail in the schedule of charges for the Port. *The Port of London Authority*, for instance, rules as follows, the rates varying according to dimension and generally increasing as the size diminishes :—

Deals, Battens and Boards (*including bundled goods*) : 6 feet and up in length, of a cross-section of 15 square inches and not exceeding 44 square inches ; 6 square inches and under 15 square inches ; over 3 square inches and under 6 square inches ; 3 square inches and under loose.

Thickstuff, Logs and Flitches. Cross-section exceeding 44 square inches but not exceeding 72 square inches.

Slating Battens, squares and strips and sawn laths ; in bundles (1 in.×3 ins. and under or the equivalent, excluding goods over $3\frac{1}{2}$ inches wide).

(iv) The *Firewood Trade.* Lengths 1 foot to $5\frac{1}{2}$ feet rising by $\frac{1}{2}$ feet.

Deals and battens—2 inches and up thick ; width plus thickness over 7 inches.

Scantlings—2 inches and up thick ; width plus thickness, maximum 7 inches.

Boards—1 inch and over but under 2 inches thick ; width plus thickness minimum 7 inches.

Planchettes—1 inch and over but under 2 inches thick ; width plus thickness under 7 inches.

4. Calculations.

Once the trade terms and units of sale are understood, timber trade calculations become merely a question of a clear brain and elementary arithmetic. Accuracy is essential. Speed in making calculations will come only with continual practice, some short cuts are described in this chapter, but the person constantly making timber calculations will evolve many short cuts of his own.

(*a*) STANDARD QUANTITIES.

In softwood calculations, the essential unit to remember is that 1 standard = 165 cubic feet. Any person can then calculate standard quantities merely by calculating the total number of cubic feet and dividing by 165. The total quantity in cubic feet is the sum of the length × width × thickness of each piece, all the measurements being in feet. Where, as in many cases, the width and thickness are constant, all that is necessary is to add all the lengths together, and then multiply by width and thickness (in feet).

E.g. A parcel of 3 ins. × 9 ins. contains 8 pieces 10 feet, 4 pieces 11 feet, 7 pieces 12 feet. The sum of the lengths is 80 + 44 + 84 = 208 feet. The quantity in cubic feet is $3/12 \times 9/12 \times 208 = 39$ cubic ft.

The standard quantity is $39/165 = 0{\cdot}236$ standards.

Standard measurements are normally made to three places of decimals only—this being accurate enough for commercial calculations.

It will be observed that in all calculations of this nature it is necessary to obtain the total lineal feet of the particular dimension. It is convenient therefore to remember what the standard of 165 cubic feet represents in lineal footage of certain key dimensions.

165 cubic feet of timber can be visualised as 165 lineal feet of timber of cross-section 12 ins. × 12 ins. For timber of 12 ins. × 1 in. cross-section the lineal feet for 1 standard is therefore $165 \times 12 = 1{,}980$ feet. For timber of 1 in. × 1 in. cross-section the lineal feet for 1 standard is therefore $165 \times 12 \times 12 = 23{,}760$ feet.

The lineal feet per standard for any dimension is therefore the cross-section of that size divided into 23,760.

E.g. 3 ins. × 9 ins. $\frac{23{,}760}{3 \times 9} = 880$ feet run.

$2\frac{1}{2}$ ins. × 6 ins. $\frac{23{,}760}{2\frac{1}{2} \times 6} = 1{,}584$ feet run.

$\frac{7}{8}$ in. × $5\frac{3}{4}$ ins. $\frac{23{,}760}{\frac{7}{8} \times 5\frac{3}{4}} = 4{,}722{\cdot}48$ feet run.

Obviously there will be twice the lineal feet per standard of 1 in. × 6 ins. (or its equivalent—say 2 ins. × 3 ins. or $1\frac{1}{2}$ ins. × 4 ins.) as 1 in. × 12 ins.—and lineal feet per standard of 1 in. × 6 ins. is therefore $1{,}980 \times 2 = 3{,}960$ lineal feet. Similarly there will be half the lineal feet of 2 ins. × 12 ins., so lineal feet per standard will be $\frac{1{,}980}{2} = 990$ lin. ft.

It is not necessary to remember any of these "lineal feet per standard" figures, provided the figures 165, 1,980 and 23,760 are remembered, particularly the last one, and the simple method of calculating the others. A calculation of standard quantity then becomes a matter of (*a*) calculating the lineal feet per standard for the dimension in question, (*b*) obtaining total lineal feet of that dimension, (*c*) dividing total lineal feet by lineal feet per standard.

E.g. A parcel of 3 ins. $\times$ 6 ins. comprises 1,815 lineal feet.
Lineal feet of 3 ins. $\times$ 6 ins. in a standard is

$$\frac{23{,}760}{3\times 6} = 1{,}320 \text{ lineal feet.}$$

Total lineal feet of parcel = 1,815.

$$\text{Standard quantity is therefore—}\frac{1{,}815}{1{,}320} = 1{\cdot}375 \text{ standards.}$$

There are several " ready reckoners " and " calculators " which set out the lineal feet per standard for various dimensions, and the standard quantity against lineal measurement. Any lineal measurement can be converted to standards merely by addition of the various equivalents.

E.g. 1,815 lineal feet of 3 ins. $\times$ 6 ins. From calculator—1,000 = 0·7576, 800 = 0·6061, 15 = 0·0114 : Total, 1·375 standards.

The fact that there are 1,980 lineal feet of 1 in. $\times$ 12 ins. (or square feet of 1 inch) in a standard of timber can be used for rapid calculations. Quick estimates of quantity where great accuracy is not required can be obtained by converting the lineal feet of the dimension into lineal feet of 1 in. $\times$ 12 ins., and then dividing by the round figure of 2,000.

E.g. 11,500 lineal feet 1 in. $\times$ 9 ins. boards, equivalent to 11,500 $\times$ 3/4 feet of 1 in. $\times$ 12 ins. = 8,625 feet of 1 in. $\times$ 12 ins. = approximately 4·3 standards. This is a calculation that can be done quickly in the head, without pencil, paper or calculators.

With a little modification this can be made into a comparatively accurate short cut. The aim is to convert the quantity to lineal feet of 1 in. $\times$ 12 ins. and divide by 2,000 instead of 1,980. In 1 standard, the lineal feet of 1 in. $\times$ 12 ins. is 1980 ; add 1 per cent. (19·8), giving 1,999·8 ; divide by 2,000 = 0·9999 standards. The error here from the exact quantity of 1·0 standards is only 1/100 per cent. Greater accuracy can be obtained by adding a further 1 per cent. of the 1 per cent., *i.e.*, 1,980 ; add 1 per cent. (19·8) ; add 1 per cent. of 1 per cent. (0·198) ; total, 1,999·998. Divide by 2,000 = 0·999999—here the error is 1/10,000 per cent.

Converting Feet Run to Standards.

The simplest accurate formula for calculating the number of standards in so many running feet of any size is :—

Multiply the lineal feet by the cross-section in inches and divide by 23,760, which, as already explained, is the number of running feet of 1 in. $\times$ 1 in. in a standard.

E.g. 6,542 lineal feet of 2 ins. $\times$ 7 ins. ; multiplied together = 91,588 ; divided by 23,760 = 3·854 standards.

Converting Standards to Feet Run.

Conversely, to find the number of running feet in so many standards of any dimension :—

Multiply the standards by 23,760 and divide by the cross-section in inches.

E.g. To find the number of running feet in 4 standards of 2 ins. × 7 ins. : $4 \times 23{,}760 / 2 \times 7 = 6{,}789$ feet run.

The conversion of cubic feet to standards may be done quickly, since $6 \times 165 = 990$ and if 1 per cent. is added to this, it becomes 999·9 or practically 1,000. Thus, if 1 per cent. is added to the quantity in cubic feet, and the sum multiplied by 6 and divided by 1,000 the answer is in standards within reasonable limits.

E.g. 3,050 cubic feet ; add 1 per cent. (30·5), equals 3,080·5 ; multiply by 6, giving 18,483·0 ; divide by 1,000 = 18·483 standards.

A greater degree of accuracy may be obtained by adding a further 1 per cent. of 1 per cent.

E.g. 3,050 ; add 1 per cent. (30·5) ; add 1 per cent. of 1 per cent. (0·305) ; total, 3,080·805 ; multiply by 6, giving 18,484·830 ; divide by 1,000 = 18·4848 standards.

(*b*) Nominal and Actual Measure.

In dealing with planed boards it is often necessary to calculate the " nominal " measure for invoicing purposes, and the " actual " measure for freight charges.

For instance take say 5,750 feet run of 1 in. × 6 ins. boards which have been planed, tongued and grooved (P.T.G.). The shipper's *invoice* will be for the *nominal* measure which will be shown in standards calculated thus :—

$$\frac{5{,}750 \times 1 \times 6}{23{,}760} = 1{\cdot}452 \text{ standards.}$$

The *freight* however will be calculated on the *actual* measure thus :—

$$\frac{5{,}750 \times \frac{7}{8} \times 5\frac{3}{4}}{23{,}760} = 1{\cdot}217 \text{ standards.}$$

(Remember the tongue takes up space and freight must be paid on it.)

A difference of 0·235 standards or over 16 per cent.

(*c*) Specification—Pieces and Lineal Footage.

Before standard quantities can be calculated it is necessary to assess the total lineal feet of the dimension. In the case of a specification of timber purchased from a foreign shipper, or from a merchant in this country, it is also necessary to check the specification arithmetically, and to see that the " number of pieces " is correct. In its simplest form this check consists in multiplying each length by the number of pieces, then totalling number of pieces (check against specification or invoice) and totalling the lineal feet (to enable standard quantity to be assessed).

3 ins. × 9 ins.	*Number of Pieces.*	*Length.*	*Total.*
	41	10 feet	410
	37	11 ,,	407
	52	12 ,,	624
	63	13 ,,	819
	42	14 ,,	588
	26	15 ,,	390
	11	16 ,,	176
	4	17 ,,	68
	276 pieces.		3,482 lin. ft.

Much time may be saved with the following quick method which checks both total of number of pieces, and total lineal footage at the same time. Starting with the greatest lengths first, the number of pieces are set down in consecutive and cumulative totals.

In this example :—

4,
15 (4 + 11),
41 (4 + 11 + 26),
83 (4 + 11 + 26 + 42),
146 (4 + 11 + 26 + 42 + 63),
198 (4 + 11 + 26 + 42 + 63 + 52),
235 (4 + 11 + 26 + 42 + 63 + 52 + 37),
276 (4 + 11 + 26 + 42 + 63 + 52 + 37 + 41).

The last total is of course the total number of pieces and is the first check required. Next, the last total (in this case 276) is multiplied by the next length *below* the shortest in the specification, *i.e.*, 276 × 9 = 2,484. The sum of all these now gives the total in lineal feet, *i.e.*, 3,482 feet.

This method can very easily be used on a calculating machine or adding machine—starting with the number of pieces of greatest length, the accumulated totals of number of pieces is added into the machine, the last total added in for a number of times equal to shortest length of specification less one, and the final total showing on the machine is the lineal feet.

Where a length is missing in the specification, the last accumulated total is repeated. *E.g.* *Long Method.*

Number of Pieces.	*Length.*	*Total.*
43	9 feet	387
27	10 ,,	270
34	11 ,,	374
	*	
17	13 ,,	221
18	14 ,,	252
	*	
11	16 ,,	176
150 pieces.		1,680 lineal feet.

* Note—there are no 12 feet or 15 feet lengths.

Quick Method.

11
11 (15 feet)
29
46
46 (12 feet)
80
107
150 (check on number of pieces).
1,200 (150 ft. × 8 ft.)

1,680 lineal feet.

In reading through a specification to be checked, some small mark should be made where lengths are missing, so that they are not overlooked when making the check.

If any ½ foot lengths are in the specification, all lengths may be doubled (there will then probably be several " missing " lengths to be adjusted) and final total is divided by 2.

(*d*) AVERAGE LENGTH.

The calculation of the average length of a parcel of timber is merely the division of total lineal feet by the total number of pieces. In the last example for instance :—

Total lineal feet = 1,680
" number of pieces = 150

$$\text{Average length} = \frac{1{,}680}{150} = 11{\cdot}2 \text{ feet.}$$

It will be remembered that in the calculation of average lengths in imported sawn goods, " ends " have to be omitted.

(*e*) AVERAGE WIDTH.

In a parcel of mixed widths, the calculation of average width is based upon the total of pieces by widths divided by total number of pieces.

Boards 1 inch thick.

270	3 inches wide	=	810
340	4 " "	=	1,360
483	5 " "	=	2,415
532	6 " "	=	3,192
211	7 " "	=	1,477
115	8 " "	=	920
1,951			10,174

$$\text{Average width} = \frac{10{,}174}{1{,}951} = 5{\cdot}214 \text{ inches.}$$

The quick method of calculation can also be applied here.

This is the commercial method of assessing average width—but it is only an *average width per piece*—it is not, mathematically, an average of the width of the whole parcel since this must take into account lengths as well.

(*f*) QUICK RETAIL CALCULATIONS.

The person who is making timber calculations regularly will evolve his own quick methods. When calculating retail invoice charges per square foot or per 100 square feet, it is useful to remember that 1d. per lineal foot is equivalent to 8s. 4d. per 100 lineal feet and £4, 3s. 4d. per 1,000 lineal feet.

A calculation of 1,342 feet at $3\frac{1}{2}$d. per lineal foot may be quickly made as follows :—

At 1d. per lineal foot :—		£	s.	d.	
1,000 feet at 1d.	=	4	3	4	
300 „ 3×8s. 4d.	=	1	5	0	
42 „ at 1d.	=	0	3	6	
		5	11	10	= 3d.
		5	11	10	
		5	11	10	
		2	15	11	= $\frac{1}{2}$d.
	=	£19	11	5	

For clarity this has been shown in rather greater detail than normally necessary.

Another quick method of calculating price *per lineal foot* from *price per standard* is based on the approximation of 2,000 lineal feet, 1 in.×12 ins. per standard (instead of 1980).

If price per lineal foot is *A* pence, for thickness *T* inches and width *W* inches, the cost per standard will be :—

$$\frac{A \text{ (in pence)} \times 2{,}000 \times 12 \text{ (approx. lin. ft. of 1 in.} \times 1 \text{ in. in a standard)}}{20 \times 12 \text{ (brings result to £ s. d.)} \times W \times T.}$$

From this it will be seen that

$$A \text{ (price per lin. ft.)} = \frac{\text{Price per standard (£ s. d.)} \times 20 \times 12 \times W \times T.}{2{,}000 \times 12}$$

$$= \frac{\text{Price per standard} \times W \times T.}{100}$$

The approximate price in pence per lineal foot is therefore the price per standard in £ s. d. multiplied by cross-section in inches, and divided by 100.

E.g. 2×3 at £49, 10s. per standard

$$= \frac{\text{£49, 10s.} \times 2 \times 3}{100} = \frac{297}{100} = 2{\cdot}97, \text{ say 3d. per lineal foot.}$$

(g) CALCULATING MACHINES.

People who use modern calculating machines now often wonder how they ever managed without them in earlier days. Without a doubt they enable accurate checks of specifications, invoices, etc., to be made, which previously were neglected or very often skimped. A trained operator can use a calculating machine as fast as a typewriter, but it must not be overlooked that any person making timber calculations should be able to use a calculating machine and that even using " one finger only " it can save time and increase accuracy. The golden rule in the use of calculating machines is that every calculation must be cross checked, but then in any worthwhile timber firm this is done anyway where longhand calculations are made. Calculating machines are particularly useful for the quick methods outlined previously in this chapter.

Multiplication on an adding machine is quite simple—to multiply 8 by 3, the figure 8 is " added " three times. To multiply 847 by 143, the figure 847 is added three times, 8,470 added four times, 84,700 added once.

Some calculating machines are capable of division, but the majority work purely on addition and subtraction. If it is desired to divide by a figure, say to divide cubic feet by 165 to give standard quantity, this is done by *multiplying* by the reciprocal of 165, *e.g.*, 1,437 cubic feet = 1,437/165 standards = 1,437 × 0·00606 standards.

The following reciprocals are used regularly in timber calculations :—

1/165 = 0·00606 = To convert cubic feet to standards.

1/12 = 0·08333 = To convert square feet of 1 inch to cubic feet.

1/12 × 165 = 0·000505 = To convert square feet of 1 inch to standards.

1/12 × 12 = 0·00694 = To convert square inches to square feet *or* to convert sum of multiplication of lengths in feet by width and thickness in inches to cubic feet.

1/165 × 12 × 12 = 0·0000421 = To convert sum of the multiplication of lengths in feet by width and thickness in inches to standards, *i.e.*, lineal feet of 1 in. × 1 in. to standards.

These are particularly useful on a calculating machine where the specification includes mixed widths and/or mixed thicknesses. Each length in feet is multiplied by the number of pieces, width (inches) and thickness (inches) and added in to the total on the machine.

Final total when multiplied by reciprocal 0·00694 gives cubic feet, or by reciprocal 0·0000421 gives standards.

Until the U.K. adopts a system of decimal coinage, the extension of prices in pounds, shillings and pence will always be cumbersome. On a calculating machine, the extension of standards, at so much per standard into a total of pounds, shillings and pence can best be done by converting all shillings and pence into decimals of a pound.

£	£	£
19/- = 0·95	9/- = 0·45	10d. = 0·0416
18/- = 0·9	8/- = 0·4	9d. = 0·0375
17/- = 0·85	7/- = 0·35	8d. = 0·0333
16/- = 0·8	6/- = 0·3	7d. = 0·0291
15/- = 0·75	5/- = 0·25	6d. = 0·025
14/- = 0·7	4/- = 0·2	5d. = 0·0208
13/- = 0·65	3/- = 0·15	4d. = 0·0166
12/- = 0·6	2/- = 0·1	3d. = 0·0125
11/- = 0·55	1/- = 0·05	2d. = 0·0083
10/- = 0·5	11d. = 0·0458	1d. = 0·0041

£67, 14s. 9d. then becomes £67·7375.

(*h*) Slide Rule Calculations.

By and large the timber trade look upon the slide rule as black magic peculiar to engineers and scientists quite outside their comprehension. This is really very foolish since the slide rule in reasonably competent hands can save many hours of work. The timber merchant is only concerned with multiplication and division on a slide rule, therefore no fancy engineering scales are required.

There are three important points concerning slide rule measurements :—(*a*) The accuracy of the slide rule depends upon its length, the longer the rule, the more accurate it is since divisions can be read off more easily ; (*b*) The slide rule is accurate to three figures only. In calculations up to 1 standard, maximum error = 0·001 standard ; up to 10 standards, maximum error = 0·01 standard ; up to 100 standard, maximum error = 0·1 standard. In calculations up to £1, maximum error = ¼d. ; up to £10, maximum error = 2½d. ; up to £100, maximum error = 2s. ; (*c*) Great care must be taken to ensure that the decimal points are taken up in their correct places in the answer.

Estimating and costing can be greatly simplified with a slide rule, particularly when sets of figures are being calculated. For instance, if a price per standard is known, and the rule is set as follows :—

$$\frac{\text{Price per standard} \times 240}{1{,}980 \times 12} \quad \begin{matrix}\text{(Scale A)} \\ \text{(Scale B)}\end{matrix}$$

then against every width in inches on Scale B can be read off immediately the price in pence per lineal foot on scale A.

One of the timber trade's criticisms of the slide rule in the past has been that it was not accurate enough as compared with longhand calculations. The fallacy of this criticism is in the fact that in estimating, the final figures are generally " rounded " up or down to the nearest convenient fraction or whole number.

CHAPTER XV

Grading Rules for Timber

1. General.

It will be seen from chapter II, section 2 (Grading and Shippers' Marks) and chapter V, section 4 (Description in Contract) that the classification of timber into various qualities and grades is of major importance. In the early days of any timber producing country, the grading of the timber into qualities must have been purely by experience and rule of thumb. In many countries it remains that way and provided that experienced grading men are available it is quite satisfactory.

With the passing of time, some of the major timber producing countries have felt it advisable to establish sets of written " grading rules " to which reference can be made by all people in the trade. In the case of Canada and the U.S.A. these grading rules are scientifically planned on a very comprehensive scale to cover a great number of grades. Grading rules of this nature are useful in that they do establish a definite basis. Theoretically every piece of timber in a particular parcel should be graded individually, but it is not truly practicable to examine each piece of timber as closely as the grading rules provide. It would simply not be possible to count the number of knots in each piece and measure their diameters. Grading is usually carried out either on a moving conveyor, or at the end of a conveyor from the mill as the sawn timber comes out. The time for inspection is very limited and so it comes back again to the experience of the man doing the grading. Grading rules can be deceptive if followed too slavishly without due regard to " grading by experience." Although the provision of grading rules has greatly improved the general quality of some of the Canadian productions, it has sometimes been found that pieces marked as No. 1 Merchantable were superior to pieces marked Selected Merchantable, which had been the result of following grading rules too rigidly.

The grading of the timber must be carried out economically without adding too much in labour charges to the cost of the timber. Planed boards from the Scandinavian mills are usually graded as they come off the planing machine at 200 to 300 feet per minute. To break the flow of production by a close examination of each board would obviously be far more costly than could be justified by any result of better grading.

There is in practice a very general but not invariable rule, which makes an essential difference between the grading of softwoods and hardwoods.

Softwoods, such as Baltic redwood and whitewood, and Canadian spruce and Douglas fir are normally used for construction work in the sizes in which they are shipped and the grading is based on that assumption. Consequently the practical reason for the de-grading of any piece, from the basic standard grade to a lower one, is the existence of any defect or combination of defects affecting the strength of the piece in its own size. For instance a batten with a very large (compared with the size of the piece) knot or group of knots near the middle making it unfit for use in normal construction work in its existing length must be degraded, in spite of the fact that, if the knotty section were cut out, the remaining pieces might be faultless.

By the way, it is not the knot which causes the loss of strength in timber so much as the divergence of the grain surrounding the knot.

The grading is based on constructional use, not on re-cutting. An example of an exception to this rule is Quebec pine which is normally used, not for construction work but for pattern making.

All the same there is nothing wrong in the practice of using Fifths in constructional work where strength of the kind affected is not required. An example of this would be battens on a concrete base, where it would be sheer waste to use a higher quality than Fifths.

Hardwoods on the other hand are graded mainly according to the amount of wood free from defects and of reasonable size which can be cut out of the piece, so that, contrary to the case of constructional softwood, the existence of a serious defect which can easily be cut out, leaving the rest of the piece faultless, would entitle the whole to be regarded as high grade. The grading of hardwoods is based on "cutting," not on "construction" value.

2. Finland.

The grading in Finland of sawn goods for export to this country is mainly confined to separating from the Unsorted quality any pieces which do not come up to the shipper's standard for that grading. Although the qualities of timber vary as between one shipper and another and also between one part of the country and another, there are National grading rules, published in 1937, laying down the general basis for grading under the title of "Grading Rules for Export Timber."

Introduction (extract).

The Committee is of course aware that the grading rules here set out cannot comply in every respect with all the ideas of the sawmillers, but the Committee ventures to hope that in any case these grading rules will be an important factor in the effort to unify and improve the quality of Finnish sawn goods and assist towards *increasing the reputation and value of these goods in the foreign timber markets.*

General Rules.

In accordance with the General Rules for the sorting of wood goods, the grade is decided mainly on the basis of the better side and edges of the piece, but if large defects occur on the other side, the piece is transferred in the sorting of export goods to that grade to which, on the basis of the defect on the worse side, it belongs according to the grading rules.

A piece must be judged as it stands adjusted to a prescribed length and not on the basis of what might be made out of it by cutting it into two pieces. A piece in which a defect occurs that brings it into the lower grade is, however, reckoned as belonging to the higher grade if in the absence of this defect the piece would rank as one of the better specimens in the higher grade.

The thickness of the piece is generally the ruling factor in deciding the size and number of the defects. Proportionately more and larger defects are permitted in wider than in narrower goods of the same thickness. This is the case both with regard to the size and number of the defects.

Defects occurring on the edges are regarded more seriously than defects on the sides in deciding the grade. Defects on the edges are considered to be greater if they occur on the corner.

When defects occur in clusters, the size and number of the defects must be less than would be otherwise allowed, also the composite effect of the cluster of defects must be taken as the basis for deciding the grade.

Two of the greatest defects allowed must not generally occur simultaneously except in fifth quality.

Wane in the middle of the piece is a greater defect than wane at the end of the piece.

The rules then go into details of the defects which may occur, dividing these into :—

(A) Defects in *Quality* which are (i) defects in the structure of the wood, (ii) defects in manufacture, (iii) shakes ; and
(B) Defects in *Condition* which are (i) incorrect moisture content, (ii) discoloration.

As regards defects in *Structure*, the description of *Knots* takes up three times as much space as all the other defects in structure, namely pitch-pockets, ingrown bark, compression wood, twisted grain, worm-holes and rot, put together. *Knots* are described as : Pin-knots (average diameter less than $\frac{1}{4}$ inch), Small knots (average diameter not exceeding $\frac{3}{4}$ inch), Medium knots (average diameter from $\frac{3}{4}$ inch to $1\frac{1}{2}$ inch), Large knots (average diameter exceeding $1\frac{1}{2}$ inches).

Knots may be round (ratio of maximum and minimum diameters, less than $2\frac{1}{2}$), oval, or spike (which spread to the edge and when in pairs are called moustache, splay, or horn knots) ; they may be sound (partaking in the life of the tree), dead (either tight or loose), rotten, or bark-ringed ; they may be distributed or cluster.

Defects in *Manufacture* are wane, contortion and mis-sawing.

Wane is the absence of wood owing to the roundness of the log.

Contortion may be either : Bowing (curvature in the direction of the length), Cupping (curvature in the direction of the width), Springing (curvature in its own plane), or Twist (distortion). It may be argued that " contortion " is not necessarily due to manufacture, but it is rightly included here, as, whatever the cause, the effect is the same as if it were due to faulty manufacture.

Shakes are of three kinds, namely : (i) Heart-shakes which occur radially across the annular rings ; (ii) Ring-shakes which follow the direction of the annular rings, both being more or less inherent in the log ; (iii) Drying-shakes, which develop during the seasoning process.

Defects in *Condition* are : (i) Moisture defects : Shipping-dry is defined as maximum 24 per cent. M/C (*i.e.*, maximum Moisture

Content 24 per cent. of dry weight); (ii) Discoloration: either log-blue which occurs before sawing, mainly during the floating period; or dealyard discoloration which occurs after sawing. To prevent the possibility of sawn goods discolouring it is customary to dip them immediately after sawing in some anti-stain solution.

Following the general rules are special rules which define precisely how many of the recognised defects may occur in the different qualities of half a dozen sample dimensions, namely 3 ins. × 9 ins., 2½ ins. × 7 ins., 2 ins. × 6 ins., 1 in. × 6 ins., 1 in. × 4 ins. and ¾ in. × 4 ins. The general rules state that the defects permitted are proportionate to the dimension.

One set of special rules, for 2½ ins. × 7 ins., are here considered in detail, being reasonably representative of the special rules for other dimensions.

Although there is practically no export to this country of Finnish sawn goods sorted into I to IV, which are shipped together as Unsorted quality, continental buyers have a much stricter interpretation of " shipper's usual bracking " and insist that when they sort the goods on arrival, the proportion of the higher qualities shall be up to standard. Importers in this country are more broadminded and look at a shipment more as a whole. In addition, importers in this country seldom sort the goods when yarding them.

The amount of defects permitted in IV and therefore in Unsorted quality may appear surprising at first, but it must be remembered that these are the maximum defects permitted in the grade, which must also contain a fair proportion of higher grade pieces. In addition, two major defects must not usually occur simultaneously.

UNSORTED QUALITY, 2½ ins. × 7 ins. The *maximum* defects may be summarised thus :—

Wane. On two corners combined 1¼ inches deep, 25/40 per cent. of the length.

Knots. On the side: Sound knots—2 or 3 fairly large and 3 to 5 medium, as well as some smaller knots well distributed in each 5 feet of length; Dead knots—the same but two-thirds of the size; Rotten knots—a few small ones; Bark-ringed knots—2 fairly small to each 5 feet of length.
On the edge—two-thirds of the size and half the number on the side.

(There are two important provisos—the knots must not be grouped in such a way as materially to affect the strength of the piece; two of the greatest defects allowed must not generally occur simultaneously.)

Shakes. On the side—combined depth maximum half the thickness and two-thirds of the length; On the edge—3 to 4 shakes to each 15 feet of the length, not too wide nor touching the corner.

Discoloration. 1 to 3 slight blue piling marks or corresponding slight dealyard discoloration on one side or one edge. No log-blue.

Rot. None.

Wormholes. Maximum 3 to 4.

Pitchpockets. Fair number of fair size.

Compression Wood. Any amount.

FIFTH QUALITY, 2½ ins. × 7 ins. This permits the following defects :—

Wane, which however must not exceed on two corners combined 1⅝ inches for 40/70 per cent. of the length.

Knots, which are unlimited except that rotten knots must not exceed 2 to 3 fairly large to each 5 feet. Knotholes going through the piece are not allowed. Knots on the edge two-thirds of number on side.

Shakes may go through, even touching the corner.

Discolouration and pitchpockets are unlimited.

Rot. Small quantities of hard firm rot are permitted.

Wormholes. Maximum 4 to 5 holes may occur.

The Table for *Wane* shows that this is permitted to increase in depth in proportion to increase in dimension and decrease in quality; and in length in proportion to the decrease in quality only.

3. Sweden.

Swedish grading rules were published in 1926, describing the sorting of wood goods which had been followed in the Härnösand District since 1880. The introduction to these rules points out that *during recent years the sorting had become much stricter*, especially in regard to wane and discolouration.

When this comment has been taken into account it will be found that the Swedish and Finnish rules are very much alike as regards the sorting of Unsorted and Fifths. The Swedish rules go somewhat further than the Finnish in describing also Utskott (VI quality) which admits a considerable amount of wane and an almost unlimited amount of other defects (except open rot holes in the ends) so long as the piece holds well together.

"HÄRNÖSAND GRADING RULES FOR SAWN AND PLANED GOODS."

Extract from *Handbok I Skogsteknologi* : (Stockholm 1922).

Translated from the Swedish.

Although the sorting of wood goods has gone on for many years there are no absolutely fixed rules for sorting into qualities. Attempts have been made on various occasions to obtain such rules, but they have failed owing to certain real or imaginary difficulties. It must also be acknowledged that a certain reasonableness must be applied in deciding the quality of wood. In various districts the sorters have developed the existing sorting tradition ; different mills have, for competition or other purposes, a stricter or less strict sorting, etc., etc.

In order to show what principles are applied in the sorting of wood, the following tables are annexed which give a good impression of the sorting rules which are generally applied in the district of Härnösand.

As a rule Upper Gulf wood is seldom sorted otherwise than by separation of Utskott : Härnösand sorts more often deals and wide boards and first at Sundsvall a more complete sorting takes place, which at Gefle goes right down to planchette sizes. In the more southerly shipping districts sorting into qualities occurs more seldom, only Utskott being separated. Sorting is usually applied to redwood and at times also to white deals. White battens and boards are seldom sorted.

SORTING RULES FOR SAWN GOODS.

NOTE.—*The defects enumerated are those of the lowest limit of the quality and must not occur all at once*, but two may well appear together, then, however, on a smaller scale.

FIRSTS (I).

Wane. About 3 per cent. of end-area, maximum 25 per cent. of the thickness and 20 per cent. of the length.

Rot. Must not occur in any form.

Knots. Only live knots in size of 3 per cent. of end-area and only on the flat, one in each 4 feet of length. Some small pin-knots may also occur.

Shakes. Only small, shallow sunshakes.

Blue. Only small slight spots.

Worm. Must not occur.

SECONDS (II).

Wane. About 4 per cent. of end-area, maximum 33 per cent. of the thickness and 20 per cent. of the length.

Rot. Must not occur in any form.

Knots. Sound knots in size of 4 per cent. of the end-area, on the edges as well as on the flat, about one in each 3 feet of length, besides small pin-knots.

Shakes. Sunshakes and heartshakes may exist to a depth of one-sixth of the thickness, and to one-third of the length of the piece.

Blue. Slight blue in spots on the edge as well as on the flat.

Worm. Must not occur.

THIRDS (III).

Wane. 6 per cent. of end-area, maximum 50 per cent. of the thickness and 35 per cent. of the length.

Rot. Hard rot may exist in spots but only on the surface.

Knots. Sound knots in size of 7 per cent. of the end-area on the edges as well as on the flat, one in each 5 feet of length, besides a similar number of 4 per cent. size and a large number of small pin-knots, also an occasional less serious tight rotten knot.

Shakes. Both sun- and heart-shakes may occur, also bright and not too wide seasoning-shakes.

Blue. Slight blue may occur on the whole of one edge or on the flat, the whole width and half the length, or else half the width on the whole length.

Worm. A few bright wormholes may occur, provided the piece is not already III through another defect.

FOURTHS (IV).

Wane. 8 per cent. of end-area, maximum 60 per cent. of the thickness and 50 per cent. of the length.

Rot. To some extent deep-seated hard rot may occur up to 20 per cent. of the end-area or even up to 40/50 per cent., if it only occurs on about 30 per cent. of the length.

Knots. Sound knots on the edges as well as on the flat in size of 10 per cent. of the end-area, one in each 3 feet of length, a large number of pin-knots, also at most one tight rotten knot in each 3 feet of length.

Shakes. Through sun- and heart-shakes, up to two-thirds of the length of the piece and seasoning-shakes on the edges as well as on the flat.

Blue. Slight blue on two-thirds of the width and the whole length, or both edges, or entire width and two-thirds of the length. Dark and mouldy blue may occur in some sticking marks.

Worm. May occur provided bright, but not quite through the piece, nor large.

FIFTHS (V).

Wane. 30 per cent. of end-area, maximum 67 per cent. of the length and 70 per cent. of the thickness.

Rot. Hard rot may occur in nearly the whole piece.

Knots. Sound knots may occur in almost unlimited number, also tight rotten knots which may be slightly open.

Shakes. Unlimited number so long as the piece holds firmly together, also seasoning-shakes on the edges as well as on the flat.

Blue. May occur in the whole piece.

Worm. May occur bright as well as dark, on the edges as well as on the flat.

SIXTHS (VI) OR UTSKOTT.

Wane } *Rot* } In Utskott may occur at the same time wane, if only a square edge occurs on some side, and hard-rot in the whole piece, besides some soft-rot, but not open holes in the ends.

Knots. Sound as well as rotten knots may occur in unlimited numbers.

Shakes } *Blue* } *Worm* } Unlimited.

UNSORTED.

This comprises saw-falling qualities down to and including IV quality and is reckoned to fall out on the average about as follows :—I—5 per cent., II—10 per cent., III—65 per cent., IV—20 per cent.

SORTING RULES FOR PLANED GOODS.

FIRSTS (I).

Wane. May occur on the back up to maximum 10 per cent. of the thickness, 10 per cent. of the width, and 10 per cent. of the length.

Knots. May occur in quite large numbers if they are bright pin-knots.

Rot. Must not occur.

SECONDS (II).

Wane. May occur on the back—in p.e. up to maximum 40 per cent. of the thickness, 20 per cent. of the width, and 30 per cent. of the length. In t. & g. the wane may go up to and touch the lower edge of the tongue and groove. For the rest the same as p.e.

Blue. May occur, if it is bright on the whole of one edge, 25 per cent. of the width and the whole of the back. Log-blue only in slight streaks on both sides.

Knots. May occur if they are bright and tight and not larger than 20 per cent. of the width of the piece and in number of one knot to each foot. Pin-knots may occur in unlimited numbers. Rotten and black-ringed knots must not occur.

Rot. Must not occur.

THIRDS (III).

Wane. May occur on the back: in p.e. up to 50 per cent. of the thickness, 25 per cent. of the width and 33 per cent. of the length. In t. & g. the wane may go up to the tongue and groove and also take away some part of them. For the rest same as p.e.

Blue. May occur if it is not altogether too dark on the whole of the back and 50 per cent. of the sap on the face. Long-blue may occur on the back and up to 25 per cent. of the face.

Knots. May occur if they are tight, bright and sound in almost unlimited numbers as well as tight black-ringed knots with about one knot to each 2 feet of length.

Rot. May occur on the back in shallow streaks, if it is hard.

UNSORTED.

This comprises saw-falling qualities down to and including III and is reckoned to fall out on the average about as follows :—

Red I—10/15 per cent., II—60/65 per cent., III—20/25 per cent.
White I—10/15 per cent., II—65/70 per cent., III—15/20 per cent.

These rules also describe the grading of first and second quality *firewood* and *cement staves* which are also subject to strict sorting.

There are other products of the sawmill which may be summarised as follows :—

Slating Battens. Often of excellent quality, being manufactured mainly from edgings and consist mostly of sapwood which is freer from defects than heartwood. Shipped as Unsorted, seldom any Vs.

Sawn Laths. Usually sorted into two qualities, the firsts being practically perfect and the seconds containing some pin-knots and discolouration.

Squares. Also sorted into two qualities, the firsts must be bright and only permit such knots in the corners as would disappear in the rounding process.

Seconds permit some very small knots.

Schaalboards. These are side boards which may be so waney that they need only be touched by the saw on both sides and edges throughout the whole length. The knot-free boards are usually sorted out and sold separately.

Halv-rena. These are waney battens corresponding to Schaalboards. They may contain any amount of wane provided the saw touches all four sides throughout the whole length of the piece. They are usually cut two ex log from small logs and are most often 2″×4″ and similar sizes.

Torrack. The product of trees which have died standing; it is sold sawfalling, usually at about the same price as Sixths.

4. Poland.

The Swedish system of grading has been adopted in Poland.

5. Russia.

There are no official published rules, so it is simplest to compare the grading with the Finnish and Swedish rules.

There are two classifications of Russian timber.

(i) *Archangel Bracking*, applying to shipments from Archangel, Onega and the Kara Sea. All 7 inch and up is sorted into five qualities:—

I—Practically free from defects, at all events on one side.
II—Contain small sound knots and other slight defects.
III—Contain a fair number of knots and a reasonable number of other defects.
IV—Defective or faulty in some way such as excessively knotty (*i.e.*, either too many or too large knots, or rotten, dead or loose knots) or log-blue, slightly discoloured, weathered, somewhat shaken or wormy.
V—The lowest grade and seldom shipped.

In any case not too many of these faults may exist in one piece, as the bracking is not according to the existence of any one particular fault, but according to the accumulation of faults, so any piece containing too many faults together is reduced to the next grade below.

6 inch and under Unsorted battens include IV quality.

6 inch and under Unsorted boards include I, II and III qualities only, the IV being sold separately.

Lengths are 9 feet and up, with 5 feet to 8 feet ends at reduced price. Unsorted 5 feet to 8 feet ends when sold separately include IV quality in all sizes.

Russian wood goods are usually cut from large logs and are therefore less waney than Scandinavian wood goods.

(ii) *Leningrad Bracking*, applying to all other ports, and also to some shipments from Archangel.

All sizes in Unsorted include I, II and III qualities only, the IV being sold separately.

Lengths are 9 feet and up with 5 feet to 8 feet ends at reduced price. Unsorted 5 feet to 8 feet ends, when sold separately, include IV quality in all sizes.

Generally the IV Russian stocks are similar in grade to V of high class Finnish stocks.

The Russian system of grading is followed generally in the Baltic States (Estonia, Latvia and Lithuania).

6. Canada—West Coast.

The principal West Coast softwoods are Douglas fir, Pacific Coast (West Coast) hemlock, Sitka spruce and western red cedar.

The Pacific Lumber Inspection Bureau (U.S.A.) published in 1951 a set of Grading Rules for these woods called the "R List" which was adopted by the West Coast Lumbermen's Association (U.S.A.) and the British Columbia Lumber Manufacturers' Association (Canada).

These are definitely named "export" grading rules and, as mentioned in the General Notes, "the grade of each piece is determined by . . . . its suitability for the use or uses for which the grade was developed."

These rules are very detailed and give 22 different gradings for Douglas fir alone. As an example only, No. 1 Merchantable grade 1½″ and 2″ thick is quoted here. The rules vary for under 1½″ thick; 3″ to 5″; and 6″ and up thick.

The grading of Douglas fir differs from European grading of redwood mainly in five ways:—

(i) Attention is paid to the growth of the wood expressed in terms of annual rings to the inch.

(ii) The dimensions are much larger on the average.

(iii) Pitch pockets and/or pitch blisters are more to be expected.

(iv) Attention is paid to the proportion of sapwood as against heartwood in the top grades (but bright sap is not limited when treated with anti-stain solution).

(v) The slope of the grain is taken into account; whether the sawing is edge, flat, or random grain.

The general description of *No. 1 Merchantable Douglas fir* 1½″ to 2½″ thick is as follows:—

"Shall be sound strong lumber, well manufactured and suitable for *good sound constructional purposes*. Must be medium grain, *i.e.*, an average on either one end or the other of the piece of not less than 4 annual rings per inch over a 3″ line measured at right angles to the rings.

Will admit the following or their equivalent:—

Knots—sound and tight, ranging from approximately 1½″ in 4″ widths to 3″ in 12″ widths. Proportionate in wider widths.

Knots—not firmly fixed, approximately two-thirds diameter of allowable tight knots.

Spike knots—equivalent.

Pitch pockets and/or pitch blisters—medium.

Pitch—streaks.

Sap—half width or equivalent (other than black).

Heart stain—firm, limited.

Split—approximately width of piece.

Wane—⅙ width, ⅓ length of the piece or equivalent. Approximately ¼ thickness.

Wormholes—pin, occasional, scattered.

Variation in sawing—occasional, slight.

When planed.

Skips—occasional, $\frac{1}{12}$ deep, 3 ft. in length; $\frac{1}{16}$ deep by ⅓ length on edge.

Sap—bright or discoloured (other than black).

Edge or surface irregularities—slight, due to machining."

In order to meet the requirements for something slightly better than "*good sound* constructional purposes" there is the *Selected Merchantable* grade which is suitable for "*high class* constructional purposes," this must be close grained and the defects allowed are less than those in the same dimensions of No. 1 Merchantable.

There are superior "*Clear*" grades and also inferior grades, *No. 2 Merchantable* and *No. 3 Common*, which together provide a range to satisfy all reasonable requirements. In addition to these, there are a number of special grades for ceiling, door stock, pipe stock, ship decking, etc., etc.

7. Canada—East Coast.

The best quality Eastern Canadian spruce comes from Quebec and is usually bandsawn. It is sorted into six qualities with I to IV together comprising Unsorted quality.

Quebec Grading Rules

$\frac{3}{4}$ inch to 3 inches. (Qualities I to IV are Unsorted.)

1st Quality. Straight grain. A few small knots, sound and solid, of about $\frac{1}{4}$ inch allowed on the faces of the piece. No dead wood and no knots in the cants. The wood must be well sawn and well butted.

2nd Quality. A few sound and solid knots, $\frac{1}{2}$ inch to $\frac{3}{4}$ inch in diameter allowed on the faces of the wood. No knots on the cants. Dead wood allowed on a quarter of the length and about a quarter of the thickness of the wood on one side in 10 per cent. of the number of pieces. The wood must be well sawn and well butted.

3rd Quality. Several sound and solid knots up to $1\frac{1}{4}$ inches in diameter allowed on the faces of the wood. Clean and solid knots allowed in the cants. Dead wood allowed on a third of the length of the piece and a quarter of the thickness on one side in 15 per cent. of the number of pieces. The wood must be well sawn and well butted.

4th Quality. Large sound and solid knots, up to $1\frac{1}{2}$ inches to 2 inches in diameter allowed on the faces of the piece. Sound knots up to $1\frac{1}{4}$ inches in diameter allowed on the cants. Dead wood allowed on half the length and on a quarter of the thickness on one side in 20 per cent. of the number of pieces. Slight shakes on one face. A little sound red streak allowed in the fir. The wood must be well sawn and well butted.

5th Quality. Large sound and solid black knots allowed on the faces of the wood and middle-sized knots on the cants. Small worm holes and shakes which do not cross the piece and red streak allowed on three-quarters of the face. Dead wood allowed on half the length and half the thickness on one side of the wood, or on a quarter of the thickness on the two sides in 25 per cent. of the number of pieces. The wood must be well sawn and well butted.

6th Quality. All kinds of knots, worm holes, shakes, gum seams, rot and dead wood allowed. The wood must have one face square, and the saw must have touched half of another face and a quarter of the width of two sides. The wood must be sound enough to stand nailing the whole length of the piece.

Shipments from New Brunswick ports, principally Miramichi, Campbellton and St. John are graded III and up as Unsorted, the IV being very similar to Quebec V.

Shipments from Nova Scotia are similar to those from New Brunswick but the average quality is somewhat inferior, the goods are mainly rotary cut and of shorter average length.

The Maritime Lumber Bureau has issued some very detailed "Grading Rules for Eastern Canadian Spruce." The following extract from these rules shows the defects permitted in

Grade III, 3 ins. × 9 ins. and up.

Knots: Sound, tight, round (face)—Large; Black, round (face)—Medium; Corner (all except defective)—Medium; Spike (face)—Medium; Defective (all, face and edge)—Medium; Edge (all except defective)—2 Large.

Wane: Better Corner $1\frac{1}{4}$ inches; Other Corner $1\frac{3}{4}$ inches; Length 40/60 per cent.

Split: Medium. (Examples—15 inches in a $2\frac{1}{2}$ ins. × 10 ins. or 17 inches in a 3 ins. × 11 ins.)

Ring Shake: Small.

Surface Check: Face—$1\frac{1}{2}$ Medium per 3 square feet; Edge—$4\frac{1}{8}$ inches parallel or $4\frac{1}{16}$ inches diagonal to corner.

Rot: Hard rot—None; Soft rot—None.

Discolouration: Sticker stain—3 per 12 feet of length; Mould—Face 30 per cent., one edge 60 per cent. (or equivalent on both edges); Blue stain—*Light*—Face, 50 per cent., one edge 100 per cent. (or equivalent on both edges); *Medium*—One half permissible amount of light; *Heavy*—One quarter permissible amount of light.

Pitch Pockets and Bark Pockets: Small—No limit; Medium—2 per 3 square feet; Large—None.

Worm Holes: Small—So placed that a single piece free of worm holes may be obtained with less than 20 per cent. waste; Medium and Large—None.

Cross Grain: Maximum slope—1 in 10.

Warp: Pronounced.

The rules define each of the defects and size of defects in great detail.

8. U.S.A.—Softwoods.

The West Coast softwoods are of course identical with those of Canada, whose grading has been set out in para. 6, except that the export of western red cedar is almost entirely from Canada, and the Ukay "A" List, under which shipments are generally made, is a Canadian production.

Another important American softwood is pitch pine, shipped from ports on the Gulf of Mexico and the southern Atlantic coast. Longleaf varieties of pitch pine are heavy to heart, and shortleaf varieties almost devoid of heart.

Higher grades of Lumber and Timbers for Export were graded on "The Gulf Coast Classification." Emphasis in these rules is upon Heart Content and Species, and the fact that the last reprint was dated 1923 points to the difficulty of obtaining longleaf pitch pine within the United States of America at the present time.

The rules in current use are the Southern Pine Inspection Bureau Rules, 1948—primarily a domestic grading. The emphasis in these is on "fitness for purpose." Heart Content and Species are of less importance than working stresses. This " Structural Grading," although well accepted in American domestic markets, is only slowly being accepted in the more conservative export markets.

Genuine longleaf has now been almost cut out in the U.S.A. and, as it does not readily regenerate itself, and has not been replanted on any large scale, it seems unlikely that it will ever again become the important commercial proposition it has been in the past.

Not unnaturally there are many small differences between the terms used in grading softwood in Scandinavia and in America, for instance the size of pin-knots (Scandinavian, less than ¼ inch; American, maximum ½ inch diameter) and knot distribution (Scandinavian, 5 feet; American, 6 feet), etc.

9. Brazil.

The grading rules of Parana pine are quite different from those of Scandinavia and Canada. They are formulated by Government decree and were revised on 21st December 1951, making them less strict than formerly, so that

GRADE I now permits some wane on one edge and small knots on one side.

GRADE 2 now permits some wane on both edges, knots on both sides and a few wormholes.

GRADE 3 now permits still greater defects, including some sap-rot on one side.

GRADE 4 approximates to Scandinavian Sixths (or Wrack or Utskott).

PRIME GRADE consists of 80 per cent. I and 20 per cent. II.

10. Moisture Content of Softwoods.

The Albion and Uniform contracts state that the timber shall be " properly seasoned for shipment to.................... " but no definite moisture content is specified.

In Finland the following definitions are given as to moisture content, which is calculated in the same way as in this country, *i.e.*, amount of water expressed as a percentage of the dry weight of the wood.

(*a*) *Shipping Dry*. 20/24 per cent. Discolouration on passage is then impossible unless the goods become superficially wet.

Re-absorption must not be forgotten; ½ inch thick strips under cover exposed to a damp winter atmosphere, have been known to rise from 8 per cent. to 28 per cent. moisture content.

(*b*) *Planing Dry*. 15/18 per cent. This is simply for successful surfacing, as the wood will normally regain moisture content on exposure. Kiln seasoning is required for this, except during summer months.

(*c*) *Outdoor Joinery Dry*. 10/14 per cent. Doors, windows, etc.

(*d*) *Furniture Dry.* 7/10 per cent. (Most Finnish houses are central-heated and very dry.)

(*e*) *Absolutely Dry.* For technical test purposes only, zero per cent. at a temperature of 100/105° C.

Pacific Coast softwoods are usually sold without any guarantee as to seasoning (except when kiln-dried) and dimensions are subject to any natural shrinkage whether "green," or partially, or wholly seasoned, the intention being to manufacture all rough lumber full size when green, but occasional variations in sawing are allowed.

For *Eastern Canadian spruce* the Maritime Lumber Bureau Grading Rules make this definition :—

(*a*) All the provisions of these rules shall apply to "dry" lumber, that is, lumber having a moisture content not exceeding 25 per cent. (based on the oven dry weight of the wood) at the time of shipment.

(*b*) Lumber of which the moisture content exceeds 25 per cent. at the time of shipment shall be classed as "green" lumber, in which case it shall be graded on the basis of those defects which occur in freshly sawn wood and not those which develop in the process of seasoning or weathering.

For Pitchpine the "Standard Specifications of Southern Pine Lumber," issued by the Southern Pine Association, U.S.A., gives clear details of moisture content for various grades and thicknesses of timber with the procedure to be adopted in inspecting timber for moisture content. Where a particular moisture content is not specified, these rules state that the following moisture contents will apply :—

2 inch thick and less—kiln-dried 15 per cent. ; air-dried 19 per cent.

Over 2 inches thick—kiln-dried 20 per cent. ; air-dried 23 per cent.

Higher qualities and other specified grades are limited to lower moisture contents.

11. Hardwoods.

The most important hardwood grading rules are those published by the National Hardwood Lumber Association (U.S.A.). These are very comprehensive, yet possibly clearer to understand than the West Coast softwood grading rules. For this reason they are often used outside the U.S.A. as a basis for local grading.

In the general instructions, the following instructions are given concerning the measurement of the goods.

Measurement and Tally.

16. Board measure is the term used to indicate that a board foot is the unit of measurement of lumber. A board foot is 1 foot long, 1 foot wide and 1 inch thick or its equivalent. In surfaced lumber the board foot is based on the measurement before surfacing, and all lumber less than 1 inch thick is counted face measure and taken as 1 inch.

In lumber measured with a board rule, random width pieces measuring to the even half foot shall be alternately counted as of the next higher and lower foot counts ; fractions below the half foot shall be dropped and fractions above the half foot shall be counted as of the next higher foot. On pieces measuring to the even half foot, the grade requirements shall be based on the lower foot count. Fractional lengths in standard grades shall be measured as of the next lower standard length.

Note : Unless otherwise specified, reference to percentages applies to board feet and not to the number of pieces.

17. Tapering lumber in standard lengths shall be measured one-third the length of the piece from the narrow end.

18. Random width lumber of standard grades and thicknesses shall be tallied surface measure and this tally shall be the number of feet, board measure, of 1 inch lumber. In lumber thicker than 1 inch the tally so obtained is multiplied by the thickness as expressed in inches and fractions of an inch. Except squares, lumber less than 1 inch thick shall be counted surface measure.

Tallying on 12 feet Basis.

21. The terms " export tally," " width and length tally " and " tally on 12 feet basis " are synonymous. The term " tally on 12 feet basis " is more definite because the width of 12 feet lumber is the same as the surface measure on the board rule. On this basis, the lengths are tallied separately. In tallying the widths, pieces measuring to the even half inch are alternately counted as of the next higher or lower width count, fractions below the half inch are dropped and fractions above the half inch are counted as of the next higher width. After the tally is figured up, the proper fraction is added or subtracted in order to obtain the correct measure, thus : for 4 feet lengths, divide the total by 3 ; for 6 feet divide by 2 ; for 8 feet subtract 1/3 ; for 9 feet subtract 1/4 ; for 10 feet subtract 1/6 ; for 11 feet subtract 1/12 ; for 14 feet add 1/6 ; for 15 feet add 1/4 ; for 16 feet add 1/3 ; for 5 feet and 7 feet multiply by the length and divide by 12.

This method of tallying should not be confused with tallying stock widths such as 1 in. × 6 ins., 1 in. × 8 ins., etc.

The rules then define a " cutting " as : " A portion of a board or plank obtained by cross cutting or ripping or both."

A " clear face cutting " is stated to be : " A cutting having one clear face (ordinary season checks are admitted) and the reverse side sound as defined in sound cutting, etc."

A " sound cutting " is stated to be : " A cutting free from rot, pith, shake and wane. Texture is not considered. It will admit sound knots, sound bird pecks, stain, streaks or their equivalent, season checks not materially impairing the strength of a cutting, pin, shot and spot wormholes, etc., etc."

Standard defects are laid down as follows :—

" (Apply to the grades established on a ' defect basis.')

36. One knot 1¼ inches in diameter is a standard defect.

When located away from edges and ends where they cannot be admitted as the equivalent to wane defects, the following shall be considered as standard defects :—

Four pin wormholes or their equivalent equals one defect.
Three spot wormholes or their equivalent equals one defect.
Two ⅝ inch diameter knots or their equivalent equals one defect.

Not more than two standard defects of this character can be admitted to the piece ; each additional pin wormhole or spot wormhole or ⅝ inch knot shall be considered one additional standard defect.

Defects larger than one standard defect, excepting wane and split, shall be considered on the following average diameter measurement :—2½ inch knots or their equivalent shall be two standard defects ; 3¾ inch knots or their equivalent shall be three standard defects ; 5 inch knots or their equivalent shall be four standard defects.

One split equal in length in inches to the surface measure of the piece in feet and diverging not more than 1 inch to the foot in length.

Wane or its equivalent in other defects, 1 inch wide, one-sixth the length of the piece along the edges, or its equivalent at one or both ends. In the wane defect, wane may extend through the full thickness of the piece showing on both faces.

Worm, grub, knot and rafting-pin holes, not exceeding in extent one standard knot defect described above."

" Equivalent defects are :—

37. Pith and other defects not defined as standard defects, that do not damage the piece more than the standard defects allowed, are equivalent defects and must be so considered by the inspector."

From the measurement of the timber, and the standard defects present, the amount of " cutting " in a board is assessed. That is the amount of clear timber if all defects were cut out. This amount of " clear face cutting " is expressed as a percentage or fraction of the total face measure. The rules lay down a method of making these calculations working on units of 12 square inches.

This gives the clear cutting in fractions of 1/12th or alternately a straight percentage if preferred. This percentage of " clear face cutting " is a major item in the definition of each standard grade.

The cuttings required by each standard grade are :—

Firsts —91⅔% (or 11/12).	No. 1 Common —66⅔% (or 8/12).
Seconds—83⅓% (or 10/12).	No. 2 Common —50% (or 6/12).
Selects —75% (or 9/12).	No. 3A Common—33⅓% (or 4/12).

No. 3B Common—25% (or 3/12).

As an example, a board 9⅜ ins. wide × 16 ft. long may contain the following clear face cuttings : 8½ ins. × 6 ft. (4·25 square feet), 3 ins. × 9½ ft. (2·38 square feet), 4 ins. × 2¾ ft. (0·92 square feet), 3 ins. × 3⅓ ft. (0·83 square feet) ; total 8·38 square feet.

The full face measure of the board is taken as 9 ins. × 16 ft. = 12 square feet. The clear face cutting is therefore 8·38/12 = 69·8 per cent. Since the board contains more than 66⅔ per cent. (8/12) cutting, it grades as *Standard No. 1 Common*, subject to certain other requirements.

In practice these calculations are made on a simple unit basis, and not in the manner shown above which has been adopted to make the calculation easy to follow. In the above calculation there are said to be four cuttings.

The *Standard No. 1 Common* grade permits up to five cuttings to be made depending on the surface measure of the board. The lower the surface measure, the smaller the number of cuttings permitted and the higher the cutting yield required to make the grade, *i.e.*,

Surface Measure.	*Required Cutting Yield.*		*Number of Cuttings.*
1 foot	12/12	100%	
2 feet	9/12	75%	1
3 feet and 4 feet	8/12	66⅔%	1
	9/12	75%	2
5 feet to 7 feet	8/12	66⅔%	2
	9/12	75%	3
8 feet to 10 feet	8/12	66⅔%	3
11 feet to 13 feet	8/12	66⅔%	4
14 feet and over	8/12	66⅔%	5

Each standard grade has its own schedule of cuttings.

The Standard Grades : National Hardwood Lumber Association, U.S.A.

The standard grades are :—

Firsts ... Seconds ...	Usually combined as F.A.S.
Selects ... No. 1 Common	Sometimes combined as No. 1 Common and Selects.
No. 2 Common.	
No. 3A Common No. 3B Common	Sometimes combined as No. 3 Common.

The following requirements for each grade are set out :— (*a*) Minimum widths ; (*b*) Lengths—giving admissible proportion of shorts ; (*c*) Limits for pith and other defects ; (*d*) The minimum cutting size ; (*e*) The percentage yield of clear face cutting.

For instance :—

Firsts. (*a*) Widths 6 inches and wider ; (*b*) Lengths 8 feet to 16 feet admitting 30 per cent. of 8 feet to 11 feet of which one-half may be 8 feet and 9 feet ; (*c*) Limits for pith, wane, splits and diameter of knots, etc., and other defects ; (*d*) Minimum cutting—4 inches wide by 5 feet long, or 3 inches wide by 7 feet long ; (*e*) Cutting yield, to admit 91⅔ per cent. (11/12), clear cutting face as follows : 4 feet to 9 feet surface measure, in one cutting ; 10 feet to 14 feet in two cuttings ; 15 feet and over in three cuttings.

It will be seen that the cutting yield figure is the basis of the grading.

The standard grades are summarised in the appended chart.

Having laid down the conditions and requirements for the standard grades, the N.H.L.A. rules then give the grading rules for each separate class of hardwood by reference to the standard grade.

For instance :—

Ash, Beech, Birch.

Firsts } Standard, except 40 per cent. 8 feet to 11 feet
Seconds } lengths admitted in Ash and 30 per cent. in other species.

Selects—Standard, except 40 per cent. 6 feet to 11 feet lengths admitted in Ash.

Other grades—Standard.

The N.H.L.A. rules cover many other specialised grades, squares, furniture, kiln-dried lumber, waggon building, cabinet, constructional, etc., etc. The last section deals with veneers, giving definitions, basis of measurements and grading, and tables of weights.

Grading rules have been established for Malayan timbers, and these are also based on a system of " cuttings." The standard grades are :—Prime, Select, Standard, Common, Sound, Merchantable, although the defects and " cuttings " vary from the N.H.L.A. rules.

These rules are published by the Department of Forestry in Malaya as " Malayan Grading Rules (Export) for Rough Sawn Timber." They represent an important advance in the grading of hardwood outside the U.S.A.

12. Plywood.

There are few set grading rules for plywood, with great variations between individual shippers' productions.

EUROPEAN grades are roughly as follows :—

A or AA—Specially selected grade with surfaces as free from blemish as possible to obtain. No joints permitted in veneers and generally machine scraped or sanded on both sides to give better finish.

B—Ordinary first-class production veneers practically free from defects. In certain timbers, such as beech, occasional plugging permissible. No joints permitted in veneers.

BB—Sound material with small knots, unsound knots replaced by plugs. Some discolouration and well made joints permitted.

BBB—Low grade. Splits and open knots permitted. Generally rejects from BB grade.

WG—Signifies that the plywood merely requires to be well glued.

Very often it is only necessary to have one good face to the sheet, the reverse side being of lower grade. The grade of such sheets is indicated by a combination of the various symbols such as B/BB. The letter J, if added to the grade, shows that the face veneer is jointed.

CUTTING REQUIREMENTS FOR STANDARD GRADES: N.H.L.A., U.S.A.

S.M. = Surface measure in square feet.

Firsts			*Seconds*			*Selects*			*No. 1 Common*			*No. 2 Common*		
Widths 6 ins. and wider			Widths 6 ins. and wider			Widths 4 ins. and wider			Widths 3 ins. and wider			Widths 3 ins. and wider		
Lengths 8 ft. to 16 ft.			Lengths 8 ft. to 16 ft.			Lengths 6 ft. to 16 ft.			Lengths 4 ft. to 16 ft.			Lengths 4 ft. to 16 ft.		
S.M.	*% Clear Face.*	*Cuts.*	*S.M.*	*% Clear Face.*	*Cuts.*	*S.M.*	*% Clear Face.*	*Cuts.*	*S.M.*	*% Clear Face.*	*Cuts.*	*S.M.*	*% Clear Face.*	*Cuts.*
4′ to 9′	$91\frac{2}{3}$	1	4′ & 5′	$83\frac{1}{3}$	1	2′ & 3′	$91\frac{2}{3}$	1	1′	Clear	–	1′	$66\frac{2}{3}$	1
10′ to 14′	,,	2	6′ & 7′	,,	1				2′	75	1	2′ & 3′	50	1
15′ & up	,,	3	8′ to 11′	,,	2				3′ & 4′	$66\frac{2}{3}$	1	4′ & 5′	,,	2
			12′ to 15′	,,	3				5′ to 7′	,,	2	6′ & 7′	,,	3
			16′ & up	,,	4				8′ to 10′	,,	3	8′ & 9′	,,	4
									11′ to 13′	,,	4	10′ & 11′	,,	5
									14′ & up	,,	5	12′ & 13′	,,	6
												14′ & up	,,	7
			6′ to 15′ S.M. will admit one additional cut to yield $91\frac{2}{3}$% clear face.			Reverse side cutting sound. 4′ and up shall grade on one side as required in seconds with reverse side of board not below No. 1 Common or reverse side of cuttings sound.			3′ to 7′ S.M. will admit one additional cut to yield 75% clear face.			2′ to 7′ S.M. will admit one additional cut to yield $66\frac{2}{3}$% clear face.		
Minimum cutting 4″× 5′ or 3″× 7′			Minimum cutting 4″× 5′ or 3″× 7′			Minimum cutting 4″× 5′ or 3″× 7′			Minimum cutting 4″× 2′ or 3″× 3′			Minimum cutting 3″× 2′		

DOUGLAS FIR PLYWOOD is graded as under :—

1. *GENERAL NOTES.*

(*a*) *Species.*—Plywood conforming with the grade requirements listed in this Section shall be manufactured from Douglas fir veneer ; veneers of other species shall not be admitted.

(*b*) *Interior Plies.*—Interior plies of grades listed in this Section shall be of a quality equivalent to or higher than that specified for the back of a Good One Side panel (see para. 4 below).

(*c*) *Gluelines.*—All panels conforming with the grade requirements listed in this Section shall be of the EXTERIOR type, bonded with approved phenolic formaldehyde resin glue, and shall fulfil the requirements for moisture resistance specified in Appendix A of this Grading Standard.

(*d*) *Size Tolerances.*—A tolerance of 1/64 (0·0156) inch over or under the specified thickness shall be allowed on sanded panels. A tolerance of 1/32 (0·0312) inch over or under the specified length and/or width shall be allowed but all panels shall be square within $\frac{1}{8}$ (0·1250) inch.

(*e*) *Marking.*—Each panel conforming to grades listed in this Section may be marked on the end with the following registered Association mark : PMBC EXTERIOR.

2. *GOOD TWO SIDES GRADE* (*G2S*).

Each face shall be of one or more pieces of firm, smoothly cut veneer. When of more than one piece, it shall be well joined and reasonably matched for grain and colour at the joints. It shall be free from knots, splits, pitch pockets, and other open defects. Streaks, discolorations, sapwood, shims, and neatly made wood inlays shall be admitted. This grade shall present a smooth surface suitable for painting.

3. *GOOD ONE SIDE, SOLID BACK GRADE* (*G/Solid*).

One face shall be equal to the face of Good two Sides. The back shall present a solid surface, free from open defects, but in addition to characteristics admitted in the Good face shall admit also neatly made repairs, as well as synthetic plugs that present solid level, hard surfaces, knots up to 1 inch if both sound and tight, tight splits, slightly rough but not torn grain, and other minor sanding and patching defects. The back shall be paintable.

4. *GOOD ONE SIDE GRADE* (*G1S*).

One face shall be equal to the face of Good two Sides. The back may contain knotholes not larger than 1 inch in least dimension, open pitch pockets not wider than 1 inch, splits not wider then 3/16 inch which taper to a point, worm or borer holes not more than $\frac{5}{8}$ inch wide or $1\frac{1}{2}$ inches long, knots if tight and not more than $1\frac{1}{2}$ inches in least dimension, and plugs, patches, shims, sanding defects, and other characteristics in number and size that will not impair the serviceability of the panel. The back may be of one piece or of joined veneers.

5. *SOLID TWO SIDES GRADE* (*Solid2S*).

Each face shall be equal to the back of Good one Side, Solid Back.

6. *SOLID ONE SIDE GRADE* (*Solid1S*).

The face shall be equal to the face of Solid two Sides. The back shall be equal to the to the back of Good one Side.

7. *SELECT MARINE GRADE.*

Both faces shall be equal to the faces of Good two Sides. All cross-banding and cores shall be equal to the face of Solid one Side. This grade is suitable for hull planking and all marine uses.

There is also a *CONSTRUCTION* (*EXTERIOR SHEATHING*) *GRADE*.

CHAPTER XVI

Softwood Surfaces

1. Sawing.

The surfaces of imported sawn and planed wood goods are a matter of interest and may be of importance where there is an undertaking that the goods shall be produced in one particular way or another, but it is sometimes a little difficult to determine how they were produced from the appearance of the finished product.

In countries exporting timber there are mainly three types of saw used for converting logs into sawngoods: *Bandsaws*, which may be single or double edged, may be vertical or horizontal and the teeth may be spring-set or swage-set; *Frame (or Gang) Saws*, which are usually spring-set; and *Circular Saws* of several different kinds.

(Note: In spring-setting, every alternate tooth is bent out in the opposite direction, so that the cut or " kerf " made by the teeth is greater than the thickness of the sawblade, giving the necessary clearance. In swage-setting every tooth has the point spread out equally, which has the same effect of providing clearance for the saw, but each tooth cuts both sides.)

I. BANDSAWS. A large bandsaw is capable of breaking down a very large log. The log is held firmly to a carriage which moves past the saw so that the projecting part of the log is sawn off in the form of a slab.

Valuable *hardwood* logs are usually converted to sawngoods on a horizontal bandsaw and the log may be cut into varying thicknesses through and through, or may be turned over on the carriage to produce desired effects in the way of figure. To obtain a smooth finish different woods require different shapes of tooth with a varying hook or rake or angle of cut and not all woods will tolerate the same rate of feed.

In this country *softwood* logs are quite often converted on a rack sawbench, but in Canada (to which the following remarks mainly apply), usually on a vertical *bandsaw* which, after removing a slab may, if the saw is double-edged, make another cut in the reverse direction and the next cut in a forward direction and so on until only another slab is left. On the other hand the log may be turned half-circle, or quarter-circle on the carriage to produce various thicknesses according to the size of the log and the dimensions required.

The big bandsaw is capable of doing very fine work and the smaller bandsaw even finer, but the production of a fine finish is dependent upon very expert attention to the saws and their tensioning and setting by the Saw Doctor.

The carriage to which the log is held travels at a considerable speed. The turning of the log is done by a mechanical " nigger " which, in the hands of an expert, does super-human work in turning the log and holding it until it is firmly held on the carriage.

Twin bandsaws are sometimes used which are very useful for such operations as converting 3 inch deals into three boards of equal thickness by making two simultaneous deep cuts, or for converting 9 inch widths into three equal widths (a pile of boards can be cut simultaneously in this way) by making two flat cuts.

" Deep cutting " sometimes called " deeping " is parallel with the wide surface, leaving widths the same. " Flat Cutting " sometimes called " flatting " or " ripping " is parallel with the edge, leaving the thickness the same.

Small bandsaws are very useful in the boxboard mill for dealing with small sizes requiring very accurate cutting and fine finish.

When the big bandsaw loses too much width by frequent sharpening, it comes into use as a horizontal re-saw for converting the larger slabs into boards.

2. Frame (or Gang) Saws are customary in the large mills of Northern Europe and these are now usually run in pairs in series, the first frame removing two slabs (and usually a couple of boards on each side of the log as well) and the second cutting the block, which has two sawn sides, into the required thicknesses of which the first frame fixed the width. This is called block-sawing. By this system the bulk of the production, at all events in the larger sizes, will be frame-sawn on sides and edges, but any pieces cut waney will be edged by a circular saw, often known as a Double Edger.

The modern framesaw is very fast and very accurate and although the sawkerf of the spring-set framesaw is greater than that of the swage-set bandsaw, it has the advantage of making several cuts at a time. In result the multiple production of the framesaw more than compensates for the greater feed speed of the bandsaw. Quite often the first frame will have six saws—three each side with a space of say 9 inches, 7 inches or 6 inches in the middle according to the diameter of the log. The second frame often has nine saws, one in the middle for the centre cut and four each side of it to produce the thicknesses required, say 3 inches, 2 inches, 1 inch, $\frac{3}{4}$ inch; in each case with sufficient excess measure to allow for shrinkage during seasoning.

3. Circular Saws are of different types according to the purpose for which they are to be used. There is the large log-saw used in South Sweden and Eastern Canada which is a fairly thick spring set parallel-sided plate saw and the customary method is to take a slab off one side of the log, turn the log over half-circle, take another slab off and continue cutting the thicknesses required. Alternatively the log may be converted by several successive cuts without turning. Very large circular saws cutting frozen logs in freezing temperatures have a hard time of it and the sawn product is frequently irregular in

thickness, in fact it is understood that if goods are described as circular sawn they are not expected to be so regular and accurate in dimension as bandsawn or framesawn.

Particularly in the production of the small circular saw mills of Eastern Canada there is a liability for occasional pieces to " run off " or taper in thickness or width towards the end. This is not considered a serious fault in such productions and it is customary to check for thickness and width a foot or two from the end and not at the extreme end.

In one of the most modern Canadian mills a big bandsaw is used for initially breaking down the logs and a pair of framesaws run in series for resawing.

In all three cases, those of the sawngoods which are cut waney are edged by circular saws and the end trimming, or adjusting, is done by crosscut circular saws, several different types being used for the latter, some of them giving a very smooth finish which is of great importance to appearance and consequently the value of the imported product, whether it has a paint-mark on the end or not.

The edger, which usually consists of two ordinary plate saws, one fixed and one movable on the same spindle, has a larger saw kerf than the re-cutting saw, but as this is at the expense of waste it is of little importance. Slatings, staves and laths are all cut on similar benches with multiple circular saws.

The re-cutting saw, principally used for " cutting for planing," is usually a special type of circular saw, thickness perhaps 4 mm. at the centre and tapering off to about 1 mm. at the rim, so that the thickness of the cutting edge of the saw, plus the set of the saw, makes a saw kerf of only about $\frac{1}{16}''$. The fineness of this re-cutting saw, in view of subsequent planing, is very important, so that the surface shall be as smooth as possible and the minimum of wood lost by the cut. It is possible to recut deals and battens into boards and plane them, with a loss of less than 3 mm. per cut.

" Ari-sawn " means that the goods have been cut on an improved type of circular saw bench called the ARI which has adjustable feed rollers enabling the wood to be sawn with much greater accuracy than on the old type of circular saw bench. It has been claimed that Ari-sawn goods are equal in manufacture to frame-sawn : this largely depends on the respective saws themselves and how they are cared for, as well as on the skill with which they are operated.

The circular saw used for crosscutting, as in trimming or adjusting the ends, is of a different type from that used for straight cutting along the grain, as in edge trimming or ripping. The crosscut saw does not need so much set as the edging saw, as less clearance is required in cutting across the fibres than in cutting along them when they have a tendency to grip : it is also a shorter cut. The crosscut sawplate may therefore be thinner at the edge, with less set and smaller teeth, which has the effect of making the end look as if it were planed, thus adding considerably to the appearance and consequently the value of the shipment.

It may be very difficult to distinguish between well-sawn bandsawn and well-sawn framesawn surfaces, since the saw marks, which are practically always visible, are very similar. However, there is nearly always at least one tooth which runs fractionally out of line making a defined scratch at regular intervals and these scratches will be much wider apart in the bandsawn goods than the framesawn goods, as the bandsaw has so many more teeth than the framesaw.

One cannot necessarily judge from the edge of a pile whether the goods are bandsawn, framesawn or circular sawn as the edges may be circular sawn however the other surfaces may have been worked. Circular sawn goods practically always show the circular saw marks fairly clearly.

4. Shrinkage. When sawing logs into deals, battens and boards, allowances are made in Scandinavian mills (but not in Canadian and U.S.A. mills) for shrinkage in thickness and width. Shrinkage in length is so slight as to be negligible.

Shrinkage is greater in the direction of the annual rings than across them—in other words wood shrinks more tangentially than radially—and this fact is applied in the case of flooring blocks and flooring strips which are usually cut " rift- " or " quarter-sawn " or " edge grain," so that when laid they not only have a harder wearing surface, but also any tendency to shrink will be more in thickness than in widths and so less likely to cause gaps between the blocks or strips.

It is estimated that Scandinavian sawngoods shrink, on the average, 3 per cent. from green (unseasoned) to shipping dry, so they are cut to a *minimum* of Norwegian inches which are 3 per cent. longer than English inches. In practice a greater allowance is usually made since it is most important that the wood shall hold up its nominal measure when shipping dry.

Boards cut from the outside of the log, consisting as they do mostly of sapwood, have a greater tendency to shrink than sizes consisting mostly of heartwood and that also has to be taken into account. Furthermore, boards shrink more than deals and battens, being normally cut tangentially, and being thinner they dry more thoroughly.

The allowance is made, when fixing the distance between the sawblades of the frame, by inserting blocks of wood which are the thickness of the deal, batten or board to be produced, *plus* the set of the saw to give the necessary clearance for the sawblade through the wood, *plus* the allowance for shrinkage.

In Canada and U.S.A. softwood lumber is sold " subject to natural shrinkage." Douglas fir is estimated to shrink on the average 5 per cent., western red cedar 4 per cent., western hemlock and Sitka spruce

6 per cent. According to the British Columbian rules Douglas fir shrinks approximately as follows :—

Thickness	1″, 1¼″, 1½″	2″	3″	4″ and thicker.
Approx. Shrinkage ...	$\frac{1}{16}$″	⅛″	$\frac{3}{16}$″	¼″ to ⅝″ in 12″ thickness.

Width	3″	4″	6″	8″ and 10″	12″	14″ and wider.
Approx. Shrinkage ...	⅛″	$\frac{3}{16}$″	¼″	½″	⅝″	¾″

It sometimes happens that sawngoods have ragged edges or ends, which is very detrimental to their appearance and consequently their value. This is a fault of the saws which, if of the correct type for the job and properly sharpened and set, should be able to cut wood cleanly whatever its moisture content or the temperature.

The amount to be allowed for the set of the saw depends upon the thickness of the blade and also the type and dimension of wood to be cut. The average framesaw blade is about 2 mm. thick and the set about ½ mm. on each side, making a total sawkerf of about 3 mm.

2. Planing.

PLANED BOARDS. These have normally a face and a back and are produced on a machine which has a fixed knife, or series of knives, set in the bed, with a rotary cutter operating as thicknesser in advance of them, and a rotary cutter or two operating above. The board to be planed normally goes through the planer face downwards on to the fixed knives whilst the upper side, constituting the back of the board, is thicknessed by the rotary cutter. The face of the board will thus have a perfectly smooth surface, but the back will show, however slightly, the ridges caused by the rotating knives of the cutter. Rotary cutting can be so beautifully done that it is almost impossible to tell the difference between the face and the back, but a wet finger wiped on the board will show up the rotary cutter marks. In some cases, as in the case of mouldings, the whole process is done by rotary cutters and not by a fixed knife, but the face can then never be quite so perfect, though commercially good.

The use of fixed knives for planing, although a standard practice in Scandinavian Planing Mills, is not so general in the United Kingdom or North America. In consequence these planed boards generally have a surface slightly inferior to the Scandinavian imported planed boards.

CHAPTER XVII

The Home Grown Timber Trade

1. General.

In the years up to 1939, less than 10 per cent. of the timber consumed in the U.K. was home grown. During the 1939-45 war over 60 per cent. was home grown. These two figures express the relative importance commercially and economically of the Home Grown Timber Trade in peace and war. The graphs in Figs. 12, 13, 14, 17 illustrate the immense increase in the home production of softwood, hardwood, pitwood and plywood during the war years. At the same time it should be remembered that the proportion of land area, about 6·5 per cent., under forest in the U.K. is very low compared with the timber producing countries of Europe (Sweden 56·5 per cent., Norway 23·8 per cent., France 19 per cent.).

At one time the country mills producing timber from trees in England and Scotland held a proud position in the internal trade of the land. The growth of the imported timber trade during the nineteenth century, enabling bulk quantities of cheap timber to be put on the market to meet the expanding trade and population of the country, resulted in the decline of the Home Grown Timber Trade, which found itself unable to compete with the low prices of imported timber.

The Home Grown Trade was in a depressed condition in the 1930's and as a result many firms further developed the side lines carried on from time immemorial such as agricultural work, gates, fencing, barrows, some extending into manufacturing of tool handles, mouldings, portable buildings and the like in order to have more than one source of income.

War-time requirements changed the position immediately. From being the smallest supplier of timber for the country, the Home Grown Trade became the largest. The trade was expanded greatly and the majority of sawmills previously handling only Imported Timber, began to handle Home Grown Timber, but of course at the first opportunity returned to the handling of the Imported Timber for which they were laid out.

The sawmills of the true Home Grown Timber Trade, that is to say the country sawmills, etc., that were established before 1939-45 and have no other normal trade, once again have a very doubtful future. The lack of any definite forest policy in the country until 1919, together with the excessively high rate of felling in both the 1914-18 and 1939-45 wars have resulted in the forest areas of the country dwindling to a dangerously low level. For many years the rate of felling will have to be drastically curtailed in order that these forest areas may regain a safe level. This immediately affects the Home Grown Trade, as this is their raw material. The immense war effort made by them during the war has been at the expense of their future livelihood.

It is always necessary to view the country's natural resources of materials in the light of defence and possible war. This produces two conflicting requirements that cannot be reconciled easily. First, the timber resources of the country must always be maintained at a safe level—so that timber as an essential material of war can be produced if and when sources outside the country fail; second, the Home Grown Timber Trade must be encouraged and maintained at a reasonable state of efficiency in order to meet a very rapid expansion should a major war occur.

A little help will be obtained from the increase in the import of hardwood logs from West Africa, but there are only a limited number of Home Grown Timber sawmills that have sawing equipment suitable for the very large African logs, and the high cost of transport prevents the sawing of these logs by country mills situated well inland.

The most encouraging development of the Home Grown Timber Trade since 1945 has been the introduction of re-afforestation schemes by the trade. In this manner the trade is taking an active part, with the Forestry Commission and the Landowners, in establishing its future supply of material.

2. Structure of the Home Grown Trade.

(*a*) *Landowner*. In the U.K., over 90 per cent. of the forest areas that produce timber are in the possession of private landowners. This is in sharp contrast to Scandinavia where the majority of timber-producing forests are state owned.

The Forestry Commission since their inauguration in 1919 have planted considerable areas of new forests, besides clearing and re-planting old forests. The first areas planted by them are still a long way from maturity, the only fully grown trees in the possession of the Forestry Commission being in existing forests purchased by them. Pending full maturity the afforested areas give a comparatively small but useful return in the way of thinnings which are in good demand as Poles, Props, etc.

(*b*) *Agent or Purchaser*. The buying of standing timber requires considerable skill and experience. Practically all pre-war Home Grown Timber Merchants are expert in this phase of their business carrying out surveys, valuations and purchasing by means of their own staff. Whilst it is unusual for them to employ outside assistance there are specialists in this work who will carry out a survey of the standing timber, and purchase it on behalf of the interested party such as a sawmill proprietor. Some of these agents may act on their own behalf and buy standing timber, arrange for it to be felled and then sell the logs to the sawmill proprietors, etc.

(*c*) *Fellers.* In many parts of England and Wales will be found felling gangs, who work either for agents or sawmill proprietors on contract to fell a particular stand of timber. They may operate over a considerable area of country, moving from place to place as required to carry out their various contracts.

(*d*) *Hauliers.* With the advent of the 1939-45 war and the impetus given to increased production, employment of haulage by contractors with their own haulage equipment developed. These generally work on contract, for which they move the logs from the woods and then haul them either direct to the sawmill or to a railway station.

(*e*) *Country Mills.* The sawmills which are to be found in the small villages of England and Wales are the oldest in the country. Many have been modernised with the introduction of the Band Rack Log Machine although some have changed little over the years and their sawmilling equipment is sometimes of a primitive nature. These usually have a local trade, specialising in agricultural requirements.

In Scotland and the North of England the country mills are rather different. These mills are portable and are set up at a central point in each felling area. When that area has been cleared, the mill is moved to the next area to be felled. Their principal raw material is softwood, following the preponderance of coniferous forests in Scotland.

(*f*) *Town Mills.* Sawmills established in the towns are usually larger than the country mills and equipped with more modern machinery, enabling greater precision and productivity to be obtained. They carry out the same function as the country mill but on a wider scale, particularly with distribution, the production being sent over a much wider area. Being better equipped and with more reliable production, greater possibilities are available to them; some balance their trade with other interests in imported timber or the manufacture of wooden articles.

(*g*) *Port City Mills.* Port City Mills is a term given to the sawmills established in major ports and cities for the sawing of imported timber, but which can be converted to the sawing of Home Grown timber. During the 1939-45 war these mills lost their principal supply of imported timber, and had to take on the conversion of round logs for which they were rarely adequately equipped. They are not really a true part of the Home Grown Timber Trade, but are a very necessary addition during the abnormal times of war.

All these sections of the trade have been detailed separately in order to define their separate functions. More often than not it will be found that one firm combines many of these functions, and some combine all of them. Port City Mills usually purchase their round timber requirements from Round Timber Merchants whereas town and country mills usually buy their own timber and have their own felling gangs and transport vehicles.

Round Timber Merchants are to be found in many parts of the country. These have no mill, but employ their own gangs of fellers and their own transport vehicles. They combine the work of the agents, fellers and hauliers, selling and delivering their logs to either the country or town mills.

3. Forestry Commission.

The Forestry Commission was set up in 1919 following the Acland Report of 1918, with these objects: (*a*) Establishing and maintaining a national reserve of state-owned forests; (*b*) Encouraging, advising and assisting privately owned forests and estates. By the end of September 1951, that is to say in the first 32 years of operation, the forest areas under the control of the Forestry Commission were as follows:—

Acquired plantations	76,400 acres.
Land acquired and planted	660,600 ,,
Land acquired, to be planted in the future	337,200 ,,
Other land acquired, but unsuitable for planting	707,300 ,,
Total	1,781,500 ,,

The total acreage of land planted by the Forestry Commission actually amounted to 696,901 acres, but in this period 36,301 acres was accounted for by losses from fire or wind or as a result of felling, disposal, etc., leaving the nett figure of 660,600 acres shown above.

The total area of 696,901 acres has been planted in the proportion of 92 per cent. (643,928 acres) conifers and 8 per cent. (52,973 acres) broadleaved trees. Of these figures, 501,645 acres represents afforestation and 195,256 acres re-planted land (including 17,711 acres replanted after fires).

The rate of planting in the five years 1947 to 1951 was considerably greater than the rate of planting in the first 27 years 1919 to 1946. The total planted by the Forestry Commission in this five year period amounted to 217,600 acres. In this same period the area of planting carried out in privately owned estates and forests was estimated to be about 62,900 acres.

The Forestry Commission programme is based upon planting 675,000 acres in the first 10 years from 1946, of which 290,000 acres was to be planted in the period 1947-1951, so that the area planted represents about 75 per cent. of the programme. Planting on private estates is expected to be 200,000 acres in the first 10 years from 1946, with 75,000 acres of this figure being planted in the period 1946-1951, so the area of private planting represents about 84 per cent. of the expected programme of planting.

Although the Forestry Commission is concerned with the major part of the extensive planting programme for the future, it will be seen from these figures that much will depend upon the development of planting on private estates and forests.

There are few landowners, however, who can afford to-day to carry out ambitious forestry schemes. In operating a forest or woodland, the principal return comes to the landowner when the trees reach maturity and are felled. There is a yearly income, of course, from the sale of thinnings and other forest products. In the case of the Forestry Commission in 1951, the sale of these items amounted to £1,517,708, the most important item being pitwood.

Nevertheless, this yearly income is usually exceeded by the expenses incurred in maintaining and operating the forest, particularly in the early stages. In the case of the Forestry Commission, in 1951 the nett excess of expenditure over income (which includes other income in addition to the sale of forest products) amounted to £5,555,144.

To assist and extend the development of private forestry, arrangements have been made to grant financial assistance in the form of loans, planting grants and maintenance grants. These arrangements are embodied in a project entitled "The Dedication of Woodlands." In this scheme, in return for financial assistance, the landowner is required to enter into an agreement or deed of covenant by which the land is dedicated to the production of timber.

The landowner undertakes certain responsibilities under these Agreements or Deeds of Covenant, such as: (*a*) To use the land in the best way for timber production; (*b*) To work to a plan approved by the Forestry Commission; (*c*) To employ skilled supervision; (*d*) To keep adequate accounts.

The Forestry Commission are closely concerned with each of these responsibilities since they must exercise supervision to ensure that the landowner is keeping to his part of the agreement and at the same time make available to the landowner all the advice possible. Such a vast increase in afforestation will naturally call for an increase in trained men to administer and work the forests. The training of men for these tasks will be largely undertaken by the Forestry Commission.

Since the "Dedication of Woodlands" scheme was initiated in 1948, the amount of private forestry dedicated has amounted to 73,731 acres, with a further 70,326 acres being in process of dedication at the beginning of 1952.

Amongst the forest areas established and controlled by the Forestry Commission are seven National Forest Parks which are open to the public, namely, Forest of Dean, Hardknott (Lake District), Argyll, Glen More (Cairngorms), Glen Trool (Galloway), Snowdonia and Loch Ard.

4. Products of Home Grown Timber.

Although much of the best Home Grown timber has been sacrificed in two great wars, it must not be thought that it is in any way inferior to the imported. Prime qualities of Home Grown hardwoods are the master of their counterpart in any part of the world.

It must be remembered that the recession of the Home Grown Timber Trade up to 1939 was principally on account of price—not quality. Imported hardwood could be brought half across the world and still be cheaper than the equivalent English hardwood. The large forest areas abroad enabled mass production methods to be used in production, with consequent reduction in costs.

Naturally there is only a limited amount of prime quality timber available, and all the lower grades have to be sold as well. Wartime uses of Home Grown timber have accentuated the lower qualities, since nothing could be wasted and all had to be used. Consumers compared the run of Home Grown timber they received, unfavourably with the equivalent Imported timber, forgetting that only the higher qualities of timber are in fact imported.

The Home Grown trade caters for several specialised products such as :—

Timber for railway waggon building and permanent way maintenance, shipbuilding, pitwood, road vehicle constructional timber, high quality timber for sports goods and tools, high class building construction, farm implements, fencing and gates (particularly for housing estates), repairs and rustic work in farm and garden, timber for coffins, box and packing cases, clogs, artificial limbs, brush backs, general turnery, handles, rollers for textile industry, bobbins, fruit storage racks and trays, ladders, furniture, cabinet work, dock and wharf construction, agricultural buildings, trawl rollers, butchers' blocks, veneers, gunstocks, airscrews and aircraft construction, telegraph poles, cooperage and scaffold poles.

CHAPTER XVIII

Specialised Branches of the Trade

1. Plywood and Veneer Trade.

(*a*) Exporting Countries.

Plywood factories abroad are situated close to the forests that supply their raw material. The most important timber for European plywood is birch. In 1938 birch plywood accounted for nearly 70 per cent. of the total import of plywood, in 1951 it was still 53 per cent. although many new supplies of plywood were opened in the intervening thirteen years. European birch grows in a broad belt from the Baltic extending into Central Russia, the most important plywood mills being in Finland, with other important mills in Estonia, Latvia and the U.S.S.R.

In 1938 these countries supplied over 75 per cent. of the U.K imports of plywood, made up as follows: Finland 44·4 per cent., U.S.S.R. 20·7 per cent., Latvia 8·4 per cent., Estonia 2·3 per cent.—Total 75·8 per cent.

In 1951 the U.S.S.R. and Finland accounted for 57 per cent. of the U.K. import of plywood, although none was imported from the former states of Latvia and Estonia.

The second most important European plywood timber is alder, growing farther South in Lithuania, Poland, White Russia and the Ukraine. Farther South still in Roumania, Czechoslovakia and Jugoslavia, considerable quantities of plywood are manufactured from the beech that grows well in those areas.

In Norway and Sweden the majority of the plywood production is from pine and spruce, although a little birch plywood is also produced. Imports of Swedish pine plywood have increased and in 1951 amounted to nearly 5 per cent. of the total U.K. import.

The export plywood industry in North America has expanded very greatly in the last ten years, and is continually expanding. On the West Coast of the U.S.A. and Canada the principal production is of Douglas fir plywood. This is produced in larger sheets than the European birch and alder plywood.

The manufacturers of Douglas fir plywood have made a speciality of marketing it in special exterior grades, in addition to the usual interior grades, and the former is being successfully used on a large scale for such items as the exterior covering of railway goods waggons, air-sea rescue launches, the sheathing of prefabricated buildings, the lining of form-work for concrete to ensure a fine surface, and other heavy duties.

This expanding industry has an important bearing on the Timber Trade, since the production of plywood calls for the highest quality of logs available. The result is that the plywood industry is competing with the normal timber trade for the limited supply of logs that will produce high quality " clear " grade timber. With the diminishing supplies of available Douglas fir, this is already resulting in a shortage of " clear " grades of Douglas fir.

From the East Coast of Canada some birch plywood is produced, also a small amount from such hardwoods as cottonwood, sap gum, red gum, etc.

Plywood imports from the U.S.A. and Canada were greatly increased during the 1939-45 war when no European plywood was available. The imports from U.S.A. have since been limited by dollar currency restrictions.

In South America there is a growing industry in Brazil producing Parana pine plywood. This also originated during the 1939-45 war but has now been firmly established.

Imports from Japan in 1951 amounted to 3 per cent. of the total import and consisted of Japanese oak plywood and lauan plywood. These are of special importance to the cabinet makers, the plywood although relatively cheap being well manufactured.

Not all plywood is manufactured from local timber resources. A large quantity is manufactured in Europe from hardwood logs from West Africa. These are mainly gaboon but several other species are used also.

The post-war development of West Africa for timber supplies has resulted in the setting up of an important plywood industry there to utilise the local timber resources. The theory that plywood cannot be produced in tropical climates owing to excessive heat and moisture has been disproved. Immense technical advances were made during the 1939-45 war in the uses of synthetic resin glues, of which special grades are available for arduous climatic conditions.

(*b*) Home Produced Plywood Industry.

The large scale commercial manufacture of plywood in the U.K. commenced in 1938, in direct competition with imported plywood. It has grown greatly since then, many new plywood factories being laid down during 1939-45 to supply wartime requirements. Up till that time only specialised plywood products were manufactured.

The U.K. plywood industry has the disadvantage of being a long way from the source of its material. Gaboon and other hardwood logs are brought from West Africa, birch and maple logs from Canada, birch and beech veneers from Europe and Canada. The additional transport and handling costs made the production of Home manufactured plywood uneconomical before 1938, but the trade has now grown to a size where the quantities of plywood produced enable it to meet the competition of imported plywood.

The Home Produced plywood industry is essential to the country in time of war. It becomes therefore a defence necessity in the same manner as the Home Grown Timber industry, quite apart from its ability to produce plywood commercially and economically.

(*c*) STRUCTURE OF THE TRADE AND MARKETING.

The imported plywood trade follows closely the structure of the other importing sections of the Timber Trade, with shippers, agents, importers and merchants.

The c.i.f. contract form follows the general terms of the timber contracts that have already been discussed, with the addition of special clauses applicable only to plywood. The contract specifies that all goods shall be shipped " under deck " and protects the buyer against the occurrence of manufacturing defects such as :—

(*a*) *Bad glueing*—for which claims may be made up to six months from date of final delivery of the goods into stock.

(*b*) *Manufacture damp*—being a defect in manufacture in which excess moisture is left in the core of the board. This may cause a fungoid growth to develop which, if not arrested, will eventually destroy the glueline and finally the whole board and spread to the boards adjacent to it in the bundle. External water damage is sometimes mistaken for manufacture damp, but the difference is evident when a bundle is opened : in the case of external water damage the boards nearest the outside of the bundle will have suffered most damage, whilst in the case of manufacture damp the boards nearest the centre of the bundle will be the worst affected. In external water damage there is also usually a waterline mark on the boards which does not occur in the case of manufacture damp.

(*c*) *Metal clips*—wire or fastenings present in the board.

If either of the defects in (*b*) or (*c*) are discovered within twelve months of the final date of delivery of the goods into stock, the buyer may reject a part or the whole of the parcel as may prove necessary.

The grading of plywood is discussed in detail on pages 263, 265.

(*d*) THE VENEER TRADE.

Veneers may be put into two main classifications : Decorative veneers (for furniture, panelling, etc.) and Constructional veneers (for manufacture of plywood in the U.K.). A large amount of decorative veneers are imported, but there is an important difference between the import of these and the import of timber, since the buyer always inspects decorative veneers before buying as it cannot be left completely to a full " description of goods " in the contract.

France is the main source of imported decorative veneers. The high average cost of French veneers in 1948 and 1951 shows the difference in cost between the French decorative veneers and constructional veneers produced in other countries.

PLYWOOD IMPORTS TO U.K. (INCLUDING LAMINBOARD, BLOCKBOARD AND BATTENBOARD)

	1938			1948			1951		
	Cubic Metres	Av. C.I.F. Value	Percentage	Cubic Metres	Av. C.I.F. Value	Percentage	Cubic Metres	Av. C.I.F. Value	Percentage
		£ s. d.			£ s. d.			£ s. d.	
Canada	10,600	12 14 2	3·4	47,900	31 1 2	27·4	14,200	59 4 5	4·7
U.S.S.R.	63,700	8 19 10	20·7	—	—	—	71,500	54 5 9	23·5
Finland	136,500	9 18 1	44·4	88,400	48 16 9	50·5	101,800	47 17 5	33·5
Sweden	6,200	10 2 7	2·0	12,200	47 12 7	7·0	14,400	49 6 5	4·7
U.S.A.	7,900	12 0 0	2·6	8,700	50 19 5	5·0	9,450	54 14 10	3·1
France	3,300	18 3 0	1·1	9,300	69 0 2	5·3	20,400	68 19 9	6·7
Japan	—	—	—	—	—	—	8,950	72 1 5	3·0
Others	*79,400	13 11 5	25·8	8,400	48 9 5	4·8	63,400	64 18 10	20·8
Total ...	307,600		100·0	174,900		100·0	304,100		100·0
Birch	214,300	9 15 10	69·6	87,600	48 17 8	50·2	161,700	50 8 6	53·2
Others	93,300	13 9 3	30·4	87,300	41 4 2	49·8	142,400	62 17 5	46·8

* Imports of plywood in 1938 from other countries were as follows :—

Latvia ...	25,900 cubic metres.	Estonia ...	7,300 cubic metres.	Czechoslovakia	2,600 cubic metres.
Poland ...	15,700 ,, ,,	Lithuania ...	3,900 ,, ,,	Japan ...	11,200 ,, ,,
Germany ...	5,600 ,, ,,	Roumania ...	3,000 ,, ,,	Others ...	4,200 ,, ,,

The import of constructional veneers is a more simple matter not requiring the same experience and judgment.

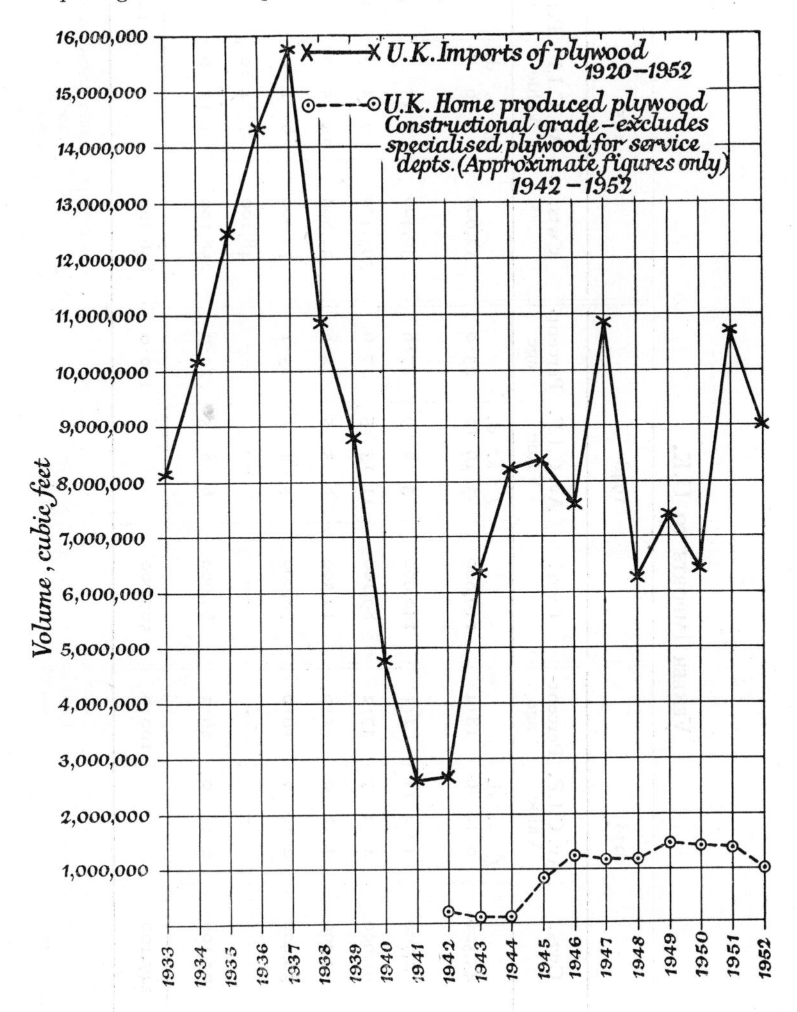

Fig. 17. IMPORTS OF PLYWOOD, 1933–1952; AND HOME PRODUCTION, 1942–1952.

The vast increase in veneer imports from the U.S.A., Canada and other Empire countries in post-war years was made necessary by the demands of the Home Produced Plywood Industry, and the Aircraft Industry both of which use large quantities of birch and beech veneers.

VENEER IMPORTS TO U.K.

	1938			1948			1951		
	Cwts.	Av. C.I.F. Value	Percentage	Cwts.	Av. C.I.F. Value	Percentage	Cwts.	Av. C.I.F. Value	Percentage
		£ s. d.			£ s. d.			£ s. d.	
Canada	45,500	0 19 6	18·4	116,800	3 16 10	23·0	12,600	5 6 7	1·5
Other Empire Sources ...	2,700	4 4 11	1·1	140,900	3 8 9	27·8	30,400	6 15 1	3·6
France	91,900	4 1 7	37·2	89,100	11 13 5	17·6	393,400	9 12 5	46·4
Italy	2,500	4 18 0	1·0	14,300	8 5 5	2·8	30,800	14 5 10	3·6
U.S.A.	39,400	2 10 7	16·0	76,900	5 4 2	15·1	72,900	6 1 9	8·6
Jugoslavia ...	—	—	—	—	—	—	48,100	7 4 10	5·7
Others	65,100	2 18 0	26·3	69,600	6 8 5	13·7	258,100	4 12 6	30·6
Total ...	247,100		100·0	507,600		100·0	846,300		100·0

A large number of veneers are also cut in the U.K., principally in London, although veneer cutting mills are now being set up in other parts of the country.

2. The Door Trade.

In Sweden and Canada, some timber shippers have set up special mills for the mass production of both flush doors and panel doors. These are exported to this country through the normal timber trade channels. It is difficult to believe sometimes that before 1939 flush doors could be imported and sold in this country for 7s. 6d. to 8s. 6d. each. Since 1939 no doors have been imported from Canada, and only a token quantity have been imported from Sweden, the price of these being found to be rather expensive compared with the equivalent made in the U.K. A special door contract form is used for the import of doors, following the general form and terms of timber contracts. " Shipment under deck " is a condition of the contract.

The import duty on doors from countries other than Empire countries is 1s. 6d. per door or 15 per cent. whichever is the greater (see page 191). The comparatively high rate of import duty is accentuated by the general increased cost of the door due to labour and material increases. It is this factor more than anything else that makes the imported door more expensive than the equivalent home produced door.

3. The Wood Fibre Wallboard Trade.

(*a*) General.

Wood fibre boards were originally a by-product of the mills producing sawn and planed wood goods. They are marketed in the U.K. by the timber trade. The wallboard mills are usually found very close to the sawing and planing mills. Waste from the latter, in the form of sawdust, planer chippings, edgings and " drop offs " are fed to the wallboard mill by conveyor, either direct or after reduction to a condition ready for pulping.

The trade, however, has now grown to such a size that there is insufficient waste produced at the sawmills that also make wood fibre boards. This has resulted in these manufacturers competing with the wood pulp manufacturers for the purchase of pulp logs, etc.

The wood chips, etc., are broken up mechanically and shredded out into pulp. The pulp is in the form of an emulsion which is fed into machines not unlike the normal paper-making machine. From this a board is produced in one continuous length, crosscut to the lengths required.

This board is soft and porous. It is marketed as " Insulation Board " since it has very good thermal insulation properties although its uses as an inexpensive building board are greater than its use as an insulating material. The most common thickness is $\frac{1}{2}$ inch though other thicknesses, such as $\frac{5}{16}$ inch and $\frac{3}{4}$ inch are produced.

Another type of board, produced in much the same way but with the addition of certain hardeners and binders in the pulp stage, is pressed under great heat and pressure. This is known as "Hardboard" or "Semi-Hardboard" depending upon the process. The most common thickness for this is $\frac{1}{8}$ inch or $\frac{3}{16}$ inch although $\frac{1}{4}$ inch boards are also produced. By producing a lower quality and thinner board, and laminating this together to form a board $\frac{3}{16}$ inch or $\frac{1}{4}$ inch thick, a very cheap building board is produced, generally known as "Laminated Board."

Wood waste is used generally for economic reasons, but actually almost any agricultural fibre may be used. One proprietory brand of insulation board is produced from "bagasse" the residue of sugar cane fibres.

(*b*) PRODUCING COUNTRIES.

The main producers of Wood Fibre boards in past years have been Canada, U.S.A., Sweden and Finland, since these are all countries with considerable softwood waste from their own large softwood sawing and planing mills. This trade has expanded greatly in recent years, the total tonnage of fibre board imports to the U.K. in 1951 of 128,000 tons being nearly five times as great as the 26,700 tons imported in 1938, although the great quantity imported in 1951 appears to have been considerably more than normal consumption. This increased demand, which is not confined to the U.K., has resulted in the setting up of new wallboard mills in nearly every country in Europe, notably Norway, Germany, Holland, Belgium and the Irish Republic. The comparative imports for 1938 and 1951 are shown in the adjacent tables.

1938 IMPORTS.

	Wallboards over ¼″ in Thickness (*i.e.*, mainly Insulation Board)			Wallboards up to ¼″ in Thickness (Hardboard and Laminated Board)		
	Quantity Cwts.	Average C.I.F. Value per cwt.	Percentage of Total Import	Quantity Cwts.	Average C.I.F. Value per cwt.	Percentage of Total Import
		£ s. d.			£ s. d.	
Canada	165,282	14 19 0	42·0	44,254	15 18 2	31·5
Finland	123,168	14 6 10	31·5	22,430	20 0 3	16·0
Sweden	80,057	16 1 5	20·5	66,318	27 12 8	47·0
U.S.A.	20,963	18 4 0	5·0	4,895	31 18 8	3·5
Norway	2,604	16 19 2	1·0	472	16 13 11	·5
Germany	407	18 13 6	—	2,180	17 0 5	1·5
Total ...	392,481		100·0	140,549		100·0
Approx. equiv. in super feet ...	58,872,000			21,081,000		

1951 IMPORTS.

	Insulation Board			Laminated Boards			Hardboard		
	Quantity Cwts.	Av. C.I.F. Value per Cwt.	Percentage of Total Import	Quantity Cwts.	Av. C.I.F. Value per Cwt.	Percentage of Total Import	Quantity Cwts.	Av. C.I.F. Value per Cwt.	Percentage of Total Import
		£ s. d.			£ s. d.			£ s. d.	
Canada	44,207	63 2 6	10·0	4,266	65 10 6	25·0	19,911	67 8 11	1·0
Finland	73,346	50 3 6	16·5	341	58 17 9	2·0	221,467	52 7 6	10·5
Sweden	232,704	52 16 0	53·5	10,500	53 1 10	62·0	1,411,778	51 19 9	66·5
U.S.A.	—	—	—	780	85 19 6	5·0	4,766	82 7 1	·25
Norway	38,228	49 14 6	9·0	351	57 5 3	2·0	118,383	49 2 9	5·5
Germany ...	28,136	56 2 10	6·5	372	62 4 1	2·0	173,246	55 8 8	8·0
Netherlands ...	10,451	50 2 9	2·5	—	—	—	45,176	52 11 5	2·0
Irish Republic ...	549	57 0 3	—	366	16 11 2	2·0	41,237	54 9 3	2.0
Austria	6,301	56 19 2	1·5	—	—	—	11,147	60 11 2	·5
Belgium	1,392	59 5 8	·5	—	—	—	50,437	56 0 2	2·5
New Zealand ...	—	—	—	—	—	—	13,020	61 0 2	·75
Italy	—	—	—	—	—	—	5,637	78 13 5	·25
Czechoslovakia ...	—	—	—	—	—	—	3,809	47 18 6	·25
Total ...	435,314		100·0	16,976		100·0	2,120,014		100·0
Approx. equivalent in super feet	65,295,000			2,547,000			318,000,000		

Statistics of wallboard imports for 1938 are not available in sub-divisions for Hardboard, Laminated Board and Insulation Board, but only in the two divisions shown above.

The major thicknesses of wallboard imported are ⅛" Hardboard and ½" Insulation Board, other thicknesses representing only a very small fraction of the total imports. In both cases there are approximately 3,000 super feet of board per ton.

Some of the earliest wallboard mills in Europe were established in the U.K., these mills also have expanded their production greatly since 1938 and supply a major part of the requirements of the country.

TOTAL HOME PRODUCTION.
(Hardboard, Laminated Board and Insulation Board.)

1938	1951
12,600 tons approx. (equivalent to approx. 37,800,000 super feet).	35,600 tons approx. (equivalent to approx. 106,700,000 super feet).

These figures should now be compared with the total tonnage of all types of imported board; 1938 approx. 26,700 tons (equivalent to approx. 80,000,000 super feet); 1951 approx. 128,600 tons (equivalent to approx. 386,000,000 super feet).

From this it will be seen that the total tonnage of imported and home produced wallboard has risen from approx. 39,300 tons (equivalent to approx. 117,800,000 super feet) in 1938, to approx. 164,000 tons (equivalent to approx. 492,000,000 super feet) in 1951.

This shows clearly the great increase in this trade and is a measure of its present day importance.

(*c*) STRUCTURE OF THE TRADE.

The wood fibre wallboard trade is comparatively young, and the structure of the trade varies slightly from the structure of the timber trade. Up till 1939 the wallboard industry was still growing and the boards were sold in the U.K. through firms acting as concessionaires for the manufacturers. These concessionaires appointed distributors and merchant stockists in the trade. They differed from the normal timber agents in importing stocks of board on their own account, taking them into warehouses and offering them as a "landed stock" when required to their distributors. They sometimes also permitted the distributors to import the board through them on normal c.i.f. terms. The position has now changed since so many new mills have been established abroad. The recent tendency has been not to appoint concessionaires but to appoint agents in the normal way.

At the present time therefore there are :—

(i) Agents—for foreign shippers offering boards on normal c.i.f. basis to any importer capable of taking sufficient quantity at one time.

(ii) Concessionaires — for the original foreign manufacturers. Offering boards either c.i.f. or from " landed stocks " imported by themselves.

(iii) Importer Distributors.—Merchants importing through agents or concessionaires on a c.i.f. basis. They may be appointed local distributors for a particular brand of board but this practice is gradually fading.

(iv) Merchant Stockists.—Merchants purchasing smaller quantities from the importers or concessionaires for re-sale.

(*d*) THE IMPORT AND HANDLING OF FIBRE BOARDS.

Generally wood fibre boards are shipped by liners, and so are automatically shipped under deck. If however a large quantity were shipped on a timber ship it would be necessary to specify that shipment must be under deck.

The description of goods in the contract, together with any questions of quality are much simpler. Wood fibre boards are manufactured articles, with their own specification and trade name, so detailed description is unnecessary.

The import duty for wood fibre boards is 20 per cent.

The principal cause of any claims on wood fibre boards is damage by crane hooks and slings. Imports of board must be closely inspected after receipt from the ship to see if this damage is present. A pair of chain slings carelessly placed on a crate of insulation board can damage every board in the crate.

The liability to damage in handling bulk quantities of board results in carriage rates being higher per ton than for timber. Road carriage rates for wood fibre board are often nearly 20 per cent. more than rates for carrying timber.

CHAPTER XIX

Trade Associations and Authorities

1. The Timber Trade Federation of the U.K.

The Timber Trade Federation (75 Cannon Street, London, E.C.4) is the organisation that deals with the commercial and economic matters of the Timber Trade, principally in connection with imported timber. Formed in 1892, the Federation has the following objects :— (*a*) To protect, promote and develop the common interests of the timber trade of the U.K. (*b*) To collect and disseminate statistical and other information relating to the English and Foreign timber trade. (*c*) To acquire, promote or support a company limited by guarantee ; with the principal objects of research, information, technical education and publicity of timber and its products. (This refers to the T.D.A. Ltd.—see page 290.) (*d*) To promote, support or oppose legislative or other measures affecting the timber trade. (*e*) To do all such other things that will be conducive to the prosperity of the timber trade.

The Federation is organised on both a National and Regional basis. It comprises National Sections for each main type of timber and also for plywood. It also includes a National Merchants' Section, Timber Agents' and Brokers' Association, Hardwood Agents' and Brokers' Association and National Sawmilling Association—the last three by affiliation.

Regionally, the interests of members are served and promoted by Area Sections or Associations—these Sections and Associations having representatives on the Executive Council of the Federation and on the Executive bodies of the National Sections.

The administration and general policy of the T.T.F. is ordered by the Executive Council which in addition to representatives from Area Associations and National Sections includes the nominees of certain affiliated trade organisations. Certain specialised subjects are dealt with by Standing Committees of the Executive Council. Among the more important of these are The National Port Labour Committee, The Transportation Committee, The Parliamentary and Legal Committee, and the Joint Standards and Technical Committee, whose function is to examine and comment upon proposed British Standards affecting timber.

There are some sixteen local area associations or sections, and fourteen National associations or sections ; of these latter the most important are National Softwood Importers' Section, Hardwood Importers' Section, Merchants' Section, Plywood Section, Timber Agents' and Brokers' Association of the U.K., Hardwood Agents' and Brokers' Association Ltd., National Sawmilling Association (this includes two sub-associations, the Kiln Owners' Association and the

Hardwood Flooring Manufacturers' Association, which look after specialised problems), Pitwood Importers' Section, National Veneer Section, Sleeper and Pole Section.

The Federation is a unified organisation recognised by the Ministries and Government Departments, foreign shippers, Chamber of Shipping, and the various Consumer Associations, as representing the interests of Agents, Importers and Merchants in the U.K. The fact that the strength of the Federation has increased from an original Membership of approximately 250 to close on 1,200 provides some evidence of the value placed by the Trade on its achievements in negotiations with such bodies.

2. Local Timber Trade Associations.

Members of the local timber trade associations or sections, which are listed below, are usually also members of one or more of the National associations or sections within the T.T.F.

Bristol and District Timber Traders' Association—Guildhall, Small Street, Bristol, 1.

East Anglian Softwood Importers' Section—7 St. George Street, Norwich.

Hants. and Dorset Timber Trade Association—31 Hanover Buildings, Southampton.

Humber District Timber Trade Association—Samman House, Bowlalley Lane, Hull.

Incorporated Bristol Channel Timber Importers' Association—Guildhall, Small Street, Bristol.

Irish Timber Importers' Association—39-41 Dame St., Dublin.

Kent Timber Trade Association—75 Cannon St., London, E.C.4.

Liverpool Timber Trade Association Ltd.—34 Moorfields, Liverpool, 2.

London Merchants' Section (Softwoods)—75 Cannon Street, London, E.C.4.

London (Softwood) Importers' Section—75 Cannon Street, London, E.C.4.

Manchester Timber Trade Association—30 Cross Street, Manchester, 2.

North East Coast Section—26 Mosley Street, Newcastle-on-Tyne, 1.

Northern Ireland Timber Importers' Association—18 Arthur Street, Belfast.

Scottish Section—116 Hope Street, Glasgow, C.2.

South Coast Timber Association—75 Cannon Street, London, E.C.4.

South of Ireland Timber Importers' Association—Waterford.

West of Ireland Timber Importers' Association—Merchants' Road, Galway.

Western Counties Timber Importers' Association—31 Cathedral Yard, Exeter.

In addition there are various merchant groups and associations throughout the country.

The functions of the local associations are as follows :—

(*a*) Discussion and negotiation between members of the local association on local timber trade matters.

(*b*) Liaison and negotiation between the local timber trade as a whole and local organisations and bodies such as :—

Area officers of Board of Trade and other Government Ministries.

Local port and dock authorities,

Local offices of railway authorities, etc.

(*c*) Discussion of National matters affecting the local trade of the association and the forwarding of the considered and representative opinions of the local association to the T.T.F.

3. The Federated Home Timber Associations.

The Federated Home Timber Associations (75 Cannon Street, London, E.C.4) are the following :—

English Timber Merchants' Association—75 Cannon Street, London, E.C.4.

Midland Home Timber Association—Chamber of Commerce, 95 New Street, Birmingham, 2.

North Midland Home Timber Association—11 Smithy Row, Nottingham.

North Western Home Timber Association—75 Cannon Street, London, E.C.4.

Northern English Timber Merchants' Association—West Bar Chambers, 38 Boar Lane, Leeds, 1.

Western and Southern Counties Home Grown Timber Merchants' Association—Chamber of Commerce, Guildhall, Bristol, 1.

The F.H.T.A. occupies the same position in the Home Grown timber trade as the T.T.F. occupies in the Imported trade. It is responsible for Home Grown timber trade matters on a National level, and has direct liaison with the T.T.F. on matters of joint interest. The Area Home Timber Associations have responsibilities similar to those of the Local Imported Timber Trade Associations, although the area covered by each Home Timber Association is much larger.

There are two specialised sections of the F.H.T.A., the Oak Waggon Scantling Section and the Forestry Section (formed 1947).

The Home Grown Pitwood Association is administered by a Joint Secretariat of the F.H.T.A. and T.T.F.

4. Timber Development Association Ltd.

The T.D.A. (21 College Hill, London, E.C.4) is a non-trading organisation, formed for the purpose of making the advantages of wood better known to present and potential users. The Association conducts research into the structural and decorative properties of timber of every kind, with the object of ensuring its most efficient, economic

and artistic utilisation. It fosters timber education and, in addition, it collects statistical and technical information, which it makes available by means of booklets, pamphlets, information sheets and by personal contacts through its permanent staff.

Its activities are therefore classified under four main headings: (1) Research into the properties and uses of timber; (2) The design of timber components and assemblies for the purposes of industry; (3) Education in the field of timber, its production, processing and use; (4) The publicising and dissemination of information on timber.

The membership of T.D.A. Ltd. is in three main groups.

Group 1, which is by far the largest, consists of firms who are also members of the T.T.F. (*i.e.*, agents, importers and merchants), and are known as "Federation" members.

Group 2 consists of firms, companies and associations of such who are engaged in the manufacture and sale of manufactured woodgoods and are known as "manufacturing" members.

Group 3 is made up of such persons, companies or associations as do not come within the definitions of Groups 1 and 2, for example: members of the Timber Trade who are not eligible for membership of the T.T.F.; overseas shippers; manufacturers of wood preservatives, etc. These are known as "subscribing" members.

All members in Group 1 and the majority of those in Group 3 pay a basic subscription to T.D.A. Ltd. and also contribute directly to a guarantee fund which provides the main part of the income of the Association. Group 2 members pay an annual contribution, in accordance with a sliding scale, which is based on turnover and a small number of Group 3 (*i.e.*, those to whom a turnover basis is not applicable) pay a fixed annual contribution, the amount of which is decided by the Council of the Association. All members have the same voting rights and are eligible to receive all the services offered by the Association.

RESEARCH AND DESIGN DEPARTMENT.

This Department carries out research in timber technology and constructional design, dealing with such diverse problems as tests on timber joints, fire resistance of timber, alternative timbers for ships' decks, properties and uses of recently imported but little-known tropical hardwoods, etc. It also promotes research through timber consuming trades.

The Design Section of the Department has been responsible for the development of the T.D.A. Roof and a great deal of development work on agricultural, horticultural, school and other types of buildings.

Booklets, information and design sheets and pamphlets on the work of the Department are prepared and distributed, both to members of the Association and to a wide range of timber users.

STATISTICS AND INFORMATION DEPARTMENT.

This department prepares and collates trade statistics and information concerning timber. It also maintains a comprehensive library of textbooks, photographs, films and lantern slides on timber and its uses.

EDUCATION DEPARTMENT.

The main work of the Education Department is in sponsoring Timber Technology classes that are held in technical colleges all over the country. There are over 60 centres holding these classes. The Education Department prepares the syllabus for these classes, and holds the T.D.A. certificate examinations for students at the end of their three year course. There is also a further two years course of study leading to the award of a higher certificate.

Although the majority of classes are held in Technical Colleges the T.D.A. assist in the training of instructors by holding a summer school each year at Cambridge University and a Post-Graduate Course in collaboration with the Forests Products Research Laboratory.

Teaching aids are provided in the form of pamphlets and information sheets. In addition it prepares wall charts and film strips, which are in general use by Education Authorities throughout the country. Advanced lecture courses on timber are organised in collaboration with local Education Authorities and specialised lectures are arranged for Architectural and Building Colleges, Universities, Engineering Societies, and Government Departments.

PUBLIC RELATIONS DEPARTMENT.

The Public Relations Department has the responsibility of "putting over" the case for timber not merely to all consumers of wood, but also to the general public. It presents the case for timber in all sections of the press by editorial reference and descriptive articles, undertakes exhibitions, film displays, distribution of literature and other public functions in various towns. The T.D.A. Ltd. has grown up through a period of trial and error into a very efficient trade organisation.

The achievement of the valuable work accomplished by the T.D.A. appears all the more remarkable when it is realised that the funds available to the T.D.A. for this work are small when compared to those devoted by other industries to the development and publicity of their product. It is indeed surprising that there should be any people in the Timber Trade who would doubt the advantages and opportunities to be gained by joining the T.D.A. Fortunately they are in the minority. It has been often stated that no business or trade stays still, it either advances to prosperity or retreats to ignominy. Without some such energetic organisation as the T.D.A. Ltd. the Timber Trade would be in grave danger of losing place to its rivals, particularly in the field of building construction.

5. Forest Products Research Laboratory.

This laboratory (Princes Risborough, Aylesbury, Bucks.) was established in 1925 as a Government department under the Department of Scientific and Industrial Research.

Its function is to carry out research into the utilisation of timber and major forest products. Research on minor forest products is done at the Imperial Institute, South Kensington. The Laboratory is organised under the following sections:—

Wood Structure. Research into the structure of wood in relation to its physical and mechanical properties.

Physics. Study of the physical properties of wood and particularly of the movement of moisture, gases and heat in wood and the relation of this to the physical properties of wood.

Seasoning. Study of the moisture relations of wood and study of the practice of air-seasoning and kiln-seasoning, together with research into kiln design. [Courses are held at the laboratory for kiln operators from individual firms.] Research into the bending qualities of timber both in solid and laminated form.

Timber Mechanics. Study of the comparative mechanical properties of various woods, plywood and other forms of composite wood.

Woodworking. Research into woodcutting principles, the behaviour of commercial timbers during woodcutting operations, and the design of machines and tools.

Composite Wood. Research and investigation into the problems connected with veneers, plywood and other composites of wood, and of adhesives used in their manufacture.

Wood Preservation. Study of the durability and resistance of woods against fire and decay.

Mycology. Study of the physiology of staining and wood destroying fungi, and of micro-organisms affecting glue in plywood, etc.

Entomology. Research and biological studies of insects attacking timber and the development of methods of control.

Chemistry. Study of the chemical properties of wood, and extractives. Corrosion of metals by wood and *vice versa.*

Utilisation. Investigation into the industrial application and uses of wood in various forms.

Publication and Records. The collection and recording of the data obtained from the above sections and other laboratories working on wood technology. The publication and dissemination of this information by means of various types of publications published by H.M. Stationery Office.

External Relations. Liaison with industry. The Laboratory provides free advice on any technical matter submitted to it. This important service is a major part of the Laboratory's work and serves to link individual firms in the Timber Trade with the Laboratory.

On technical matters the Laboratory works closely with the T.D.A. Ltd. and assists in providing training for the T.D.A. Instructors.

6. Wallboard Importers', Distributors' and Merchants' Association.

This Association (3-4 Newgate Street, London, E.C.1) was formed in 1944 for the purpose of co-ordinating the interests of importers and merchants of wood fibre wallboard. It works on a National level for the trade, and collaborates closely with the following Associations :—

Insulation Building and Hardboard Association. Representing the interests of the original " Concessionaire " importers, etc., of wood fibre board.

Fibre Board Agents' Association. Representing the interests of the agent for wood fibre boards. This Association was formed following the great increase in the agencies set up in the U.K. for imported wood fibre boards.

Building Board Manufacturers' Association. Representing the interests of the United Kingdom manufacturers of wood fibre boards.

It is divided into :—(1) *Importers' Section*—being persons, firms or companies who import fibre building board on f.o.b. or c.i.f. terms for re-sale in the United Kingdom, and who carry stocks ; (2) *Home Produced Section*—being persons, firms or companies who are distributors and who carry stocks of Home Produced fibre building board for re-sale in the United Kingdom ; (3) *Merchants' Section*—being persons, firms or companies purchasing fibre building boards from Importers or Distributors for re-sale.

7. Federated Merchant Freighters Association Ltd. Hardwood Legal Protection Association Ltd.

Both these associations have similar functions and use the T.T.F. secretariat at 75 Cannon Street, London, E.C.4. The F.M.F.A. Ltd. caters for the softwood trade and the Hardwood Legal Protection Association Ltd. for the hardwood trade. Their services are only available to their members, and not all the members of the T.T.F. National Softwood Importers' Section or T.T.F. Hardwood Section are members of these associations. They provide legal advice to their members on all matters concerning marine insurance and shipping. Where disputes arise, particularly those where there is a matter of principle involved, they undertake to stand behind the member concerned who is fighting the case, paying a large proportion, if not all, of the legal charges.

These associations have grown up through the need for importers to be able to face similar associations of shipowners, etc. Although they are affiliated to the T.T.F., they do not overlap the existing work of the Federation committees and sections.

8. British Wood Preserving Association.

This association (6 Southampton Place, London, W.C.1) was formed in 1929. It collects, promotes and spreads knowledge of all methods of wood preservation, including the protection of wood against fire, and it promotes the standardisation of preservative specifications. Its members include the research bodies concerned with timber preservation, the manufacturers of all types of preservatives and fire retardants, the users of timber and of course members of the timber trade who are particularly concerned in timber preservation—including those firms operating preserving plants. With the growing interest being displayed in wood preservation, this association is now expanding rapidly.

CHAPTER XX

Developments in the Timber Trade

1. New Products.

(*a*) Utilisation of Wood Waste.

The grave shortage of timber both during and immediately after the 1939-45 war focussed attention on the large amount of wood waste in the form of planing chips and sawdust, for which there was apparently no outlet. The manufacture of "synthetic wood" from wood chips or sawdust is by no means new, in fact anybody can experiment with sawdust and waterglass and produce a solid material. From 1946 however, wood waste boards began to be manufactured on a large scale commercially.

The process is not very complicated, but requires powerful heated presses. The main constituents are either wood chips or sawdust, and a bonding agent such as urea-formaldehyde. This is a synthetic resin greatly used in the manufacture of plywood. By this method a board may be produced in any thickness from $\frac{1}{4}$ inch to say $1\frac{1}{2}$ inches in dimensions up to 8 ft. or 9 ft $\times$ 4 ft., the maximum size being limited by the dimensions of the press.

The advantages in, say, partitions, of using a solid board of 8 ft. $\times$ 4 ft. are considerable. The other materials available are insulation board (much more fragile), wood fibre hardboard and thin plywood (not self supporting), plywood blockboard (more expensive) or timber matching (more labour required for erection). There are many applications for wood waste boards where they can do the job adequately and save a certain amount of cost.

One of the most interesting structural uses of chipboards in recent years has been for domestic flooring. When $\frac{3}{4}''$ thick it has been laid on timber joists at 16″ centres. Tests have shown that it has ample strength, and in times of high timber cost it can be a competitive material to P.T.G. flooring.

These materials are as yet in their very early stages and there are many developments still to be seen commercially.

The synthetic resins used as a bonding agent for the board are themselves expensive. Experiments have been successfully carried out in the U.S.A. whereby the lignin in the cell walls of the wood chips has been made to "run" under heat, pressure and solvent, and has formed the bonding agent. The plant required for this process is very expensive and cheaper production methods yield materials which, though having somewhat different physical properties, are in general satisfactory.

There have been many critics of wood waste boards in the last few years, but in reality these boards are now in the same position as plywood was thirty to forty years ago. In a few years time they will doubtless be accepted as one of the normal specialities of the Timber Trade. In a world of rapidly dwindling capital resources of materials, it is difficult to see how it can be considered reasonable to continue wasting 30 to 40 per cent. of a natural product like timber. Here is a fundamental that still has to be fully appreciated by a great section of the trade. Wood waste boards are only a part solution of this problem, since they can only absorb a fraction of the total waste produced. The future for the utilisation of this waste and the balancing of the world's economy of raw materials would appear to lie in the hands of the chemist. The development of chemical products from wood waste offers immense possibilities and grounds for scientific research for a long time to come.

(*b*) IMPROVED WOOD AND OTHER RESIN IMPREGNATED MATERIALS.

In recent years there have been considerable advances in the production of specialised wood products. These are important since they show the ultimate technical achievements with wood, and are the outward signs of the never ceasing research work that is carried out to improve the utilisation of wood.

Improved wood is manufactured from hardwood veneers (usually beech, birch or maple). They are impregnated with synthetic resin and then subjected to great heat and pressure, resulting in a very dense laminated product very much heavier than natural wood.

There are many trade names for improved wood, each produced in a particular manner, but all of them have the following basic properties: They do not suffer from the normal defects of natural timber, *i.e.*, no longer hygroscopic, so changes of moisture will not cause swelling, shrinkage, twisting or shaking, etc.; not attacked by fungi or insects, and practically fireproof. Strength properties are improved since normal timber defects such as knots are cut out before the improved wood is made. They are excellent electrical insulators: this primarily on account of the synthetic resin. Lastly, they are very hard wearing.

If the same process is applied to paper or to linen, thin flexible sheet materials of considerable strength are produced. They can be manufactured from $\frac{1}{32}$ inch thick to 3 inches thick and in sheet sizes up to 9 ft. × 4 ft.

The thicker sections of improved wood, paper, or linen base plastic sheet are used for silent gears, and any working part taking a great amount of wear. Although heavier than wood, all these materials are much lighter than metals, being about one-sixth the weight of steel and one-half the weight of aluminium although their strength properties are comparable.

The quantities of these materials used for mechanical, electrical or gear components is not very large, but in recent years the use of paper based sheet plastic material in thickness of $\frac{1}{16}$ inch and $\frac{1}{8}$ inch has grown considerably. There are certainly some classes of work where this is more effective than the more traditional materials, plywood and wood fibre board.

The additional cost of paper base plastic sheet is often more than offset by the saving in labour cost on a finished article since its surface is harder than that of plywood or wood fibre board and does not require the same paint treatment.

The normal resins (phenol or cresol formaldehyde) are used to produce a material either brown, or with the addition of pigment, black, or other dark colours. Lighter colours may be obtained by using a different resin (urea formaldehyde or melamine formaldehyde).

It is possible to incorporate in a paper base plastic sheet a top veneer of a decorative wood. This is particularly useful where surfaces that receive a great amount of wear are concerned. These sheets can be made proof against blistering from burning cigarette ends.

The final result therefore, is that a table top may now be produced with a veneered " real timber " surface, but with qualities of resistance to heat, fire, acid, spirit, alkali and mechanical abrasion such as never before has been possible with varnishes, or lacquers, or waxes applied to a natural wood surface.

2. Timber Preservation.

Although there have been no major technical developments or improvements during the past few years in wood preservatives or their application, there has been a considerable increase in the country of the capacity for carrying out wood preservation and many new plants have been laid down.

In the past, the economics of wood preservation have been accepted by many but practised by few. The application of a wood preservative means an additional cost which is recovered over a number of years through the increased life of the timber. Users of wood in large quantities, such as the G.P.O. for telegraph poles, or the railway authorities for railway sleepers and fencing, etc., have long appreciated this point, and have been the greatest users of preserved timber in the past. For the average building or constructional work however it is a different matter. Builders have not been in the habit of fitting preserved wood fittings and carcassing timber in houses in the past, since the extra cost can rarely be recovered from the purchaser of the house.

During the 1939-45 war the facility for the preservative treatment of wood became extremely important in connection with the packing of stores and equipment for the Burma and Far East campaigns. Unless the timber for these cases and boxes, etc., was treated, it was often completely destroyed by insects or fungi before the stores reached their destination.

Apart from the demands of the large users mentioned above, the use of preservative treated wood depends largely upon some competent authority, such as a Government department, a local authority, or a private architect, specifying that it shall be used. It is not suggested that every piece of timber, wherever it is used, should be treated with preservative, but all building timber in situations liable to become humid or damp should be so treated. This is particularly the case where dry rot damaged timber is being replaced. The lack of proper maintenance to buildings during 1939-45 together with the "unseen" damage by enemy action (loosening of roof tiles, etc., admitting water) has resulted in an immense increase in the rate of attack and destruction of timber by fungi and insect pests. One authority has estimated this to be at the rate of over £20,000,000 per year for dry rot alone.

The cost of wood preservative depends upon the method of treatment and the type of preservative.

The methods of treatment are:

(*a*) Brushing the surface with the preservative.

(*b*) Dipping the timber in a tank of preservative.

(*c*) Dipping in a tank of preservative which is heated and then allowed to cool (alternatively the timber may be removed from the hot tank and dipped in a tank of cold preservative).

(*d*) Pressure treatments of various kinds.

These methods have been placed in approximate order of cost and *effectiveness*. Brushing is the cheapest, but the least effective. Pressure treatments are the most expensive, since a fairly extensive plant is necessary and much more preservative will be left in the wood, but timber treated in this manner will last several times longer than if untreated. Much however depends upon the species of timber being impregnated. Whereas whitewood (spruce) is a difficult timber to impregnate even with pressure treatment, there are others such as Scots pine and beech which can be completely impregnated by the hot and cold tank method, (*c*) above.

More complete penetration may be obtained by incising the timber beforehand, but this also adds to the cost. Douglas fir railway sleepers are generally treated in this manner, as that wood is more resistant to impregnation than Baltic redwood.

There are three main classes of preservatives, which are placed below approximately in order of cost.

(*a*) *Tar Oil Preservatives*—including the familiar creosote. This is the cheapest and ideal for exterior work—but suffers from the disadvantages of a strong smell (which can be absorbed by fatty foodstuffs *without* their being in direct contact with the timber); a dark colour which has a tendency to spread to untreated wood causing discolouration where it is not required; and it cannot easily be painted over.

(*b*) *Water Soluble Preservative.* These are concentrated mineral salts dissolved in water. Treated timber can be painted and is odourless. Care has to be taken in using this type of preservative for exterior woodwork as some of these preservatives will " leach " out under the action of rain, etc. There are others however that produce water-insoluble substances inside the wood that can be used safely externally.

(*c*) *Solvent Type Preservative.* These are also toxic mineral salts but are dissolved in a volatile oil or spirit. These are particularly useful for treating timber in existing buildings, etc., since this class of solvent permits a reasonable penetration of the preservative by brush treatment. Since the solvents are usually highly inflammable they cannot be used with safety in pressure treatments.

3. Stress Grading and Laminated Timber.

The use of stress graded timber in the U.K. is at present in its elementary stages. Much has yet to be learned about it and many people have to be converted to appreciate its possibilities but, since stress grading moves hand in hand with the modern conceptions of the use of timber as a structural engineering material, it will inevitably have a major place in the timber trade in the future.

Stress grading is simply the grading of a piece of timber for strength. The structural engineer when using steelwork or reinforced concrete can calculate accurately from tables of dimensions of these materials exactly what load or strain they will bear before breaking. He knows the load or strain that has to be carried and therefore, after making a liberal allowance for a " safety margin," he uses no more material on the job than is necessary. In the past the use of timber in such circumstances has been governed by traditional practice and rule of thumb methods. The uses of stress graded timber, together with the great advances that have been made in " timber connectors," enabling efficient timber joints to be made, now introduces timber as a direct competitor to light steelwork in roof sections, etc.

The stress grading of timber is based on the following factors: Density and rate of growth, knots, checks, shakes, splits, slope of grain, decay and insect attack, and sapwood.

Stress grading is carried out extensively in the U.S.A. and in the West of Canada for their domestic markets. At one time it was considered that timber could be imported into the U.K. as " stress-graded " timber and domestic grades were in fact imported during the war, but recent experience has tended to indicate that stress grading will have to be carried out in the merchants' yards in this country. This will naturally add to the cost of the timber, but in comparison with steel, reinforced concrete or aluminium, timber is a very cheap material and this additional cost will be more than covered by the total saving in the use of timber.

Considerable efforts have been made, particularly in Eastern Canada, to establish stress grading for export. This movement has had the excellent effect of improving the grading of the smaller productions of East Canadian spruce. It should not be forgotten that most imported timber is already " graded " and the difference between Scandinavian Unsorted and Fifths and also between Douglas fir Selects and Merchantable is mainly a question of the existence and extent of defects affecting the " strength " of the piece and is to that extent a form of " stress grading."

The use of laminated timber beams in constructional work is another example of the modern conception of timber as an engineering material. Laminated timber beams are built up from laminations of small sections of timber, the completed beam being considerably stronger than the equivalent beam in one piece of timber. Although the timber used for the laminations does not require to be of such a high structural grade as the solid piece would be, it is not possible to use very low grades for this work and it is certainly not an outlet for low grade timber.

The cost of laminated timber beams is therefore high, since each lamination must be machined before the whole is bonded together, but a little of the labour cost is offset by a saving in the cost of the timber, since the value of the timber laminations will be less than the equivalent in solid timber.

Laminated timber beams may easily be produced in parabolic curves and other shapes for roof construction, enabling great weights to be supported over considerable spans with pleasing architectural design. In work of this nature, the cost of a laminated timber beam cannot truly be compared with the same beam in solid timber: comparisons can only be made with the cost of other materials that can be used in the same form of construction (*i.e.*, reinforced concrete and steel) and indications at the moment show that laminated timber can be very competitive in price with these other materials.

The country is becoming increasingly " timber conscious " and much of this is undoubtedly due to the increasing efforts of the T.D.A. Ltd. This belated appreciation that one of the oldest building and industrial materials available can compete with the most modern man-made materials, must eventually have a great effect on the trade, since where timber is eventually used to replace steel, the trade will have to supply not merely timber but stress graded timber or laminated timber. This demand will obviously not come quickly, but will be gradually built up as architects and structural engineers are converted to the new uses of timber. This in its turn will create a demand which eventually can affect a great many merchants throughout the country.

General Index

CARPE
DIEM
B·I·E·T

Ravensdale Wharf, Stamford Hill, London, N 16. Tel: Stamford Hill 6611

PUB. S.E.D.I.
YES!
Here is the solution
to your problem of
LOGS' PRESERVATION